D0998554

**SEMATECH**

*Number Ten:*
*Kenneth E. Montague Series in Oil and Business History*
*Joseph A. Pratt, General Editor*

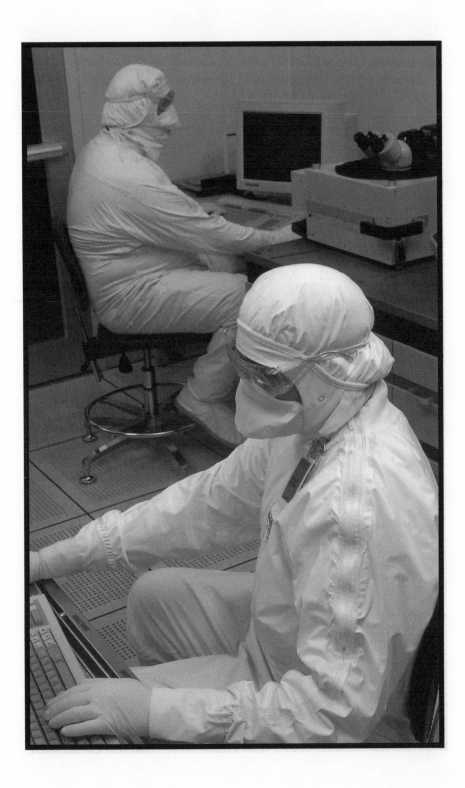

# Sematech

## Saving the U.S. Semiconductor Industry

LARRY D. BROWNING AND JUDY C. SHETLER

Texas A&M University Press
College Station

The paper used in this book meets the minimum requirements
of the American National Standard for Permanence
of Paper for Printed Library Materials, Z39.48-1984.
Binding materials have been chosen for durability.
⊗

For a complete list of books in print in this series, see the back of the book.

Library of Congress Cataloging-in-Publication Data

Browning, Larry D.
    Sematech : saving the U.S. semiconductor industry / Larry D. Browning and Judy C. Shetler.
       p. cm.—(Kenneth E. Montague series in oil and business history ; no. 10)
    Includes bibliographical references and index.
    ISBN 0-89096-937-X (cloth)
    1. Sematech (Organization)—History.   2. Semiconductor industry—Government policy—
United States.   I. Title: Saving the U.S. semiconductor industry.   II. Shetler, Judy C.
III. Title.   IV. Series.

HD9696.S4 S453   2000
338.7'62138152'0973—dc21

               99-057068

# Contents

# Preface

On a fall day in 1994, Dr. William Spencer, chief executive officer (CEO) of Sematech, startled many observers by announcing that his organization would soon relinquish its federal funding. Sematech, a semiconductor manufacturing consortium, had been created only a few years before as a collaborative effort between semiconductor makers and the U.S. government to counter the imminent threat of foreign domination of the global microchip market.

This threat was still a grave one. By the mid-1980s, foreign competition, notably from Japan's government-subsidized collaborative production, was rapidly overrunning the global market for semiconductors, especially with their aggressively priced memory chips. The goal of recovering competitive leadership in this vital economic sector supplied the rationale for establishing an American chip-making consortium. Its founding charter in 1987 was a sweeping pronouncement: "To provide the U.S. semiconductor industry the capability for world leadership in manufacturing."

By 1994, pressure from global competition was even more widespread. It thus caused consternation when Sematech's CEO said: "The industry can afford to support the consortium and we should. We are setting an example for other U.S. industries and for the world. We never intended direct federal funding to become an entitlement program."[1] His announcement was all the more startling because federal funding is seldom given up after it has been gained.

The collaboration had been unusual from the beginning. Sematech was the desperate marriage of suspicious and unaccustomed bedfellows: fourteen of the major American semiconductor manufacturers and the federal government. Until then, the American semiconductor industry had been inventively entrepreneurial in design, fiercely competitive in practice, and resolutely self-reliant in nature. Rivalry and antitrust history limited communication within the industry and tainted trust in government intentions. Old habits died hard, and it was a struggle for industry rivals to connect with each other and to win and accept organizational legitimacy and official support for collaboration from Washington.

The new Clinton administration gave Sematech enthusiastic approval in 1992. The microelectronics industry was enjoying fuller recognition of its embedded importance in every sector of the nation's industrial strength. Vice President Al Gore called semiconductors the "V-8 engines on the information superhighway" because they were driving the U.S. economy and making military weapons "smart." He committed the administration to helping U.S. firms to "develop the computer chips of the 21st century."[2] Sematech was being cited as a role model for future collaboration between the government and other threatened sectors of the U.S. economy.

It took two years after Sematech's official chartering in 1987 for the U.S. share of the global microchip market to halt its downward slide and start creeping back up. The picture had grown much brighter by the time of Spencer's announcement in 1994, with U.S. chip makers once again ahead in global market share. They were one of the few American industrial groups ever to rebound from loss of their lead to Japan.

Astonishment that Sematech planned to wean itself from federal support at this point sparked new interest in what the consortium actually was and what it had achieved to that point. How much of the semiconductor industry's ongoing recovery could be attributed to Sematech's role? Had it already accomplished its sweeping mission? Could domestic collaboration really turn the tide of global competition? If so, what had Sematech done and how?

Sematech has been called an "experiment that had to work":[3] a trial marriage of unlikely partners, brought to the altar by their desperate drive to survive, but with no guarantees of success. Detractors called the consortium an un-American form of "industrial policy"[4] that would choose to support only the most likely technology winners. It was criticized for "giving suckers to 300-pound kids."[5] Such collaboration among major rivals had been unthinkable and illegal in the United States before 1984.[6]

Even after achieving industry and federal support, Sematech's course was not clear, and its success was not assured. The consortium's founders were aware that consortia emphasizing cooperative research had been frustrated in accomplishing their aims.[7] Sematech represented a different approach. It was a manufacturing consortium strictly limited to precompetitive collaboration—that is, companies working together to improve core manufacturing competence rather than on making breakthrough end products with competitive features.[8]

What had this experimental body done to help the semiconductor industry recover, coming back from death's door and declaring itself ready to pick up its own bed and walk? Because Sematech's approach was new, what it did and how are questions of vital importance to the economic health and security of the United States in an increasingly multinational competitive environment. It is more important, as well as more difficult, to trace the strands of Sematech's contribution to America's diverse economic fiber before they become indistinguishable.

One clear advantage to the historical view of any enterprise is that, in retrospect, choices that led to fortuitous outcomes often appear to have been logical and even inevitable, whereas choices with bad results either sink unnoticed or look like obvious blunders that should have been avoided. In real time, however, those entrusted with making directional decisions on foggy paths find it much harder to foresee the consequences and predict the long-term implications of any choice.

Because Sematech was a national initiative, it became a focal point for public and private agendas to interact in new ways, generating an array of novel choices and opportunities. At the organizational level, small and large members' interests often differed in fundamental ways, making agreement on choices of internal agendas and courses of action problematic.

To integrate the long historical view with the confusing daily picture of how Sematech had to deal with many urgently demanding alternatives, it helps to develop overlapping viewpoints for looking at chronological events. The major areas of interaction can be grouped into three domains. First, there was the internal matter of organizing the consortium itself: the issues involved in the structuring, developing, and managing of organized cooperation among competitors. The second, wider, area of interaction to consider was the nature of the consortium's business-government relations within the shifting context of national and international economic and political pressures. Finally, there was the overriding need to achieve timely and substantive manufacturing technology goals. The simultaneous push and pull from these three contingent areas (consortium management, industry-government relations, and technological performance) affected every decision and choice that Sematech's leaders had to make and carry out, and they inform the three themes of our analysis. The pressure-cooker stress and high visibility of having a mission of national scope—the rescue of a vital industry—further magnified the interdependence of these three domains.

Sematech, as the first manufacturing consortium, had to create itself with no blueprint to follow as it went along while simultaneously creating its own competitive/cooperative environment. As with evaluating a baseball team's statistics, none of the consortium's accomplishments can be interpreted as isolated absolutes. They must instead be measured as collective performances against adversaries with their own strengths and weaknesses. The world did not stand still waiting for Sematech to work. Many other factors affected industry recovery, and Sematech's contributions are interwoven with them.

Even our trithematic analysis of chronological events does not uncover any straightforward historical thread of achievement to follow. Instead, the story of cooperation skeins out into an enlarging narrative as the consortium's scope spreads beyond the originally stated mission, supporting a wider effort than its founders could predict. The long-term effects and influence of the consortium are not yet fully realized, but the time has come to begin looking at what has been gained and learned from the experiment.

## Statement of Method

The first theme, the management perspective of the chronological events involving Sematech, is the anchoring focus of this book since the formation of a manufacturing consortium was an organizational experiment. (For a chronology of major events related to Sematech, see appendix 1.) The political and technological viewpoints from the two other major domains listed above (i.e., the consortium's government-industry relations and its technological performance) provide essential interpretive context. Seeing how these three thematic domains operate together allows even the most deeply intertwined of Sematech's contributions and their significance to emerge from its story.

## Acknowledgments

We want to thank Sematech for research and financial support, including paying travel expenses and covering the costs related to completing transcriptions of interviews, as well as providing full access to Sematech documents. Our appreciation for the research support does not alter the interpretations and analysis that unfolds in this book. They are our sole responsibility.

We also want to thank the people who worked at Sematech whose observations are offered throughout this book. Without their willingness to share their experiences at Sematech and their analysis of what went on there, our ability to write this book would have been severely limited. We owe a special debt of gratitude to Turner Hasty. Hasty was one of the original forty-four Sematech employees in Santa Clara, California, and served as chief operating officer (COO) under both Noyce and Spencer and as interim CEO following Noyce's death. He acted as our informal sponsor during the project and spent endless hours helping us to understand microelectronic manufacturing sufficiently to write about it. We also would like to thank John Trimble in the Department of English at the University of Texas at Austin for help in sharpening the manuscript.

Finally, we would like to acknowledge family support in completing the book. Larry's brother Jerry, who spent most of his career as a regional manager in the U.S. Department of Agriculture, copyedited the book for us and affirmed that our analysis of good management practices are applicable to a wide variety of settings. Judy's husband, Paul, a physicist, surgeon, and medical management consultant, reviewed early drafts of several of the chapters and also helped with the final copyediting. In addition, Paul's intellectual, financial, and, especially, his moral support throughout this project were crucial to Judy's participation, and we owe him special thanks.

We would like to dedicate this book to Vickie and to Paul, for being there.

**SEMATECH**

## CHAPTER I

# Long-Established Relations Drive Cooperation

O nce there was an American industry, grown hugely successful through making very small integrated circuits (ICs), but rapidly dwindling under the double jeopardy of its own exuberant short-sightedness and the calculated long-term strategy of foreign competition. Integrated circuits are an all-American invention, composed of multiple electronic transistors. Transistors were invented in 1947 at Bell Labs and by the mid 1950s were a standard component in radios, hearing aids, and other electronic devices.[1] On integrated circuits, transistors are combined on a single etched silicon chip instead of having to be wired together. This ingenious device is usually called a semiconductor or microchip, and is now made in many increasingly miniaturized and powerful types, such as various memory or logic chips, microprocessors, and so on.

However, in 1959—when the microchip was invented—big, cheap, reliable vacuum tubes ran America's radios and television sets, and there was natural market resistance to replacing these workhorse tubes (and the many products they already inhabited) with the newfangled microchips. The semiconductor industry gained momentum slowly at first, finally gathered speed, and then grew exponentially to become a huge enterprise on which today's advanced industrial economy depends. In less than thirty years from the invention of the first handmade integrated circuit, the essential semiconductor industry was even bootstrapping itself, using computer-aided design and automated manufacturing to generate the next generation of chips.

From its inauspicious beginning, the semiconductor industry erupted in an expanding pattern of unfettered and brilliant innovation coupled with Yankee entrepreneurialism, and urged on by eager American venture capital. Once in the race, no chip maker could afford to slow down long enough to perfect the manufacturing of soon-to-be-obsolete inventions. Manufacturers swiftly and repeatedly leaped to the next exciting and promising divide, forming aggressive new companies around the latest idea, constantly vying to stay ahead of the others.

Each company's unique innovations had to be kept secret, of course, because without time for manufacturing refinement or performance quality, competitive advantage lay almost entirely in product innovation. If a novel product was first to capture a market-share threshold, it forced other companies to make their products compatible with it or forget about competing. A popular, well-advertised innovation could capture the market, force product compatibility, snowball with increasing returns, and repeal the traditional law of diminishing returns associated with product maturity.

If proprietary secrets could be successfully guarded, other companies' potential product compatibility could even lose "cadence," lagging a generation or more behind the leader—or at least until the next clever innovation made all previous ones obsolete, when the race would be up for grabs again. Companies scrambled fiercely to be first, balancing precariously, but often temporarily, on the top of the heap.

This speed and secrecy of innovation by which the market could force product compatibility, along with antitrust laws forbidding collaboration among companies, regulated the industry both internally and externally so effectively that the government mostly ignored chip makers during the early years. This held true even though the fierce competition did not always guarantee semiconductor customers access to the best product, but only to those products that could compel market domination. The competitive process forced the best to the top just often enough to keep customers coming back, but also just seldom enough to encourage rival entrepreneurs to try again and again.

For microchip makers, taking time to refine the quality and manufacturing competence of yesterday's innovation could mean losing the race for market share in the next device generation. Many a start-up company formed around an entrepreneur's new idea, financed its invention with funds from venture "vultures," mushroomed into quick profitability, went public with its stock to make its founders' fortunes, and withered as the next start-up with a new idea overtook it.

Some companies that survived did so by huge and cumbersome vertical integration that through sheer market share could at times force compatibility of others' new products to the volume standard. Some smaller companies survived with strategies such as developing niche markets with customized microchip devices, or by supplying unique national defense requirements. The government hindered monopolization by large companies as much as it could through antitrust regulation and tax laws. Capital and tax breaks were more available to small companies and start-ups to use for research and development (R&D) than for investment in manufacturing improvement by established firms. Large or small, all the companies that survived became increasingly skilled both in maneuvering the proprietary regulation of the marketplace, and in using antitrust and patent laws to exclude potential follow-ons or even would-be innovators. Relationships among microchip firms and with the government grew increasingly adversarial as the industry grew more practiced in these business skills, and both antitrust and patent litigation began to flourish.

Equipment and material suppliers felt the effects of a life defined as adversaries, as they were forced to respond to different secret standards and specifications for each semiconductor manufacturer. Equipment and material requirements changed rapidly due to constant increases in miniaturization and sophistication, with no pause for manufacturing refinement or effective feedback, so that responses leading to improvement always lagged behind. Microchip makers demanded nonstandardized, uniquely and secretly designed and calibrated, instantly operable equipment for making the newest innovation tomorrow, and then would do it all over again the next day—all the while pitting suppliers against each other to get the lowest price. Because the industry required instantly operable equipment to meet its fast pace, it claimed to need top quality. However, it was not prepared to pay for it or to openly provide the feedback suppliers needed to respond with quality improvements. American-made equipment became less and less reliable, even as the demands on it became more sophisticated.

With unresolved equipment and material problems, manufacturing costs rose, eating into the industry's market size and reducing the resources available for R&D—the driver for any company based on continuous innovation. Much finger pointing ensued, and U.S. customer-supplier relationships grew increasingly adversarial, in step with the growing government-industry hostility.

Nevertheless, the creative and potentially lucrative challenge of this inventive U.S. industry was heady stuff, and for a while it captured not only domestic but also global market share with the brilliance of its innovation, egged on by the excited pace of competitive pressures. Agile and inventive entrepreneurship seemed to be the exciting formula for success, even with its exasperating problems.

Then the shadow of doom fell over the frenetically fragmented U.S. semiconductor industry. Global competition, mostly from Japan, arrived in the form of huge, government-supported, vertically integrated manufacturers of previously developed U.S. innovations. Within a decade the Japanese, through cost-effective and quality manufacturing, overtook American chip makers in the race for global market share in this U.S.-originated industry. Moreover, Japan accomplished this takeover without introducing a single product innovation of its own.

Japan also began to dominate the equipment and material supplier infrastructure through integration and/or supportive customer-supplier relationships and quality assurance based on effective feedback. American industry

5

increasingly turned to higher quality, more reliable Japanese equipment, and the U.S. equipment supplier infrastructure situation worsened as it lost U.S. customers.

These upward and downward spirals favoring Japan increasingly allowed the Japanese to engage in the short-term predatory pricing (below cost) practice known as "dumping," as they sought not only to take over the chip-making industry but also their actual target, the worldwide computer industry. Since computers are totally dependent upon microchips, whoever controlled the global semiconductor industry would also have global computer dominance.

The incredible achievement of taking over market share without one innovation challenged nearly all embedded U.S. industrial assumptions about: (a) the priority of R&D innovation over engineering production performance; (b) the effect of rapid return on investment demands; (c) the value of zero-sum competition; (d) the meaning of a "free" marketplace supported by industry-government hostility; and (e) the cost advantage of exploitative customer-supplier relationships.

The challenge was not merely a philosophical one, however. By 1986 the U.S. semiconductor industry was calculated to be within eighteen months of irrecoverable loss of production capability, closely linked to the rapid deterioration of its equipment and materials infrastructure. Desperation now made unfamiliar but committed partners out of former adversaries—including industry rivals, government agencies, and equipment and materials suppliers.

That their desperation brought competitors together in cooperation is well known. What has not yet been fully told is the tale of how these anxious and unaccustomed partners accomplished, with government sanction and support, a working collaboration in a manufacturing consortium called Sematech. There was no blueprint to follow; they had to discover how to do it by just getting in and doing it. The Sematech story cannot be told as a simple linear recounting of serial events. It takes many turns, being indirect, complex, and evolutionary in nature—an appropriate response to Japan's complex and indirect global competition strategy.

The story also has a surprising, miraculous quality. The routes that Sematech took to become a viable organization were not predicted and cannot be traced to singular causes. Sematech required the best efforts, commitment, and hard work of many gifted individuals as they brought forth a new kind of organization. This is that story.

## Early Connections

Nothing comes from nothing, however, and at this desperate stage the failing U.S. semiconductor industry was fortunate to have some earlier connections on which to draw. In 1971 the youthful U.S. semiconductor equipment-manufacturing industry had formed its own trade association, the Semiconductor Equipment and Materials Institute (SEMI). At first the group consisted solely of its American founders, but as international equipment makers penetrated more of the market, SEMI went through a three- to four-year period of debate that led to opening up membership worldwide and changing the "Institute" in its name to "International." Sam Harrell describes this action as simply "following the boat to the marketplace."[2] As of 1994, six years after Sematech was founded, 850 of SEMI's 1,450 member companies were American; the rest were mostly European and Asian.[3]

In the U.S., SEMI's official attitude came to reflect the alienation between chip makers and material and equipment suppliers. Many suppliers felt they were being weakened by having to pay the price for the U.S. chip makers' own short-term entrepreneurial divisiveness, fierce competitiveness, and secretive business practices. With the U.S. suppliers preferring more supportive Japanese customers, and the U.S. chip makers preferring often more reliable Japanese equipment, it was not easy for the various American industry sectors to agree on their real adversary, especially since they were already treating each other as the enemy.

## The Semiconductor Industry Association

A few years before their precipitate loss of market share in the mid-1980s, U.S. chip makers also began to establish a network. They wanted to establish industry communication with each other and to develop a voice for lobbying for trade controls as Japanese competitors began to flex their muscles.

In 1977, leaders of five high-volume merchant producers of microchips— Wilfred Corrigan of Fairchild Semiconductor (in 1980 the founder of LSI Logic), Bob Noyce of Intel, Jerry Sanders of Advanced Micro Devices (AMD), Charlie Sporck of National Semiconductor (NSC), and John Welty of Motorola—founded the Semiconductor Industry Association (SIA) as a specialized offshoot from their umbrella trade group, the Electronics Industry Association. The other four asked Noyce to be president because they believed he was the most politically aware member of their group. He declined the post but continued to work behind the scenes.[4] The SIA's early efforts were directed toward collecting and communicating business data from among its member firms about sales, market share, start-ups, etc., which established a role from the outset for reporting quantitative performance data on industry health.

Although many American semiconductor firms had partnered in joint projects with each other and also with Japanese firms at various times, the United States had not seen any systematic, industry-wide data collection or sharing. There was little sense of interdependence and little recognition of the benefits of cooperation. The SIA was a major step toward communication, but collaboration was still strictly limited by law.

## Technology Leakage

During this time American companies with Japanese allies eventually discovered to their dismay that their skillful Japanese partners seemed to benefit more than they did from their alliances. As the Japanese grew in manufacturing competence, they naturally improved their ability to exploit the innovations of their American partners. The U.S. companies' assurance of maintaining the competitive edge through innovation at first led them to devalue anything they learned from the Japanese about manufacturing. The U.S. companies' reasons for forming these alliances were often either to license innovations and establish their own proprietary standards in Japan, or to gain access to Japanese capital and market distribution for American products.[5]

In the early days, the Americans were hasty and naive. Says 1988 SIA director David Metz: "U.S. firms didn't sense their Japanese partners would be using their technology to sell on the outside market. They might not have licensed to the degree they did had they known this." An analyst at Salomon Brothers noted that in their early alliances, "American companies made absolutely no attempt to defend themselves. Many hadn't even patented their designs."[6]

However, toward the end of the 1970s and early 1980s the atmosphere of secrecy and protection of intellectual property within the U.S. industry heightened, feeding growing suspicion and fears of "technology leakage" to Japan. This was exaggerated by differences in attitudes and policies toward patent rights between the two countries. The U.S. emphasis on design innovation gave high priority and confidentiality to establishing proprietary architectures (electronic device designs) and increasingly to their patent protection. The Japanese emphasis on product quality and dependence on manufacturing performance to give them a competitive advantage meant that their attitude toward technological innovation was more open.

Japanese partners with high-quality production skills freely turned what they learned about advanced design into a low-cost, high-yield commodity, as they did with dynamic random access memory (DRAM) semiconductors. They could then sell these chips for less than their production cost abroad to develop foreign market monopolies. (To be fair, however, one must compare this pejoratively termed foreign-market dumping with the respectable U.S. strategic practice of "forward pricing": creating a domestic market for a new product by introducing it at a cost below the initial price of production.)[7]

Technology flow in the direction of the Japanese had many more intricate aspects, of course, but the net effect was that Japanese firms during the 1970s and early 1980s learned and exploited more from joint projects with U.S. firms than vice versa even though Japan apparently practiced less industrial secrecy. According to Sematech CEO Bill Spencer, "The most important lesson the Japanese taught the U.S. was that high-volume production and high quality go hand in hand." This lesson reversed the conventional wisdom that dependence on high-volume economies of scale could compensate for performance flaws. The lesson expressed a new relationship: a high-volume, steep learning curve enabled continuous improvement, minimizing the variations that jeopardized high quality.

But Americans were slow to recognize the lesson since their faith in their proven innovative ingenuity made it easy to believe that it was the Japanese and not they who had more to learn. It is a widely recognized problem that implementing change is difficult when a firm, for instance, wants to put a new design into production on the factory floor. However, given human nature, change is relatively easy to achieve when the novel idea has been gleaned through technology leakages from the competition. Nobody wants to be told; everybody wants to find out and then mimic.

Not all the technology flow came from joint projects, however. American semiconductor firms historically practiced widespread licensing of innovations, encouraged or even forced to by the antimonopolistic regulatory atmosphere, such as happened in the 1950s when the Justice Department forced IBM to license all of its patents from basic research in computers to all comers, including the very interested Japanese. In 1956, AT&T was forced by a consent decree to license its microelectronics patents to others, and in 1984 the huge company was broken up into smaller firms.[8] Many smaller U.S. start-ups were also willing to license their design innovations to gain working capital. The Japanese also had different attitudes toward intellectual property and patent laws. Americans often were outraged by the apparently acceptable Japanese business practice of skillfully reverse engineering—that is, copying (and perhaps even patenting in Japan) whatever they could obtain on the open market.

Japanese firms had the process know-how, manufacturing skills, and vertical integration that allowed and motivated them to turn U.S. innovations into the large-scale, high-yield production of reliable chips.[9] Japanese economic policies created the support and capital resources to temporarily market those chips at a loss. American alarm and resentment of this trend grew, often interpreted as one of stealing Yankee ingenuity and turning it into a Japanese commodity. There were fears that the United States would soon turn into a sort of Third World idea colony for Japan, exporting innovation as a cheap raw material for commercial exploitation elsewhere.

## Early Trade Lobbying

The young SIA, representing only a small population of merchant chip makers in a nonunionized, politically inexperienced industry, floated some lobbying efforts in Washington near the end of the 1970s, helping to urge trade sanctions against what they recognized as Japan's growing market encroachment. However, those early efforts to obtain trade sanctions were derailed when congressional leaders did what they invariably do—they checked with their other constituencies. Congress discovered that other firms in the same industry, like Digital Equipment Corporation (DEC) and Hewlett-Packard, who bought semiconductors in high volume for their electronic systems products such as computers, naturally opposed the sanctions. They liked the flexibility of buying wherever they could get the best price, of course—including from Japan. So the SIA's earliest lobbying efforts failed.[10]

The SIA needed a broader forum for communicating within the industry, both to compile a representative sample of across-the-board data and to hash out industry differences privately among themselves rather than publicly in Congress. These problems, created by widely varying needs among the different firms in one industry, underscore the challenges of achieving cooperation among them.

Seeing how industry differences undermined SIA effectiveness, the group began a recruitment effort and gained a valuable member when IBM joined in late 1980. At the time, IBM was both the world's largest producer and the world's largest user of semiconductors for its own electronic systems needs. The powerful image of "Big Blue" carried weight in Washington. Later, when the idea for a semiconductor consortium was being floated, the first question was always, "Is IBM in on this?" Understandably, IBM did not always support protective trade initiatives, but because of its membership IBM could tell the SIA, rather than Congress, what initiatives it could accept and what ones it would decline.

Texas Instruments (TI) initially avoided SIA membership partly because the secrecy requirement of its many defense contracts restricted its data-sharing ability. However, TI finally joined in 1985, when the competitive threat grew starker for everyone, even for military suppliers. By 1985, SIA had a membership of forty-eight firms with combined revenues of more than $100 billion.[11] The SIA's effort to create an inclusive forum among its diverse membership set a pattern for later cooperative efforts.

The expanded SIA grew more effective, giving a unified political voice to an industry known for its stalwart independence both from each other and the government. The SIA's larger membership made its data more significant while at the same time creating a forum for discussing common issues among its diverse firms—be they merchant or captive,[12] large or small, niche producers of specialized chips or systems makers who bought them, or located in the East along Route 128 or out West in Silicon Valley.

The growing association was developing a more consistent, credible political voice, but proprietary secrecy and antitrust fears still limited the member firms' technological and financial discussions. In 1984 the SIA helped lobby for passage of the Cooperative Research Act, as did the Microelectronics and Computer Technology Corporation (MCC), a computer industry R&D consortium that had been established in 1983 without federal financing. The Cooperative Research Act lifted industry barriers to communication and cooperation, at least in basic research, by exempting registered R&D consortia from the treble damages provision of federal antitrust law.[13] Cooperation in such a research consortium was to be precompetitive—which in effect limited collaboration to such areas as basic research or to its applications in such areas as establishing standards or formulating processes rather than focusing on developing marketable products.

## The Semiconductor Research Corporation

In 1982, even before the Cooperative Research Act, the SIA established the Semiconductor Research Corporation (SRC), a continuing consortium whose participants sponsor generic research at various academic and laboratory sites and disseminate results to all members. The SRC operates as an administrator and information clearinghouse for its researchers rather than as a physical entity, but its successful operation provided valuable experience in collaboration for consortium organizers to draw on. The SRC became a major force supporting the founding of Sematech, and SRC president Larry Sumney acted as Sematech's first managing director.

Another early collaborative effort in semiconductor research should be mentioned: the very high speed integrated circuit (VHSIC) project established by the Department of Defense (DOD) in 1980.[14] The VHSIC's purpose was to revitalize the isolated and cumbersome military microelectronics programs by reintegrating them with the increasingly more active private sector. Military projects, particularly the Minuteman missile, and the National Aeronautics and Space Administration's (NASA) Apollo program provided crucial early support to fledgling semiconductor research and development until commercial spin-offs grew into the huge and pervasive consumer microelectronics market.

The VHSIC was an attempt to reverse the earlier flow from military development into commercial uses by spinning private sector innovation back to benefit military R&D. The VHSIC sponsored several phases of projects between teams of merchant chip makers, defense contractors, and suppliers. Although the VHSIC eventually spent five times as much as originally planned before being phased out, its R&D programs did not manage to overcome the difficulties of achieving an effective military-industry interface. Observers concluded that the barriers to technology transfer raised by the difficulties of military procurement could not be solved by more cooperative R&D alone.[15]

Sematech, as a partnership between industry and government that focused on manufacturing competence rather than R&D, was still an untried experiment, but it was one whose time had come. Michael Borrus, deputy director of the Berkeley Roundtable on the International Economy (BRIE), observed: "The Japanese production advantage is much less a product of better tooling or better technology than of better implementation. Among other things, the

Japanese advantage has been obtained in the careful management and operation of its production processes, in the close working relationships between producer and supplier, in rigorous quality control and in the continuous tinkering
that provides slow but sure improvement. The lesson for American companies
is that the greatest gee-whiz technology in the world will not substitute for
competence in these areas."[16]

For leaders in an American industry where winning and losing depended
on singular leaps of revolutionary brilliance, it would take a transformation to
believe that evolutionary change grounded in multiple, participatory processes
could be a better competitive strategy. However, by the mid-1980s, pain and
fear in the U.S. semiconductor industry and government created a critical mass
of individuals willing and able to look at things differently.

This became their greatest innovation of all: learning to depend not only
on inventiveness but also on performance, not only on individual brilliance but
also on participatory learning and shared competence, not only on being first
to the finish line but also on ensuring that others get there. The conceptual
difficulty of making this cooperative turn and making it a globally competitive
strategy can hardly be overestimated. It did not come as a flash of insight, but
as a thoughtful, emergent response to the Japanese strategic threat that was
using the splintered and adversarial relationships of the U.S. semiconductor
industry against it.

## Acknowledging Interdependence

As the industry took its first steps toward working together, obstacles to cooperation were still high, rivalries fierce, and customer-supplier and industry-
government relationships anything but cordial. However, SIA members'
persistent attempts to work together on common problems signaled not just a
political strategy but acknowledgment among chip makers of their interdependence and shared danger. The classic conditions for cooperation are said to be
facing high stakes and having high interdependence.[17]

Although in the early 1980s the United States still looked good on market
share graphs, American companies knew that their R&D spending and capital
investments in fabrication facilities and equipment were falling behind those
of the Japanese. They also knew that the strength of their equipment infrastructure and their ties to it were deteriorating. The industry trend was toward
developing microprocessor chips around which systems were designed, but the
U.S. emphasis on innovation began to look like a retreat on some fronts,
as many American manufacturers increasingly gave up DRAM (memory
chip) manufacture and turned to developing a variety of lower-volume niche
products.

In 1984, American chip makers were still barely ahead on market share
charts, although they were losing ground fast, a result of the 1982 recession that

had decreased U.S. demand and the ever-increasing competitive pressure from Japan. Then, in 1985, the bottom fell out. From owning 85 percent of the world market in semiconductors at one point, the United States share fell to 43 percent—surpassed for the first time ever by the Japanese. One unmistakable sign of the spreading effects of semiconductor market share loss was that by 1985, the Silicon Valley real estate market was glutted with 20 million square feet of excess space due to shutdowns or canceled expansion plans. A dynamic industry at the heart of a high-tech economy was, as more than one observer noted, "suddenly staring straight at the gallows."

## Better Trade Protection

The state of the industry generated great worry among SIA leaders—and in discussions among economic and military leaders in Washington as well. Debates revolved around what could or should be done, and by whom. The SIA members began planning a total strategy package, beginning with a concerted lobbying and legal effort in Washington for trade initiatives, both to prevent foreign chip dumping and to develop better trade positions in other countries. Even those who realized trade protection was not a total solution believed they needed it to buy time for longer-term efforts to improve American competitiveness.

In June, 1985, the SIA filed allegations of unfair trade practices against Japan. Citing the Section 301 Unfair Trade Regulation, which provides for punitive damages against nations convicted of violation, the SIA suit claimed that Japan was illegally restricting U.S. chip makers' access to the Japanese domestic market.

Separate firms and then the U.S. government soon filed legal claims as well. The press reported: "Micron Technology filed an antidumping complaint against Japan on 64K dynamic random access memory semiconductors (DRAMs). An antidumping charge filed by U.S. industry [the SIA suit] alleges that a foreign industry is selling its product in the United States for less than fair value—that is, less than the foreign industry's domestic selling price—or in some cases, for less than its cost of production, and that these sales are injuring a U.S. industry."[18] On the heels of this action, Intel, Advanced Micro Devices, and National Semiconductor also filed an antidumping case, this time for erasable, programmable, read-only memory (EPROM) semiconductors, another type of memory chip. The U.S. government also filed a suit against Japanese DRAM chip makers. A cabinet-level Trade Policy Strike Force recommended that the president take this unusual action even though opponents of drastic trade protection measures argued that they would backfire against ongoing industry attempts to penetrate the Japanese market.

It is interesting to note that although the SIA instigated the first suit, the company actions were still brought by merchant producers. For them, Japanese memory-chip dumping was directly injurious in the fairly short term. For the big electronic system makers in the United States, dumping offered the direct, short-term benefit of cheap chips, although it undermined them indirectly by creating a long-term monopoly. Also, antidumping duties are paid by the importer, which hits the U.S. systems customer right in the wallet. The captive semiconductor manufacturers had to take the long-term view—that they were more threatened by bargain price dumping than by import tariffs—in order to make common cause with the more directly injured SIA merchant members.

The concerted broadside coming from the SIA, from several private firms, and from U.S. government charges was more firepower than Japan had faced in this trade area. Before punitive tariffs were assessed, though, the U.S. Department of Commerce and Japan signed a Semiconductor Agreement. Japanese DRAM and EPROM producers agreed that they would sell their products in the United States only at prices at or above the applicable fair-market value. In effect, they agreed not to violate United States antidumping law.[19] This was to some extent a Pyrrhic victory for the United States because setting price floors in the late 1980s actually led to huge profits for the Japanese.

While protesting Japan's predatory competition, the industry also had to acknowledge that it had brought on some of its own troubles—and would have to help itself out of them. Chip makers recognized that they could not compete on innovation alone, no matter how brilliant. They realized they would have to cope with the encroaching maturity of their technology by improving their manufacturing skills. It is one thing to relinquish an established device and move on to newer developments, but quite another to give it up because your manufacturing skills fail to match your competitor's. American semiconductor industry leaders also knew that they would have to nurture a healthier domestic infrastructure, with diverse sources for reliable manufacturing materials and equipment. But they feared the industry would not survive long enough to correct its weaknesses without the time that trade protection could provide.

## Survival Strategies

As worried discussions about the American semiconductor industry's threatened future took place at SIA and SEMI meetings, and also at the Department of Defense, Sandy Kane, an IBM vice president, privately undertook a gloomy initiative: to prepare what he called an "obituary" for the U.S. semiconductor industry—a comprehensive survey compiled from many areas of easily available information that no one else had put together in the same way.

Kane's presentation dealt with the whole industry perspective—including the big financial picture, manufacturing capacity, and capital investment—for the U.S. semiconductor industry versus Japan, as well as for the materials and equipment makers. Kane shared his story with other IBM executives, saying:

"There's no date on the tombstone because I don't know how long it's going to take. But unless something changes to cause the trend to shift, we are looking at a disaster for the U.S. semiconductor industry."

As part of a company-wide competitive analysis, Kane circulated his dark prophecy through IBM and finally to the Management Committee, which included John Akers and Jack Kuehler, then serving as IBM's CEO and president, respectively. This February, 1986, meeting was different from the ones Kane had experienced at lower levels, however. A prolonged policy discussion followed, and Akers directed that the concerns should be discussed outside the company.

To go public was risky. The obituary summarized a great deal of grim information potentially very upsetting to shareholders. Also, IBM had a reputation for playing its cards close to the vest. As a captive chip producer, largely vertically integrated, and seventy years past being a start-up, it had never shared much of its closely related history with the rest of the industry. The company's engineers, for instance, tended to stay with the East Coast–based firm throughout their careers rather than join in the constant flux of the professional community that seemed the norm in California's Silicon Valley.

However, Kane's obituary matched with other analyses, both internal and external, that IBM was doing. Since IBM was so large, with great electronic product diversity, it had to balance out other variable factors. For example, IBM did not make chips for sale as the merchants did; it made its own or bought them from other semiconductor firms—both American and Japanese. Although IBM did not make its own equipment and had a reputation for having better long-term relationships with its suppliers than some others,[20] it knew it could not support the U.S. infrastructure alone. The company was keenly aware that the ultimate goal of an indirect Japanese strategy, apparently aimed at monopolizing semiconductors, was actually to attain supremacy in the global computer market, which was IBM's forte. In a sense, IBM's size and diversity made it more rather than less vulnerable to such a long-range competitive strategy.

Although the merchant semiconductor firms had a more immediate vulnerability, technology law expert and SIA advocate Clark McFadden says IBM's view was changing: "In the past, most of the initiatives, certainly all the collaborative ideas, had been a function of merchant initiative. The captives had been present, but never supportive, never enthusiastic, and certainly never innovative in bringing this forward."

According to McFadden, IBM's competitive analyses, dramatized by Kane's obituary, brought about a "decisive and clear change in IBM's attitude on this question." They realized that U.S. semiconductor companies were dying off at an alarming rate, and soon would be too few to support a healthy infrastructure. Looking ahead, the leaders of the world's largest computer manufacturer recognized that the major connecting link between the health of

U.S. merchant chip makers and IBM's own survival as a systems maker was a viable American semiconductor equipment and materials supply industry.

Related to recognition of this important link was the realization that the problem was one that not even IBM could solve alone—nor would it want to try. As McFadden observes of IBM: "They did not want to get into the equipment business themselves. They recognized that if they were going to try to sustain this very disparate and far-flung group of U.S. suppliers alone, it would be an enormous business distraction for them."

So John Akers and his committee took the long-term view, extending beyond IBM's image, its shareholder's worries, or proprietary borders. Kane describes their vision: "They thought this was important enough that we should run that risk because it was clear that this was something where others had to get involved. IBM could clearly not do it alone. It was an important enough issue that it was worth taking the risk."

IBM knew it would have to use discretion communicating this message, however. At Akers' behest, Sandy Kane took his show on the road. "Over the next three or four months, from February to June of 1986," he said, "I showed the obituary briefing to almost every chief executive of the major semiconductor companies in the United States, a number of the equipment companies, a number of people in universities, and a number of people in the government. I think in the course of those 3 months, I probably showed the pitch in the neighborhood of 25 times."

In May, 1986, the SIA public policy committee met in Boston, and George Scalise gave a challenging talk. Scalise was chairman of the board of the SRC, the SIA's research consortium, and chaired the SIA board's public policy committee. He committed the SRC to providing $100,000 to study what should be done to save U.S. semiconductor manufacturing.[21]

The day after Scalise threw out the SRC challenge, the SIA board met. Most of the board members had seen Kane's presentation and were shocked by the picture that emerged from his accumulation of separate facts. Other voices of warning spoke at this meeting. Jim Peterman, an SIA board member from TI, remembers a series of speeches, including one by technology consultant and author Charles Ferguson of the Massachusetts Institute of Technology, describing the industry's imminent doom unless it improved its performance in relation to Japan's.

Gary Tooker of Motorola chaired the next SIA board meeting in June, 1986, following the one that fielded Scalise's challenge. There was general agreement that something must be done. Charlie Sporck of NSC was asked if he would determine what was needed and report back to the board at its September meeting. According to Peterman: "Charlie hit the road in the summer of '86 and it took 50 to 60 percent of his time. It was a tremendous effort. George's [SRC] $100,000 offer would have meant nothing without Sporck's effort."

Sporck met personally with the directors of the semiconductor operations in all the major companies. He also lobbied in Washington and polled the science and business research community. He encouraged high-level people constantly to develop support in the government. Sporck's vision was clearly focused on the connected goals of improving American chip makers' manufacturing processes and improving the manufacturing equipment built by their U.S. suppliers. He was quoted as saying: "SIA companies must work together on common specifications for new equipment needed to build next generation devices. This will allow our equipment suppliers to devote the resources they need to develop new systems. It will also give us economies of scale to produce equipment effectively."[22]

Sporck's commitment set a precedent for high-level advocacy for the collaborative proposal. During this time he even appointed two vice presidents to manage the semiconductor and computer divisions of his own company so he could devote his time to shuttle diplomacy, seeking support for a consortium first within the industry and later in Washington.

To many observers, Charlie Sporck was a natural champion, an industry pioneer who had branched out from Fairchild Semiconductor where Bob Noyce's silicon version of the integrated circuit was invented, to establish his own successful Silicon Valley manufacturing firm, National Semiconductor. Sporck was known for his willingness to be involved in anything that he thought was important, even though he did not spend months planning something before he did it. "His spontaneity was something I always found fascinating and charming. That part didn't surprise me at all," says Sandy Kane. According to Sam Harrell, president of SEMI at the time: "Charlie Sporck was willing to take the task of communicating with his peers on the SIA board and other leaders in the industry. Sporck really was the first one to look at the magnitude of the task."

Clark McFadden describes how support emerged from the interactions among Kane's obituary, the SIA proposal, George Scalise's SRC challenge, Charlie Sporck's mission, IBM's subsequent involvement and its influence in the industry, and many other factors: "The captive producers [such as IBM, AT&T, and DEC] really came together with the merchant semiconductor firms at the time that Charlie Sporck, in particular, had articulated a proposal. He was obviously someone who not only had great experience in manufacturing, but was a recognized leader in that area. He felt a strong commitment, and it was something that he believed in very deeply. He illuminated the issue for a lot of folks."

Sporck urged the creation of a manufacturing consortium. When it became known that IBM was taking Sporck's idea seriously, McFadden adds, "I think there was a qualitative change in the effort to go forward. Suddenly, everyone realized that not only was this important, but it was something that could be done and needed to be done. And Charlie was able to harness that realization

17

in a way that brought people together, rather than letting them go off in their own directions."

Once someone of Sporck's stature and enthusiasm championed the idea of an SIA manufacturing consortium, IBM no longer felt constrained by the need to keep a low profile. Indeed, because of IBM's size and importance, not only to the industry but also to the national economy, its visible involvement triggered support from others as well. Even as Sporck embarked on his journey to gain industry consensus for a cooperative mission, various government agencies were also studying what could be done on several fronts, especially in the areas of defense, commerce, energy, and trade.[23]

## Trade Negotiations

For the threatened industry to look to the government for trade protection was a natural defensive move, especially since the recent agreement had not put an end to Japan's dumping as intended. Rather than just file complaints, in the summer of 1986 the SIA succeeded in getting Congress to pass a trade legislation package that included sanctions against Japan that prohibited dumping DRAM chips in the United States at below fair-market value. The bill also required Japan to increase its importation of U.S. semiconductors incrementally, with a target figure of 20 percent by 1990.[24] Passage of this benchmark trade bill was a signal that Washington and Japan heard the SIA speaking with a single voice in spite of the differences among its members. It also showed growing awareness in Congress that nearly every aspect of the U.S. economy and national security depended on America's ability to manufacture silicon chips.

This meant that in Congress, at least, a more connected view of the economy was beginning to replace the old one, in which separate technologies had been valued according to their asset sheets rather than by their ability to amplify the worth of many other industry sectors. Some high technologies are "pervasive and essential," says Michael Borrus of BRIE.[25] Silicon chip making enables developments in everything from milking machines to satellites to hair dryers, not to mention the factory machinery for making all this equipment, including designing and manufacturing more chips. The old zero-sum competitive assumptions with "winners and losers" were beginning to look inadequate to describe the embedded market effects of these little pieces of silicon in both domestic and foreign trade.

The Reagan administration continued to take a more traditional market sector stance publicly—not actively supporting the SIA's initiatives toward protection and collaboration, but not blocking them either. One analyst characterizes the White House's hands-off attitude during this period as being based on the beliefs that: "(1) the fundamental U.S. technology position was sound; (2) in the long run there's no reason to lay emphasis on technological develop-

ment, as there aren't any transformative sections of the economy; (3) government probably can't do very much that's positive anyway; and (4) trade policy
is not an instrument of technology policy."[26] These views betray a lack of com-
prehension of the economic leveraging provided by healthy semiconductor production, the impossibility of not having a technology policy in a technology-
driven economy, and the inescapable connection of such a policy with trade,
even if only by default.

American trade and regulatory policy had not yet adjusted to the new challenges of global competition. Looking back, Michael Borrus now says: "A lot
of what has passed for industrial policy in the U.S. . . . was in essence a reaction
to failed trade policy. If the trade issue had been addressed in the early 1980s,
Sematech might not have been needed."[27] One can also speculate that if there
had not finally been some trade protection, Sematech could not have helped
the semiconductor industry when it was needed.

## Government Involvement

By 1986, the Defense Department, relying more and more on the high-tech
abilities of its advanced weapons and communications systems, also saw a grave
threat to national security in depending on Japan for essential chips. Just as
IBM's CEO Akers was initiating corporate policy support of Sandy Kane's
grim presentation, the military's Defense Science Board (DSB) convened two
task forces. One was to take a broad look at the threat to microelectronic commercial components under the direction of Dr. William Perry, a consultant and
former undersecretary of defense for research and engineering who later became defense secretary during Bill Clinton's first term, and Bob Burnett, a
TRW vice president. This group was to study the cost savings that could result
from the military's purchase of commercial components rather than customized military ones. It focused on semiconductors as an example of cost savings,
and its findings could strongly affect the structure and defense production of
the semiconductor industry. This group's report was scheduled for release in
March, 1987.

The other DOD Science Board task force was focused specifically on semiconductor dependency. Chaired by Norman Augustine, president and CEO of
Martin Marietta, this group worked throughout the fall and summer of 1986,
while Charlie Sporck was traveling around trying to gather a favorable consensus for collaboration within the industry. This DSB report was scheduled for
release in January, 1987, but was leaked to the press in December. *Electronic
News* headlined its article on the report: "DOD task force urges $1.7 B for five-
year semicon thrust: seeks $250 M/yr for DRAM consortium," and claimed that
the recommendation was for establishment of a semiconductor manufacturing
technology institute, with yearly contributions of $250 million a year from
DOD, and $250 million a year from industry.[28] The *Wall Street Journal* ex-

pressed doubts that Congress would want to "embrace such an expensive proposal," and quoted a cautionary Bob Noyce as saying, "The board's plan won't happen if the industry won't provide substantial support, and that's questionable."[29] The $250 million a year each in contributions quoted by the press daunted both Congress and industry leaders.

The DSB task force reported findings at least as alarming from a national security viewpoint as Kane's obituary had been from an industrial one, and its primary recommendation was surprisingly similar to the one emerging out of the SIA discussions. Both called for a collaborative effort under the auspices of a Semiconductor Manufacturing Technology Institute sponsored and funded jointly by the government and industry. The task force supported its recommendation with the observation that "a direct threat to the technological superiority deemed essential to U.S. defense systems exists [since]:

- U.S. military forces depend heavily on *technological superiority to win.*
- *Electronics* is the technology that can be leveraged most highly.
- *Semiconductors* are the key to leadership in electronics.
- *Competitive, high-volume production* is the key to leadership in semiconductors.
- High-volume production is supported by the *commercial* market.
- *Leadership* in commercial volume production is being *lost* by the semiconductor industry.
- Semiconductor technology leadership, which in this field is loosely coupled to manufacturing leadership, will soon reside *abroad.*
- US Defense will soon *depend on foreign sources* for state-of-the-art technology in semiconductors. The Task Force views this as an unacceptable situation."[30]

The DSB report used militant language to declare that a "threat" to U.S. technological superiority existed. The DOD was not the only one using martial language in referring to the Japanese semiconductor industry. In a widely quoted (and often misquoted) comment on the DSB task force report, Shintaro Ishihara, a member of the Japanese Diet wrote: "In short, without using new-generation computer chips made in Japan, the US Department of Defense cannot guarantee the precision of its nuclear weapons. If Japan told Washington it would no longer sell computer chips to the United States, the Pentagon would be totally helpless. Furthermore, the global military balance could be completely upset if Japan decided to sell its computer chips to the Soviet Union instead of the United States. (Some Americans say that if we contemplated such action, US forces would reoccupy Japan.)"[31]

Ishihara's book met with popular acclaim in Japan and appeared in bootleg translations in Washington for some time before it was published in English in the United States. Although Ishihara professed to be making an overture toward more respectful U.S.-Japan communication, his language contributed to an already rising level of American nationalism that was creating bonds of patriotic fervor between groups that were traditionally suspicious of each other, such as chip makers and government officials.

Patriotic fervor created a paradox, however, since most American chip makers had various kinds and degrees of offshore alliances, mostly with Japanese firms, but a growing number with Korean companies, and some in Europe. With one arm they were holding hands with their Japanese partners, and with the other arm enlisting public and political support to oppose them. Managing this paradox to satisfy both Congress and other consortium members would be essential if any government funds were involved—and any meaningful information shared.

## Sematech Is Christened

Meanwhile, in September, 1986, the SIA convened again and found its initial resolve to form a manufacturing consortium strengthened by the positive consensus that Charlie Sporck brought back from his industry-wide shuttle diplomacy. The SIA formed a Manufacturing Initiative Working Group to study the idea and prepare specific recommendations for an organizational plan at a special session to be held at the end of October. The group consisted of seventeen representatives from eight of the most interested member companies, including Sporck, and Larry Sumney to represent the SRC. It also included SIA legal advisers from the firms of Dewey, Ballantine, Bushby, Palmer, and Wood of Washington, D.C., and Ware and Friedrich of Cupertino, California.

A Technology Group chaired by Ian Bell of NSC began looking at the feasibility of possible semiconductor devices that a consortium could produce as a vehicle to develop and demonstrate manufacturing advances. Choosing a product that many diversified and proprietary competitors could use as a manufacturing demonstration vehicle (MDV) posed a difficult challenge, one that would take a while to solve.

The name Sematech (an acronym for Semiconductor Manufacturing Technology) also surfaced at the special SIA session in October. Charlie Sporck is generally credited, or blamed, for coining it. Although not everyone was thrilled by it, the name stuck.

The founders of the newly named consortium began to take advantage of the collaborative experience gained by organizing their research consortium, the SRC. A manufacturing consortium, however, would have to carry out actual manufacturing processes in a semiconductor fabrication facility (fab). Every semiconductor manufacturer knew that the difficulties of achieving effective cooperation among secretive, often adversarial competitors would be enormous. There simply was not enough trust in the industry to overcome the fears of jeopardizing proprietary secrets. Even if representatives of fellow

21

companies were allowed into another company's fab, on-site security would be so high that nothing worthwhile would get done. The work-site issue epitomized the underlying fear that others would exploit their cooperation by learning their secrets and thus gain a free ride at their expense. It all centered around three questions: What technology could they use for the mission of improving performance? What firm would want to contribute a cutting-edge proprietary process? What would be the use in working on anything else?

The consortium planners faced the challenge of balancing safeguards of information security and investment risk against obtaining technology sufficiently advanced for practicing manufacturing. However, the fear of the gallows that had brought the members together reminded them that they might have nothing to lose if they did not take the chance.

Sandy Kane brought a thorough and specific set of recommendations to the October, 1986, organizational meeting. "Our presentation was carefully structured to make sure we covered all of the points that the task force was designed to cover," he recalls. "This structure became the straw man for the discussion for the next two days. Everybody picked apart things that were wrong, added things, changed it around, and focused off of it." The unusual diversity of the semiconductor industry, with merchants and captives, component makers and systems makers, niche players and military contractors, and so on, complicated the discussion. All recognized that improving manufacturing meant improving manufacturing equipment as well, but vertical integration with suppliers in a consortium seemed to be impossible. Figuring out a mechanism for horizontal integration of a group of varied chip makers was going to be difficult enough.

Discussion of commercial aspects concerned how much it would cost to create an effective consortium, which was hard to foresee, and how that cost would be funded. Would they really need a fabrication facility? That depended on their mission. Jim Peterman of TI remembers: "The discussion was lively. Lots of 'we want to do this' and 'We want to do that.' Lots of differences were aired. The biggest single issue was several folks believed you could not solve manufacturing problems in the lab, that you had to use the factory. Therefore, you had to build a large DRAM factory." The opposing view was that making a factory work would swamp long-range solutions to manufacturing problems. The solution was a compromise: Develop a fab capability, but instead of using it as a full-run production factory, use it for short-run equipment tests. Problems of mission focus and how it related to the fab question continued on well past this planning stage and complicated later execution of the plans.

Building a consortium fab—or, as originally suggested, a series of three fabs for each of the three phases of chip development—would be expensive. That issue led to discussions of how to formulate proportional dues for large and small member companies. What about companies that couldn't afford dues? Although everyone agreed the consortium was necessary, would enough members put their money and personnel on the line to make it work? Other even more difficult questions concerned intellectual property: How could enough technological information be shared to be able to work? Who would have rights to new data coming out of collaboration? Who would hold any patents awarded for consortium work? How could developed knowledge be effectively disseminated to make the hoped-for difference in competitiveness? Many of these questions again revolved around one or another aspect of what is known as the "free rider" issue. Here the question was: Will my company's "crown jewels" be exploited by other members with no comparable return if I share proprietary information? The even larger question was: If the whole semiconductor industry can benefit from the knowledge created by my investment, why should my company be the one to join, take the risks, and pay the dues?

The discussions and planning continued and became even more urgent at the November 19 meeting. Everyone felt the time pressure to mount a rescue before it was too late for the industry. "This is our last chance," one member said, "If we lose the ability to make this (manufacturing) equipment in America, we might as well fold up the tent." In November, Charlie Sporck was commissioned to develop an operating framework and to initiate a broad recruitment-and-funding campaign. He and Sandy Kane were cochairmen of a steering committee tasked with gaining political support and lobbying the various interested government agencies for the financial help the SIA's members were becoming convinced would be essential.

## SIA and DSB Recommendations Converge

When it came to seeking support from the White House, Congress, various cabinet departments, and agencies of the government, the semiconductor industry as a whole had little depth of experience on which to draw. The SIA represented a fairly young and nonunion industry, which meant it had not been a major player in the type of political networking that traditionally establishes a well-connected presence in the halls of power.

This was not all bad, though, as Clark McFadden commented: "The SIA had not been a major participant in governmental affairs over the 1960s and 1970s, and didn't have big elaborate contacts with Washington. What they did have was the benefit of a very intense focus by the government on the importance of this industry, its impact on the future, and its vulnerability."

The SIA by now had organized a two-pronged approach to its predicament, both parts requiring government consensus. First, the industry needed immediate protection from the aggression of Japan's trade practices. Second, the industry needed support for its own efforts, meaning legitimization of industry cooperation through antitrust relaxation, with financial backing to match industry investment. Potential consortium members from the SIA were wary of what form government funding might take—and of the cumbersome oversight that could be attached. It required some finesse between asking the government for trade measures and financial backing, and initiating what the industry wanted to do for itself. The SIA wanted to remain in control.

One early participant observed: "The leadership recognized that we had two problems: we were not playing on a level field, [and even] if we were, we would still not be able to compete from a quality and productivity standpoint yet. Sematech was set up to assure that somehow the SIA would get the government to help us level the playing field and apply antitrust laws across the board so we could address the quality and productivity problems."

The White House, Congress and several of its committees, the Departments of Justice, Defense, and Commerce, and the U.S. Trade Representative topped the list of those particularly interested in the consortium for economic, technological, or commercial reasons. Then the list began to snowball. Those officials in favor of government-industry collaboration had their own idea of how a consortium should be made up and supervised, how to fund it, and what its mission should be. The possibility of building a nationally supported high-tech facility would mean local popularity for the state and district that could eventually acquire it. For the SIA leaders, attempting to enlist support while avoiding pork-barrel traps must have felt like negotiating a minefield daily.

The law firm of Dewey, Ballantine, Bushby, Palmer, and Wood was there to help. They were the SIA's advocates in Washington, and many of their specialists in antitrust or trade law quickly became involved in helping the SIA make its official case while avoiding ethical entanglements. Allan Wolff and Clark McFadden are two of the firm's experts in the field of technology and its military applications. Both knew where valuable support could be found in Washington, especially in the Departments of Defense and Commerce. They worked through the complicated, shifting maze of private- and public-sector interests to help create a legitimate, workable, beneficial combination. McFadden recalls that "as the industry talked to the various departments, there were advocates who said, yes, the government ought to join and take an activist position here. There was [also] some very clear and determined opposition to the government doing anything. It led to extensive analysis and debate in the Economic Policy Council at the time. The Treasury and the Council of Economic Advisors were adamantly opposed to moving forward with any kind of government funds going into a collaborative effort with the government."

The DSB task force on semiconductor dependency was finishing up its study, due in January, when its report was leaked. The recommendation in the DSB report calling for an industry-government Semiconductor Manufacturing Technology Institute was heartening to the SIA, since it represented a potential convergence with its own developing ideas and possible official support for combining forces. As the SIA looked at the cost of establishing and equipping a fab, getting some help with government funding looked better even to those originally opposed to the idea.

## Differing Visions

The DSB report added a major impetus to the idea of collaboration between industry and government from DOD's viewpoint. However, another semiconductor study failed to arrive at the same conclusions. The National Security Council had been studying the current state and probable future of the U.S. semiconductor industry ever since the fall of 1985, the year of precipitous market share loss. This interagency panel consisted of members of the Departments of Commerce, Justice, and State, the U.S. Trade Representative, and the Office of Management and Budget (OMB), as well as various White House staff members and advisers.

Because it reflected so many viewpoints and interests, the group was reportedly plagued by divisions and unable to produce a consensus on recommendations. According to the press, "National Security Council staff members have been able to agree on the poor health of the industry, but not its future ability to be competitive internationally without federal aid."[32] The panel could not agree on such issues as the impact of the cost of capital on the U.S. semiconductor industry, the impact of the effective monetary exchange rate, the actual success of Japan's system of private sector consortiums, the relevance of the theory of "technology drivers,"[33] and the extent to which an uncompetitive U.S. semiconductor industry would compromise national security.

It is small wonder that the multiagency panel could not come to a clear consensus on these knotty issues, which collectively express the range of controversy over the political, economic, technological, and security problems that the prospect of government legitimization and support of an industrial consortium raised nationwide.

As we have seen, the semiconductor industry had enjoyed mushrooming growth in an overtly laissez-faire atmosphere in which venture capital rewarded the creativity of the entrepreneur. The individualism of the U.S. semiconductor industry seemed intrinsic both to its innovative design advantage and to its vulnerability when faced with Japan's vertically integrated production juggernaut. No one wanted Yankee creativity to suffer defeat from foreign competition, but no one wanted its spirit destroyed through domestic application of industrial policy welfare either.

How, then, to save the threatened industry without destroying it, or disrupting the cherished free market in which it had developed its technological achievements? There was no precedent for authorizing and supporting a manufacturing consortium, no matter how precompetitive, in a previously independent industry now suffering in part from the consequences of the very entrepreneurial practices that had brought it success.

Industry leaders like Sumney and Intel's Washington representative Mike Maibach continued to work alongside McFadden, Wolff, and other legal experts from Dewey, Ballantine in lobbying key administrators such as Dr.

Robert B. Costello, assistant secretary of defense for acquisition and logistics; Ronald Kerber, deputy undersecretary for research and advanced technology; E. D. Maynard, director of the DOD Office of Computer and Electronic Technology; Robert C. McCormack, deputy assistant secretary of defense for production support; and Richard E. Donnelley, director of the DOD Office of Industrial Resources. The lobbying schedule grew more intense in January, 1987. By then, Congress had returned from Christmas recess, and the DSB report was officially released.

In a cover letter to Charles Fowler, chairman of the DSB, task force leader Norman Augustine said, "The Task Force concludes that procurement by the Department of Defense is a relatively insignificant factor to the semiconductor industry; but, in contrast, the existence of a healthy U.S. semiconductor industry is critical to the national defense." Besides urgently calling for government-industry collaboration, the report recommended:[34]

- The establishment of "university centers of excellence" for semiconductor science and engineering at a cost of $50 million per year.
- A gradual increase from $60 million to $250 million in DOD spending over four years for R&D of semiconductor materials, devices, and manufacturing technology.
- The provision of a source of discretionary funds to DOD semiconductor suppliers to support R&D at a cost of $50 million.
- The creation under DOD auspices of a joint government-industry-university forum for semiconductors at $200,000 per year.[35]

This DSB study, after analyzing causes for the semiconductor industry's predicament, concluded: "The major reason for the relative inadequacy of technology development in the U.S. vis-à-vis that in Japan has been the difference in the industrial practices and structure of the two countries."

The comprehensive nature of the study, including its attention paid to training, industrial and business practices, and up- and downstream connections with suppliers and end users, made it a useful document for anyone trying to understand both the complicated situation and its possible remedies. Many of these task force recommendations gave timely help to consortium planners, especially as they sought to formulate an initiative that could win government support.

The National Security Council panel was a different story. No one knew when, if ever, the group would come to any publishable conclusions. The SIA members were very concerned about what government agency would interface with Sematech and what form the involvement would take. McFadden remembers: "We spent a lot of time arguing, writing papers, and making an intellectual case of why the government should be concerned, why we had a problem, why we needed to do something about it, and why collaborative action was appropriate. That took the form of both dealing directly with government officials, but also trying to generate, in public press and intellectual community in Washington and elsewhere, a rationale that was defensible for government participation. This was something that was not tightly controlled by any means. Lots of people contributed to it, and there were lots of nuances and variations on it."

Even though the SIA had officially agreed to establish a manufacturing consortium called Sematech, and even though the working committees were developing a plan, they still faced differences among their own interested members about the desirability of having the government as a partner. There was also a question as to whether the consortium should focus on recovering DRAM manufacturing for the United States or instead on raising general competitiveness. Obviously, asking for trade protection against Japan's cheap DRAM chips if there was no surviving DRAM manufacturing capacity in the United States would be ironic, but the systems makers in the SIA were still nervous about losing their sources of inexpensive Japanese DRAM chips. Would these American firms support a consortium effort to reestablish U.S. DRAM production?

On March 3, 1987, with the official DSB task force report in hand, and with positive results in from feasibility analyses done by several SIA committees, the SIA board formally approved establishing a consortium to be known as Sematech. The venture was to have a $200 million budget, with half coming from dues-paying members and the remainder, the industry hoped, coming from the federal government, aided by other sources such as the National Science Foundation (NSF) and state funds where Sematech would locate. The organization was born with the creation of a steering committee that would report to the SIA board. Larry Sumney, president of the SRC, chaired the Sematech steering committee. It was time to begin acting on all the talk.

However, before the organization could act, it needed an operating plan incorporating the basic agreement hammered out by the SIA the previous fall, and developing all the ideas suggested, fought over, and agreed upon in the ensuing months of study and talk. The recommendations of the DSB task force were also a valuable resource. On March 10, a planning task force of thirteen volunteers from ten SIA firms, chaired by Norm Argast of IBM and Ted Malanczuk of NSC, was formed to write the operating plan. Called the "Black Book," it outlined Sematech's goals and the organizational, business, and technological strategies for achieving them.[36] Jonathan A. "Skip" Greenfield, of Ware and Friedrich in California, helped them create a legal structure for incorporation.

The Black Book not only was intended to cover everything, it also "offered everything for everybody," as one early observer commented. The authors of the Black Book were in a bind: The plan had to appeal to potential members with various competing needs, but since their membership or financial contributions were as yet unconfirmed, it was difficult to be precise about expectations.

As the Black Book team set to work, well-known members of the SIA public policy committee continued to lobby for the federal funding that even the most reluctant members now agreed they would need. Key to Sematech's success was the fact that, rather than sending professional lobbyists to do the job, top industry champions devoted themselves to gaining the ears of government leaders, thus bypassing much of the turf rivalry of the usual agency and subcommittee politics of Washington. People like Robert W. "Bob" Galvin of Motorola, Bob Noyce of Intel, Charlie Sporck of NSC, and many others spent countless hours lobbying.

For instance in March, 1987, Jonathan E. Cornell, senior vice president of Harris Semiconductor, testified before a Senate subcommittee that recent efforts to revive U.S. chip makers had failed because of the redundant use of entrepreneurial resources and a lack of coordination between the government and industry. Cornell could now point out that both the DSB and the SIA were making specific recommendations for government-industry collaboration.

McFadden, commenting on the power of the simultaneous initiatives supported by the intensive lobbying and publicizing effort of the SIA, observed: "Had it not been that the industry, at the same time, was engaged in a very concerted effort to address the same problem, and came to essentially the same conclusion, the DSB report would probably have had the same fate as countless other Defense studies. It is an interesting study; thank you very much. Then, it disappears."

This time, however, the study did not disappear. On April 7, Secretary of Defense Caspar Weinberger, in a talk before the American Electronics Association, publicly endorsed Sematech, saying that the United States could not afford "to rely on other nations, no matter how friendly, for the technological innovations that are fundamental to our defense." The following day he sent a memo to Undersecretary of Defense for Acquisition Richard P. Godwin, requesting policy recommendations to implement the DSB semiconductor dependency report. Lobbyists, including George Scalise and McFadden, also met in April with Defense officials, including Craig Fields, from interested areas of Defense Research and Technology and the Strategic Defense Initiative (SDI). Fields was later to lead the Defense Advanced Research Projects Agency (DARPA), which became the government's representative in Sematech.

On April 28, the Senate Armed Services Committee (SASC) met in executive session, marked up the fiscal year (FY) 1988–89 Defense Authorization Bill, and recommended a funding authorization for FYs 1988 and 1989 for "semiconductor manufacturing technology." Senators Tim Wirth (D-Colorado) and Jeff Bingaman (D-New Mexico) championed the bill and managed to raise the suggested funding level to $100 million by stressing the urgent need for immediate, effective action.

Even given the political boost of Weinberger's endorsement of Sematech, his official move to implement the DSB report, and the fact that DOD technology needs were closely connected to the industry's, many SIA members were not convinced that collaboration with the cumbersome DOD bureaucracy would work. These skeptics thought the Department of Commerce, led by supportive Secretary Malcolm Baldrige, would be more compatible with private industry. The House of Representatives passed an omnibus trade bill on April 30 that allocated $100 million a year from the Department of Commerce for the next five fiscal years to aid the semiconductor industry's comeback. Bipartisan champions of the bill were Rep. James J. Florio (D-New York), chairman of the House Energy and Commerce Committee, and Rep. Don Ritter (R-Pennsylvania). However, the bill did not include spending authority. Whether Commerce or Defense, or both, would become the government's partner in Sematech was not clear. The Senate leaned toward DOD, whereas the House supported Commerce involvement. The Department of Energy's (DOE) interest came from its authority over the national laboratories and their microelectronics research.

The funding amounts recommended, allocated, and finally authorized by groups from the first DSB task force to congressional subcommittees fluctuated up and down depending on who was talking and at what point in the budget process. The $250 million originally advised by the DSB board—an arrangement that made both Congress and the industry cringe—might not look so bad if it could be shared. The language and dollar amounts in the various proposals slowly grew closer together as the seemingly endless discussions went on and plans became more focused.

The Black Book writers had to consider the as yet unspecified and unconfirmed nature and amount of government support in the consortium's organizational and financial plan. However, they were determined not to let official oversight dominate and doom the project. A key worry about government interference was the antitrust dimension. Before Sematech could exist and operate as a legitimate organization, it needed assurance of antitrust exemption. Here the level of official support served to clear the path.

McFadden recalls that there was a series of complaints at the outset about government participation: "We can't deal with them on a contract basis. The cost accounting standards in a consortium are absolutely too prohibitive. It is too inefficient in most of our own businesses. If we have to deal with all of the international controls on this technology that we have to deal with in our normal export administration and international traffic and arms regime, we'll never do this. If we have antitrust concerns, if we can't get some general relief there, we'll never go forward." Although different companies had different views, all agreed that if the current regulations were not relaxed, the consortium was doomed.

Legal experts and industry leaders began working together with the regulatory officials in an effort to solve the problem. Using their SRC and trade lobbying experience, they nurtured the growing attention to the industry predicament in Washington. They needed to, because, as McFadden reports: "In terms of the Sematech proposal, we were vastly beyond anything that had ever been attempted in collaborative R&D under the 1984 Act. There was really no experience for that. It took quite a leap for the Justice Department to see [their previous monopolization targets] AT&T, IBM, and all the others in this; why would Justice take an open mind to that?" Why, indeed? It is worth recalling that both AT&T and IBM had long, costly histories of antitrust prosecution by the Justice Department.

Nevertheless, McFadden says that, given the importance of the industry to America's overall economy and trade balance, the Justice Department had participated in the earlier high-level, interagency deliberations on the trade side and on the Economic Policy Council. When the Sematech advocates came to the Justice Department looking for regulatory relaxation, McFadden notes: "Instead of just the head of the Antitrust Division, who takes a very skeptical view of any of these matters, we had two Deputy Assistant Attorney Generals who had participated in this whole general issue. They were very familiar with the urgency and the importance of this to the nation, and with the trade problems and the international scope. We got a reception and analysis from the Justice Department that showed interest in helping us solve this problem, rather than telling us why it couldn't be done."

The National Cooperative Research Act of 1984 exempted R&D consortia from antitrust penalties, but it did not exempt manufacturing or joint-production initiatives.[37] Because of the Justice Department's positive attitude, McFadden says, new amendments were eventually worked out that made it possible to include Sematech as the first U.S. manufacturing consortium under the antitrust protection of the original National Cooperative Research Act. As a nonprofit corporation, Sematech would be allowed to produce its not-for-sale manufacturing demonstration chips in the fab, inasmuch as these chips were considered an essential element of developing improved manufacturing processes.[38] These processes were still to be precompetitive—that is, focused on generic improvements that members could apply to their own proprietary products back in their fabs.

Other government leaders also lent their support, particularly Secretary Baldrige, for whom the Malcolm Baldrige National Quality Award is named.[39] Ambassador Michael Smith, the U.S. Trade Representative, helped to smooth regulation negotiations, and the DOD's national security concerns about semiconductor dependency continued to impart a sense of urgency.

## CHAPTER 2

# The Black Book Sets the Structure

**A**s the negotiating, recruiting, lobbying, and publicizing intensified, and the possibility of Sematech looked more real day by day, attention focused more and more on the Black Book. "It was about a four-inch thick set of detailed plans, descriptions of tasks, and descriptions of approaches to the solutions," Jim Peterman recalls. The four main areas it covered—and the men responsible for them—were: government affairs under Jon Cornell of Harris Semiconductor and George Scalise of SRC, legal-organizational structure planning under Bill Sick and Jim Peterman of TI, a funding task force led by Sandy Kane of IBM, and a human resources task force chaired by Bob Jenkins of Motorola.[1] Peterman remembers subdividing the tasks, and says that the book eventually had at least a dozen tabs, with separate sections for issues like Total Quality.

A steering committee of Peterman, George Schneer of Intel, and Sandy Kane met with the Black Book team as often as possible. Their parent companies were paying them to concentrate largely on consortium planning. But not all of the steering committee members were able to give Sematech first priority, despite their commitment to the cause. For some it was an added responsibility on top of their already demanding corporate jobs.

The Black Book grew into a document so sweeping in scope that it later became a burden when the organization trying to implement it had to face funding realities. One assignee later said of the book: "It was a typical case of a group of engineers getting together to write a task for another group. No stone was left unturned, even recognizing that there was no way to focus a mission on something that broad."

The Black Book established a key framework, however. It presented a road map for three projected phases of technological achievement, each phase increasing the miniaturization of features on silicon chips—and using American equipment exclusively to do it. It allotted a five-year federal budget horizon for these phased goals. The three phases corresponded with Sematech's three-stage overall strategic objectives. Those objectives, to be achieved by 1992, included recovering global competitiveness, maintaining a globally competitive position, and regaining global leadership in semiconductor manufacturing. Once those phases were completed and once the progress achieved for the first five years had been evaluated, two more phases would be drawn up for a ten-year horizon, assuming approval had been gained for continued support.[2]

The Phase I goal was to master the technologies of .80 micron[3] width features on a silicon chip; the Phase II goal was to reduce this size to .50-micron lines; and Phase III to .35-micron lines. Competitive analysis by member companies and industry analysts showed that accomplishing these three technological goals by 1992 would be necessary for the United States to recover and maintain global leadership in semiconductor manufacturing. The ability to keep decreasing the size of circuit lines or features on a chip depends on continual refinement of processes and manufacturing equipment. Simply measuring something as fine as a thousandth of a millimeter requires ultramicroscopic precision.

Sematech's planners recognized that in addition to cooperation the industry needed a stronger infrastructure to reach the micron-feature objectives of its planned phases. The Black Book did not specify how to achieve that infrastructure; that would take more negotiation and experimentation. Charlie Sporck understood the difficulty of connecting semiconductor process technology and production equipment expertise. "I don't think the solution exists," he said. "We're going to have to build one."[4]

## Financial and Legal Issues

How to handle intellectual property issues in a consortium was the task not so much for those writing the Black Book as for those charged with structuring the organization. Intellectual property became one of the key problems needing resolution before an acceptable members' participation agreement could be drawn up. This agreement defined the requirements, rights, privileges, and responsibilities of the members and of Sematech, and the relationships between them. Modifying the agreement could only be done with a unanimous vote of the members, so it needed consensus on its structure from all fourteen members and the DOD right from the beginning. When one company objected to a specification or requested an item change it triggered other changes, leading to what seemed endless controversy and revision.

Underlying these structural difficulties was the members' recurring question: "How are we going to do this and not give our own technology away to our rivals and/or to the Japanese counterparts in their alliances?" This was uppermost in members' thinking primarily because almost all the industry spokesmen believed that the market share problems were technology problems. "No one expected any gain by changing the way we did business," recalls one of the participants in the process. Business was typically done through rivalry over technological innovation, thus the emphasis on guarding against free riders and on practicing secrecy. The limited domestic partnerships previously allowed under U.S. antitrust law operated on trade-offs of calculated exploitation. A different basis for creating benefits was emerging, but how to construct a mechanism that people could trust was not yet clear.

The organizational differences of SIA members heightened the free rider and secrecy concerns. In 1987 IBM was nearly as large as all the other members put together, a few members had defense contracts with tight security classifications, and many firms had valuable Japanese alliances. For instance, Intel had no DOD contracts, 10 percent of Motorola's were with DOD, and TI inked about 50 percent of its contracts with DOD agencies. Texas Instrument's Peterman recalls his company's concern was that "This [lack of secrecy] might make it impossible for TI to participate in Sematech, depending on how the participation agreement was written. Also because of TI's relationship with Hitachi, the company had to manage two contracts that had little overlap. The issue was how to manage both agreements. TI would not give up Hitachi for Sematech and would not give up Sematech for Hitachi."

Talks were both careful and contentious on all sides. Early participants recall about a dozen major issues, with no pattern of coalitions among members. On one issue, the differences would be between Company A and Company B; on another issue, it would be Company C versus Company X.

Jim Peterman remembers that "Bill Sick from TI was given the task of working the legal problems, the biggest of which was on intellectual property. In one meeting in New York there were thirty-two lawyers in the room and me. Intellectual property lawyers for individual companies are a tough group to work with. If you're looking for consensus and agreement on wording, you can spend a lot of time on what seems to be very little. It went on and on." The development of a participation agreement required members to resolve these issues before they could sign. Fortunately, the firms had a strong incentive for reaching a consensus: Besides their similar manufacturing technology and equipment needs, they all faced the haunting specter of imminent demise.

In addition to the intellectual property free-rider issue there was concern over the relationship between the size of investment different companies would make and how that would affect their influence on the consortium's strategic choices. McFadden recalls: "For the most part, there was full participation of major players in the industry and the major contributors to SIA. There was tremendous financial pressure on all of them, especially the merchant firms, and they were asking, 'We want to do this, but how much is it going to cost us?' Smaller firms were very willing to receive the advantage of the big captives' high dues and technology donations, but didn't want them to dominate the agenda. . . . It was curious to watch the negotiations, because it was against the interests of a number of these smaller companies to say, 'We've capped the contributions of the big players, and that means now we're going to have to pay more.'" This paradox was doubly painful for the smaller companies, which were already suffering financially but stood to lose more if the size of their own membership contribution did not carry any clout.

Motives for the larger captives' cooperation were still suspect to many smaller merchant players, one of whom likened the experience to being offered bananas by a gorilla. "There was a healthy skepticism," McFadden concurs. "A remarkable part of this was that, while there was great rapport and an ability to work together, there was clearly a lot of acrimony and controversy in the marketplace among these folks. They are fierce competitors. Different lifestyles were visible just sitting at the table. They did things differently, and they approached problems differently." Trade-offs were required of everyone in order to include all the players at all the levels necessary to make the consortium work. Admission of their interdependence was a good starting point.

## Striking a Balance

The common danger that drew participants together affected them differently, creating barriers to cooperation. The merchants liked the technological process and the financial support that the big captives like IBM would contribute, but they did not want the captives to dominate Sematech's agenda. The captives, meanwhile, wanted to benefit from the merchants' innovative drive and agile management practices, but they feared that the merchants might not pull their own weight.

Because these needs varied as widely as their uses, the consortium needed a balanced support of semiconductor makers nationwide, with no sector left out. A demonstrated need for semiconductor manufacturing technology was reason enough for any given firm's cooperation. Major uses for microchips include computers and electronic controls of many kinds, DOD systems, and automotive components. However, except for Motorola, which has a huge microelectronics auto business, the automotive sector was never persuaded to help. For instance, efforts to woo Delco into becoming a member failed.

Important also was the determination that no one without a demonstrable need should be using the consortium for other purposes, such as for political domination. McFadden puts it plainly: "We didn't want to have any free riders, large or small. We didn't want to have a big chunk of the industry excluded from participating in the effort while participating in the benefits. Jerry Sanders of AMD made it very clear that he didn't want anybody getting a free ride, and several others supported that conclusion. Even without the automotive sector, we had 80 percent of the [microchip using] industry and that was sufficient."

The financial incentives for securing government participation were convincing, however. Industry members realized that their investment share might be, for example, $55 million without any government help but only $15–25 million with it. "SIA members started looking at this and saying, 'Wait a minute. The numbers don't add up here,'" McFadden recalls.

Trade officials encouraged the industry to abandon its traditional standoffish attitude and not try to do it all alone. Government participation would give the consortium national credibility and improve the chances of passing through many official hurdles, like the relaxation of antitrust laws or legislative authorization. Several people remember feeling: "Well, if all this comes together in a balanced way, we're for it. If it becomes lopsided in any sense, it's gone."

## Getting Started

Leaving negotiation of many of these differences to be settled by the participation agreement allowed the Black Book to be written rapidly and presented to the SIA board at a special session in Dallas, on May 12, 1987.[5] The board approved the first draft of the $250 million budget and operational plan, with half to be provided by the industry and half by the government. The plan was subject to revision and finalization in June, but the board authorized the steering committee to begin implementing it immediately. The participation agreement would come later. First there had to be an organization for companies to join.

The SIA board would still supply direction during the organizational phase, and the SRC would provide an institutional interface with the research community, including universities and labs. Larry Sumney, head of the SRC, was to serve as acting head of the start-up operation from May to September, the target date for incorporation.[6] Company membership in the SRC was to be a requirement for Sematech membership, a provision that effectively raised the cost of participation and angered some smaller companies.[7]

Other resolutions in the Black Book plan included a formula for member contributions, calculated at 1 percent of semiconductor sales, with a $1 million minimum and a maximum contribution of 15 percent of Sematech's $100 million member share, which was to be matched by DOD. The SIA member companies guaranteed $1.5 million for start-up funding to cover expenses before incorporation and government funding could be achieved. Those funds were to be managed by the steering committee, with Sporck and Kane serving as cochairs,[8] and were crucial for running the technical planning workshops.

The plan also established two committees—one charged with finding a CEO and COO for Sematech and one to select its permanent site. Bob Noyce of Intel and Jerry Sanders of AMD were cochairs of the executive search. They were joined by George Bodway of Hewlett-Packard and Robert Palmer of Digital Equipment (DEC). Sandy Kane headed the site selection panel.[9]

At the same May meeting, board members committed to the formation of a team to get things rolling. The start-up team would consist of engineers and scientists supplied by Sematech's potential member companies, and would be the first short-term example of the technical and managerial assignees that member companies would eventually send to the consortium. IBM's Jack Woods and AMD's Colin Knight became the team's two COOs. National Semiconductor contributed space for an interim headquarters in its Santa Clara, California, offices and Sematech's wheels began to turn at last. Over the summer, some twenty-five assignees collected in Santa Clara. Their salaries and expenses were still being paid by their member companies as Sematech was not yet a legal entity with its own money. Lillie Haynes came from TI to act as financial officer and comptroller to help sort out the ambiguous situation.[10]

Most assignees came without their families, renting small apartments for short leases. No one knew yet where Sematech would be permanently located, but it would probably not be Silicon Valley, which was strongly associated with the merchant firms and had an exceptionally high cost of living.

Turner Hasty of TI was assigned two early organizational tasks required by the Black Book. First, he was to establish Sematech Centers of Excellence (SCOE) at research universities. The SCOEs were specifically recommended in the DSB report and will be described in more detail below. Second, he was to develop a peripheral system of advisory boards of industry experts that would be responsible to the Board of Directors for providing counsel to Sematech's management and for assisting with the external leverage of resources. The Board of Directors would set policy, while Sematech's management staff was charged with making operational decisions. The advisory boards, meanwhile, would advise them both, as well as provide high-level contacts with outside agencies. Chief among these boards was the Executive Technical Advisory Board (ETAB), consisting of high-level representatives from each member company and the DOD. The ETAB would receive recommendations from its subboards—called Focus Technical Advisory Boards (FTABs)—each responsible for specific areas of technology. Industry specialists from each area, usually from firms with particular expertise or interest in the area, would serve as members of the FTABs. However, FTAB meetings were open to any company that wished to send someone.

The ETAB and FTABs were intended to play an external communications and advisory role, with advice coming into Sematech from the outside, up from the FTABs to the ETAB, and then to either the Board of Directors or the CEO. In practice, however, it was often difficult for a high-ranking FTAB representative from a company with an assignee at Sematech not to feel an urge to meddle, or just to give the assignee a little proprietary direction. Since assignees planned to return to their parent firms, they could hardly ignore this advice, and dealing with the back-channel interference was sometimes a problem.

As with so many other cooperative issues, working out the difficulties came with practice, and the advisory boards proved to be a valuable part of the process. In the summer and fall of 1987, the framework for the TABs was still being worked out, with staffing to follow as member firms signed on and began paying dues. The SIA Board of Directors was still acting as the Sematech board because there was a strong overlap between the companies supporting the initiative and their representation on the SIA board.[11]

## SEMI's Involvement

The Black Book specified the absolute necessity of including not just chip manufacturers, but the industry's supplier infrastructure as well. Improving manufacturing processes would be manifestly impossible without the involvement of the makers of manufacturing equipment and materials. Their trade association, SEMI, was the logical cooperative interface. As the initiative for Sematech had formed and grown, several SEMI leaders, especially Sam Harrell and Scott Kulicke, of Kulicke and Soffa Industries, lobbied effectively for it in Washington. However, one of the biggest hurdles to SEMI's official participation was that as relationships weakened between the U.S. semiconductor industry and its infrastructure throughout the 1980s, and ties with Japanese, Korean, and European chip makers strengthened, SEMI had become an international organization. Harrell notes that it changed its name from the Semiconductor Equipment and Material *Institute* to Semiconductor Equipment and Material *International,* which remains its name today.

Including an international association in a consortium dedicated to regaining national leadership in the global market appeared to present conflicts of interest for both SEMI and Sematech, and might cost them the support of their constituents. In addition, the animosity that had developed between U.S. chip makers and suppliers could not be overcome immediately. Their history made them vulnerable to "Othello's Law," which states that there is always a reason for distrust and doubt in a relationship if one looks hard enough for it.[12] According to Harrell: "There [was] a series of meetings between the SEMI board members and the SIA board members, which were strikingly adversarial. Strikingly adversarial on both sides. Everyone had a set of wounds and war stories that reinforced their preconceived notions about one another. There was plenty of data to reinforce the no."

Clark McFadden also recalls the hostile nature of the meetings that occurred in the course of strenuous, all-day negotiations: "We had all the lawyers from all the different companies and several from equipment companies. Finally, after a lot of acrimony, one of the company guys, who happened to be the head of intellectual property for one of the big companies, gets up and says, 'Look, I don't want to take any more of this crap. We all know you equipment guys are thieves, you've been stealing our technology for years, and we're the ones who are keeping you guys in business. I'll be damned if we're going to finance this, and turn it all over to you.' When he said, 'We all know you're a bunch of thieves,' everybody said, 'Yeah!' It really captured the essence of the relationship between the supplier and producer in American industry." The suppliers shared that sentiment. They were convinced the chip makers kept them weak and vulnerable in order to exploit them.

Still, both sides knew they would have to work together to survive, and American SEMI leaders decided to become involved in Sematech. Harrell describes how hard the decision was: "You have to understand that, by now, the Japanese were the equipment community's largest customer, the best partners they had. The majority of the wafer starts were taking place in Japan, and American customers were losing American share. It was a serious debate: If I partner with Americans, I'm partnering with the losing team instead of the winning team. At the same time, the Japanese semiconductor community is trying to drive me out of business in parallel with all of this."

To become a legitimate member of the consortium, the supplier group formed a separate, American-only branch, called SEMI/Sematech in the summer of 1987. (Many feel that this lumbering acronym only compounds the offenses of the name Sematech, but it sticks, too.) This branch shared many members and leaders with SEMI, but none of its international concerns. This branching off was a major organizational transformation for SEMI/Sematech, and it began the evolution of an even closer working relationship with the consortium.

After the first draft of the Black Book was approved at the special May 12 meeting, the steering committee began to develop its provisions, including figuring out a way to include the interested supplier infrastructure. The headquarters for SEMI was located just down the road from the interim Sematech offices supplied by National Semiconductor, and a SEMI team held weekly meetings with Sematech's start-up team. The results of these meetings were reviewed by the steering committee and discussed by the Sematech board.

## The Problems of Sharing Information

The same old problem of proprietorship of interests and information soon resurfaced. "In many ways, the biggest problem was intellectual property rights at the interface between the vendors with the contractor's equipment firms and the device firms," remembers McFadden. For example, consortium members would not obligate themselves to purchase manufacturing equipment developed in joint projects. However, they originally demanded that they have exclusive option on it for eighteen months. But equipment makers saw this as punishment rather than a reward for consortium involvement. This particularly acrimonious debate continued for a long while. Much later, as we will see, the members' lack of commitment to purchase developed equipment created business difficulties for one of Sematech's technological successes.

The early planners were not able to come to a complete resolution of some of these differences, but they worked out in practice. In the middle of June, 1987, SEMI/Sematech was offered a seat on the Sematech board and the vertical concerns of equipment and materials suppliers became an integral part of the horizontal consortium of chip makers. The visibility of SEMI/Sematech's participation gave credibility to the consortium's claim that it aimed to benefit the entire industry—"raising all boats" and not just a few, as early planners like to say.

The involvement of SEMI/Sematech also helped to counter fears that Sematech would be an expensive and unjustified way for the government to pick winners and losers, and thus encouraged political support. Representatives of SEMI/Sematech, most notably Sam Harrell and Scott Kulicke, became key supplier spokespersons in Washington and throughout the industry, just as were Sporck, Noyce, Galvin, Sumney, Scalise, and other major chip manufacturers. Soon, SEMI/Sematech published a summary of its new role, stating: "For Sematech and the semiconductor industry to be viable there must be a real partnership between the semiconductor manufacturers and the semiconductor equipment and material manufacturers [therefore]:

- A Sematech chapter of SEMI is being established.
- The chapter will be a member of Sematech with a seat on the Sematech board of directors.
- The chapter and its members will participate in Sematech technical planning workshops.
- The chapter will provide the vehicle for Sematech to reach potential vendors for development projects and encourage teaming of vendors."

Even before its authors made the final revisions and formulations, the Black Book, which spelled out the working relationships between Sematech and SEMI as well as between Sematech and the SRC, was approved by the SIA board in June. But an organizational structure for collaboration still had to be constructed, and it had to be reflected in a participation agreement for members to sign when they paid their dues and committed themselves to the organization. Also still to be resolved were such issues as legal rights and obligations, intellectual property and patents, and access to consortium development for member companies and for suppliers involved in Sematech projects. Meanwhile, however, there was an immediate constructive role for the start-up team, aided by SEMI representatives, in conducting the technical-planning workshops mentioned above.

These workshops were among the earliest activities organized by Sematech's founders. The SIA provided start-up funds for the workshops, which were held not so much to explain the consortium as to pinpoint and gather specific data on the key technical problems in all areas of semiconductor manufacturing. The workshops were designed to accumulate this information from the industry rank-and-file so that Sematech could concentrate on what was actually needed rather than dictate unwanted prescriptions.

Colin Knight, as a co-COO of the start-up team, organized the series of workshops. He also conducted several, including the introductory workshop conducted June 8–10 at the Naval Postgraduate School at Monterey, California, just down the coast from Silicon Valley. This kick-off workshop was jointly sponsored by the steering committee and the Institute for Defense Analysis, and consisted of a briefing on Sematech for all interested parties, followed by seminar sessions to organize and schedule the planned strategic workshops. Sixty representatives from the semiconductor industry attended the workshop, along with 120 more from various universities, national laboratories, and the government.

Bill George, who in 1991 would become Sematech's COO, had just begun an assignment for Motorola in its new alliance with Toshiba. He attended the kick-off workshop and was excited by what he saw. The Japanese engineers he had been working with for six months had told him that the biggest difference they saw in working with an American firm was "the lack of a partnership between the IC companies and their suppliers. We just didn't work with each other, and we fought all the time. That was an interesting perspective. I came down to the workshops and began to see, in fact, that there were suppliers here and supplier companies. I said, 'Here's our opportunity. Finally we can get together and begin to work together on these things. Sematech has one real opportunity: to get the semiconductor producers speaking with one voice to their suppliers.'"

George's Toshiba assignment kept him away until Motorola allowed him to become Sematech's COO in 1991. By then, relations between U.S. manufacturers and suppliers were steadily improving, along with their share of the market.

## Technology Workshops and Road Maps

Beginning with the June, 1987 Monterey workshop, the start-up team, guided by the steering committee, then organized a series of thirty-four such gatherings (later extended to over a hundred) to design the technical specifications for Sematech's manufacturing agenda, based on the extensive objectives listed in the Black Book. Two to four of these early workshops were held monthly, each typically lasting two days. They ran through April, 1988, at several sites from coast to coast. Members of the start-up team, as well as experts in at least thirty different technical areas from companies committed to Sematech, conducted the sessions, then assembled and interpreted the data they generated for the consortium to use, sometimes in the form of a technology road map. Feedback from these meetings continued to come in for more than a year. The practice of holding workshops continues today, although their purposes are different from the early planning sessions. The continuing workshops vary widely— from user group forums to technology transfer sessions.

Besides developing Sematech's technical agenda, the workshops provided a valuable forum for sharing ideas—something that had never been available, or even possible, before the new level of antitrust protection. The workshops publicly signaled a new era of cooperation. They brought together people who ordinarily had no chance to meet and provided a noncompetitive arena for discussing common problems and working out potential solutions.

Obi Oberai of IBM made a key presentation at the first workshop. His job at IBM involved talking with people in the various divisions and technical areas of the huge company, collecting information for road maps for coordinating in-house efforts. IBM had already asked him to talk to other chip makers, just as it had sent Sandy Kane around with his forecast of the industry's fate. Oberai, however, was to put together a picture of what the industry needed to do to survive. That report became his contribution to the first workshop.

Oberai, who had done all of the IBM semiconductor road-mapping activity—including introducing its technical and philosophical components—was accustomed to telling why it was necessary to get together with other people in the company and share details. He describes how he went about mapping the industry's potential future: "So now I was out in the industry saying, 'Here's what you've got to do and how we've got to change in the next ten years.'" Oberai presented his road map at the June, 1987, Monterey meeting and attended all the other workshops that followed. He eventually became one of the first assignees to come to the consortium's permanent site when it was chosen. He also became Sematech's first director of strategic analysis.

During the continuing effort to negotiate the consortium's participation agreement, Oberai's skills also helped to overcome an impasse by creating an innovative technology-sharing road map that ingeniously enabled member companies to cooperate on information without betraying proprietary secrets. Later, as guarding technological secrets became less important, this particular map was outgrown, but it set a precedent for future work.

The value of Oberai's first Sematech participation road map was that it showed member-company leaders how they could cooperate even without total consensus and without betraying the proprietary information that they believed gave them a competitive advantage. Each firm, in other words, could see niches where it could usefully cooperate even at partial levels. The road map didn't resolve all of their differences, but it did something almost as good: it incorporated them into a pattern of possibilities.

The workshops also helped attendees understand what technical problems they shared before they attempted to develop solutions. In fact, the workshops inspired Sematech's first comprehensive road maps correlating the collective technological needs of various sectors of the entire industry with programs that addressed them, and their projected timetables. For many rank-and-file industry members, the workshops and their resultant road maps were the best thing to come out of the start-up period. As Harrell recalls: "Those were working sessions which drove to some conclusions about the needs and requirements of the industry and what was most likely alternatives to meet those needs and requirements. Those were very powerful interactions that had never been able to happen before."

Even before the consortium's incorporation and financial arrangements were in place, the workshops began providing a leveraging effect never before possible. Says Harrell: "They empowered enormous amounts of investment to get focused on those problems. Sematech's [proposed] $100 million from the government and $100 million from industry was peanuts compared to what the industry spends on its own balance sheets. Suppliers alone spend $1.4 billion a year on RD&T [research, development, and testing]. The member companies spend $6 to $7 billion a year on RD&T in a comparable basis. What the strategic workshop road maps did was to set in motion a bunch of focusing activities of $8 or $9 billion worth of effort, not just $200 million worth of effort."

## The Executive and Site Selection Searches

While the workshops were providing a forum for technical communication, other committees were busy as well. The executive search committee headed by Bob Noyce and Jerry Sanders was charged with finding a CEO ready to lead Sematech once it was incorporated and able to operate as a legal, independent entity—a milestone that was expected to be accomplished by the early fall of 1987. Nominated candidates were to be submitted for consideration by the end of July.

Having the steering committee act as the CEO during the interim start-up phase was unwieldy enough, but it would become infinitely more awkward when the organization started coming together and needed leadership. The number of top-level semiconductor executives who traveled, testified, lobbied, negotiated, and recruited for Sematech made an undeniable impression wherever they went, but Congress and DOD were pressing to discover who the consortium's real leader would be. Furthermore, recruiting consortium members and their assignees would be easier if a well-known industry leader headed Sematech.

As it happens, it was a long time before Sematech's CEO was finally chosen. Those who were willing to serve were never asked, and those who were asked were not willing—at least for a while. The search was to go on for over a year. Fortunately, no one knew that at the time.

Sandy Kane's site selection committee, organized at the Black Book approval meeting, reflected IBM's desire to assume a strongly supportive but less aggressive role in Sematech. He recalls: "We had a top-level discussion before the meeting at IBM that said that one of our concerns was that we had a company that has facilities all around the country. We were concerned that IBM executives, because of IBM's visibility in Sematech, would be calling and saying, 'Hey, can you help me do this so we can get Sematech to come to our site?'"

The thinking at IBM was that one of the best ways to avoid internal arm-twisting would be to take a visible role in the site selection process. "Then, the party line that could come from [CEO John] Akers would be that it would not be proper for us to get involved in that because we're participating in the selection process. This was a way to say no and be clean and have a legitimate excuse," Kane added.

The site committee went right to work, sending out letters on May 20 to the governors of all fifty states and Puerto Rico. The letters announced the establishment of Sematech, included a synopsis of site criteria, and invited site-location proposals. The criteria included the physical and environmental conditions for operating a fab, such as a vibration-free site, clean water and air, and energy resources. The proposals were to describe whatever incentives the states could legitimately offer, such as the donation of existing buildings or real estate, potential tax benefits, research and university connections, the availability of a skilled local workforce, and a desirable quality of life for attracting assignees. All the SIA member companies were sent letters inviting them to participate in their state's proposal if they so desired.

The response was not exactly what Kane and his committee had pictured. "We thought that we would announce the opportunity for people to submit bids sometime in May," he says. "We would ask for them to have the bids into us by the end of June. We figured we'd get six or eight proposals, and half of them would be worth reading. We'd send out a technical team to those places; go kick the tires and whatever. By the end of July, we'd make a decision." However, by the June 30 deadline thirty-five states had responded with proposals for 134 sites. In some cases, competing sites within a state engaged in internecine warfare, hurting their state's overall chances in the process.

A subcommittee met for a week, winnowing the proposals down to the thirteen best. It then asked the frontrunners for more data. By July, it was ready to present the thirteen proposals to the full site selection committee. Meanwhile, congressional delegations from the finalist states became actively involved in the process—a happy reversal of the usual Sematech lobbying efforts. Many congressional members were already strong supports of the consortium, and their interest in its success was only heightened by the site competition. Meanwhile, consortium leaders were determined to get the best deal possible while avoiding any pork-barrel odor. It wasn't always easy.

Kane has rich memories of this period: "The connection between the site selection and the political process was a difficult one at best. I was regularly down in Washington lobbying for that money during the time we were doing the site selection process. I was in and out of an awful lot of congressional offices pushing for that thing. It was going pretty well until our friends from one state tried to screw us."

43

When Kane and his team made a site selection visit in early October, they brought out all of the politicians:

> The governor was there, and their senator on the Finance Committee that was going to be instrumental in what funding we needed was there, along with their representative on the House Defense Appropriations Subcommittee. He was literally going to write the bill that included our monies.
>
> They had this whole day planned. We had lunch, and most of the politicians had left by this time because the press was gone. A staffer came up to me after lunch and pulled me aside. He said, "Sandy, we need to talk. What do you think is the possibility that, by November 14, you can give us a positive response with regard to our state proposal?" I said, "What's so magical about November 14?" He said, "On November 15, we're going to start marking up the appropriations bill and we need to know whether to include $100 million or $0."

Kane responded by saying:

> Oh. You need to understand that we are doing this site selection based on the merits, not politics. It is going to be the site that makes the most sense to us. At the same time, I will tell you that we're not stupid. If, in fact, your state is one of the top few on the list, the fact that you guys have the ability to be of such help to us in Washington will not be lost on us and that will be an important criterion. But if you guys are near the bottom of the list, or even in the middle of the pack, that particular aspect of your qualities isn't going to make such a difference as for us to move you to the top. I could never defend to anybody why some place that's got an existing facility that is in great shape that we could walk into tomorrow is better than you guys who don't have anything.

Kane continues:

> He says, "Well, that gives you quite a dilemma. We're going to need to have an answer." I said, "I'm telling you that the likelihood of us having an answer by then is not very high, and the likelihood of us having an answer based purely on your political clout is nonexistent." He says, "I'm just telling you the facts." I said, "Well, where I come from, that sure sounds like extortion." That's what I said to him. He said, "Here, we call it politics."
>
> I was astounded by this conversation, and I walked away. Six weeks later, November 14 comes and goes, and, of course, we've had nothing to say to that state. . . . They started the following day on a campaign to make it $0! That's the way they were working on it. If it weren't for work from good supporters to get the bill fixed again, they would have won. Even after the appropriations bill was done, the Senate, because of some of the work these guys did, screwed it up again so it had to go to conference committee. That's when it really started getting heavy, and we were in there lobbying with various guys on the commit-

tee and so on. Our law firm in Washington set up an appointment with Senator D'Amato from New York, who was on the conference committee.

My recollection is that we're sitting in his anteroom, and D'Amato walks in. He just comes up to me, and the first words out of his mouth were, "I want you to know I'm pissed." Before I had a chance to react to that, he unloads for about ten minutes. He's going on and on about this whole business with Sematech and how the site selection is a sham. It is purely a political circus. We have already made our decision, he says, and the answer is California. He's been told that from reliable sources. The reason we've done that is because we've already picked the CEO, and he's in California and he doesn't want to move. He goes on and on like this. Finally, after about ten minutes, I interrupted him and said, "Senator, if everything you were saying was correct, you would have every reason to be as upset as you are. Fortunately, however, most everything you've said is wrong and therefore you have no reason to be upset. But I do. You obviously got that information from someplace, and I need to ask you where you got it from." He says, "What do you mean it's wrong?" I said, "First of all, I can tell you with assurance that neither the committee nor the board has made a decision. We haven't even recommended a decision. Second, we haven't even come close to selecting a CEO, so the connection between the CEO and the site doesn't make any sense either. That's the facts; that's the truth. You can verify that anyplace you'd like. Please tell me where you got that information." . . .

It turns out that he got it from the staff of the guys in that other state, who were spreading this to see if they couldn't do anything to get people on their side. We then explained to the senator what was going on with them, and he was incensed. Now, he wasn't mad at me, he was mad at them. He says, "I'm going to help you guys. I want you to draft a letter for my signature that states what the facts are with some basis of being able to show that clearly, and I will personally see to it that it is given to every member of the conference committee by first thing tomorrow morning." We said, "Great!" We rush back to the law firm, type up a letter, and get it back to the senator's office. Sure enough, he did this. I can't tell you whether or not it made any difference in the end result at all, but this guy went from being purple with rage to wanting to be our best friend, and the other state's maneuvering backfired.

Sandy Kane and his committee were well aware of the political minefield they were being forced to negotiate. However, knowing that any hint of cronyism would seriously compromise Sematech's long-term effectiveness, they were careful to ensure that the process was scrupulously fair.

Kane recalls the difficulties: "None of us had ever done this before. Even if we had ever been involved in any kind of site selection from a business standpoint before, this one was unique. We did our damnedest to keep politics out of the site selection process. In the end, we were successful with it, but it was a very painful process to go through."

In refreshing contrast to the pork-barrel maneuvering was the behavior of members of Congress whose support for the consortium initiative was based on a larger vision of what would be good for the country. Many senators and representatives worked throughout 1987 to improve cooperation between the government and the semiconductor industry. Representative J. J. "Jake" Pickle of Texas was known for his strong support from the beginning, and when Texas became a site contender, he helped the state put together an attractive incentive package for its proposal. So did Texas governor William Clements. A former deputy defense secretary, he was naturally sympathetic with DOD's fight to prevent semiconductor dependency. He asked Willis Adcock, a semiconductor pioneer at TI who was then teaching at the University of Texas, to help prepare an analysis of the opportunity afforded by the site proposal invitation.

Adcock's memo to Clements was favorable, but it contained a pointed warning: "This requires a major concentrated program to prepare a response suggesting Texas. . . . Texas would have to select a manufacturing facility that can be readily adapted and a financial support package of about $20–50 million, depending on the scope of the project. . . . Texas would have to move very fast with a complete proposal to be delivered within thirty days." Even so, he said, the project was still shaky: "The industry is divided on the project's scope and funding, and federal support is very uncertain."

Almost immediately a group of business, governmental, academic, and community leaders banded together to develop a proposal centered on Austin. Heading the group were the "P twins": Pike Powers, then the managing partner in Austin for the law firm of Fulbright and Jaworski, and Peter Mills, the economic development representative from the city's Chamber of Commerce. Representative Jake Pickle added national expertise. Pickle had previously helped Austin win the computer MCC consortium in 1983, and Bobby Inman and Grant Dove, MCC's former and then current CEOs, confirmed from their experience that Texas not only could come up with good promises, it was able to keep them. Powers's group had the advantage of working together on previous initiatives, such as attracting MCC and the supercollider-superconductor site to Austin, and the help of many highly placed people. Their supporters included Hans Mark, chancellor of the University of Texas system; William Cunningham, president of the University of Texas at Austin; and University of Texas professor Al Tasch, who helped set up a mock clean room for the committee to view. Meanwhile, Judge Bill Aleshire of Travis County helped win county approval, and Frank Cooksey, the mayor of Austin, expedited incentives through the city council.[13]

The Texas incentive package came in at a whopping $468 million when all the mortgage incentives, spousal job assistance, and tuition breaks at local schools and the university were added to the $68 million in funding assistance offered by the state. Powers's committee identified an empty 285,000-square-foot Data General building suitable for fab renovation. The University of Texas then offered to purchase it, lease it back to the consortium for a nominal fee, and help with construction costs.[14] The proximity of a major research institution, the University of Texas right there in Austin, with another research dynamo, Texas A&M, nearby, was another cornerstone of the proposal.

By September, the 134 written proposals from thirty-five states had been reviewed, and a comparative analysis of the benefits and financial incentives calculated. During September and October the subcommittee then visited the thirteen sites that made the final cut. Every hopeful state went all out to make a good impression on the subcommittee members. The subcommittee labored through November to consolidate all the information gained from the on-site visits, and then it was up to the full committee to decide among the three closely matched finalists: Arizona, North Carolina, and Texas. However, the committee still wanted to wait for the larger decision of federal backing to be made before it chose the site.

At 3:00 A.M. on December 22, 1987, Congress passed the Defense Appropriations Authorization, which included $100 million for Sematech. Later that day President Reagan signed the bill into law. A week later, the site selection committee reviewed its process and criteria with the DOD to assure fairness, and gained its approval. With federal support now a certainty, it was time for the final decision on location. The site selection committee and Board of Directors met together for one last time in Dallas. No one, including Kane, knew going into the meeting which site candidate would be chosen. Nevertheless, they planned to inform the winner immediately to avoid speculation and leaks.

Kane therefore made only his potentially more difficult flight reservation from Dallas to Raleigh, knowing it would be easy to get to either Austin or Phoenix from Dallas, if necessary. An enterprising reporter sniffed out that fact and decided it meant good news for Raleigh. He spread the word, and when the plane arrived there, a jubilant contingent was waiting, waving a huge banner that read, "Welcome Sematech!" Unfortunately for the North Carolinians, Kane was not on the plane. Charlie Sporck's congratulatory phone call went to Texas governor Bill Clements's office right from the Dallas meeting room immediately after the site decision was made. In a ceremony on January 6, 1988, Austin was officially notified that it would be Sematech's home.

Senators Lloyd Bentsen and Phil Gramm, House Speaker Jim Wright, and Rep. Jake Pickle, had been loyal Sematech supporters long before the site competition. They and other Texans carried much influence, holding seats on various congressional committees: the Senate Finance, Armed Services, and Commerce Committees; and the House Ways and Means, Appropriations, Armed Services, Science and Technology, and Energy and Commerce Committees. They used it effectively right from the beginning. Kane remembers: "Texas didn't get the site because of men like Jake Pickle and Jim Wright and their ability to make things happen in Congress. What was most impressive to us was their understanding that Sematech was important enough to make sure it happened even though they weren't sure it was going to Texas."

The site selection process had been an extensive, emotional courtship and marriage, replete with rival suitors and political drama. The breadth of public interest and feeling surprised Sematech's founders. If it was any consolation to the runners-up, the SCOEs slated to be established in 1988 were in many of the states whose proposals had included good research and university connections.

Ironically, perhaps, but not surprisingly, once the inevitable site selection was made, congressional support from many states cooled noticeably, making the next battle in the continuing fight for government support harder to win.

## Technology Gifts

Meanwhile, during the summer of 1987, the technical-planning workshops continued to be held every week or two. For the consortium to capitalize on the data the workshops were yielding, though, Sematech still had to choose what semiconductor device it could produce as its manufacturing vehicle. Since the consortium was to begin at a dead run in the middle of the semiconductor race, the technology for its first product would have to be brought in from somewhere.

Led by NSC's Ian Bell, the Product Vehicle Subcommittee held its first meeting on August 5 in Santa Clara. When Sematech was first conceived, both the industry and the DSB task force focused on regaining U.S. production of the workhorse memory chips that Japan was so effectively exporting. Early on, Gordon Moore of Intel urged, "Let's go into the business of building DRAMs in a big way to develop manufacturing skills and to make a statement by establishing a world-class DRAM." Although the military also wanted advanced design for various other kinds of customized chips, it was most worried about foreign DRAM dependency.[15]

In 1986 the press had reported on this convergence of goals: "The scope of the [industry manufacturing initiative] venture, which is expected to include a major wafer fabrication unit for 16-megabit dynamic RAM production in the U.S., will be determined in great part by the extent of government financial participation. . . . As part of an evaluation program, the Defense Science Board (DSB) has drafted a study for government-subsidized semiconductor production of 16-megabit DRAMs."[16]

By the fall of 1987, however, Sematech's founders had scaled down the declarations that the consortium would be a sort of Japanese-beating super-manufactory of advanced DRAM chips, and the DOD also publicly acknowledged that overall industry improvement in manufacturing competitiveness would best serve their interests. Their willingness to tone down the rhetoric calling for breakthrough victory, and instead to take on the less dramatic, workaday challenge of improving performance, prefigures the many adaptive changes in Sematech's evolution.

Meanwhile, in late 1987 and early 1988, as the Product Vehicle Subcommittee and the steering committee studied the choice of a device to practice on, interested SIA member companies were paying dues and committing themselves for the next four years. As firms made their investments, they naturally began to assert their individual interests in what they expected back from the consortium. Their assertions and demands moved the early planning right along toward the implementation stage, with heated discussions of how to execute the broad mission of improving the industry. Practical issues, such as the pending choice of a product vehicle and the nature of the use of the site (e.g., how much production), became part of the new operational agenda discussions.

## Incorporation and Funding Accomplished

As the end of the third quarter of 1987 approached, the SIA members that had committed to becoming Sematech members were negotiating final plans for legal incorporation. Various interested government agencies also came closer to defining both what their interests in the consortium were, and what means of support they could offer. Jack Woods, who shared start-up team COO duties with workshop director Colin Knight, was developing a six-month projected budget and an operational and business plan for publication by the end of November.

As early as June, 1987, Gil Amelio of Rockwell, the funding chairman of the committee, and Charlie Sporck had requested written formal pledges from the members who planned to join Sematech upon incorporation. In July, Skip Greenfield presented the proposed corporation bylaws to the steering committee. In order to form a collaborative organization, this document had to include nondisclosure agreements for outside employees and strategic workshops, as well as antitrust guidelines.

On August 6, the task force handling legal and organizational structure matters was still working on tax matters and antitrust concerns, but it reported that the incorporation documents were in order. The steering committee met at the Washington offices of Dewey, Ballantine to discuss and approve the incorporation, as well as the ongoing progress of the legal and organizational structure group.

Charlie Sporck signed the Certificate of Incorporation the next day and Sematech, Inc. was born as a not-for-profit corporation in the state of Delaware.

Now the die was cast. The $100 million in committed fees from industry members was due during the fourth quarter of 1987, and there was a legal entity for the government to partner with—when and if the other half of the consortium's funding survived the federal appropriations budget process. At the next SIA board meeting, held jointly in September with the SRC and the Sematech steering committee in Research Triangle Park, North Carolina, Sematech's original separate Board of Directors was formed.

Other key events occurred on that same hot August day in Washington

49

when the consortium was incorporated. The steering committee met with Secretary of Defense Weinberger at a Capitol Hill luncheon hosted by Sen. Pete Domenici (R-New Mexico) and seven other senators. Charlie Sporck and Jon Cornell briefed the gathering, which included Dr. Costello, Weinberger's assistant for acquisition and logistics. The senators presented Secretary Weinberger with a letter strongly urging DOD support for Sematech. It said, in part, "We are writing to ask your support for Sematech, an industry-driven R&D consortium designed to restore the United States to a position of international competitiveness and self-sufficiency."[17]

The letter concluded: "The Defense Science Board recommended that DOD commit $200 million a year to upgrading semiconductor manufacturing technology. The Senate Armed Services Committee has authorized $100 million in FY 88 and $100 million in FY 89. With industry's commitment to provide fifty percent of the necessary funding, Sematech provides DOD with a cost-effective vehicle in which the government's investment can be leveraged."[18]

The issue of which government agency would partner with Sematech became more acute as the language of the two legislative initiatives supporting it—the House Trade Resolution and the Senate Defense Appropriations Bill— grew closer together. During this time Sematech's founders lost a friend and the consortium lost one of its champions when Secretary of Commerce Malcolm Baldrige was killed riding in a rodeo.

While Sematech was being put together, trade issues with Japan had grown very heated as it became apparent the Japanese were not living up to the stipulations of the 1986 agreement. The SIA passed an urgent resolution in September, 1987, citing Japanese noncompliance, and presented it to Ministry of International Trade and Industry (MITI) Vice Minister Makoto Kuroda of Japan, Undersecretary of Commerce Bruce Smart, and U.S. Trade Representative Clayton Yeutter. The trade furor underscored the importance of government support for Sematech just as the appropriations decisions neared.

First, however, Undersecretary Smart spoke individually with various semiconductor manufacturers about each company's plans for future manufacture of DRAM chips and other semiconductor products. He held personal meetings with top executives of NSC, Motorola, and TI, and spoke with Intel and AMD officials by phone.[19] If the U.S. government was going to regulate the flow of essential DRAM chips into the country and support a memory-chip manufacturing consortium, it wanted assurance from individual manufacturers that they were serious about regaining DRAM market share. Everyone knew it would not be easy to retool and restart DRAM production.

Smart was apparently satisfied with the answers he got.[20]

Meanwhile, membership fees were not due until the end of the fourth quarter, and the consortium was getting its organization done on the $1.5 million in start-up funds contributed by the SIA, plus the donated hours of executives working on their own company salaries from offices provided by NSC. In December, Carroll Nelson, a start-up team assignee from Motorola, succeeded Colin Knight and Jack Wood as the COO. Larry Sumney, still the acting director, had been working for months on the reallocation of some FY 1987 funds, which were finally released. In October the NSF announced that Sematech would get approximately $3 million in funding through a grant to the SRC. This grant was made from reprogrammed funds transferred from the DOD to conduct manufacturing technology analysis and planning. It was the first tangible government support for Sematech. Sumney worked with DOD representatives and with NSF director Erich Bloch, a former IBM vice president and member of the DSB task force, to arrange the grant.[21]

This was a heartening sign of the official support that was building. The president's Economic Policy Council, which had held out against *industrial* policy, finally recommended that the DOD participate in Sematech as a matter of *national security* policy. Secretary of Commerce–designate William Verity publicly testified in confirmation hearings that he personally supported a private sector–public sector partnership of the sort envisaged by Sematech.

There was constant jockeying over consortium support going on both within and between the Senate and the House and their various committees. Mostly, however, the debate focused on the amount Sematech would get, or who would oversee government participation, rather than on any actual threat to deny funding. Sematech supporters weren't the only ones lobbying in Washington, of course. Opponents of the consortium criticized the plan as a scheme for helping the companies that could afford the $1 million minimum dues get bigger and richer, and shutting out smaller companies that they considered more nimble and innovative.

One of the most colorful and vocal antagonists from the beginning was T. J. Rodgers, president of Cypress Semiconductor, who didn't join the consortium, but who has continued to criticize it from the outside. Rodgers mixed his metaphors with relish: "I think Sematech is dog meat. . . . Sematech is a well-lobbied subsidy to a group of companies. Even for our own industry, I don't like pork barrel."[22] Still others predicted it would be a costly boondoggle, pointing to previous expensive failures like the VHSIC. An effect of this opposition was that one version of the House Defense Appropriations Bill recommended that $10 million of the $100 million be awarded to companies who were not members of Sematech.[23]

Eventually, committee recommendations from the Senate and the House got close enough for members to be able to confer on final language and conditions of participation. The Senate still favored DOD participation, whereas House opinion remained divided. The DOE, with its national laboratories' involvement, and the Commerce Department, with trade and economic responsibilities, had obvious interests in the project.

Several factors finally tipped the scale in favor of DOD. First, the military had a history of supporting "dual-use" technology development, notably in microelectronics, and the SIA believed that the DOD's demonstrated need for technology was the most closely aligned with theirs. Second, Sematech leaders preferred having just one agency with which to deal. Third, the DOD's enlightened leaders, including Secretary Weinberger and Dr. Costello, acknowledged the importance of giving financial support to the consortium as a grant, rather than doling it out in micromanaged doses. A further practical consideration was that the DOD had funding mechanisms and funds readily available to commit, whereas the other departments did not. More weight was added in favor of DOD when the Economic Policy Council announced it supported DOD participation as well.[24]

When Congress passed, and President Reagan signed into law, Public Law 100-202 in the wee hours of December 22, 1987, it was a great Christmas present for all who had labored to make Sematech a cooperative reality in the face of competitive habits, adversarial histories, and differing political agendas. The consortium still lacked a CEO, and its founders faced the challenge of setting the whole thing to work without one, but their sense of having accomplished so much together gave them a new basis and new energy for their next efforts. They were going to need them.

## CHAPTER 3

# Collaboration amidst Controversy

*Working the Issue of Secrecy*

The pressure of lobbying for political support and industry participation to establish Sematech had been intense, right up to the 3:00 A.M. authorization signing at the very end of 1987. As 1988 dawned, so did a new kind of excitement. Sematech was becoming a reality, and its demands were even greater. The thirteen original founding firms began investing their membership dues, joined in February by the fourteenth and final member company, NCR (National Cash Register).[1] Industry dues would provide half the $200 million annual budget for the remaining four years of Sematech's first five-year charter, ending in 1992. The federal government, through the DOD, was committed to underwriting the other half of the budget. However, the DOD would be a nonvoting member, as would the SRC. Larry Sumney stayed on as Sematech's managing director under the Board of Directors's steering committee, but as the organization became an official entity, the fruitless nationwide search for a permanent chief executive continued.

Other activities centered mainly on running more workshops and developing an organization ready to receive assignees. Carroll Nelson of Motorola had been named acting COO in December, 1987, freeing Colin Knight and Jack Woods to go back to their primary duties. Knight was still overseeing the many workshops and accumulating valuable technical feedback from the industry, while Woods was working to establish an administrative and financial structure for the consortium's new Austin home. Meanwhile, the Santa Clara start-up team was busy planning the April move to Austin and starting to recruit assignees from member firms.

Once these individuals began arriving from their member companies, coming together for the first time to try to make this experimental cooperative organization work, they proved, not surprisingly, to be far from a neat, congenial fit. An observer of Sematech in early 1988 recalls, "There was pure chaos everywhere." No longer just an idea, the consortium began to embody and carry on all the various agreements and disagreements of the planning stage. A ferment of competition and cooperation, common and opposing interests, and differing strengths and needs began brewing.

As far back as the summer of 1987, industry planners foresaw the inevitability of turbulence during organizational start-up, despite the urgency everyone felt. So although Phase I's .80-micron objective was a demanding goal, it did not represent a great breakthrough. In fact, some member firms could already produce chips with lines as small as .80 and even .70 of a micron—and they were approaching even smaller sizes.[2] Phase I thus was a training exercise for establishing procedures for working together. For assignees from competing companies, learning how to work together was the first real task.

The Federal Advisory Council's review at the end of Sematech's first working year called the .80-micron Phase I goal an organizational accomplishment as much as a technological one since it served to establish three things: (1) a benchmark for measuring the consortium's common technological achievements; (2) a discipline for rapid start-up—an occasion to create and drill an organizational team, and (3) an opportunity to establish and season working relationships with vendors, the R&D community, and the DOD.[3]

However, this disciplined start-up drill couldn't happen as planned until Sematech accomplished some other things. It had to move into its own site, construct a fab, and develop an operational plan and work schedule.

## Commitment without Consensus

As we have seen, Sematech's broad mission—to save the semiconductor industry through improving manufacturing performance—brought both agreement and controversy about how to help and be helped. As Sandy Kane says, "The SIA board agreed that what we were now doing was agreeing that we should move forward with this." Rockwell's Gil Amelio, the SIA chairman in 1987, said very simply that, when they were faced with imminent extinction, industry firms had to find a common purpose. Then they all had different ideas about how to achieve it.

Still underlying many of the operational suggestions was the desire to beat the Japanese at the game that Americans felt had been stolen from them. Early planners kept remembering how Gordon Moore, chairman of Intel, had urged early on, "Let's go into the business of building DRAMs in a big way, and develop manufacturing skills by establishing a world-class DRAM!"

The press hyped this idea, predicting that by 1988 Sematech would be running a twenty-four-hour-a-day, twenty-thousand-square-foot fab, filled with seven hundred workers who would be producing two hundred wafers per day.[4] Some taxpayers hoped that these two hundred wafers would represent a state-of-the-art product that Sematech could sell to become at least self-supporting—while still retaining its nonprofit status! But such a vision failed to take into account the fact that, besides violating the provisions of the Cooperative Research Act, selling chips would have put the consortium into direct competition with its own members. Another suggestion was that the wafers might only be demonstration prototypes, to be ground up and discarded later. Since Sematech's purpose was to help the industry be more competitive, rather than be competitive itself, it required a new mind-set in an industry accustomed to striving for excellence through competition.

Many proposals ignored Sematech's financial limitations. Intel's vice president, Craig Barrett, described the problem: "The original goals were all things to all people. It took the group a year or so to get its priorities aligned, with a lot of spirited discussion about what it should focus on. Sematech was bandied about as everything from a high-volume dynamic RAM producer to a learn-by-doing type of consortium. At first, it was a grandiose scheme to do everything that the member companies couldn't do—but all with a total investment of only $100 million per year, a lot less than many of us were spending and not even doing a portion of this." The growing realization that Sematech couldn't do it all spurred rivalry among the agendas that different kinds of semiconductor firms put forward. Although by as early as mid-1987 DRAM chips were no longer the official focus, the notion that they would be Sematech's primary mission lingered on, affecting both internal negotiations and public perception.

## Manufacturing Differences

Sematech's choices of operating focus were complicated by the differences in members' semiconductor products. This went beyond the more visible industry distinctions (e.g., merchant versus captive, commercial versus defense contractors, large versus small). The type of chip a company makes largely determines the way its production is organized, the firm's potential for innovation, the kind of fab and equipment it has, and the nature of its technological processes.

Because of the ways they are made, chips are of two major types: DRAM and others. The DRAM chip had historically not only been a major product for the semiconductor industry, it had also served as its principal technology driver.[5] In nearly every case before 1986 the development of a new process technology had been done around the DRAM chip. They had become the workhorses of microelectronics, needed in almost everything, and thus produced in the greatest volume. Their innovation has been mostly related to increasing miniaturization—and thus the possible density—of the circuit features that are etched, by an intricate sequence of processes, in layers on a silicon wafer. Miniaturization and increasing the density of the etched features requires sophisticated fabrication facilities and equipment that conform to incredibly small tolerances for any contamination, vibration, or malfunction of the slightest kind. Such defects tend to show up late, toward the end of the line, where high-volume mistakes are the most expensive.

The DRAM chip has characteristics that make it easier to distinguish design defects from manufacturing defects. This proved to be a learning advantage for engineers. Expertise gained from high-volume DRAM production was then applied in other areas, such as engineering design and function, equipment development, and testing and operation.

The need to raise yields led companies to manufacture high-volume products that could act as technology drivers for other products. Skills learned in manufacturing large quantities of a simple product could be transferred to more complicated, higher-value-added devices and help reduce the company's learning curve.

Since it was agreed that Sematech was being established to improve manufacturing ability industry wide, it had originally been taken for granted that the technology-driving memory chips would be the demonstration vehicle of choice. As analyst David Yoffie explains: "One of the industry's most striking characteristics is that production costs for most products declines by 30% for every doubling of cumulative volume. This is because semiconductor manufacturing lines frequently turned out more defective chips than sound ones. With new products, yields were often as low as 25%, even for the best companies. As products matured, however, yields would run as high as 90%."[6]

Although the need to improve U.S. DRAM production had at first appeared paramount, there was an increasing demand for developing other kinds of increasingly important chip processes, especially the application-specific integrated circuit (ASIC). This view was becoming more popular within much of the DOD as a whole—a marked contrast to the 1986 DSB focus on DRAM dependency. Naturally, the smaller companies already making various niche products favored developing transferable manufacturing processes for them. These firms were also being squeezed by the tighter patents and copyrights on both hardware processes and software microcodes, making it harder for smaller firms to capitalize on the developments coming from the larger firms' R&D efforts.

Thus, by the time Sematech was established in 1987, its manufacturing emphasis was, in fact, also beginning to shift away from DRAM technology—a reflection of the changing trends in a fast-paced industry.[7] However, there was still controversy over what the focus should be. The advisory council reported in 1989: "A different perspective, shared by small custom-chip firms outside Sematech, their philosophic admirers, and most importantly, DOD, is that the consortium's initial planning underestimated the growing importance of markets for small-lot special application chips and the potential of ASICs as drivers of flexible manufacturing technology."[8] This comment shows how opinions were changing, despite the fact that national security concerns about foreign DRAM dependency had been persuasive in obtaining government funding.

Sematech had to be born on the run, as it were, keeping pace with a rapidly changing technology, operating in a changing political and economic environment. Semiconductors are an archetypal bootstrap industry—that is, one that continually builds on its own advances. For instance, during the 1980s the creation and fabrication of more powerful chips was in the process of being revolutionized by the increasing use of chip-driven computers in everything from computer-aided design (CAD) to computer-integrated manufacturing (CIM).[9]

In particular, larger firms with more sophisticated R&D capabilities were just beginning to explore the potential of CAD to model new chip architectures and their processes. By successfully simulating standardized basic process designs for products that could be differentiated farther down the line, CAD eventually opened new avenues for precompetitive collaboration that no one had envisioned, thus influencing the direction of Sematech's evolution. At first, however, the sophistication that computers brought to the more advanced chip makers highlighted the differences among the founding firms. It was not immediately apparent how Sematech could help the industry overcome such differences.

A related change was taking place in the political and economic environment during this same period. At the time of the 1986 DSB task force report on semiconductor dependency, another group led by William Perry[10] was studying the feasibility of relaxing strict military specifications so that more commercial components could be used off the shelf, rather than paying $1,000 for a screwdriver, for instance. Semiconductors were included in the study, although they were not specifically targeted, and defense contractors in the SIA were becoming alarmed.

The SIA officially opposed a complete shift, although it did support some utilization of commercial procurement. The standardization of basic manufacturing design that CAD could facilitate would further eliminate some differences between commercial and military development. However, this environmental change threatened the status quo, and its technological benefits were not yet clear.[11]

## Choosing a Manufacturing Demonstration Vehicle

In practical terms, some differences among member firms affected the choice of a manufacturing demonstration vehicle (MDV). Because Sematech had to be jump-started without any of its own R&D leading to the Phase I ramping-up, Ian Bell's Product Vehicle Subcommittee had been working since August, 1987, to find a manufacturing process that the consortium could import to begin operations. Sematech's two largest captive members offered MDV contributions. It may sound easy to begin with a ready-made process handed over, but cooperatively using proprietary technology that is ordinarily surrounded with great secrecy created some of the worst early difficulties of operation, triggering fears that it might be impossible to accomplish Sematech's primary mission. At a minimum it would be difficult to follow all the operating recipes laid out in the consortium's Black Book.

One proffered contribution for the MDV came from AT&T. The AT&T proposal called for making a sixty-four kilobyte (K), six T, static random access memory (SRAM) chip, which would be followed by a 256K, 6T, SRAM chip as soon as it became available. AT&T was prepared to share the full details of this process with Sematech. But the 64K SRAM chip had only just been designed, and its manufacturability had yet to be proven. Later it was determined that it had not been designed for a sufficiently high production yield.[12]

The other offer came from IBM, which promised an MDV process for making a four megabyte (Mb) DRAM chip. It was hard for IBM to give—and hard for Sematech to receive—this technology gift. Although it had been tested and qualified for manufacture at IBM, the company decided at the last minute not to make available to Sematech a crucial step relating to a secret technique called planarization. Therefore, in addition to installing the donated part of the process in the forthcoming line, Sematech would also have to develop its own version of this critical step before the line would be fully operational.[13]

Even worse, IBM's whole process initially came with such strings of proprietary secrecy attached that it was nearly useless for workbench collaboration within the consortium. IBM stipulated that only IBM assignees or directly hired Sematech employees were to be allowed access to the technology. Moreover, IBM would allow only the knowledge gained at Sematech to be disseminated to other member companies. This limitation could undermine the worth of the technology transfer to members, which Sematech considered the ultimate goal of its knowledge production.

Hearing of IBM's restrictions, AT&T tightened the secrecy requirements on its own process. Both firms were to send engineers familiar with their contributions to supervise—and safeguard—their use. These difficulties spread ripples of tension into other areas, particularly in assignee recruitment. The fear of free riders took on a new guise because at this point it was not clear whether engineers from other member companies would be able to share enough details of what was going on to work effectively at Sematech. The problem of giving proprietary information to engineers from competing member companies had another side as well, since there was a chance that any engineer who did have the desired access to such information might be under some type of legal restraint upon returning to the parent firm. Assignees themselves feared they would be relegated to a well-informed but prohibitively secretive no-man's-land, no longer welcome anywhere else. The greatest fear, though, was that Sematech's ultimate goal—the transfer of its collaboratively produced knowledge to all member companies—would be seriously jeopardized.

Simultaneously during this frustrating period in early 1988, the steering committee was making decisions concerning the configuration and equipping of the fab,[14] which was supposed to be ready for Phase I operation by February, 1989. The decisions related to setting up the fab depended on what technology processes would be used, and the equipment choices associated with donated proprietary technology brought with them financial and political contention.

On January 26, 1988, Charlie Sporck reflected the board's decision to avoid choosing between the AT&T and IBM contributions when he officially announced acceptance of both: "We have selected two MDVs to facilitate the fast start-up of a flexible manufacturing capability that can meet the industry's needs for a wide variety of product families. The MDVs will allow us to demonstrate a baseline against which we can measure progress. . . . Sematech's product is manufacturing knowledge. This cannot be expressed as a single deliverable product, process, statement, or strategy."[15] The steering committee thus accepted both the AT&T SRAM and the IBM DRAM contributions without specifying how either would be used. However, the SRAM process, in addition to having fewer proprietary restrictions, also had the advantage of being more easily applicable to the manufacture of other types of chips, including microprocessors, logic chips, and the ASICs that were especially desired by the military and the consortium members with defense contracts.

## Practical Choices Highlight Differences

The January, 1988, choice of two MDVs raised additional questions. Most members expected Sematech to develop its own fabrication facility, actually producing improved chips on site if it was to prove anything. In fact, the original plan called for the consortium to build a fab for Phase I and another for Phase II, perhaps to be followed by another for Phase III. The Austin site had an empty Data General warehouse waiting to be turned into a fab, and there was the promise of $38 million from the University of Texas to help with initial building costs.[16] Others argued that building even one fab was too expensive and beside the point anyway, since Sematech did not have the resources to be technologically ahead of its larger members.

Differences among member companies again affected expectations. AT&T and IBM, for example, were supplying MDV technology that was more advanced than some of the smaller merchant firms had. Would this lead to exploitation? Charlie Sporck voiced what was on everybody's minds: "Stronger companies were asking, 'How would firms play here? If everyone contributed technology, would all members fairly contribute?'"

Texas Instruments, for example, took justifiable pride in its reputation for developing strong technology. One TI assignee recalls how the company at first felt a great reluctance to hand its hard-earned knowledge over to smaller, weaker, lower-dues-paying member companies. American habits of esteem based on individual achievement were hard to subordinate to group aspirations. Andrew Grove, Intel's CEO, saw this as the emotional issue of giving up individual interests for group agreement, now being played out in a national arena.[17]

The participation agreement specified that collaboration would meet the precompetitive definition of the 1984 Cooperative Research Act. What would this mean in terms of on-site manufacturing activities, information sharing, and using the proprietary MDV processes being donated? Between the research act and the participation agreement there existed only a narrow line to walk between sharing too much and sharing too little. The consortium would be liable for antitrust prosecution if it overstepped the provisions of the act. On the other hand, member companies would be released from their collaborative obligation—free to walk away from the consortium at any time—if proprietary secretiveness limiting access to information violated their participation rights spelled out in the agreement.

If the definition of precompetitive had been hard enough to determine at the time of chartering, it became even more elusive in practice. The location of what is considered to be competitive shifts along a continuum between design and manufacture, and approaches the product end of the line as production investment costs rise.[18] Companies may become more willing to share information when they need to share higher costs.

Thus, the term precompetitive means different things to different companies, depending upon where their greatest investments lie—with innovative R&D, with high-cost manufacturing control, or with flexible production—and especially with their answers to the question, "What is our competitive differentiator?" For example, when chip makers designed and made their own manufacturing equipment, as they did in their early days, their proprietary tools embodied competitive differentiation and created potential advantage. By the time Sematech was formed, with most equipment made by the infrastructure, the chip makers' competitive differentiators lay much farther toward the product end of their lines. Quality standards for equipment could now be of precompetitive benefit to the entire industry and its infrastructure—*if* habits of secrecy could be overcome.

Sam Harrell, as the SEMI/Sematech representative on the new board, saw these broad differences firsthand. "Sematech was down here beginning to carry on the wars over the fact that they hadn't agreed on which turf to fight on," he recalls. "During the first couple of years at Sematech, there was a tremendous amount of right-turn, left-turn, uphill, downhill to try to narrow down what could be done." In early 1988, this was mostly seen in the agenda conflicts.

## Competing Agendas for Direction

The agenda differences among the fourteen members eventually boiled down to three major issues, influenced by company size, position, and products. These three main program issues were improving equipment, improving core technology processes, and developing a model fab. Obviously, these agendas overlap, and progress made in any one would help the others, but without unlimited resources it was a question of which should take priority. All parties involved were keenly aware that it would be easy to take Sematech in a direction that could lead to a literal dead end for an industry struggling to survive.

The largest companies—including IBM, Intel, Motorola, and TI—lined up behind the equipment-improvement focus. They wanted improvements in the all-new equipment they had to put into each new fab to produce the next generation of increasingly miniaturized and sophisticated semiconductors. They were most affected by the difficulty of obtaining dependable, ready-to-use units of American manufacturing equipment (called "tools") that were compatible with each other and that could be linked for automated production. Larger companies could only achieve the lead by bearing the brunt of expensive evaluation and qualification of new equipment in their fabs. This was currently taking up to eighteen months with U.S. equipment. Other companies followed later, building on large company results, like a bicyclist following another rider into the wind. The biggest chip makers were thus the consortium members most painfully aware of the U.S. equipment problems.

Some of the companies with smaller semiconductor operations—including Micron, LSI Logic, NCR, and Hewlett-Packard—argued for their need to have Sematech help with basic process-technology research, since they more often purchased equipment after the bigger companies had gone through the difficulties of ironing out all the bugs. Even for smaller companies, core process development and training was growing prohibitively expensive. Some firms depended on hiring trained talent away from bigger companies. However, with the increasing pace of technology sophistication, a defecting engineer could no longer bring away enough in his head to cover everything. The goal of sharing process knowledge was a strong small company agenda. AT&T supported this agenda at first, despite its large size, but eventually switched its support to the equipment-improvement focus.

Craig Barrett of Intel describes how large and small company differences created their agenda needs: "Larger, here, is almost synonymous with state-of-the-art manufacturing technology. Smaller is staying a year or so—or a generation—behind in the technology. The larger companies were interested in a strong process-equipment industry, because it is the process equipment that drives the technology forward. The smaller companies had more interest in manufacturing know-how, the secret Black Book recipes that make things work and make you more competitive and more productive."

The third major agenda was put forward mostly by chip makers specializing in military contracts, especially Harris Semiconductor, but also Rockwell to some extent. Although the military's need for American-made DRAM chips was well publicized, military contractors also needed customized chips, like those in some of the so-called smart bombs employed in the Gulf War and the more recent air campaigns in Bosnia and Kosovo. At the same time, cumbersome military procurement practices require long-term, low-volume production and support of specialized chips—some of them long obsolete anywhere else. Military contractors thus wanted help with "flexible manufacturing," a computer-aided form of factory floor control. They had an urgent interest in developing automated manufacturing processes for small runs of over 150 different devices—some highly advanced, and others dating back to the 1960s.[19] There were still mutual suspicions that the military might either dominate the consortium or else be exploited by the private sector. Eight of the ten largest U.S. military electronics suppliers were Sematech members.[20] Although everyone expected magic solutions from the consortium, the nature of those solutions could not be fully foreseen.[21]

The flexible-factory issue caused pressures within the military for more direct oversight of Sematech. Even before DOD's funding request was approved in 1987, a senior military official declared, "It's not clear that we're prepared to give money to a project headed in the wrong direction." A Prudential-Bache analyst scoffed at that position, claiming, "That's like saying, 'The hell with making Chevys—we'll get by making Ferraris.'"[22]

These tensions kept alive the private sector's fear that having the DOD as a partner would force the consortium to give military interests priority. Turner Hasty recalls that during the 1987 planning stages for technology Phases One–Three in Santa Clara, word was funneled back to the steering committee through the SRC from the Defense Nuclear Agency (DNA) that unless Sematech agreed to develop hardware for military and space needs, the DNA would not support government funding for the consortium. Hasty remembers refusing: "We're not going to do that. We've got to work on real, honest-to-God processes. Fortunately, the Department of Commerce was very concerned that the Sematech mission would be guided or misguided by the military."

Differences of opinion among DOD agencies and among military niche contractors were predictable, but high-level supporters in both Commerce and Defense tried to avoid enmeshing Sematech's operation in interagency-level politics. Defense procurement czar Robert Costello took the large view and articulated a frequently repeated metaphor, saying that defense needs depended on the structural strength of a healthy industry, just as the tenth floor of a tall building (analogous to specialized military chips) needed the nine floors below for support. The federal advisory report on Sematech confirmed this, stating: "Sematech's own purposes are chiefly commercial. The consortium will bolster U.S. military strength primarily by contributing to a strong U.S. electronics industry."[23]

Consortium members—whether merchants or captives, small or large, military contractors or the DOD itself—had overlapping but not convergent needs. The biggest player of all, IBM, with many diversified products and customer requirements, still supported all three major agendas—developing process equipment, manufacturing skill, and automated, flexible manufacturing simultaneously—apparently convinced that the resources to accomplish them would be found.

## The Search for Clarity

Priorities clashed at Board of Directors meetings through the fall of 1987 and into 1988 as Sematech picked up steam. In February, 1988, the first ETAB meeting was held in Austin, and the first FTABs were formed to consider developments in the major areas of lithographic technology, etch and deposition processes, and equipment and manufacturing systems. Nationwide requests for universities to submit proposals for establishing SCOEs were sent out on schedule. Progress on internal and external matters was also made, despite the unresolved agenda and mission discussions.[24]

As the consortium grew, the board's work became more complicated. The whole board was trying to give operational direction to all the start-up activity without a single leader or clearly defined mission. The directors were caught between the ambivalence of their companies' strongly agreed upon commitments to Sematech and their conflicting expectations. One participant describes their dilemma: "Companies wanted to cooperate, but they were afraid to; they had put their money in, and they wanted to get their money's worth back." They were under pressure from their own companies to champion their own agendas because, in effect, each company had taken 10 percent of its R&D budget and handed it over to Sematech. This created pressure and conflict back home because the parent companies' performance expectations for their own R&D programs remained the same despite having only 90 percent of the budget they would have had without Sematech.

The members' hope that having the freedom to cooperate would overcome the difficulties of execution highlights some of the basic ambiguities of freedom and of cooperation. It was hard to freely share *and* continue to believe that collaboration would benefit their separate needs. It was also hard to learn new ways of working that were based on sharing and interdependence. The first ETAB also found it difficult to provide technical advice openly to Sematech's board and management, especially in the absence of an established leader. Executive group facilitator Diane Verden remembers that the early meetings were often marked by long periods of silence. Hostility and distrust were often so great that members felt that even discussing controversial topics might be too revealing.

Discussions at all levels were still hampered both by secrecy and lack of information. Participants were reluctant to share information about their manufacturing needs, so no one knew what they might realistically expect as a return from their investment or how it could be measured. The situation was not typical of a start-up with a clean slate, nor of a new venture by insiders with something on which to build. Ironically, although the Black Book had promised everyone everything, a majority vote would decide the agenda, even if it did not address all of the member companies' needs. Later, as better ways of sharing information and measuring return on cooperative investment developed, so would more representative methods for including more members' priorities.

## Agenda Alternatives Focus and Expand

In early 1988 the two proposed agendas of focusing either on tools or processes began to move ahead of the third alternative (i.e., flexible manufacturing in a model fab). The board majority favored the first two ideas because they were less specialized and offered more timely aid to the industry. Also, CAD might change the nature of solutions that depended on automated control for flexibility. Accepting both IBM's DRAM and AT&T's SRAM technologies as demonstration vehicles also helped to bridge some differences. The fab line was being planned to have a flexible, modular architecture that would allow for the manufacture of DRAM, SRAM, or logic chips with only minor changes in process sequence.[25]

This choice of a focus for Sematech also would determine how the fab would operate. The choice was still open between focusing on better manufacturing equipment or emphasizing improved process development, the same tools-or-process controversy that remained evident in meetings four years later.[26]

Differences between tool or process focus carried other implications, such as whether the emphasis would fall on short-flow or full-flow operation. An agenda calling for core process development would require Sematech to run three eight-hour shifts a day, producing a full-flow manufacture of chips on the fab production line (i.e., running chip fabrication all the way through to final testing) in order to determine how all parts of the process would work together. It was estimated that it would cost $3 million a week to run a full production fab. Furthermore, doing so would preclude setting up the fab for development because production efficiency and new development typically get in each others' way.[27] Opponents of the model fab agenda argued that all the U.S. firms had to do was look at Japan's efficiently automated fabs to learn how it was done, instead of spending Sematech's whole budget on it.

Focusing on equipment quality and compatibility could be accomplished mostly in the testing facility section of the fab (and later in members' own fabs). Since there are about 250 process steps employing at least twenty generic processes, each requiring specialized equipment, in the production of a chip, there were plenty of areas for improvement even without taking chips to the level of full production. There were hopes that computer-aided design and modeling would eventually be able to simulate full iterations from combined projections of short-flow segments. As already mentioned, only the larger and more advanced companies had begun to develop this modeling capability. Smaller firms were not convinced of its value, and were still looking for computerized ways to control many different, specialized, full-flow manufacturing lines.

Full-flow production is by far more costly than short-flow, which is one reason smaller companies were having difficulty developing core processes by themselves. They wanted the consortium to develop turnkey processes that they could take home to their own fabs. Now the arguments that erupted over full- and short-flow operation triggered new fears of free riding. Would smaller companies simply use Sematech to do the hard work they didn't want to invest in? Would larger firms drive the direction of research into areas too advanced to be of benefit to smaller firms? Perhaps smaller companies might unwisely divert all their funds available for R&D into Sematech programs and do none of their own research. A compromise could be a dead end for both more- and less-advanced firms.

Political dramas underscored the intensity of the feelings behind technical arguments. At one point in the discussions, Intel grew impatient with the seemingly interminable irresolution. Intel CEO Andy Grove paid a visit to Sematech and laid out the best path for the consortium to follow. When that did not have the desired effect, Grove convened the member companies that collectively paid 60 percent of Sematech's dues: Intel, Motorola, TI, and IBM. All but IBM agreed on a position paper recommending prioritizing 75 percent of Sematech's funding to be spent externally (i.e., mainly on strengthening the manufacturing equipment infrastructure through such things as development projects). When IBM weighed in, however, it insisted on restoring most of the other priorities, believing, as it had all along, that resources would be found to accomplish everything necessary.

The other three firms privately blamed IBM for reducing the intent of their paper back to an unfocused hodgepodge, but nobody was willing to take on IBM openly. Then word of the large firms' agenda-setting meeting leaked out, creating a backlash of resentment among the others, who reacted by attempting to create some ultimatums of their own. One insider calculates that with some skillful coalition-building at least 85–90 percent of the member firms could have been persuaded earlier to support a more external focus, since probably only about 5 percent were violently opposed to it and committed to an internal focus on full-flow production. There was no clear answer to be found in planning; it had to be created by doing something and making it work.

Proponents of full- and short-flow production still sometimes argue the merits for each at ongoing meetings at Sematech today as the lines for any given project are never as neatly drawn as they might appear on paper. However, the arguments always circle back to the fact that limited resources forced the setting of priorities. Full-flow model fab production could absorb most of the funding internally without doing anything really new, whereas short-flow production and testing would allow a combination of internal and external funding, with the goal of simultaneously developing a product ready for flexible manufacturing along with standardized equipment ready for dependable operability. Eventually, as the consortium focused more on supporting the infrastructure, short-flow production would become more suited to most of its operations, but this commitment was only beginning to emerge.

Observer Bill Daniels, who worked during this period as a management consultant to Sematech, neatly summed up the differences in internal consortium objectives: "From my understanding, the early board was split between two alternatives: either Sematech was here to design processes, or Sematech was here to raise the quality of vendors who manufacture equipment for the industry. The smaller members wanted process; the larger members said, 'We have twelve times the budget for that in our own organizations than Sematech has, and it is very unlikely they will develop anything we'll be interested in. What you could do is something to help with the vendors and suppliers out there from whom we need equipment for our next generations.'"

This approach would help all chip makers, despite their differences, and provide a nexus for cooperation while strengthening the U.S. infrastructure at the same time. Strengthening this argument was the widespread recognition that Japan's cartel-like aggressiveness was targeting the U.S. manufacturing and materials infrastructure as the weak link in the American semiconductor industry. Factoring the supplier infrastructure needs into the agenda discussions helped to push the consortium toward a focus emphasizing equipment improvement, and foreshadowed the direction Sematech's evolution was to take.

## Assignment Paradoxes

At the same time that the Board of Directors was tied up with the ongoing policy conflict over consortium agenda choices and their implications, individual agendas became an issue. The earliest assignees formed the growing start-up team in Santa Clara. The first visible sign of Sematech's progress, before it had any output to be evaluated, was its ability to attract top-level industry champions. The drive to survive pushed them together, and the vision of a new freedom to share ideas drew them on.

Like all freedoms, this one had many faces. One question that haunted all of the early assignees was: "If I were really very important back home, why did my company send or allow me to come here?" The most satisfying answer to this question was: "Because Sematech is enormously important and you were chosen because of your special abilities." But only a few of the initial assignees bought that answer completely. Knowing that coming to Sematech might derail their careers from corporate tracks made it harder to accept and publicly acknowledge the Sematech assignment.

Many committed themselves fully to the consortium's goals in order to assure the success of their efforts. Others hedged their bets, with one foot back in their parent company and one foot in Sematech. This was especially the case before Sematech had a home of its own because most start-up team members maintained offices at their own companies and were paid by them. A significant number of assignees, especially those from nearby Silicon Valley firms, spent a great deal of their time away from Sematech. Those coming from other areas of the country naturally did not want to relocate to the temporary California site, and commuted a great deal, making for long weekends.

The individual assignees' ambivalence epitomized the difficulties faced by competitors attempting to cooperate. Daily participation became a visible measure of commitment. The federal advisory report noted: "Member commitment, expressed especially in the contribution of able staff, is crucial to the success of the consortium model."[28]

In Santa Clara, the half of the assignees who showed up on a daily basis found their colleagues' frequent absences both annoying and de-energizing. The rule of thumb was that the higher a person was in the management chain, the more likely he was to be absent. Rick Dehmel, a program manager from Intel, began a morale-building weekly "lunch bunch" on Wednesdays over a sandwich in the conference room, to rehash the events of the previous week, plan the next one, and air issues. These often turned into gripe sessions about absent colleagues, which became a good reason to be present.

Two unifying effects on assignee morale during the Santa Clara period came from the ongoing technology workshops, as recalled by one observer: "They [the workshops] were the ideal team-building exercise. First, they provided a well-defined work schedule, outlining tasks on which assignees could work together without being concerned about their need to push company agendas or protect company secrets. Second, in providing a public forum on the issues, they also provided the catalyst for nationwide support for the idea. This support, garnered from industry, government, and the universities proved to be very important in establishing the worth of Sematech."

## Growing Pains

On April 18, 1988, Sematech officially changed its address from Santa Clara, California, to Austin, Texas. Forty-four of the fifty-five members of the start-up team moved almost en masse, and most stayed on the same floor of a local hotel until they could find housing, increasing their sense of solidarity. An advance party led by Jack Woods and Nick Nicoson had already made good progress on modifying the previous Data General warehouse so that offices could be used, although the fab was far from finished. The Austin move signaled that Sematech had graduated from its planning stage.

The assignee picture rapidly became even more complicated, as the consortium was deluged with job applications. An average of over five hundred unsolicited semiconductor engineer résumés arrived each week, and an equal number of phone calls came from local residents seeking employment on the support staff. Sematech grew from the forty-four who moved to Austin in April, 1988, to 175 by September, to over five hundred the next year.

Even with a strict understanding that Sematech would not "raid" member companies for personnel, the chance to be on the cutting edge of freely shared technology was hard to resist.[29] Intel, for example, reckoned that it would officially assign twenty-five people to each two-year assignee tour, staggering their leave times to absorb the loss, but that it would probably lose more than a hundred people to the consortium within the same period. Member companies were obligated to send assignees to the consortium, although the number varied proportionately with the size of a company's dues, and was capped, as were the dues, thus preventing any one company from swamping the organization with its own personnel. Member firms' dues were correspondingly reduced as an in-kind contribution, since parent companies underwrote the salaries of the people they sent.

Assignee commitments to Sematech have continued to mirror the dilemma that companies faced in sending the very first representatives to do consortium planning and write the Black Book in the spring of 1987. All had sent top people in record time, even though, as IBM's Sandy Kane remembers: "It was a bit of a paradox. If the guy is that terrific [to be needed at Sematech], you can't afford to let him go." On the other hand, said Charlie Sporck: "We [at NSC] are going to put in something like $10 million or $12 million. It would be insanity to do it without putting in good people along with it. We have got to be awful damn stupid to put in that kind of money and not put in good people."[30]

Attracting good assignees had been difficult for MCC, another Austin research-based consortium, which ended up with only 20 percent of its scientist slots filled by assignees and the rest directly hired.[31] However, a manufacturing consortium like Sematech would acquire knowledge as its assignees collaborated at the workbench. Both the value of the knowledge produced and the quality of its diffusion would depend on the caliber of the assignees that actually worked together on site and then became vectors for technology transfer as they returned home.

Thus, for a number of reasons, the company assignees who made it to Austin ranged from idealistic misfits eager for the freedom to prove themselves in a new setting to carefully chosen top performers sent to ensure the consortium's success and a good return on their parent companies' investment.

Sporck himself epitomized the highly placed industry champions who invested personal effort as well as company resources to making interfirm cooperation work on a national level. At the operational level within member companies the selection of technical assignees fell to middle managers who found themselves caught in a cross fire. Charged with sending good assignees to Sematech, they were still responsible to their firms for successful operations in hard times. Although managers were understandably reluctant to give up their best people for at least two years because of the value of continuity, the assignees' professional and personal caliber was generally high, and they worked hard.

Methods of assignee selection varied. Sometimes firms simply posted notices of Sematech openings on the bulletin board. More often they hand picked their representatives. It is rumored that a few assignees were organizational exiles banished to this new corporate Siberia. Assignees who might not have gotten along back home were more likely to suspect this of each other at Sematech as well. An unspoken identity question among assignees was, "Why are you here? What kind of assignee are you?" They wondered, "Did you come with a personal ax to grind, and were they glad to let you go, or are you a competent, committed, and trustworthy collaborator?"

## Assignees' Dilemmas and Direct-Hire Stability

Some assignees feared they would not have a job to return to after spending two years away, especially if the company had to find someone else to do their job for that long. Although it was not supposed to happen, some early high-level assignees were not welcomed back to their parent firms, and sued them. Other assignees, who returned to parent firms, brought back valuable technical information and management skills, but also an altered outlook, which occasionally made their return problematic.

Intel's Deepak Ranidive describes how turbulent these cultural changes felt at the time: "You don't realize the importance of corporate culture in the organization until you don't have one. When we started Sematech, we did not have a Sematech culture, or an organization that was a well-oiled machine. We started in chaos, with people coming from totally different companies with different operating cultures and management styles for day-to-day operations." Assignees found communication a major issue initially. Whereas newcomers to a firm face adjusting to the majority culture that surrounds them, consortium assignees faced a Babel of corporate languages and styles.

Ranidive recalls: "When I got expense accounts from one of my engineers, he had a very large amount of money for dinner. 'I"m not going to sign this,' I said. He said, 'But, my company doesn't mind. They don't have any problem with this. I can go by my company's guidelines or by U.S. government guidelines, or I can go beyond that.' I just didn't think that was right. We had a lot of argument about that, and I made that person very unhappy." Authority was another issue at Sematech that stemmed from assignees coming from different corporate cultures. "There used to be a problem," continues Ranidive, "although I think it is better than it used to be, of assignees coming here and a

69

Sematech manager, who may be a direct hire or another assignee, would say, 'Your project is this.' The assignee would say, 'Sorry, that's not what my company sent me here to do and I'm not going to do it.'"

Direct hires[32] formed a more stable subculture as the consortium grew, providing administrative continuity to the organization as the assignees came and went on staggered individual schedules lasting an average of two years. The direct hires understood from the beginning that, due to the temporary nature of the consortium's charter (five years authorized, but with a ten-year planning horizon), their jobs had no guaranteed future. They felt the excitement of being part of the experiment, but they sometimes felt like second-class citizens, holding the fort for the more glamorous and rewarding jobs that the assignees could waltz in and out of—and hence back to their parent firms with job security.

## Commitment Needs Reinforcement

As Sematech grew, member firms started looking for a tangible return on their investment, and the problem of developing a focus became even more crucial. For one thing, data was starting to come in to Sematech's leaders from the nearly concluded series of off-site technology workshops set in motion in June, 1987, to assess what the industry rank-and-file needed and wanted from the consortium. It was rapidly becoming plain that Sematech's funding would cover only about half of the urgent recommendations coming out of the workshops. The board and Sematech's leaders were faced with refining an affordable working plan from all the contending urgent claims produced by the workshops and agenda drives.

Sam Harrell says of this period: "A lot of the start-up team felt that whatever amount of money was necessary would be found. The SIA leadership felt that $200 million [a year] was enough. That was a disconnect between the people writing all of the programs to be attacked and those who were setting boundary conditions.[33] That disconnect is a direct result of the fact that there wasn't a leader in the beginning."

With so many clashing company cultures, and with no leader as yet, disconnects persisted at many levels, from the overall agenda issue to how best to manage the MDV implementation problem. The more people who arrived on-site, the more progress and problems both became apparent. On the positive side, face-to-face contact at the physical site began to reinforce a sense of organizational solidarity. As the advisory council observed, "Members interact within the Sematech framework on a daily basis and that familiarity, in this case, breeds cooperation."[34] It also bred a sharpened awareness of their differences.

The activity immediately following the move to Austin centered on readying the site for the Phase I ramp-up. Turning the physical facility into a fab with an office tower was on schedule, showing that choosing Nick Nicoson as the builder had been prudent. Given the resources, Nicoson would finish on time.

The only major problem identified was the mismatch between the overall plans and available funds. Building fabs for each technology phase would be a large expense, so the board decided in the spring of 1988 to modify Fab One, extending its suitability for use in Phase II, instead of building another new fab. The savings would more than offset the expected overrun on Fab One. As it turned out, another fab was never needed.

The DOD was pleased with the progress Sematech was making toward establishing a permanent site, refining the budget, and recruiting a skilled staff, but it was increasingly unhappy that a permanent leader had not been found. Hoping to satisfy DOD's complaints, the Board of Directors appointed Jim Peterman, Sandy Kane, and George Schneer to serve on an executive committee that would take over from acting manager Larry Sumney. The committee became known as the "troika."

## Black Book Danger Revealed

Although acceptance of both of the MDV contributions in January, 1988, revealed a lingering hope that the consortium could do it all, by April there was worry that if the Black Book's road map was strictly followed Sematech's survival might be in danger.

Carroll Nelson, the acting COO, knew that he would be replaced when permanent leaders were found, so he was reluctant to take a strong stand on how the MDVs should be used to begin Phase I operations. Nelson's position was further weakened by the fact that he had no plans to remain at Sematech since he was not being considered for the permanent COO position. In fact, he had begun actively seeking employment outside of Motorola. In June, 1988, he announced that he was resigning from that company to join VLSI Technology, making him ineligible to remain at Sematech.

The troika hurriedly met to choose his replacement. The only remaining member of the start-up team with division-level management experience was TI's Turner Hasty. But he had promised to TI management (namely, George Heilmeier) that he would not take an active role in managing Sematech.

Knowing this, troika member Peterman, vice president of TI's semiconductor group, got permission from TI to allow Hasty to serve as interim COO. One of Hasty's qualifications for acting COO, at least in the eyes of the troika, was that he had no aspirations for the job. Hasty's appointment was announced at one of the periodic "all hands" meetings held at the Hyatt Regency Hotel in June, 1988. By then the number of "hands" had roughly tripled, to about 125 employees.

The troika also chose that meeting to unveil Sematech's first organizational chart. The chart had been devised in Santa Clara. Now, as personnel arrived in

Austin, names were slotted into positions for the first time. It was also officially hinted that the permanent CEO and COO would soon be named. That news was met with some skepticism, as similar announcements had been made in the past.

The problem of implementing the MDV technology could not wait on the executive search, however. The fab, already being built, was scheduled to be ready for use in less than a year—by February, 1989. The Black Book called for Sematech's Phase I to demonstrate the capability for producing a chip with .80-micron features, and the process technology for it was to come from the IBM 4Mb DRAM or the AT&T 64K SRAM donations. Something had to be done promptly.

The proprietary problems with implementing these contributed processes were further complicated by the disparity between goals and available resources. "Realistically," Hasty recalls, "we had no chance of building a factory and building up a capability here that would allow us to build the IBM 4Mb DRAM. It would have completely consumed all of our resources." Moreover, nobody had yet figured out how the consortium could actually utilize either of the donated MDV processes in a collaborative organization.

As it turned out, Sematech was never able to use the IBM DRAM process, although it managed to adopt some of its technology. In fact, the consortium that many thought was established specifically to recover U.S. DRAM manufacturing capability has yet to produce a single DRAM chip. To ensure readiness for the Phase I start-up drill, the more accessible AT&T process was used, even though certain proprietary aspects of it were forbidden to disseminated. This was bad enough for Phase I, but the situation could not be allowed to continue into the next phases without defeating the consortium's purpose.

All agreed that Sematech would have to derive its own process for Phase II, the .50-micron objective, and so on through subsequent phases. On the positive side, the Sematech-derived MDV design and its technology process would then be open to all member companies—both to their assignees working on site, and for complete technology transfer back to parent firms.

This account of how the wholly Sematech-derived processes developed was one of the first revelations to many participants that, as they now say: "The biggest secret is that there is no secret." Its accomplishment became a powerful incentive for further lowering proprietary barriers and communicating more freely.

## From Two Secrets to None

The change began with the Phase I plan to provide practice and a technology base for the next more ambitious step in Phase II. In that phase, the fab was to operate as a manufacturing center, duplicating all of the demonstrations called for in Phase I, but this time using an MDV and .50-micron process developed by Sematech. Planners projected this to happen just twelve months after the completion of Phase I.

If Phase I's goals seemed unrealistic, Phase II's were doubly so. According to conventional wisdom, a skilled, well-coordinated team would need at least five years to develop such a process from scratch—and then only if they already had access to a first-class research lab. By 1988, Sematech had—or was acquiring—expert personnel with the necessary individual skills, but assignees were still reluctant to share enough of their knowledge to form an effective team. And the proprietary restrictions on the donated MDVs hardly encouraged such sharing.

The Black Book called for Phase I to be executed with a donated process technology rather than its own R&D because Sematech was still two years away from having the lab capability to develop such a process. But Phase II was another story. Although it was acceptable for the Phase II MDV chip design to be contracted out, the transferable technology process for it had to be developed at Sematech.

These were some of the problems confronting Sematech in the summer of 1988. As program manager Rick Dehmel and his team tried to fit all of the tasks required for Phase I and Phase II into a an operational schedule, the goals laid out in the Black Book looked even more impossible. Nevertheless, no one on the team was willing to give up. The threat to their industry was real, and they were determined to do something about it.

At that moment, a decisive shift occurred. Rather than openly questioning or criticizing the Black Book's goals, the management team quietly began to reassess the mission and whether those goals were really best for the industry. Team leaders concluded that Sematech could not become a viable organization until all of the proprietary processes were gone. It did not make sense then, to spend a lot of time on the still partly secret Phase I. They also concluded that the desired Phase II process could not be developed from scratch in time unless they built on information from an existing process.

At this pivotal moment, AT&T provided the path to a Phase II process. It offered to stipulate that while the originally donated Phase I process would remain proprietary for three years, any process derived from it at Sematech could be considered open for collaborative work and technology transfer. Although Sematech still did not have all the details of the AT&T process, enough had been published about it to satisfy the program team that the process was sound. After some thought, the team members decided the only way Sematech could develop a suitable process for Phase II on time was to map the .80-micron process onto a .50-micron process.

There was just one catch: They would have to do it without benefit of experimental verification since Sematech would not possibly have the needed research labs set up in time. Sematech's development staff would have to accurately model the changes in the process required for the transformation, and

73

verification would have to come from assignees from the member companies that already had some experience with .50-micron technology.

Tom Seidel was asked to head the task force that would attempt the mapping. Seidel was spent twenty years working with semiconductor technology at AT&T before going to the University of California at Santa Barbara on a research appointment. He was hired directly from there—not as a member-company assignee, but as the first Sematech Fellow. Professor Al Tasch of the University of Texas was also hired as a consultant, and since neither he nor Seidel belonged to a member firm, they could have complete access to the AT&T process. Hasty himself, although acting COO, was still a TI assignee and thus could not. He was careful to confine his contributions to exploring the published literature. Seidel and Tasch, with the help of some of Tasch's students, developed a list of the steps needed for the Phase II process. No one expected it to work very well, though, because of the uncertainties in the modeling process.

The Design Rule and Process Council (DRAPAC) was formed in answer to this predicament, with Seidel as its first chairman. The DRAPAC was made up of process and design experts from the member companies that already had .50-micron processes. The Phase II process flow model was presented to the council. Although none of the member-company representatives on the council would have volunteered their own proprietary information on how to develop a .50-micron process, they were quite free to offer advice about how *not* to do it. With technological projects, knowing what paths not to take can be very valuable because it narrows the direction and simplifies resource allocation.

This shared advice, gained from criticism of a theoretical model, proved enormously informative. The Phase II process, created from mapped technologies derived from the AT&T gift, actually worked so much better than anyone had dared to hope that it eventually became the basis for the Phase III (.35 micron) development program as well. Thereafter, the Sematech process could be freely worked on by all assignees and disseminated to member companies.

But there was considerable resistance within the consortium to this unorthodox method of arriving at the MDV process, especially from people who had looked forward to spending the next three years developing it. In fact, when Paul Castrucci became COO in the late summer of 1988, these fledgling task force and DRAPAC results were shelved in favor of developing a more traditional development program, including working with the IBM 4Mb process. The results were revived again after a period of tumultuous change among the executive group.

# Start-up Struggles

*Noyce Becomes CEO*

**S**ematech was growing fast. It was building an organization of experts, constructing a fab, developing skills, and striving to accomplish something quickly, but it was also struggling to decide just what that something should be—all within the context of a competitive industry that was continuously and rapidly changing itself. A participant describes how the turbulence fed on the urgency: "The organization was very mixed up, and nobody knew what they were there for. What is Sematech? It had not been worked out, and that problem existed up to the board level." A willingness to move forward under time constraints with only an agreement to agree and the freedom to experiment carried them as they learned how to take action on their commitment. But the lack of a leader and a clearly defined focus was costing precious time.

One time delay led to another. When the executive search committee headed by Intel's Bob Noyce and AMD's Jerry Sanders could not find a CEO for Sematech by the end of the first quarter, 1988, the DOD held up the much-needed disbursement of authorized government funds. Noyce himself was an obvious choice, but he repeatedly declined the CEO position, saying that at age sixty he was too old for the job. Perhaps he felt he could continue to be more useful where he was.

As a stopgap measure the board created the executive troika of Kane, Schneer, and Peterman—each still a full-time executive at his own firm. Because the troika was heroically doing double management duty, it was all the more imperative that Sematech have its own leader, something DOD was beginning to insist on.

## Organizing Without a Leader

The DOD's active involvement in the process started in March, 1988, when its oversight of Sematech under E. D. "Sonny" Maynard was passed to DARPA (later known simply as ARPA). The DARPA took a more stringent look at the way the consortium was developing than Maynard had, and demanded that all conditions for the funding be fulfilled as planned. A month later, the DOD put a temporary stop to the funding, citing the lack of a "disciplined planning process," including having no leader.[1]

Although the DOD dollars were a grant and not specific project funding, the authorizing legislation required a Memorandum of Understanding (MOU) between the DOD and Sematech. The MOU laid out certain criteria that had to be met before the authorized monies would be released.[2] The MOU thus became, in effect, the government's participation agreement with the consortium. Negotiators drew it up in January, 1988, to become effective on March 1, and it had a number of provisions that were either required by the Defense Authorization Bill or had already been agreed upon. These included:

- An Advisory Council on Federal Participation in Sematech would submit an annual report to Congress on the consortium.
- Industry would provide at least 50 percent of the budget and have a charter guaranteeing representation of all members.
- National labs and universities would be included in the initiative.
- The DOD would approve the site selection and operating plan, including the R&D strategy and the leadership structure.

The operating plan and leader, two key elements of the agreement, were not yet in place.

Although the DSB recommendations had stressed American recovery of DRAM manufacturing leadership, the DOD itself was also concerned with the increasing importance of ASICs. The DOD also felt that the consortium should commit more of its budget to long-range R&D than was reflected in the planned objectives for Phases I–III.

Although Sematech had not been able to deliver a leader by the government deadline, their shared danger, common interests, and many personal friendships held the member companies together. An early direct-hire employee remembers how he felt: "Things were getting done typically in a matter of minutes or hours as far as the decisions were concerned. At first, at Sematech, we just *had* to do it because we didn't have the time or the structure. Everybody just pitched in and did it." This willingness to keep going was as true of the early individual participants as it was of member companies that kept supplying operating money when government funds were delayed. Even when some of the early activity was judged as less than productive, dedication kept Sematech alive. Still, it had to respond to DARPA's requirements.

## DARPA's Influence

Clark McFadden, who negotiated the many agreements between Sematech organizers and the DOD, recalls that "After two years of formulation working with Defense [by the SIA champions and their Washington advocates, including McFadden] there was a major reorganization and the project was turned over to DARPA, which was a very independent, very specialized place, with absolutely no previous contact with Sematech, and no involvement in the formation of it."

McFadden and others had worked since 1986 to educate various DOD figures on the development of Sematech, only to find that the consortium had suddenly become somebody else's program. Craig Fields, the acting DARPA director, was now responsible for the Sematech project. Without trying to change the consortium's essential industry-driven character, Fields imposed a series of demands and disciplines that provided a helpful push toward more specific planning and structure. This was an unusual achievement, because, as McFadden says: "The founders had set up a structure for government to participate, but at the same time be spared the normal governmental procedures [i.e., for obtaining a grant]. I'm not sure it could ever be fully duplicated again—nor has it been, to my knowledge." This official freedom—first from antitrust prosecution, then from the usual funding oversight—was the government's counterpart to the semiconductor industry's unprecedented attempt to freely share ideas. This new freedom also required a new kind of self-discipline.

Sematech's first strategic planning director, Obi Oberai, recalls what it took to convince Craig Fields: "We presented a rationale for what we were doing. After he saw that presentation, he said, 'I understand your methodology. I understand what you're doing. Go do it.' After that, we had a very strong, supportive role from him."

With Field's support, Sematech's operational plan came closer to meeting the MOU requirement for receiving DOD funding. Leaders worked closely with William Bandy, DARPA's single-project officer for Sematech's entire operation.[3] The DOD's insistence on what it described as "a more disciplined and structured plan" helped the consortium to define itself, although in expanded terms.[4] Specifically, the decision to focus the fab line more on the SRAM production process than on DRAM accommodated the wishes of the smaller contractor member firms since the SRAM process could also be applied to microprocessor, logic, and ASIC products. Although DARPA had neither project oversight nor a vote on the board, the MOU requirements certainly gave the DOD some leverage on the consortium's agenda. On May 12, 1988, a new MOU was signed, and the federal share of the 1988 operating budget was released, even though Sematech still did not have a CEO. However, until it did, the delicately balanced interaction between the industry and government grant remained in jeopardy.

## The Search for a Leader

Finding a leader became even more difficult as the problems of making the consortium work became more evident. The site selection process drew a nearly overwhelming response, with many states bidding to be chosen, and the final pick made from many attractive choices. The choices for a CEO lacked the same unity and pursuit. Some who might have been willing to tackle the challenge were often not acceptable to one or another of Sematech's many "bosses"—fourteen highly individualized companies led by accomplished men of strong wills and egos, plus a powerful government agency.

Part of the problem lay in Sematech's participation agreement, which gave each industrial member an equal board vote and restricted the DOD, the SRC, and SEMI/Sematech to advisory roles. While these terms established its freedom both from internal domination by any single member company and from specific government project oversight, they also prevented any one party from solving the leadership crisis. Both the DOD MOU and the participation agreement called for a leader acceptable to all parties.

Sematech's ferment throughout this early period made clear what it needed in a leader. The individual selected to fill the post would have to be strong enough to bring order out of the consortium's chaotic potential—someone respected within the industry as both a creative scientist and a trusted corporate leader, and recognized in Washington as wielding exceptional skill and power.

Beyond identifying these desired CEO characteristics, the original plan specified that Sematech's three chief executives were not to be assignees—that is, people with ties to a parent company and plans to return to it. This limited the CEO pool to candidates who were at the pinnacle of their own corporate achievements, yet ready to serve the consortium as a capstone to a successful career.

In June, 1988, the executive troika, with Hasty as COO, was still running things. The press reported: "The search committee, which was co-chaired by Dr. Noyce and Mr. Sanders, who is chairman of Advanced Micro Devices, had run through a list of some 200 candidates for both the CEO and COO positions and had made 'a few offers,' according to Dr. Noyce. Earlier it had been confirmed by Dr. Noyce and others that Digital Equipment Corp. vice president Robert Palmer had been offered the CEO job but declined, and Rockwell executive Gil Amelio also reportedly was approached for the post and turned it down."[5]

Top candidates got where they were through demonstrated scientific and technological expertise combined with organizational skills, but not all of them suited the entire board. Others were not free, and still others weren't interested in tackling the unwieldy, unpredictable job of leading the consortium under a severe time constraint that was growing tighter with every passing day.

Sematech needed a leader of vision whose influence would be strong, because its founding charter and member participation agreement established the consortium's freedom from governmental project oversight, as well as freedom from internal domination by any single member company. The government and the member companies granted that ongoing freedom only if there was a leader capable of handling it. The leader must be someone respected within the industry as a creative scientist and trusted corporate leader, and also recognized on the political scene in Washington as someone with skill and vision.

The participation agreement specified that the top three consortium executives could not be assignees with ties to one company and plans to return to it; this requirement meant the CEO should be someone at the pinnacle of his own corporate achievements, ready to serve the consortium as a capstone to a successful career and then retire. Top chipmakers get where they are through demonstrated scientific and technological expertise, combined with organizational skills, so there were a number of possible candidates among industry leaders. In the view of the Board, however, not all of them met Sematech's need, or they were not interested in taking on the unwieldy, unpredictable effort of leading this consortium under a severe time constraint that was growing more urgent every passing day.

An early observer says, "They had done a search for a year for a leader for the organization. Of course, with 14 member companies, it was very difficult to reach a consensus. The candidate that one company liked, another company didn't like for a whole bunch of reasons. The process dragged on, and in the meantime, the organization was clearly suffering." As Sam Harrell pointed out, there was "a disconnect between the people writing all of the programs and those who were setting boundary conditions. That disconnect is a direct result of the fact that there wasn't a leader in the beginning. . . . all the guys who felt they were supposed to get the benefits that fell off the list [of consortium goals] were coming back to do guerrilla warfare against having their thing lost, and so on. It was a tremendously difficult time. In all of that, Bob Noyce came to Sematech."

Noyce was known not only as the coinventor of the integrated circuit, but also for his concern for the ways in which people worked together, inside the organizations he helped to run and outside them, in the public arena. He was known as the "mayor of Silicon Valley," an unofficial title bestowed on him by the local press because of his involvement as a citizen in his community. Having been one of the early entrepreneurs who bounced from Philco, to Shockley, to start Fairchild Semiconductor, and then to help found Intel, Noyce epitomized innovative entrepreneurship and was known for his democratic management and engaging, fun-loving personal style. His reputation for brilliance and integrity extended internationally; it was said that many Japanese engineers from archrival firms would refrain from washing their right hands for days after shaking his.[6]

Although Noyce was a hugely successful entrepreneur, he had grown increasingly concerned about the direction that competitive fragmentation was taking the U.S. industry. In a 1981 acceptance speech for the Achievement Award from the Industrial Research Institute (one of many honors from industry and government), Noyce described, firsthand, the conflicting drives of a competitor: "The primal urge of the competitor is to be a monopolist, to drive other competitors out of the area he considers to be his own. We all dream of the day when we can cease beating each other's brains out (as the victor, not the vanquished) and relax, basking in the sunshine of limitless profits."[7] Although Noyce had a history of commitment to varied causes, such as education, tort reform, or improving investment practices for the industry, he preferred to work outside the limelight. He did not accept the first presidency of SIA after helping to found it, and he removed himself from the presidency of Intel in 1975 to be chairman of the board and to have more time to devote to industrywide concerns. As much effort as he had also invested in getting Sematech established, he was not seeking its chief executive role.

When Bob Noyce finally agreed to leave Intel and become Sematech's first CEO, his personal qualities as an ethical, brilliantly creative, egalitarian, and fun-loving leader came with him, and they were sorely needed. Interest in Sematech had been dwindling, as reports were coming out about how its lack of direction was affecting productivity, diminishing assignee enthusiasm, and even jeopardizing the government funding. In fact, Charlie Sporck states flatly, "If Noyce had not accepted the job, Sematech would have faltered from falling off of interest."

Sam Harrell speaks of the inspiration of Noyce's appointment, even before he arrived, because of the strength of his image: "What Bob Noyce did[,] in addition to his wisdom and his ability to speak in public circles and to influence government[,] which was very powerful, was that he basically made it okay for people in the industry to come to Sematech. If Bob Noyce was willing to come to Sematech and it was that important to the industry, then maybe I should leave my job for two years and go serve a national cause which is also a cause for my company. He made it okay to be at Sematech." When AT&T metrology expert Tom Ellington came as an assignee, he found that "Bob's personal prestige and importance in this industry was a major factor in attracting top-level people to Sematech. A lot of people here told me that either they wouldn't have come or friends of theirs would not have considered Sematech other than the fact that Bob Noyce thought it was a great thing to do." Noyce was known for his motto, "Go out and do something wonderful."

In spite of Noyce's impressive reputation, consultant Bill Daniels remembers, "He didn't go around pretending to know. He did know a lot because we all taught him our best. He was always asking questions and people just brought their treasures to him all day long. It was a brilliant way of managing, and I never saw anybody else do it more effectively than Bob. . . . One of the thrills of working with Bob was that he always seemed to be learning. I find out that almost everybody has had this experience with Bob. In my experience, you would get such attention from Bob when you talked to him that you wanted to tell him everything. It was such a joy. He was quick to hear what you were saying, to give evidence of his understanding, and to question you in such a way that you knew he was taking you seriously. He was such a joy to work with. As much as he will be one of the great historic figures of this industry, there was nothing intimidating in Bob Noyce."

## Bob Noyce's Decision

From the beginning, Bob Noyce had been everyone's choice for the job, but he had consistently declined, saying, among other things, that he was too old for the job. Ann Bowers Noyce describes the moment he changed his mind and decided to take the job: "We went to Aspen specifically for the purpose of making the decision. We postponed it until Sunday afternoon. Finally, we went up [on the mountain] and sat up there in this howling wind, and decided. We came down off the mountain, and Bob called Charlie Sporck. It was in July, 1988. A week later we were in Washington making the announcement, and Bob was physically on the job the first of August. It was like a two-week time span from *yes* to *here*."

When Bob Noyce called Charlie Sporck to announce that he was willing to become Sematech's first CEO, he embodied the hopes of many for the consortium. He was known throughout the industry for his motto, "Go out and do something wonderful."

Sam Harrell speaks of the inspiration of Noyce's appointment, even before he arrived, because of the strength of his image: "He basically made it okay for people in the industry to come to Sematech. If Bob Noyce was willing to come to Sematech and it was that important to the industry, then maybe I should leave my job for two years and go serve a national cause which is also a cause for my company."

Many people have said that they chose to come to Sematech not just because Noyce thought it was okay, but because it gave them a chance to be associated with his efforts and to work for him. Early participants agree on the importance of Noyce's acceptance at this critical moment. Fewer people had expressed interest in coming to Sematech as reports started to come back about how its lack of direction was affecting productivity, making personnel uncertain, and even jeopardizing government funding. Charlie Sporck flatly states, "If Noyce had not accepted the job, Sematech would have faltered from falling off of interest."

Soon after Noyce announced his decision to become CEO, the advisory council noted an increase in member commitment due to "the organization's success after considerable travail in recruiting highly respected top leadership."[8] His decision also enhanced the consortium's national and international visibility as well.[9] Says Craig Barrett: "There were things which, I think, were key in

Sematech's history. One was Bob Noyce's decision to pack up and go to Austin. Sematech was certainly struggling at that time."

## Building a Leadership Team

When Bob Noyce agreed to become the consortium's first CEO in the summer of 1988, he had not yet met IBM's Paul Castrucci, the man the board had chosen to be his COO. However, Noyce did get to ask Peter Mills to round out the executive team as the chief administrative officer (CAO) and handle financial administration, in particular. At the time, Mills was an economic developer in Central Texas, and his effective role in the selection of Austin had impressed Noyce.

With the board's consent, Noyce took a surprising step: He established a three-part Office of the Chief Executive (OCE), bringing together the separate positions of the CEO, COO, and CAO. An integrated OCE, he felt, more nearly represented the democratic leadership essential to Sematech's cooperation. As Mills notes: "Bob thought it very important that the OCE reflect a very collegial, egalitarian approach to tasks. He hoped that it would be reflected throughout the organization." Another observer remembers: "That was very typical of Bob. It was saying, 'This is the team, these are the objectives, you're the people who can make it work.'" Paradoxically, it was Noyce's individual charisma—what Tom Wolfe had called his "halo effect,"[10]—that made his cooperative teamwork so effective.

Noyce's and Castrucci's appointments were announced with great fanfare in Washington in July, 1988, where they met each other for the first time. They then went to Austin together for introductions at the new site, but did not begin working together at Sematech until October. During the interim, although fab construction and the work of the MDV task force were proceeding, attempts to come to terms with overall organizational direction inevitably had a lame duck quality. Hasty, as acting COO, held a planning meeting in July to sort things out before the new executive team arrived. He remembers that the session consisted of "just trying to sift through the enormous number of plans and ideas we had. If we had done everything we had originally written down, it would have been an effort about three times the size of Sematech. So we had to get our arms around it."

When Noyce and Castrucci arrived, Hasty briefed them and they agreed to follow his plan, which prioritized the most urgent objectives. An early observer describes Noyce's ceremonial first visit at Austin following the big political hoopla surrounding the Washington announcement: "He went from Washington and the press announcements directly to Sematech. It was a Friday morning. Everybody was totally suited and tied, which was very unlike Silicon Valley and very unlike what Bob had gotten used to. We were standing there talking, and all these guys were looking at him. I don't remember if anything was actually said, but the first thing I knew, he was taking his tie off and putting it in his pocket! They kind of looked at each other, took their ties off, and stuck them in their pockets, too! Everybody who was standing around did the same—the whole executive team. Sematech needed to be an open, cooperative, collaborative organization to fulfill its mission. All those little things are very symbolic." In the same vein, Noyce changed the executive offices to be the open, egalitarian cubicles he had earlier helped to establish at Intel. Noyce made himself available to everyone.

Noyce, by openly modeling respect for others and a spirit of cooperation, inspired his colleagues to want to share and enact those same values themselves. He literally taught them how to act. He set the tone for the consortium.

## New Leaders, New Problems

As they soon discovered, Bob Noyce's egalitarian style differed notably from the style of his COO. Paul Castrucci remembers their first meeting: "I had been told only two days before that [the new CEO] was Bob Noyce. I made some phone calls around, and everyone said, 'This is a cast made in heaven. He's a thinker, you're a doer. Mr. Outside and Mr. Inside.' This is going to work like a charm. That's great! A couple of hours went by when the phone rang. 'This is Bob Noyce. Ann and I are in the hotel, how about going to dinner with us?' We were a little nervous and concerned. Is this thing going to work? This was serious stuff. I wanted it to work. After dinner, I told Margaret, 'This *is* going to work!' The feeling there was just fantastic. There was a good match there. The next day, we went to the Press Club and made the big announcements."

Paul Castrucci is an American archetype, the son of poorly educated Italian immigrants. Proud enough of his heritage to have "PAISANO" on his license plates, Castrucci worked his way up from design to manufacturing in thirty years at IBM. Since American semiconductor engineers have typically considered research design and engineering intellectually superior and more glamorous than manufacturing, Castrucci's career track reflects his unusual priorities. Sematech's goal of improving manufacturing was clearly one that he could throw himself into wholeheartedly. But he has a researcher's credentials as well: He personally holds twenty-four microelectronics patents. So his skill and commitment augured well for the cause.

It didn't take long, though, for problems to surface.

A highly placed early observer says: "Never in my wildest dreams did I assume that the problem would get to be as bad as quickly as it got. What you had with Paul and Bob was kind of like oil and water. It was two totally different management styles and two totally different personalities. Paul was the furthest from consensus that you'd ever want to see. You gave him something to do, and he was going to do it no matter what it took. His dedication was incredible. But he rolled over people to get it done. In our kind of environment [at Sematech], that didn't work."

Another insightful observer comments: "When Paul's style conflicted with Bob's, I would say, 'Paul, you are dealing with a guy who is a living legend. He isn't going to change; he doesn't have to change. You do. If you don't, you're not going to be here.'" Bob Noyce had a long-established reputation for democratic management. His egalitarian support for cooperative interaction set a tone that clashed with Castrucci's approach.

A highly placed IBM assignee says: "Obviously, when Castrucci first came in, he had a large hand in looking at this equipment industry business and defining some very important concepts. A very dynamic and tremendously inventive individual. Unfortunately, he was a lot bigger than most people can deal with. In a fourteen-member-company environment, it was a disaster."

Whereas Noyce intended to develop something new, Castrucci insisted on using proven formulas for success in building a fab and structuring the organization. "I was always involved in leading-edge technologies," he says. "I wasn't going to leave that behind. I was going to do the same thing here. In my view, there were two missions to Sematech: one was to do joint development projects (i.e., develop new and better equipment), and the other one was to make this fab down here be the leading fab in the world, bar none, in terms of its capabilities, organizational concepts, defect density, throughputs, cycle times. . . . Those are the two things I was going to make happen."

Obi Oberai, who headed the IBM assignee group and was the first Sematech person to show up, buy a house in Austin, and report for duty, says: "In hindsight, we had a lot of wrong notions about how to go about solving big problems. So the facility got going, but we did not define the problem adequately before we got on to the solution. Most of the churning that went on in the next two years was due to the [lack of] problem definition."

Castrucci's statement of two organizational missions, both to be solved by building a fab, is a reminder that even in late 1988, problem definition was still unclear. Sematech's equipment improvement mission was only beginning to come into the sharp focus it had later. The ambiguity that earlier had served well to attract membership from differing viewpoints now offered the new, hard-driving COO the chance to make his mark. Paul Castrucci threw himself into building a fab that could do everything everybody wanted, both equipment development and leading-edge process, and show the world what America could accomplish with the right kind of management.

## Harnessing Cooperation

Castrucci gave it his all. "I'm the kind of guy that doesn't want to false advertise," he says. "I want to deliver, and I've always done that at IBM. I knew that Sematech was important and I was going to do everything I could to make it happen. I also knew that good people were here. If you could somehow harness those guys, man, what you could do! I was looking forward to helping lead and manage this group to see what it could do."

The unused Data General building the University of Texas helped Sematech buy was so basic that Michael Dell of Dell Computers had previously considered it as a factory site for his start-up operation. Yet the site selection criteria show how stringent the requirements are for a completed fab. A Class One "clean room," such as Sematech needed, has carefully controlled access, and its atmosphere is continuously filtered and cleansed so that there is no more than one particle larger than .5 microns per cubic foot of air. This is comparable to having one dried pea in a cubic mile of air. Computers must aid the tightly controlled processes; hands and eyes are far too clumsy and imprecise. Metrology, making fine measurements, grows more difficult with miniaturization. To test a chip holding millions of transistors for defects takes equipment that can sense and measure in microns.[11]

Building and equipping such a fab grows increasingly expensive with each generation of greater miniaturization of design features and denser packaging on more and more sophisticated chips. In addition, Sematech's highly visible fab also had to meet or exceed strict environmental controls. The existing floor, for example, had to be torn out, and a new, vibration resistant one put in. It had five separate layers to protect the ground from any possible manufacturing contamination. To construct such a fab under fierce time constraints, with limited resources, in a fishbowl, with a start-up staff, offered a challenge that Paul Castrucci accepted with typical gusto. Construction of the fab began on February 14, 1988, and Castrucci arrived at Sematech in September of that year, so his contribution came about during the finishing stages.

"We met some of the troops, including Nick Nicoson," recalls Castrucci. "Nick was responsible for the fab. The previous Saturday, he had been in a boat accident. The gas had flared up and burned his face and his ears, and half his eyebrows were gone. Not even a week later, he's making a presentation out at the fab! There is no doubt that this fab is going to happen because this guy is committed."

Another informant notes: "Nick was the person who was our builder, our facilities manager when we built Sematech here in Austin. Nick knew how to build the fab. He built the AMD fab here in Austin, and he built part of the Motorola Bluestein.[12] He'd done it before, and he did a good job. Nick is one of the people you'd have to list as one of the reasons Sematech was able to get off the ground."

In just thirty-two weeks—about half the usual time required to build a fab—the sixty-thousand-square-foot, $75 million fab was far enough along to begin limited operation. On November 15, 1988, it was dedicated at a festive, by-invitation-only ceremony, with limited tours of the facility. Because some of the fab's features were secret, available only to member companies, this was the last time the public was granted access. More than thirteen hundred people attended the gala dedication, including industry, education, and government leaders. The ceremony included the Austin Symphony Orchestra, and a flyover by jets from nearby Bergstrom Air Force Base.[13] Robert Costello and Robert McCormack, deputy undersecretary of defense for industrial programs, both of whom had been instrumental in obtaining grant funding, represented the DOD. They were impressed with the consortium's progress, and Costello declared, "Sematech can and should become a true national asset."[14]

## First Technology Transfer

Soon after the fab was operational, Sematech performed what amounted to its first technology transfer: It held a workshop on how the fab had been built in record time. Many member companies saw this fab workshop as a major return on their investment and say it was the biggest return for a while, until longer-term projects began to prove successful.

Building costly new fabs is a constant for semiconductor manufacturers because each generation of miniaturization requires still more sophisticated processes and equipment. Complicating matters, the new generation of chips overlaps the old one that pays for it by still being profitably produced in the existing fab. It is difficult to upgrade a fab incrementally, but if chip production is discontinued while the old fab is rebuilt, it halts the flow of money that pays for the new facility.

Many companies feared that they soon would not be able to afford to build new fabs by themselves. Thus, even as Sematech's facility was being built, chip makers had begun looking at various other alliances to share costs. According to a news story appearing shortly after the clean-room dedication, "U.S. companies are finding it harder than ever to justify investments in large-scale chip-making facilities, which now cost between $200 million and $300 million and could cost as much as $1 billion by the next century."[15] It is easy to see why member companies were interested in how the consortium's fab construction was done in record time for $75 million, and why they valued a "lessons learned" workshop about it.

The advisory council cited some of these lessons when it reviewed the fab, attributing the speed and cost savings to "a widely shared sense of urgency; the fact that builders were converting an already existing structure; slack in Austin construction market—crews worked on the fab in two 10-hour shifts, 7 days a week—and strong support from local officials. Also, the fab designer set up offices on-site to speed consideration of requests for changes and clarifications in building specs."[16] The close integration of the fab's design and construction foreshadowed how Sematech's founders hoped their work would be accomplished within it.

The Phase I–III plans had called for two more fabs to be built, but with growing awareness of budget realities, and with attention focusing on development, improvement, and testing of manufacturing equipment, the board had already scaled back building plans. In fact, in addition to the single-wafer production line for the DRAM, SRAM, and ASIC chip projects, one third of the clean-room space was designated as a tool applications process facility (TAPF). The TAPF was scheduled to begin operation in April, 1989, and would allow Sematech and supplier company engineers to jointly develop and test new equipment. They soon forgot its unwieldy name, simply calling it the "testing facility," or "Fab B" (Fab A was the chip production line).[17]

Building in the test site as part of the fab, where suppliers and chip makers could work side-by-side, became an integral part of Sematech's plan to establish open and regular communication with suppliers. They could consult together about manufacturing priorities and equipment needs right at the chip makers' R&D level. This prepared the way for the development of "common performance objectives"—that is, setting uniform industry standards—for equipment and materials, which had been one of the consortium's original goals.

Although Sematech had an operating fab, because knowledge was supposed to be its output, the consortium did not face the same bottom-line requirement for wafer production that a commercial plant faced. It was able to concentrate on developing improved manufacturing processes and on trying to integrate them with equipment and material development in new ways to shorten product cycle time.

The existence of Sematech's fab accomplished three important things. First, it created a visible, centralized focus for an expensive investment, encouraging member companies to continue investing more money to make it worthwhile. Second, as an important part of the Phase I start-up drill, it provided a learning experience for collaborators, both in the construction process and from the workshop that followed. Third, and probably most important at this stage in Sematech's evolution, it demonstrated remarkable technical prowess on site with the achievement of a structural success. Observers credited the centralized plant with increasing member commitment.[18]

The rapid creation of the fab was even more remarkable considering it occurred while the consortium was still struggling to become a coherent whole. The authoritarian drive pushing fab construction, and the teamwork and collaboration that got it done, represented the uneasy marriage of tried and true ways yoked with the new vision of freely shared cooperation that had inspired Sematech. At the same time that Castrucci was harnessing the fab effort, Noyce was nurturing the new processes in quite a different way.

## Reorganization Aligns with Planning

While Castrucci was concentrating on building the fab, CEO Noyce, CAO Mills, and Turner Hasty, now the director of external resources, concentrated on what they saw as the other most urgent issues. First came the creation of the 1989 operating plan, which had won DARPA approval. Second came the development of cooperative practices for implementing the operating plan, practices that would be able to integrate all the talent and intelligence concentrating in Austin without stifling their innovation. The existing organizational practices had either been imported along with various assignees or had grown up without the benefit of a plan. During the last quarter of 1988 and the first quarter of 1989, Sematech's first major reorganization took place, this time designed around the official operating plan.

The 1988 operating plan had finally been approved and agreed to by DARPA in May of that year, before Noyce's appointment. Between August and December, 1988, Noyce oversaw development of the 1989 plan. It incorporated the lessons learned so far, and reflected the previous year's accomplishments: the movement toward Phase I goals and the beginning of Phase II.

The 1989 plan also stated Sematech's three basic operating modes for working toward Phase I–III manufacturing goals. First, the consortium would engage in leveraging and networking by contracting for technology R&D on a cost-sharing basis with suppliers, federal labs, and universities. Second, accelerated learning would be the core of Sematech's initiative to "compress development schedules for achieving high-yield production of advanced devices."[19] The third goal was to give priority to identifying "the most promising technology paths" in all the major areas of lithography, etch and deposition processes, and manufacturing systems.[20] These three modes were then tied together in the following five-step approach:

1. Conducting ongoing competitive analysis to identify the best way to develop and deliver the most needed manufacturing capability improvement, continually defining the areas for the next steps.
2. Achieving maximum leverage of external resources available through member companies, the supplier infrastructure, national labs, universities, and related industries. (This would include close cooperation with SEMI/ Sematech and require close interfacing with the ETAB and various FTABs.)
3. Demonstrating proof of leading-edge manufacturing capability, showing the technological accomplishment of each phase's objective by increasing the miniaturization of circuit lines.
4. Transferring knowledge generated at Sematech to its members at the successful completion of each phase.
5. Identifying and implementing new management technologies that would accelerate learning and reduce cycle times. (This would require learning cooperative communications practices among competitors in a high-technology arena and pooling knowledge for productivity.)[21]

Although this last objective might be the most important in the long run, it undoubtedly would be the most elusive to achieve—and the most difficult to measure.

The DARPA participated in the 1989 organizational planning sessions and gave its full approval on December 1, 1988. The plan would subsequently be updated by March of each year in order to get DOD approval in advance of Congress's annual consideration of the federal budget, rather than face yearly funding emergencies. Following approval by the Board of Directors and DARPA, the 1989 plan was presented to the consortium's top managers. They were then asked to prepare their responses to its strategic objectives and be ready to share them at a meeting scheduled for February, 1989.

Important factors reflected in the new plan were the decision not to build another fab, and to trim the projected total employment from 750 to 650. This would free more funds for long-term R&D, which still concerned the DOD. Budget concerns, along with a growing emphasis on developing and improving manufacturing equipment, influenced the decision not to build a new clean room for each projected phase. Noyce, with the board's approval, decided to complete only half of the TAPF in 1989, which was proving adequate for starting up. The other half was scheduled for completion in 1990. Funds were to be leveraged more effectively through off-site projects (such as with companies and/or national labs). Fully 40 percent of the 1989 budget, or $104 million, was designated for this purpose.[22]

It was now possible to assess some of the progress made, and senior leaders, top managers, and project officers gave briefings in November, 1988, to the Advisory Council Report on Federal Participation in Sematech, summing up the current state of accomplishments, ongoing problems, and future goals. The council gave the consortium high marks, saying:

> By the close of 1988, Sematech had made significant progress toward Phase 1 objectives and established elements of the groundwork for Phases 2 and 3. Construction of a state-of-the-art fab had been completed in less than half the time normally needed. All equipment for Phase 1 had been ordered; most had arrived in Austin; and partial wafer processing had begun. The consortium had also used its extensive advisory apparatus to develop consensus R&D agendas for Phase 2/3 and establish six university-based research projects.[23]

Nevertheless, the council added that in this, Sematech's first year of operation, its most important accomplishments "probably had less to do with meeting operational goals than with the difficult and occasionally contentious work of self-definition." This work included expanding the strategic focus to include the flexible manufacturing of ASICs; developing a detailed operating plan and more disciplined planning processes (with DARPA's help); increasing the proportion and leveraging of R&D spending; strengthening members' commitment by winning DOD approval, getting good leaders, and working together; and improving relationships with suppliers and other key constituents.

## A Crucial Breakdown

The work of "self-definition" that the council noted was requiring managerial integration of all the separate initiatives, projects, and agendas that had taken on lives of their own before Sematech's leadership was fully in place. The fab-building blitz brought both organizational solidarity and polarization at a time when Castrucci's crew was growing more dominant. The first step toward reorganization was to aid cooperation by establishing effective communication among the diverse elements.

To help him accomplish this, Noyce called on Bill Daniels, who had previously done consulting at Intel and who became one of Noyce's most valuable on- and off-site advisers during his first turbulent year as CEO. Daniels introduced a training program designed to improve teamwork and develop communication skills. To emphasize the importance of the training, Noyce and the rest of the OCE served as guinea pigs for Daniels's first training exercise. They all witnessed an event on the very first day that illuminated a growing conflict within Sematech.

Daniels describes it: "Bob understood the training meetings as a place for us to talk about and lay down some of the basic ground rules so we have places where we can start working together, talking, and making sense. Our first seminar with top management met for two days, and Paul Castrucci announced about two-thirds through the first day that he was going to a meeting with George Bush and some other people, and he really thought he should be there instead of staying for the second day, and was up and gone. Castrucci had not informed Noyce or anyone else of his leaving."

Noyce was stunned speechless. Ann Bowers Noyce recalls: "Bob always counted to ten, and would never make a public display. I would have fired Castrucci on the spot. Bob did not do that." Noyce agonized over the incident most of the night, then personally apologized for Castrucci's absence to the group the next day. Noyce felt so strongly about the importance of the training that he asked Castrucci to attend a remedial session upon his return. Daniels noted that the event had two important consequences for the rest of the watching organization: it dramatically highlighted the conflict between Noyce and Castrucci, giving it wide visibility, and it reinforced the importance of the training.

Some people, believing the differences in the OCE to be insurmountable, began asking, "How can this all come together as long as we've got such really dramatic and different styles?" Charlie Sporck had warned Noyce that an early firing of his IBM-supplied COO after such a long wait for leaders could create a public relations problem. However, the personally unpleasant situation became a policy problem when Castrucci began authorizing the purchase of expensive equipment for the fab that was not in any official budget.

At least two positive outcomes grew from the pressures of Castrucci's unapproved spending. First, a Government Accounting Office (GAO) investigation was launched. By statute, the GAO, like the National Advisory Council on Semiconductors (NACS), was obligated to issue periodic evaluations because of government participation. However, this investigation into reports by Sematech's congressional opponents was different because it addressed uncontrolled spending. Hasty describes how Sematech welcomed the investigating team, gave its members their own office in a central location, opened all files and information to them, and eventually received an "all's well" report (apparently to the chagrin of the sponsors, who withdrew their allegations). Second, an internal Investment Council was established. The council was composed of the members of the OCE and several of the top-level managing directors working directly under them, with Bob Noyce as chair and Turner Hasty as secretary. The council provided an orderly network covering all the steps in launching a sponsored development program. This began with determining the program's importance, and continued through program definition, and then proceeded up to and including the award of the contract.

## The Investment Council

The idea for the Investment Council grew out of the pressure Turner Hasty was feeling. As the director of external resources, Hasty had overall responsibility for outside contracts. Sematech needed a consistent system for submitting the requests for proposals, grading the proposals, and choosing who would receive contracts (a political and legal minefield). Not only were there strict legal requirements for an organization operating with government funds, but the contracting process brought it the closest yet to the role of "picking winners and losers"—something that Sematech's critics had often prophesied. Hasty remembers trying to exercise control over this tricky operation, but it was hard. "In the background," he says, "Paul [Castrucci] was out making deals right and left and sideways, and although he was the most visible, he wasn't the only manager doing this." The Investment Council made it possible to develop a framework for requesting proposals, and for reviewing them as a group to compare strategies and resources.

The council's chief function was not to determine where money would go but to legitimize and integrate the mechanisms for the consortium's contract allocation and spending. One of the early assumptions—that the industry's problems were technological ones and that Sematech would solve them through technological means—had loaded the consortium with technical assignees. Not all the skilled engineers who came to Sematech with project dreams were practiced in forecasting costs, managing allotted funds legiti-

91

mately and effectively, or integrating projects with an overall strategic plan. They came from parent firms with established administrative and legal structures. Sematech did not even have an internal attorney on the staff until 1989, when Bob Falstad, secretary of the Board of Directors, became the consortium's chief counsel.

The Investment Council quickly became a key element in the new organizational structure—Hasty calls it "an engine to get us started"—and it overcame the strategic conflicts and dangers running through the uncoordinated activity. Hasty again: "We discovered about seven requests for proposals that had been coming out of the woodwork, that didn't have anything to do with strategy. We had some managers with strong wills and strong personalities and all their programs were coming up." Although Castrucci's unreviewed major spending had been the biggest problem, other managers had been creating similar, smaller difficulties. The council instituted openly understood fiduciary mechanisms and strategic guidelines that reduced the detrimental effects of having managers in various areas competing to dominate the contract allocation process. Hasty now views the council as one of the consortium's first milestones: "That, to me, was really the beginning of Sematech as an organization. . . . This is when it really began to crystallize as to what we were going to do." The development of a systematic business methodology coincided with and complemented the sorting out of jobs, projects, and activities soon to take place.

## Structure with Reorganization

The OCE met off site with the consortium's entire technical and administrative staff in February, 1989, to hear feedback to the proposed operating plan. The meeting was held in the Burnt Orange Room in the Frank Erwin Center, the University of Texas's basketball arena. Participants recall this historic assemblage as the Burnt Orange Meeting—a fitting term for what became a confrontational scorcher. As feedback from staff attendees hit the proposed operating plan head on at the Burnt Orange Meeting, one thing became painfully obvious: The rapid increase in the number of assignees and their accompanying pet projects had surpassed the establishment and integration of an effective organizational structure. To include even the top priority projects in each manager's plan for achieving the consortium's strategic objectives would far exceed the available budget. When the confrontational smoke cleared, an aftermath of worry and doubt about the magnitude of this mismatch emerged.

Back in 1988 there had been concern about an unlimited mission and limited resources. This time the mismatch was brought into operational focus. Although the consortium's goal was now more realistic, there was still a discrepancy between its resources and the multitude of specific projects it inspired. The most urgently required resources now were not just funding, but a sound business methodology and an integrated organizational structure. Contributing to the operational discrepancies was the almost total lack of job definitions throughout the consortium. Assignees' understandings of their jobs and purposes at Sematech had to be reconciled with the clarity of mission being forced by the financial realities of operation.

Consultant Daniels observed the lack of structure when he arrived at Sematech: "They stacked five hundred people out there all at once in what seemed to be a two-week period, and there was no structure. Literally, there was no management structure to speak of. I'd never seen anything like it before." Structural clarification was not going to be simple in an experimental consortium with a burgeoning population of assignees still arriving from diverse, competing organizations, but it was becoming more urgent daily.

Daniels describes how the situation came about: "Part of the problem arose because people were being hired for their talents and being offered positions that required nine scalar levels to get the person to take the job, but with maybe only one other person in that department, and no employees between. It was very mixed up, and nobody knew what they were there for." Another problem he observed was that the "folks that were building the fab had their one act, and the rest of the folks were trying to build their kingdoms."

The struggle for clarity and purpose had begun with the Santa Clara start-up team in 1987, moved to Austin, and now came into operational focus with Noyce's leadership. Of the various groups at Sematech in early 1989, the successful fab-building team appeared to have the clearest goals, but it was using tactics that did not serve a cooperative effort well, and its aggressiveness was fueling other turf battles.

## Overlaps, Disconnects, and Fistfights

Following the Burnt Orange Meeting, Daniels, as an organizational consultant to the OCE, suggested a sort of shakedown strategy for sorting out all the diverse organizational behaviors and job jockeying. Proponents were asked to justify their individual projects in the light of overall consortium goals. Daniels got Noyce and Hasty to put their performance plans together with the strategic objectives of the operating plan. Then he suggested a plan for going down from the top to each level of the organization and requiring all personnel to discuss with the manager at the next level their individual goals in conjunction with those established for their team. Once this was completed, everyone could go back and look at the "overlaps" and "disconnects."

Daniels explains that overlaps occur when two or more people discover that they each thought they were doing something independently and there is a need to decide who will—or whether they should—team up. Disconnects, on the other hand, occur when there is a requirement in the performance plan that is not being accomplished. After individual plans were generated, says

Daniels, "Everyone would list these, and after they'd negotiated individually, they'd come in and show their plans to each other."

This effort to connect technology with job performance resulted in some long-distance consultation between Daniels and Hasty after the process had gone down two layers in the organization. Daniels remembers a call from Hasty that began: "Let me tell you about the stuff that's going on, and you tell me what you think of it. You know, every week, it's just a fistfight. They're bashing the heck out of each other. There are people that are really talking about leaving Sematech because they are in such terrible disagreement with the goals."

Daniels responded with support for staying the course: "Are they following the format? Are they listing key results? Are they still doing overlaps and disconnects? Are they trying to list their plans so they cooperate with their leader's plan?" Hasty affirmed the steps: "Yeah, we're doing all that. But we sure are finding out that there's a lot of funny stuff going on in this organization. We've got a lot of people that didn't know what they were here for. Is it supposed to go like that? Was that in your mind for the process?" Daniels affirmed the need to work through the difficult process, and Hasty replied: "It seems like the right problem for us to have right now." That ended the conversation; the shakedown was achieving its purpose.

There was fear and trembling at all levels in the organization as assignees began to wonder: "Wait a minute! Where's *my* work? I don't see my work coming down in any of these goals and objectives." Pinpointing the confusion meant leaving many of the assignees literally not knowing to whom they reported. As this struggle for self-definition coincided with the beginning operation of the Investment Council, business methodology and job performance began to converge.

Clarifying the process for doing the consortium's work continued. As described earlier, the initial organization plan called for Sematech to have a CEO and COO answering to the Board of Directors. The ETAB and FTAB lateral advisory groups were to help leverage external resources and supply counsel on policy and technological operations, and to communicate the results of those efforts to the board. Because of the TABs' lateral nature, they tended to break up hierarchical distinctions as well. By the end of 1988, these advisory boards had been filled and had begun to operate. The organization's own functions were originally envisioned as a type of matrix design of related internal and external programs.

In the summer of 1988—under the Kane-Peterman-Schneer executive troika, with Hasty as acting COO—this matrix had been simplified to a three-layered design that laid out the objectives required to accomplish the mission, strategies for achieving objectives, and tactics for enacting the strategies.[24] In practice, however, the importation of a variety of people into the fledgling consortium, which had no clearly defined management structure or discernible organizational culture, resulted in the advancement of individual agendas and the formation of cliques.

When Noyce arrived in the fall of 1988 he reorganized the top posts into the three-part OCE and the consortium's senior executives began working in open cubicles, as did everyone else in the organization. In the February, 1989, Burnt Orange reorganization, all the managers at the technology strategy level were made an extension of the OCE staff. This effectively expanded their scope by making them accountable not only for their own areas, but also across the boundaries of their separate management sectors. The effect of this integrated management structure was that, rather than simply flattening the hierarchy structurally, it made it more permeable. Individual turf distinctions soon became less important than Sematech's overall mission and objectives.

This organizational restructuring was combined with the ongoing training in meeting management and communication skills Daniels introduced with the OCE and other senior staff. This training covered much more than how to run a meeting, it showed participants how to be effective members of a collaborative group effort. It included the technique of "constructive confrontation," in which anyone with a relevant contribution to the discussion of an issue was not only permitted, but obligated, to offer it, even in opposition to a "higher level" opinion. The only ground rule was that a contribution could contain no personal attacks (See appendix 3 for an outline of these principles).

Another key feature of Sematech meetings was the use of facilitators to help sessions flow effectively. A good facilitator can make sure everyone with something to say is heard and, if possible, understood, so that all sides of an issue are aired without engaging in useless conflict or name-calling. Diane Verden, a Sematech administrator who has facilitated many high-level meetings, says that one of her major roles has often been to "elevate an issue" that, for some reason or another, the representative of a competing firm does not want to bring up with rival members. During the early days of hostile silence, Verden, acting in her third-party role, would get a controversial issue on the agenda for discussion and even introduce other viewpoints to the group anonymously when necessary. This expedient grew less necessary as openness increased, but there were continuing conflicts requiring clarification. The facilitators at Sematech, most of them direct hires, were a key factor in getting competitors to cooperate.[25]

## Castrucci Resigns

During this period of accomplishment and redefinition, Noyce's and Castrucci's differences became more painfully evident, particularly when the effects of the reorganization of spending and job definitions began to limit Castrucci's activities. Although some valuable unplanned-for outcomes had emerged from this contention, eventually its potential for damage grew greater than any possible benefit. On March 16, 1989, Paul Castrucci resigned. It was a relief to many insiders, but from the outside it looked like fresh evidence of Sematech's managerial difficulties.

The press observed that Noyce's style was that of a consensus leader, and Castrucci did not fit well in that environment. It quoted Castrucci as saying, "Leaving Sematech is the most difficult decision I ever had to make. For Sematech's good, I felt it was important for me to resign in order to allow Bob Noyce to install a management style which he believes is necessary for this consortium. I wish Sematech well; no one wants Sematech to succeed more than I."[26] However, even those most critical of Castrucci's management style agreed that his creativity, level of effort, and commitment were above question.

With Castrucci gone, Noyce asked Hasty to return permanently to the COO position. Hasty was reluctant. He knew he was not popular with a few of the board members, a consequence of his sometimes brusque style and of his having run interference for the OCE with the board on the issue of realistic expectations. The board, encouraged by the Black Book vision, sometimes appeared to feel that the legendary Noyce could stretch resources in ways no other executive could. Noyce persuaded Hasty to try the job until his retirement became official. As it turned out, Hasty's practical organizational skills were a good supporting match for Noyce's charisma, and the board confirmed his appointment as COO at it July, 1989, meeting.

## A Balanced Team

Turner Hasty, a thirty-year veteran of TI service—most notably in R&D and new product development—had also worked on joint projects with the Japanese. Although he felt honored by Noyce's choice, he says: "I thought it was a tremendous challenge. I felt that what we were trying to do was almost impossible, but we had to do it."

Bill Daniels was still advising and watching the new team of Noyce, Hasty, and Mills with an organizational analyst's eye. "Bob embodied the values and was really the only representative of the values that came to predominate," he says. "Turner built the system that allowed those values to actually come into practice. He laid some things out to the board, especially the limited nature of the resources and the need to focus on one or the other goal, instead of trying to do it all." The consortium was developing focus and self-discipline as it reorganized its projects and personnel to conform to its strategic plan and stay within budget limitations.

Noyce, as a consensus leader, was sympathetic to the conflicting priorities represented by the various board members, and had wanted to try to accomplish all of them. But Daniels saw that the pragmatic and tough Hasty refused to budge, both with the board and with outside contractors. According to Daniels, Hasty would say, "We're not going to do the design process here; we're not going to build model fabs here; what we can do is we can become a light to those who build equipment for the next generation."

Hasty brought in Scotty Rogers from TI to help with the business part of the ongoing reorganization. The two men wanted to give the Investment Council a sound basis, with financial and legal consistency in members' actions as they developed their team projects. Sematech had some harrowing near misses from legal scandals and suits as inexperienced participants tried to hurry contracting procedures along. Hasty recalls:

> We were letting projects out with government funding, and we had to follow very detailed procedures with the Department of Defense to make sure we were not showing favoritism. We looked at six or seven of these proposals, and could see lawsuits all over the place—letters, for example, from Sematech to Perkin-Elmer telling them that their bid was too high; they needed to bring it down. The writer was innocent, but he didn't understand that this will get you in jail! I called up Jim Greed, who was with Perkin-Elmer at the time, and I said, disregard that letter, and we're going to stop this request for proposal totally, please accept our apologies. These companies that would have had legitimate lawsuits didn't push them because they knew we didn't know what we were doing. We started over from scratch, to do it right with the Investment Council.

While systematic ways of handling these equipment and technology issues were being developed, CAO Peter Mills, was also busy. Daniels observes that "Peter [Mills's] strengths were a sense of the political necessities—the relationship with the federal government and Sematech. His skillfulness was a kind of entrepreneurial skillfulness of working that network of contacts, the pressures, and understanding of the complexities of the political arena." The area Mills took on had almost no structure and had very few personnel to balance the swelling ranks of technologists.

All early observers talk about how much Sematech suffered from a lack of human resources direction. Sematech did not have human resources functions clearly defined at first because, as originally conceived, the consortium was to consist mainly of technical assignees from member companies that had their own administrative functions, including human resources. Whatever Sematech needed in the way of support personnel—such as in the human resources area—could be hired later. In retrospect, the lack of early attention in this area handicapped Sematech's evolution, and certainly made it harder to manage the 1989 reorganization effort. Early on, the consortium had depended to a large extent on several external consultants, including Ann Polino, who had brought in Bill Daniels, and Cecil Parker.[27] Castrucci had brought in a personnel manager from IBM, but he did not work out and was also gone by this time. The early efforts at the strategic use of human resources knowledge in the Sematech's early development were, for many of those involved, one of the big disappointments and missed opportunities.

## Energy for Growth

With the conflict between Noyce and Castrucci resolved, the consortium began a healthy growth spurt, but this growth exacted enormous energy. Hasty remembers: "I don't think I have ever been involved in such intense activity as from the time I became COO in March, 1989, until I left. In building Sematech, we were trying to build a business that was a little bit different." Participants discovered that much of the experience they had gained in the operations of their parent companies did not apply at Sematech. A key difference was that they were not manufacturing and marketing products in the conventional sense. They were not profit driven; they were time driven. This called for a different organizational structure and a new management style in which manufacturing people were as high in the pecking order as design and development people. This last requirement proved to be Sematech's biggest cultural barrier.

By the early summer of 1989 Sematech could point to the accomplishment of some important early milestones, mostly related to the establishment of its collaborative organization. It was prepared to begin work with industry, the government, and the academic and research community. Establishment milestones included the Austin site selection and move, followed by building and equipping the fab for Phase I and constructing an attached office tower. A senior executive team was in place at last, and the consortium was attracting expert assignees, staff, and support personnel from member companies and the local area. An effective working relationship with DARPA had been created, and the first six SCOEs established, with various research projects begun under the supervision of the SRC. External advisory boards, one at the executive level, and fourteen in technical focus areas, had been formed with experts from throughout the industry to provide input and help leverage external resources. All these milestones contributed to producing the desired transferable technology on the Master Deliverables List (MDL), which in turn provided member firms the expected return on their investments.

First on the MDL had been the fab-building workshop, with knowledge transferred to member companies in the fall of 1988. This was followed by the first run of high-yield silicon wafers in the new fab in March, 1989, less than fifteen months after the site was selected.[28] These accomplishments were a major achievement for an experimental organization, especially considering the short period involved. The 1990 operating plan, produced in the third quarter of 1989, summarized the nature of the consortium's achievements up to that point, saying, "The 'fast track' construction and organizational setup have forced Sematech to grow up fast, undergoing intense activity and organizational introspection."[29]

The coalescence of the consortium's membership under the inspiration of Noyce's leadership, the fab's record accomplishment, the Burnt Orange shake-up, Castrucci's resignation, and the reordering of the entire organization all epitomize the extremes of this rapid growth period. As the end of 1989 approached, the consortium could take credit for achieving milestones and creating major deliverables as it matured among the thicket of economic, political, and structural difficulties.

In practical terms, the expectations for what such a manufacturing consortium could actually hope to accomplish were becoming much more clear. There was something uniquely American about the freedom to cooperate that Sematech offered and had adhered to in its many struggles. Sematech continued its shift away from the early plans of creating dramatic breakthroughs that would beat the Japanese, such as revolutionary chip design innovations, and more toward advancing the use of management technologies (i.e., freeing people to do things better technologically). Areas like CAD, for example, were growing in importance for their collaborative potential and their second-order effects on learning.

Improving management technology entailed a wider outlook. It should increase manufacturing competence and accelerate organizational learning and cycle times, but not without timely access to reliable, state-of-the-art manufacturing equipment and materials. To be sure of such access, Sematech recognized it would have to give emergency aid to the ailing U.S. supplier infrastructure and then continue to support its long-term health through partnerships and alliances. Just as packing electronic circuits ever closer together on a microchip gives rise not only to greater computing power but also to unexpected complications, so this closer collaboration between industry members and their suppliers would multiply Sematech's strengths and the difficulties that lay ahead.

## CHAPTER 5

# Reaching Consensus on Standards

F ollowing the Burnt Orange reorganization in 1989, the dream of creating a functional consortium out of competitors seemed increasingly attainable. The intensity and idealism that had driven the consortium now began to be redirected to practical questions of how best to design and implement actual projects of value to the entire industry.

Thanks to the leadership of Noyce and his OCE, useful applications for strengthening the equipment and materials infrastructure started to proliferate, sometimes taking unexpected turns, and Sematech's organizational structure necessarily had to branch out as well. With these new projects, the consortium undertook a broader kind of collaborative work that involved the chip makers and their material and equipment suppliers.

This story begins with a 1988 survey done when the ETAB sent IBM's Obi Oberai, Sematech's first director of strategic analysis, on a road-mapping expedition throughout the industry similar to the one that IBM had commissioned him to do in 1987.

## Road Mapping Shows Gaps

Creating road maps that integrate information about all the pieces necessary for future manufacturing was becoming an increasingly important strategic tool for many businesses at this time. An experienced strategist for IBM, Oberai was instructed to collect information from Sematech's member firms identifying the main causes of their manufacturing problems and how the consortium could help with them. The questions on problems were more focused than the broad technical queries put to members at the early planning workshops, and the clear answer Oberai and his team got back from everyone was that the chip makers' biggest headaches stemmed not from technological problems but from difficulties with suppliers. The unanimity of their response was striking to the surveyors.

Oberai visited all fourteen member companies and talked to many people, mostly in small meetings. He sat down with the managers responsible for manufacturing semiconductors and asked them a variety of questions, but the focus was on these three: "How do you manage your quality? How do you work with the suppliers? How do you buy equipment?"

Oberai and his staff found the answers to be very interesting. What struck them was the curious discrepancy between their espoused practices and actual ones. Oberai recalls: "My staff and I would get back to the hotel and sit down and say: 'This is what they're saying, but when you look at the words you copied down, it actually says the exact opposite of what they are saying.'"

When Oberai asked the manufacturing managers about their equipment selection criteria he was consistently told how much they valued quality and reliability. Then, when he asked them how they actually did their purchasing, he found that most of them were "beating the heck out of the supplier" for their lowest price. His review was revealing: "We put down on one side all the words they were saying, and on the other side we put down what mechanisms they were using. They were always in conflict. Firms said they wanted quality, but their message to the supplier was always: 'Give me the cheapest.'"

After discovering this anomaly Oberai tried a new tack: he took his survey to some major supplier firms. "Fortunately, they were all old friends, senior executives, who were quite open," he says. "I asked the same set of questions: 'How are you managing quality? Reliability? How do you deal with your customers?' It was very interesting. I heard the exact same bitter complaints from suppliers that I heard from the member companies, but this time in reverse!"

The correlation between poor quality and low reliability on the one hand, and the poor relationships between chip makers and suppliers was a significant finding. But for a time this nexus remained overshadowed by the consortium's need to develop its own technological capability and help the infrastructure by improving equipment technology. During the technology-focused processes of equipping the Sematech fab and initiating equipment-focused projects, the management implications of the interrelated problems of quality and customer-supplier relations continued to grow clearer. Their better understanding eventually led to one of Sematech's most successful programs.

## Equipping for Cooperative Technology

However, even before reaching that understanding, Oberai's findings proved helpful during the turbulent period when Sematech was negotiating the purchase of equipment to run its own fab in the same hostile environment that the members and suppliers had described to his team. Sematech urgently needed equipment that could run the proprietary Phase I MDV processes from IBM and AT&T. Then, once Phase I was underway, the plan was either to upgrade this initial equipment and/or develop new tools as necessary for each Sematech-derived phase to follow.

Thus, another thread in this story begins with choosing and purchasing equipment capable of handling two different proprietary technology processes in the consortium's unique collaborative fab. The choices were made trickier by the lack of communication among member companies. Before Sematech, competing chip makers never disclosed to anyone which supplier's equipment they were purchasing, and suppliers never disclosed the identify of their customers or what they bought. But that very data—long considered a confidential element of proprietary product information—was essential if the cooperative effort was to succeed.

Deepak Ranidive, the Intel assignee managing Sematech's fab, remembers how thick the veil of secretiveness was at trade meetings: "It was ridiculous because the suppliers of the equipment certainly knew who their customers were; they had the list. Sometimes other people knew who was using what equipment, but they still didn't talk about it when they ordered it. So nobody else knew whether a firm was supporting this equipment or just evaluating it or what. There was no communication on something as simple as what equipment you are using." This secrecy complicated Sematech's use of technology contributions from more than one source because it meant having to make common choices based on private information. The consortium's collective ignorance was a drawback. Resolving this issue would be a key cooperative lesson for the organization.

## Narrowed Focus, Broader Scope

Oberai's map of the difficulties member firms were having with suppliers, combined with the consortium's own struggle with industry communications barriers, showed that the problems of the weakening supplier infrastructure were hardly Sematech's alone. They would have to be included in the chip makers' cooperative manufacturing effort. If not, the equipment makers' weakness could cause the grand plan to fail. However, Sematech's 1989 Burnt Orange conference convinced most participants that trying to do everything the Black Book prescribed was not only impossible, it was potentially fatal. How could they even think of adding more?

Bob Noyce kept Congress abreast of the change in thinking when he testified before the House Budget Committee in 1989: "I think that the job that we have to do has become somewhat more difficult in the two years that have passed since the original plan was put out. As a result of that, we have been moving our emphasis to the semiconductor equipment and material suppliers because we see that as more critical now than the job that we were going to do—more in the manufacturing technology, manufacturing methods, quality methods, the techniques, if you will, of high-volume production."

Noyce explained that, with more money, Sematech could come closer to accomplishing its original job. Still, supporting the infrastructure now seemed absolutely essential—and it was proving more expensive than originally expected. "With more money we could do both of those jobs," he told the committee.[1]

Congress had overcome the 1989 federal budget cut scare by restoring full funding, but it was not prepared to come up with more money. The 1989 consortium reorganization and budget realignment thus had to take into account the need to include supplier support, which meant coming up with the resources to integrate the industry both horizontally and vertically. The grand goal of reestablishing America's lead in global semiconductor manufacturing remained the same, but it was being reframed as an initiative that included working with the semiconductor manufacturing equipment and materials infrastructure. The consortium's focus narrowed even as its scope of collaboration increased.

## A New Mission

As a goodwill gesture toward improving communication, Sematech and SEMI/Sematech jointly hosted the first "President's Day" in April, 1989, inviting top executives of supplier firms to visit the consortium, attend workshops, and meet and talk with each other. As we will later see, this event had the unexpected effect of symbolizing that old wounds between manufacturers and suppliers were being healed.

Even more significantly, as the 1989 reorganization effort concluded in June, Sematech added an important word to its mission statement that more accurately reflected its current emphasis. It now read: "To provide the U.S. semiconductor industry the *domestic* capability for world leadership in manufacturing."[2] By adding this one word, the consortium committed itself to using, developing, improving, and testing U.S. equipment as an integrated part of its technology phases. Since no new funding had been added, this commitment meant planners would have to balance internal and external efforts and further scale back the proportion of in-house, full-flow production in the Sematech fab. It also meant reallocating resources so as to maintain operating capability for the various phase processes on site while also supporting external equipment projects off site. The operating plans for 1990 and 1991 reflected the board's decision to evenly divide the internal and external allocations.[3]

Although the Black Book had called for doing everything, the decision to allocate more money to outside spending than anyone had originally envisioned caught many observers by surprise. Also, although the technology phases remained the same, putting more emphasis on equipment required adjustments in staffing, both for assignees and direct hires. Staffing and assignments had been planned for running a more internally focused organization, and changing them was slower and more difficult than redirecting financial resources. For example, the equipment focus urgently required project engineers—a scarce commodity on the now nearly full staff—and member company assignments were typically locked in for at least two years. Thus, the mismatch between personnel structure and mission focus persisted for a while.

The mission change had an immediate positive effect at another level. It led to renegotiating the early member participation agreement, giving more equitable intellectual property rights to suppliers. For instance, one supplier, Applied Materials, insisted on the right to implement improvements learned at Sematech with all its customers. According to Sam Harrell, the new approach helped break the gridlock that had developed in negotiating equipment development contracts. Only three such contracts had been in place by June, 1989, but there were five more by the third quarter, with the momentum increasing. By 1990, a total of fifty-seven projects were underway. The pace was expected to ease by the completion of Phase II, and pick up again in preparation for Phase III.[4]

## Less Glamour, More Risk

Although the consortium's shift from emphasizing cutting-edge, memory chip technology to supporting its supplier infrastructure might appear less glamorous than making global DRAM breakthroughs, it actually incurred greater economic and political risks.

Economically, Sematech would begin to share some of the development risks that U.S. material and equipment suppliers traditionally had borne—often with poor technical and commercial feedback from their customers. Now the consortium would model customer-supplier partnering projects, with suppliers chosen from the "best of breed" in key technology areas. Of course, there was no guarantee of technological or financial success for these partnerships—either for Sematech or for participating suppliers.

Politically, as in the agenda controversies, some members objected that scaling back production would make it even harder for them to recoup their investment in Sematech with transferable turnkey technology. Political jeopardy also arose from Sematech's increased power to affect the direction, nature, and makeup of the infrastructure. The 1989 Federal Advisory Council reported: "In carrying out its mission, Sematech intends to sustain or create one world-class U.S. producer in each major category of chipmaking equipment, second-sourcing only in special cases where the back-up firm uses an entirely different tool architecture or represents a particularly high-risk/high-return investment opportunity. The strategic objective for Sematech's members as a group, which none has the capacity to achieve alone, is *freedom from the potential dangers of dependence on foreign sources of supply.*"[5]

Taking this step was politically dangerous because Sematech was openly acknowledging its intent to influence the economic pace and technological character of the semiconductor material and equipment (SME) infrastructure. The advisory council's report minced no words: "The consortium's mission statement and contracting practices acknowledge implicitly that key segments of the U.S. equipment and materials market can support only one or a few strong vendors."[6] Sematech faced the danger of making bad choices, whether in partners, technology processes, or equipment types—any of which could prove disastrous for both the consortium and for suppliers that became involved in its projects. This step brought Sematech even closer to practicing the kind of industrial policy that would create winners and losers within the infrastructure, precisely as consortium critics predicted would happen at the chip-maker level. But two fundamental reasons for the step were compelling.[7] First, the weakness in the U.S. infrastructure made American supplier firms an increasingly tempting target for foreign takeovers. Second, internal to Sematech, the SME infrastructure's secrecy made it harder than anyone had expected to get a cooperative initiative going among the chip makers themselves. A willingness to select and then support selected firms to develop needed technology answered both problems.

## Tough Decisions

These difficulties complicated Sematech's own fab-equipping decisions. Despite its commitment to domestic independence, Sematech needed to use some non-U.S. tools to start up, just as it had needed to begin Phase I with donated proprietary technology. However, it still planned to have equipment projects completed in time to use all-American tools for its Sematech-derived Phase II process.

But first it had to set up the fab. And to do that, it had to determine what equipment would work best. In light of this, Deepak Ranidive says he faced a tough situation: "If we had to run the complete AT&T [SRAM] process, then we had to use the equipment AT&T was using. Or, if we were just going to do the [DRAM] back-end from IBM, we had to find out what equipment was compatible to IBM's process. But a lot of the member companies weren't using either process. How do you decide in terms of equipment which to buy?"[8]

Ranidive participated in numerous discussions with the companies and their suppliers just to understand what equipment to start with. Neither IBM nor AT&T actually gained any advantage from the use of donated equipment. The decision had to be made on the basis of what was best for Sematech. However, this was not always easy to determine. Even most of the specs on equipment were customized, proprietary secrets. There were no standardized specs on tools from one firm to another, even when the tools came from the same supplier.

Sematech had come to a crucial working point because companies' willingness to share equipment information would determine the success or failure of this cooperative community.[9] Because the financial contributions had been structured for fairness, the only way for companies to gain an advantage was in the information exchange now taking place in the consortium. The competitive action would have been to "sandbag"—that is, to send less than one's top performers and to tell them, as one informed observer recalls, "to keep their ears open and their mouths shut." Now, however, companies would have to share proprietary information basic to equipping and operating Sematech's fab.

The member-company representatives in these equipment discussions found themselves caught between the old code of not revealing too much, and two new goals: having their company's best interests represented, and agreeing on what was best for Sematech. Research on intergroup conflicts has confirmed that a by-product of intensely cohesive at-home groups, which many of Sematech's member firms had, is distrust of the decision-making of their representatives abroad.[10] Fortunately, however, the representatives that member firms sent to sit on the ETAB and other advisory boards at Sematech were already powerful in their own companies, which helped make board policy decisions more palatable back home.

Still, the discussions about what equipment to buy were anything but pure cooperation. Suppliers, for example, lobbied for their own equipment. There were power issues to be resolved among manufacturers who had clear tool preferences because of their previous knowledge. Still, Ranidive's group was able to follow the plan of working "off the known tools, until some technology transferred internally."

Sematech finally came up with a consensus list of equipment that both IBM and AT&T agreed on. The proprietary technology gifts from IBM and AT&T made their agreement necessary, but it politicized what should have been merely a technical decision because other members feared being dominated by the two bigger firms.

Ranidive says great care was taken to ensure the equipment chosen was acceptable to all members. First, he and his group used consensus methods to combine the AT&T and IBM lists into a Sematech list of the best equipment in the industry. Then, at a one-day meeting at Sematech attended by representatives of all member companies, Ranidive and his group presented to each fab area manager a listing of what equipment had been used by AT&T and IBM, and then compared it to the Sematech equipment list his group had developed. Ranidive asked for feedback from the attendees to see if his group was on the right track. He was pleasantly surprised when no one showed an attachment to a particular type of equipment or supplier.

According to Ranidive: "That is different than what I've seen in the past—it's not easy to get people to work that way, coming from such diverse backgrounds. The attention to the good of the industry was a commitment that they had already made by coming to the consortium." In short, the good of the industry had become a goal that unified members of the organizations.[11]

Ranidive's consensus-building took place during the early months of 1989, foreshadowing what Tom Seidel described as the standard "cooperative practice" at Sematech by 1993.[12] The equipment selection process was going on simultaneously with the consortium's renegotiation of rights with suppliers, which was aided by the improved contracting procedures the Investment Council established.

Once the equipment decisions had been made, it was time to inform all the hopeful suppliers what the choices were—and in more detail than an ordinary company would normally provide. The shared information and communication of fairness to all had to be tied to the requirements of Sematech's overall mission while remaining totally free of bias. Having this information come from an impartial third party, suppliers could more easily understand that even if they were not on the list, they could still benefit from and help accomplish the mission. This was an early step toward much greater communication and collaboration between chip makers and suppliers. Suppliers were convinced the decisions were fair and that they would have a chance to participate in the future if they changed their practices.

## Snowballing Benefits

The cooperative decision process that Ranidive and the other fab managers and member-company representatives worked out for purchasing equipment proved time consuming up front, but the effort was more than recouped later—with far-reaching effects.

This new cooperative practice exposed not only how much the lack of shared information had previously crippled the industry but also how unnecessary it was, for when the sharing began, people discovered that most of the knowledge viewed as proprietary was actually generic—or at least widely known. Most of all, they began to see the high costs of secrecy. It was actually far better for chip makers if their best suppliers were well supported by other customers than for them to be an exclusive customer.[13] Standardized specifications also brought an end to an enormous waste of time and effort. The practical accomplishment of collaborating on equipment choices began a pattern of cooperation based on what would be best for all concerned.

Publishing the equipment decision information to all suppliers, whether they were among those chosen or not, also established a prototype for the standard-setting procedures and quality control programs that Sematech eventually developed. All of the suppliers gained from learning how their equipment stacked up against that of their competitors. They also learned the direction that equipment development was taking in the industry. Previously, such information was not freely available.

The consortium developed a request for proposal (RFP) procedure for getting the word out to suppliers. This involved providing suppliers with detailed documents specifying the equipment's intended uses, Sematech's expectations of the equipment and of the supplier, and what the suppliers had a right to expect from Sematech.

According to Ranidive: "We said, 'Look, this is what we are looking for: this type of technology and this type of application.' You need to reply to us, 'What do you have?'"

The RFP procedure, besides being open, also formalized the purchase specifications that the supplier would have to meet. Thus, when suppliers were building or marketing their equipment, they could know exactly what was expected from them to be competitive. Sharing this purchase information with suppliers had the effect of increasing the population of firms that might compete by offering a product in a particular niche. This example shows how cooperation among manufacturers increased competition among suppliers; it also follows the economic dictum that the more information competitors have about each other's products, the more competitive they can become.[14]

## Keeping Pace

Besides having its own difficulties contracting for reliable equipment, Sematech faced another huge problem: Member companies would not be able to use its Phase I–III submicron technology if U.S. equipment development failed to keep pace with what was needed. Industry leaders recognized the need to synchronize the "cadence" of development of tools and manufacturing processes with advances in chip design, as well as to make timely purchases of the new equipment required.[15] Sematech needed to both lead and be in step with the industry, rather than become isolated from real-time commercial urgencies.[16]

Every generation of technological advance in semiconductors—it typically takes three years to achieve the next smaller size for chips—called for having not only chip-manufacturing technology, but also having all the tools and materials needed for production ready for starting up the next generation's production facility. In fact, in early 1990 the consortium was having to race just to try to get in step with industry timing. Sematech's more advanced member companies were already well past the purchasing window for the Phase I demonstration vehicle. Indeed, they were already making equipment choices for the next .50-micron line widths projected for Phase II.

The next big marketing window for the recovering U.S. suppliers would be at the .35-micron product generation—the Phase III goal scheduled to be achieved in 1993. It would not substantially help either the semiconductor industry or its SME infrastructure for Sematech alone to achieve this goal with U.S. equipment if the purchasing window for that equipment had passed for member companies—or if they did not trust the U.S. tools. The collaborators would have to be simultaneously involved and invested in the processes of developing, improving, testing, and core standardization. They also would have to be convinced of the equipment's value before they would be willing to buy it from its U.S. suppliers.

## Threatened Survivors

Because the microelectronics "food chain" extends from systems makers (like computer manufacturers) to electronic component manufacturers (like chip makers) to manufacturing equipment vendors (like material and suppliers), it is pretty clear that any global competitor gaining control of even one level of the chain can eventually monopolize the entire market. During the 1986 planning for Sematech, the founders had focused on avoiding dependency on foreign chips. However, the new mission now focused their attention on a still deeper dependency: the foreign equipment used to manufacture those chips.

As the consortium's leaders contemplated what could be done, the situation seemed truly alarming. For one thing, the supply industry was even more splintered than the chip makers themselves. The supplier infrastructure consisted of many relatively small companies, which in the 1980s had also begun losing their dominant global market share to the Japanese. In 1980 the first nine of the top ten worldwide SME suppliers were American, and the tenth was Japanese. By 1990 only Applied Materials remained in the top five, and the four other U.S. firms in the top ten ranked behind five Japanese firms.[17]

A 1989 MIT study highlighted this stark reality: "The capital equipment and service sectors in the United States [semiconductor industry] parallel the semiconductor sector in its entrepreneurialism. There are a few stable, reasonably large equipment firms . . . along with hundreds of smaller firms, many of them start-ups. In 1986, 55 percent of the American firms supplying capital equipment and services to the semiconductor industry had sales of less than $5 million, and many of them were on the verge of failing."[18] A resulting trend toward consolidation or acquisition, often by foreign firms, seemed to reflect U.S. weakness rather than strength. Typical of this weakening was the purchase of Monsanto Electronic Materials Company, the last major U.S. supplier of silicon wafers, by the German firm of Huels AG in November, 1988. Neither Sematech nor the DOD could persuade any American corporation to buy the firm.[19]

Sematech's member companies, who represented 80 percent of all U.S. chip makers, reportedly had planned to buy more than 60 percent of their equipment for the next two chip generations from Japanese suppliers.[20] This created a precarious situation in which, according to the advisory council's report, "The immediate issue is not strength but survival, i.e., sufficient revenue in the near term to support the development of next-generation production technology."[21]

For example, in the crucial technology area of lithography—the photolike process for printing circuits on silicon wafers invented and developed in the United States—American equipment firms had only 29 percent of the market by 1990, compared to the 59 percent share of such foreign firms as Japan's Nikon and Canon.[22] This threatening environment forced Sematech to concentrate its resources on the firms most likely to survive. A series of major threats and/or losses to the U.S. SME infrastructure occurred during this period, with tense international dramas played out among what one journalist referred to as "Big Bucks, big stakes, and big egos."[23] These events highlighted the cost of cooperation versus the price of competition for Sematech members, and undoubtedly influenced public perception and government support.

Both the general public and the government expressed approval of the consortium's new mission with its widened scope. Despite the risks generated by picking "best-of-breed" suppliers to support, extending a helping hand to them made U.S. chip makers appear less self-seeking to their critics because larger resources were focused on something other than themselves. When the sale of Monsanto Electronic to Huels AG was proposed in late 1988, Sematech spoke up in opposition. It petitioned the Committee on Foreign Investment in the United States (CFIUS) to recommend that Pres. George Bush block the sale. The petition was the first test of the Exon-Florio amendment to the 1988 trade bill, which authorized the government to stop foreign purchases of American firms if the sale threatened national security.[24] However, a little over a year later, President Bush, acting on the CFIUS's recommendation, declined to block the sale. Then, almost in the same breath, he submitted his 1990 budget with the full $100 million for Sematech renewed. The government's position seemed clear: The industry's bailout, if was to get one, would have to come from Sematech.

A similar case occurred in May, 1989. Sematech had just awarded its first development contracts to suppliers, among them Semi-Gas Systems, of San Jose, California. Semi-Gas was to make and install the systems for routing and maintaining the high purity levels of gases needed for semiconductor manufacture.[25] Less than a year later, however, the Tokyo-based firm of Nippon-Sanso announced that it would purchase Semi-Gas Systems from Hercules Corporation. Sematech immediately opposed the threatened sale on both antitrust and national security grounds.[26] Once again Sematech petitioned the CFIUS to intervene, citing confidentiality concerns as well as fear of losing a top U.S. supplier. In response, the CFIUS stated that a mutual agreement could supply adequate confidentiality. It also noted that Semi-Gas was not yet the sole surviving U.S. supplier of its type, so its sale did not pose a national security threat. It took the 1990 CFIUS committee and President Bush only until July to announce they would not block the sale. The Justice Department then sought an antitrust injunction, but it also lost its case. Almost a year later, in April, 1991, Nippon-Sanso bought Semi-Gas. A month after the sale, Sematech canceled its Semi-Gas contract after having invested $4 million in development—undoubtedly to Nippon-Sanso's benefit.

These two highly visible cases exemplify the relentless pressure on the SME infrastructure as well as the government's curiously mixed response. While the semiconductor industry expected more active help on the foreign trade front, the government expected the industry to restore itself and its infrastructure solely with domestic financial aid. This was the long-term trend that Sematech faced as it studied how to help rescue the infrastructure from its fading market-share predicament in 1989.

## A Four-Part Mission

Sematech's reassessment of this precarious environment, as well as its recognition of its own internal equipment difficulties, led to the new supplier emphasis in the mission statement. To accomplish this outreach during 1989 and into 1990, the consortium's activities began to fall into four major categories: (1) external development contracts for new equipment; (2) improvement of existing equipment, with the development of partnered core standards; (3) schedules or road maps for anticipated innovation, including manufacturing methods and future factory design; and (4) methods for strengthened two-way communication, both for receiving feedback and disseminating produced knowledge.

The first formal groups to emerge at Sematech, like the Investment Council, had established the organization's working machinery, and they continued to drive it. The Competitive Analysis Council (CAC) quietly held its first quarterly meeting at the end of 1988, but received more notice as it continued to grow in importance. The CAC was created after a series of meetings held by member companies to discuss establishing a system of competitive analysis that would ensure "Sematech goals and strategies might be intelligently driven from an information database on the leading edge foreign competition."[27] It was an effort to collect competitive information from varied national resources, then disseminate it in a timely manner back to member companies. The goal was to synchronize Sematech's ongoing technology transfers.

By mid-1989, the CAC was initiating market research in areas such as manufacturing tools, materials, systems, and methods, concentrating on firms with proven successes in key technologies like lithography in order to make development contract recommendations to the Investment Council and the Board of Directors. The CAC became an integral component of Sematech's strategic planning process. It combined with the Investment Council and became the organization's compass for charting a new course.

## Program Priorities

Sematech began looking at how to create equipment-related technology programs in the sectors where the CAC's analysis showed the United States was lagging, and how many materials and equipment suppliers could hope to survive in a given sector. The CAC also pointed out potential blind alleys of technological innovation—a hard and sometimes apparently ruthless call to make, but a crucial one since the directions not taken can have as many consequences for resource allocation as the ones that are pursued.

The CAC's analyses helped sort Sematech programs into three priority levels.

In Noyce's terms, first came the "show stoppers" or "critical equipment and materials for which the United States is in danger of losing timely access or technology leadership." Next in line came "key enablers"—that is, "equipment and methods that can give members the greatest advantage in the least amount of time." In third place were the "high-risk, high-return" manufacturing projects that would be hard for individual firms to tackle on their own.[28] Ongoing technical workshops, user groups, and road-mapping forums also gave members input about priorities, but as the project-based equipment mission grew, some members were unhappy.[29]

More dangerous still, 1989 was the first year when it became possible for members to give the required two years' notice of withdrawal from the consortium. Given the mission change, this became a real possibility among disgruntled firms that wanted turnkey technology processes. Because of budget constraints, focusing on equipment inevitably meant cutting back production capacity. The Phase I, II, and III chips with their .8, .5, and .35 submicron features would still be produced as fully working devices—but more as prototypes, not manufactured on an efficient, high-volume, high-yield production line, as some had previously hoped. In semiconductor manufacturing, the yield performance curve (the rate of defect-free devices manufactured) is linked to production volume as the difficulties for each new generation of miniaturization are overcome. While Sematech would develop and demonstrate the fully proven manufacturing technology with U.S.-made equipment for each process advance, it could not reproduce the volume of a commercial fab running three shifts a day, seven days a week.

On the other hand, Bob Noyce told the Federal Advisory Council that he had always believed that the only way Sematech could finance a fully integrated production line would be to manufacture semiconductors for the market, which of course had never been an option for the consortium.[30] Aside from other legal complications, putting Sematech chips on the market would mean competing with member firms' products. So the choice was not as clear-cut as simply giving up high-production volume to support the infrastructure. Still, there were obviously other trade-offs to consider.

Sematech's new project-based operations now aimed at three areas where analysis showed the United States had major, equipment-related weaknesses. These were in manufacturing operations, technology development, and systems control.

Within these sectors the consortium formed "thrust areas"—five of them by 1990—beginning with the biggest and most worrisome show stopper of all, optical lithography. Lithography was followed by thrusts in multilevel metals; furnaces and implant; manufacturing methods, processes, and systems; and the SCOE and national labs research (which included such things as X-ray lithography). Each of these thrust areas generated numerous development projects with chosen suppliers and specific applications. Joint Development Projects (JDPs) that were typically conducted off site—with tools inserted into a member-company fab or in an interested federal facility—made up over half of these by 1990. The JDPs aimed to develop new kinds of equipment and processes in partnership with a chosen supplier, including necessary training. Depending on the supplier's strength or weakness, the development costs and the rights to jointly developed technology would be shared, according to a case-by-case, negotiated formula. This was an improvement over the original member participation agreement, and helped to motivate suppliers.[31]

After JDPs, the next most numerous kind of operation was the Equipment Improvement Project (EIP). The EIPs helped supplier partners improve and extend the life of their existing equipment, some of it operating directly on Sematech's fab line and some of it off site. Sematech's previous technology focus had been on next-generation and new technology development, but the industry still had billions of dollars of installed equipment that was not getting any better, and chip-making companies could not afford to simply throw it away. For its own start on equipment improvement, the consortium planned to model how to upgrade and adapt some of its Phase I equipment as it moved to running the Phase II fab line. Other EIPs would follow. As a bonus, equipment makers could often apply lessons learned from the EIPs to the design of better quality, more reliable equipment for the future. Supplier training, in fact, was an important part of the EIP approach.

The Tool Application Program (TAP) complemented and completed both the JDPs and EIPs. The TAP helped suppliers and member companies test and qualify both new and improved equipment while working together on the line in the Fab B clean room. The time thus saved by standardizing and sharing the results of all the programs, especially the TAP, across all Sematech and SEMI/Sematech members, as opposed to many individualized tests by single members, could be very great.

## The Master Deliverables List

The Master Deliverables List brought order to the JDP, EIP, and testing programs. Known as the MDL, it was made up from smaller lists of deliverables that existed for each thrust area, showing schedules, projects, specific tools, sites, and participating suppliers. The MDL made sense out of all these elements by summing up explicitly what and when members and suppliers could expect from each of Sematech's equipment projects. This master list became a catalog of the consortium's products: an inventory of all proven manufacturing knowledge that was ready for transfer. The MDL showed the relationship of the phase goals to the state of the joint equipment development and/or improvement of the specific tools required by the phase goals. Achievement milestones for the consortium could then be marked off on the MDL.[32]

Member firms also began looking to the MDL to estimate their own return on investment in the consortium, so the list continued to grow in importance. The first MDL was a consensus document, with the projects on the list arrived at by majority approval. Later, leaders developed a system for incorporating more of the individual member firms' priorities, and of using the list as an effective instrument for calculating and demonstrating investment returns.

## Training Programs

Two related training programs operated in conjunction with the equipment projects. The manufacturing specialists' course was designed to give Sematech's direct-hire technicians an understanding of the total context in which they worked, including responsibility for the operation and maintenance of their equipment. The other course was for new college graduates. Sematech placed them in the field, to receive "fast track" semiconductor manufacturing training at Sematech, and then rotated them to member companies after three years.[33] Both training programs reflected the industrial nature of Sematech's commitment to education and complemented the research-oriented university SCOEs. The manufacturing specialists' program failed to live up to its expectations, however. It never did prove to be effective, primarily because machines were increasingly replacing technicians.[34]

## Cooperation Breeds Cooperation

Each of these project-based activities created new interfaces between the consortium and the industry's infrastructure. The equipment and materials supplier firms belonging to SEMI/Sematech constituted a large proportion of the total U.S. supplier industry and the association's president, Sam Harrell, represented the suppliers' interests as a member of Sematech's Board of Directors. Now some of these supplier firms began to participate in JDPs, EIPs, and ongoing equipment testing.

By May, 1989, the first contracts for JDPs had been signed with selected firms. Hewlett-Packard, ATEQ, Graphics Corporation of America (GCA), and Westech Systems would provide equipment and services in the fabrication facility; Semi-Gas Systems, Union Carbide Industrial Gases (Linde), and Wilson Oxygen and Supply would develop specialty gases, an ultra-pure gas system, and other associated technologies.[35] Information from these project developments would then be disseminated to other SEMI/Sematech members, benefiting the industry as a whole.

Sam Harrell notes that a policy of mutual commitment to improvement had begun to supplant the previous entrenched hostility between chip makers and suppliers. The policy was simple but uncompromising: *If it is not competitive, it has to change.* Harrell says this motto made all the difference: "That's just a small phrase, but it was a very empowering phrase. The leaders of Sematech and the leaders of SEMI/Sematech together discovered that if it isn't competitive, it has to change. Out of that, we have seen some dramatic changes occur that companies never thought they would do—things that were their practices for a very long time, that were dear to their hearts."

What facilitated this change was that the commitment was shared. Previously, even those chip makers that had tried on their own to support and improve suppliers had often felt compelled by market pressures to participate in the competitive behavior that was undermining the U.S. infrastructure. Since 1980, many U.S. chip makers had relied on the willingness of Japanese chip makers to bear the expense of nurturing, testing, and breaking in equipment, giving their suppliers valuable feedback data in the process. Then American producers could buy this tested equipment, even if it was late, rather than go through the expensive debugging process themselves.

Nobody in the entrepreneurial U.S. industry wanted to be the one bearing this burden for others, but when they relied on Japanese efforts, they traded a short-term advantage for long-term weakness. As the Japanese continued to work with suppliers to develop more types of equipment with better quality, greater sophistication, and more reliability they could temporarily withhold test results to gain even greater advantage.

Craig Barrett, Intel's executive vice president, tells a story about this: "I was at a SEMI meeting in Japan where the representative from Nikon stood up and said, 'When appropriate, we may even tell our foreign customers about our new equipment.' I can't say it any better.... A public statement like that to a bunch of U.S. and Japanese folks says it pretty clearly. Nikon happens to be our supplier, and it's nice to know that 'when appropriate' they might even tell us about the next generation."[36]

On the other hand, Japanese firms that still needed U.S. suppliers were helpful customers—but only until Japanese equipment became available. Sematech's new project collaboration, equipment testing and qualification, and industry standardization aimed to break the pattern of noncommunication and devaluation between American semiconductor and equipment manufacturers.

Member companies also began talking to each other more about equipment. In August, 1989, the consortium invited key manufacturing managers (none of them Sematech assignees) to a workshop on trends in managing contamination during the clean-room production of greatly miniaturized chips—a process known as contamination-free manufacturing (CMF). Because particle contamination of even molecular size can cause defects in a chip's silicon surface and lower the yield of usable wafers, this workshop was considered a high-profile milestone of technology transfer. One way a fab's clean room can be operated without contamination is with increasingly automated clusters of advanced equipment, thus reducing the human presence. This CMF demonstration workshop, sharing equipment information, was one of the first to bring member-company manufacturing managers together at Sematech.

## Intel Sends Help

As the number of contracts for tool development, improvement, and testing projects began to grow, the consortium needed to call on member-company experience. The major help from members, besides dues and assignees, had been the donations of IBM's and AT&T's technology design. Now Intel, which had particular expertise in managing supplier-customer collaboration in equipment testing and improvement, came up with a different kind of contribution.

Intel's manager of manufacturing operations, Dean Toombs, had represented Intel on Sematech's Board of Directors since 1988, and had become chairman of the consortium's ETAB in 1989. In 1990, the company agreed to loan him to Sematech full time to share Intel's unique program of working with suppliers to test and qualify equipment. As Toombs tells it:

> In 1989–90, I was thinking about retirement. I had been working in the industry for more than thirty years—twenty at TI, then fourteen at Intel. When Bob Noyce took over Sematech, I wanted the chance to work with him, to help him make a success of it. Craig Barrett [Intel's executive vice president] agreed that for the last two years of my career I would go to Sematech and help them. I had enough breadth of knowledge—and of people in the industry—to take this on as a last challenge, realizing what a job it would be to put together and bring a consortium into effectiveness. Also, my long-time personal friend and colleague Turner Hasty was at Sematech. At TI, I had pulled him out of R&D, where he was really good, and made an applied-development guy out of Turner. [At Sematech, Toombs would now be working under COO Hasty— no problem for either of them.] I felt I wanted to give something back to the industry.

Intel had developed the program Toombs was bringing to Sematech in response to a devastating experience in 1986. The company had suffered a multi-million-dollar loss when it attempted to open a new fabrication facility fitted out with American equipment that proved unready for use and unreliable.

In response to that near-disaster, Intel developed a rigorous equipment qualification procedure (EQP), and began to require it of all new equipment purchases. As a result, some suppliers regarded Intel as a difficult customer, whereas others came to value the improvements in their tools that grew out of having to make adjustments for their customer. Now Toombs came to Sematech, bringing with him Intel's EQP to be openly shared in the consortium. The EQP would complement the various supplier-related development and improvement projects.

Toombs describes the demands of the EQP: "It begins with how Intel has changed its manufacturing plants. We bring all new equipment into each new Intel plant and subject it to testing in an extensive qualification process—'burn-in' is the jargon term. Even before buying equipment, you thoroughly evaluate it, run extended-period 'marathon' runs to wring it out, find weaknesses, then supply feedback to the maker. No one but Intel was doing it in late eighties. When I came to Sematech, none of the other member companies did it. Even the best and biggest did only a very cursory evaluation before actual installation."

However, at the time of Toombs effort, much new equipment was unreliable and did not perform to specifications. So, from 1986 on, with Intel's new qualification program, the supplier base looked at Intel and "thought we were crazy" because of the demands placed on them, Toombs recalls. Suppliers tried to get around the standards by going directly to Intel's factories, but found they could not do that and still do business with Intel. According to Toombs, "They thought we were strange and arrogant, an antagonistic bunch of guys who wanted something special, but we felt we could bring the rest of the industry to use the same techniques."

At first, Intel had carried this torch alone. But the company's leaders believed that if they could get even six major companies to join them they could have a much greater impact on the health of the supplier base. Sharing the program with Sematech's fourteen companies created the opportunity. Intel's tough program, which it then shared with the consortium, illustrates how members could leverage the return on their own learning by sharing it. By helping its rivals, Intel benefited more than it would have by guarding its secrets.

As Toombs says, "Someone has to step up and say 'I think I know how to do it the right way,' and then share it. Even then, everyone doesn't buy everything, because many of their cultures are different, but some have taken up the practices that were shared and made them work." Intel, in sending someone of Toombs's caliber and experience to offer the EQP as an open contribution, was making a statement that could not be ignored.

## A Larger Strategy

At Intel, the EQP thrust was part of a larger strategy for developing design, manufacturing, and equipment processes in parallel. A technical development team would follow a project from initial testing to production. Then a production team that had been working in parallel with it would take over the project, including any existing problems. The technology development team would continue to work with the production team for a while, which gave them a total eighteen-month overlap. Simultaneously (this is where the EQP fitted in), new equipment that would be needed was being tested and qualified so that it would be ready when production began in a new fab. The idea was to discover and simultaneously correct the kinds of problems that otherwise would show up as wafer defects on the production line. Defects happened when the manufacturing engineers were obliged to produce whatever design the R&D engineers "threw over the wall" with new, untried equipment.

According to Toombs: "Intel's whole process is carefully documented, and brings the product right to the production ramp, with the equipment tested and ready. The methodology used to go through this transfer is actually a complex orchestration, with an all-new, large production fab, and very costly. People ask how we can afford it; we answer that we can't *not* afford it." Obviously, bringing in the new equipment for the next-generation product being developed so that the equipment can be qualified and evaluated to determine its reliability and capability is a crucial part of this orchestration.

This rigorous practice was what made Intel's suppliers think the firm was strange and arrogant, although by the time Toombs came to Sematech in 1990, Motorola was also learning a nearly identical process from Toshiba, its partner in a joint venture. However, the procedure was not yet familiar in the United States, nor were there industry-wide standards for equipment to help with it. Clarifying the impact of Intel's contribution to Sematech on the equipment qualification process, Bob Galvin, Sematech board chairman and a long-time Motorola leader, when asked if he thought it was accurate to credit Intel with such major influence on the improvement of the supplier industry, said: "Yes it is fair to acknowledge Intel in this way, in part because of Motorola's support for their effort. Because of our experience with Toshiba prior to Sematech, we knew Intel was on the right track." Motorola's support not only validated Intel's contribution, it helped fulfill its worth.

## A Basis for Standard Setting

The equipment qualification practices that Toombs brought to Sematech grew into the Sematech Qualification Methodology, contributing to a continuing effort toward collaborative standard setting. In industry jargon, equipment qualification involved: "pre burn-in" verification (testing before doing the establishing run); (b) "burn-in" (the establishing run); and (c) "post burn-in" (retesting after the establishing run.) User groups from member companies, along with someone from the equipment manufacturer, ran the consortium tests. Consortium leaders were determined that labeling equipment as "Sematech

Qualified" should signify a top industry standard rather than a standard compromised by conformity and groupthink. It has been estimated that individual testing of a piece of equipment costs $2 million, or roughly equal to the original cost of the equipment, when it is repeated at each customer's site.[37] When Sematech sponsors or performs an official, standardized equipment test, it spreads the cost throughout the industry.

## The Cost of Ownership Model

Another practice used by both Motorola and Intel, called the cost of ownership (COO) model, was also adopted at Sematech. Owen Williams came from Motorola to work on this project with Toombs. The COO model can be used to evaluate the economic potential for any piece of equipment by calculating and determining what that equipment can and should do in terms of its real-time cost. Real-time cost includes such factors as quality, reliability, and service support in addition to the purchase price. Toombs developed a COO software model on a floppy disc, which he eventually presented at a 1990 trade show in Dallas. Sematech made the model available to suppliers and taught them how to use it.

The COO model has become a Sematech gauge—used as part of the evaluation of all tools coming into the consortium. Following the COO assessment, a plaque is installed on each tool stating its officially calculated ownership cost. Widespread knowledge of comparative long-term ownership costs that reflect the quality and support of tools offers a potential marketing advantage for suppliers of manufacturing equipment.

At the time Sematech was established there was a general lack of standardized specifications throughout the semiconductor industry, a direct result of its secretively proprietary nature. Looking for ways to overcome this situation without stifling entrepreneurialism was one of the original goals spelled out in the Black Book. Now the EQP and COO programs began what would become a process for negotiating shared industry-infrastructure technical standards on common ground at Sematech, rather than having them imposed by an external regulatory body, or having them emerge preemptively from marketplace competition. More advances in negotiating standards were to come as the payoffs for mutually advantageous relationships between chip makers and their suppliers continued to grow.[38]

## Improvement Is Not Enough

Of course Sematech was not the only place where joint development or equipment improvement initiatives occurred. Individual JDPs involving an SME supplier and a chip maker also occur in the private sector. However, these require real-time testing of equipment on line—that is, in the fab as chips are made. A plant manager has to believe in the worth of the equipment before he will invest his company's time, money and effort in such an uncertain process. Bottom-line pressures require that managers must look for the sure thing, which in 1989 and 1990 often meant Japanese materials and equipment.

In Japan, the strength of the vertical integration of customers and suppliers and the long-term relationships between them support this effort. A Nikon manager says joint testing can only work "where both parties are interested in the success of each other and of the customer's customer. Otherwise it would be very difficult for anybody to be successful in this business." He points to a wafer stepper (an optical lithography tool) that Nikon tested in five U.S. and six Japanese fabs: "That's a difficult concept. A customer gets early access and headaches. Before we do that, we've got to be convinced our relationship will survive some of the bumps. It can affect your long-term business."[39]

He goes on to say that because they have ongoing commitments to the supplier for equipment selection, purchase, and service, Japanese chip makers are more tolerant of early equipment problems that occur. "In Japan, it would be almost impossible to believe that certain customers would buy equipment from someone else. It just isn't done," he explains. "In the U.S., they're more likely to get their head turned by the shorter skirt."[40]

There are other differences in the role and potential of JDPs in a consortium as opposed to those conducted by a private manufacturer. On the positive side, a consortium can offer groups of suppliers and customers centralization of testing, a common interface with shared information, and wider industry exposure and leverage of resources than possible in independent alliances.

On the other edge of the collaborative sword, however, a consortium can mislead a whole generation of its participating cohort by making poor development choices and thus get bypassed by the competition. Because a consortium may be more detached from market pressures, it can also sidetrack progress by isolating technology improvement rather than by keeping pace with equipment purchasing windows, for instance, as an independent firm would have to do.

Perhaps the most potentially self-defeating problem of all is that group collaboration can allow for a diluted sense of commitment from individual members that is unlikely between two private firms invested in a joint project and, as a result, have greater interdependence on outcomes. A developmental project is not successful until consortium members adopt and use it. At Sematech, member companies had the right to jointly developed technology processes and tools, but there was no requirement to purchase them. Therefore, a consortium member, when in the role of a customer, might not feel as great a financial stake in, or responsibility for, a supplier's success as an independent customer would. Individual firms still remained free to buy from foreign suppliers, thus leaving the goal of strengthening the infrastructure to the consortium, with its all-American charter.

The selection of appropriate and potentially worthwhile development projects, therefore, was difficult, and being involved in one meant risk both for the consortium and the invested supplier. Although suppliers' intellectual property rights were now better protected, suppliers still had no assurance that members would purchase the equipment that was developed or improved at Sematech. A look at how a couple of actual projects worked out illustrates how being awarded a development project could promise—but not guarantee—success. First we look at a JDP that eventually had positive results after a rocky start, and then at an EIP that achieved technological but not market success.

## A Joint Development Project

Typical of a JDP was Sematech's January, 1990, contract with an innovative company named Lam Research of Fremont, California.[41] The contract, Sematech's second with Lam, was for developing a manufacturing process called chemical vapor deposition, which prepares silicon wafers for etching. Lam already had an EIP contract with Sematech for improving existing tools used for advanced metal etching technology. Both these technologies would help to achieve Phase II goals, and were considered essential for moving on to Phase III.

The chemical vapor deposition JDP aimed to design, develop, and fabricate an all-American tool. It would then be evaluated in the consortium's TAP using Intel's EQP on Sematech's Fab B line. This JDP collaboration connected Lam's own investment in engineering resources and process expertise to Sematech's funding, engineering staff, facilities, and extensive process testing and data analysis capabilities.

At the time of the 1990 signing, Lam's CEO, Roger Emerick, commented, "This joint development program with Sematech is exciting and complements Lam's long-term product strategy of developing core technologies that can be integrated in a modular, open architecture."[42] Making this particular JDP work was not easy, however. It was one of the consortium's early collaborations and required much learning on both sides. At first there were unfruitful discussions, conflict, and contention among members of the Lam and Sematech project team. This resulted in renegotiation and some personnel changes on the team. The project was nearly scuttled before persistence and commitment on both sides won out.

Lam's previously threatened business position brightened considerably as the JDP with Sematech successfully achieved timely development of equipment that was subsequently purchased by member companies. By early 1993, three years after Lam's JDP began, Lam spokeswoman Karen McLennan said, "They (Sematech) have definitely augmented our competitiveness, not only domestically but globally."[43] Reversing the previous downward trend for SME suppliers, Lam by then was headed toward $200 million in sales of its chip-making tools, up from $170 million in 1992. The increased revenues allowed Lam to invest in further improvements.

The "modular, open architecture," Lam's Emerick referred to foreshadowed the direction of Sematech's equipment focus. The factory of the future would consist of clusters of modular, automated tools, with standardized specifications. Tools from different suppliers would be compatible with each other in various, flexible configurations, depending upon the demands of a chip maker's product. The evolution of Sematech's programs over time would come to include the concurrent development of many compatible elements from various suppliers to make this possible. Creating standardized, core manufacturing equipment technologies that can be customized later by chip makers for their proprietary products fulfilled Sematech's precompetitive requirements because such tools and processes can benefit the entire industry. Before Sematech, secrecy barriers had made such compatibility and standardization difficult if not impossible.

Unfortunately, even enormous investment by the consortium could not guarantee that every JDP would be as successful as the one with Lam. The story of Sematech's support of equipment maker GCA and its wafer stepper (a camera tool used to print precisely registered successive circuit patterns onto silicon chips) did not have such a happy outcome.

## Technology Success, Business Bust

Sematech's EIP with GCA was also among its first supplier partnerships. The advisory council reported that in 1989 the project plan was to "buy 15–20 wafer steppers at an estimated total cost of $24 million to $32 million from GCA, a subsidiary of General Signal Corp[oration]., and consign them to five or more member companies. With technical support from GCA, members will use the machines on their own production lines, compare them to foreign alternatives, improve them, and share the resulting technology. Benefits to GCA include the revenue from the sale itself, technical feedback that should help the company to extend the shelf-life of its current stepper and improve the design of more advanced models, and the opportunity to restore customer relations that had been virtually severed."[44]

However, after several years and a large amount of money, GCA's parent firm General Signal announced in March, 1993, that it felt forced to sell off its lithography division or close it down. If GCA were to cease making lithography equipment or be sold to a foreign buyer, only one U.S. stepper maker, Silicon Valley Group Lithography (SVGL), would remain in business—a situation considered precarious for national defense, and a clear defeat of Sematech's goal of achieving domestic capability.

The GCA announcement set off wide-ranging political controversy. Various agencies in the new Clinton administration that had vowed support of high technology criticized the private sector in the semiconductor industry for not showing good faith by supporting GCA with sufficient equipment purchases to keep the company afloat. They also criticized Sematech for focusing too narrowly on technological aspects of cooperation while ignoring its business implications.[45]

The *Los Angeles Times* reported in April, 1993: "It is not at all clear how to rescue GCA. Chip companies have not taken the obvious step of giving GCA the benefit of the doubt and buying its equipment. Sematech itself will not get involved in business rescues."[46]

How could GCA be in such a bad position after five years of equipment improvement help through a JDP with Sematech in which at least $30 million and possibly as much as $80 million (depending on whose figures are used) had been spent? Was the equipment still not good enough to compete? Or did the problem lie elsewhere? Many people wanted to know.

In Massachusetts, whose economy was threatened by GCA's loss, the *Boston Globe* reported: "If, as expected, GCA Corp. of Andover closes later this month, the loss will be far greater than the 430 jobs that the firm provides. The shutdown will punch a hole in the widely held belief that all Washington needed to do was help produce world-class technology and the free market would take care of the rest. 'It quite profoundly illustrates that technology is not all you need,' said Deborah Wince-Smith, a former assistant Commerce secretary."[47]

Loss of faith in costly technical betterment hurt all the more because the project was reportedly a technological success: "Quality is sharply better and the company's newest machine is considered by many to be superior to anything Nikon and Canon can offer."[48] Furthermore, according to some experts, the improved stepper was also four times less expensive than a similar Japanese model.[49] It seems difficult to understand why member companies were not lining up to buy GCA steppers. What did cooperation among competitors really mean in business terms?

## A Question of Risk

In the late 1970s, GCA's founder, Milton Greenberg, invented the photolithography process. The company dominated the world market during the early 1980s, not bothering to patent the process, and became so self-confident that it even turned down a Toshiba suggestion for equipment improvement. Essentially, GCA said, "Buy what we build and don't bother us," recalls G. Dan Hutcheson, president of VLSI Research, a San Jose market research firm.[50]

Toshiba wound up buying a GCA stepper and had Nikon modify and improve the unpatented tool. By 1986 Nikon and Canon began to dominate the global lithography equipment market. Not only was GCA in trouble by then, but the U.S. firms that had invested in GCA lithography equipment were being hurt in competition against firms using the better tools coming from Japan.

Michael J. Cullinane, a seventeen-year veteran of GCA and its manufacturing director, says the reason is plain: "We had become arrogant, very arrogant."[51] Many of Sematech's member companies that were hurt would have a hard time forgiving and forgetting GCA's history.

Sematech felt GCA's stepper could be made competitive again, and the consortium and GCA worked very hard together to turn the picture around. In fact, in 1989, to help "prime the pump" for acceptance of the improved GCA stepper, Sematech offered attractive leases, or even free use, to member firms and some defense agencies willing to participate in the EIP. Only four of the fourteen members—Motorola, NSC, Harris, and Micron—accepted the offer.[52]

Despite Sematech's sponsorship and some members' willingness to help, old memories of unreliability and unresponsiveness to customer needs died hard. Dan Hutcheson recalls that there were "a lot of people who won't buy from GCA because they got burned ten years ago when GCA was shipping junk."

Company attitudes alone cannot be blamed; timing was also a crucial factor. Chip-making equipment purchases occur in cycles that are tied to the development of each generation of smaller, more powerful, and sophisticated chips that require new tools and processes and often entirely new fabs to manufacture. In 1990, GCA's equipment still had a few technical glitches. Bill George, Sematech's COO, recalled that GCA had made great strides as a supplier of wafer steppers: "The latest results indicate that they're state-of-the-art. Unfortunately, they missed the I-line window in 1990 (I-line refers to a specific non-visible wavelength of light). We don't control the marketplace."[53]

George's comment refers to the fact that the glitches caused GCA to miss a critical contract window for major new fabs being built by member companies. Still, if GCA had had a better history of customer responsiveness, chip makers might have given the company a chance at that point. Some of them, like Motorola, had even participated in the EIP for GCA's steppers, and bought them for a fab where there was already some GCA equipment. Nevertheless Motorola bought mostly Canon steppers in 1990 for its big new MOS-11 fab in Austin, citing Canon's good after-sale support as a major reason for its choice.[54]

Significant new orders were not expected for perhaps two more years, even though improved GCA steppers were an essential factor in Sematech's achieving its Phase III milestone of .35 micron circuit etching with U.S.,-made equipment in January, 1993. The press commented on the dilemma: "Meanwhile, GCA is caught in a Catch-22: Chip companies do not want to buy from a vendor that may not be around in a few years, and, by not buying, they virtually assure that GCA will not be."[55]

In 1993 GCA's severe difficulties shed a harsh light on the story of Sematech's development. They show how hard it was to try to strengthen an entire industry in which the problems were interconnected. They also reveal the intricate dance involving these unfamiliar partners—each willing to contribute to the initiative, but always hoping that the other will take the risky step that will make things work.

The GCA problems brought the semiconductor industry, and consortium member firms in particular, harsh criticism for being willing to put money into Sematech but unwilling to support its efforts wholeheartedly. The press scolded: "Sematech's task to help save the U.S. infrastructure is superhuman. Obviously, the consortium by itself can't stem the erosion, particularly if critical production equipment and materials suppliers are increasingly taken over by foreign buyers. . . . The consortium's member firms could do a lot more to help the Sematech effort, particularly in setting up strategic partnerships and long-term teaming efforts with U.S. equipment and materials suppliers."[56] Yet as the JDPs and EIPs went forward, GCA's untoward outcome was still in the future—as was Lam's success story.

Sematech's original move to support the infrastructure did signal its recognition that the chip makers' problems could not be solved by simply collaborating on technical breakthroughs alone. It still had to integrate, in a timely fashion, the many other factors involved. As CAO Franklin Squires commented in 1992, "At the beginning, everybody thought the problems that were to be solved were technical. Sematech would just develop new technologies enabling Phases I, II, III, and IV integrated circuit manufacturing and transfer those back to the member companies."

Recognition that technology was not enough sparked the struggle to integrate research with performance, customers with suppliers, and technological advances with manufacturing equipment and processes. This recognition underlay the evolution of JDPs and EIPs. It also meant that there had to be synchronization with the pace of customers' business pressures. Soon more attention was being devoted to ways of improving these interactions.

## CHAPTER 6

# Supplier Relations Lead toward Partnering

**E**arly in 1989, assignee Keith Erickson arrived at Sematech to head up the supplier management and improvement areas, which had been his area of expertise at Intel. Erickson's arrival coincided with the establishment of the Investment Council to oversee capital purchases, so his primary responsibility for the first six months was to develop cooperative contracting protocols with Sematech's own suppliers. To do that, he says, "I was developing a network with the purchasing people of the member companies. [I was] also understanding and developing a network within SEMI/Sematech with Sam [Harrell]. We did some pretty high-level assessments of the capability of our supply base." This led to a broader understanding of customer-supplier problems in general.

Erickson also had access to Obi Oberai's survey of member companies and suppliers. Erickson recalls: "We had this piece of paper that said something to the effect that suppliers were the problem and so were the customers. Everybody was pointing their fingers." The blaming on both sides undermined attention to quality, reinforced by a lack of communication that prevented resolving the problems.

Sematech member companies complained that the U.S. suppliers did not have either the quality knowledge to avoid potential equipment problems or the ability to solve problems quickly after they were discovered. American suppliers, for the most part, did not have, or did not use, some of the basic quality tools such as statistical process control or benchmarking their competition. But the Japanese did, so many U.S. customers turned to Japan. The U.S. suppliers, for their part, complained that chip makers were no longer providing data or giving them information about equipment problems. In fact, they said that the manufacturing doors were closed to them, and they thus were unable to observe their current products working on the floor or foresee future equipment requirements.

"In a nutshell," observed Erickson, "we had this issue that both of us [chip makers and suppliers] weren't doing the best thing. That screams for some kind of partnership." His conclusion was based on a comparison of Intel's partnering experience with the conclusions drawn from Sematech's survey data. At Intel, besides pressuring suppliers with its unique EQP, the company had also been partnering with them for several years in order to gain competitive advantage as a preferred customer in a volatile environment. At Sematech, as the consortium had shifted to supporting the manufacturing equipment infrastructure, the mission became focused on technology and technical tool-development programs like the JDPs, EIPs, and EQPs previously described. These were providing valuable pockets for practicing improved communication, but they still were not creating a larger framework for it. At the same time that Erickson was reaching his conclusions about Sematech's need to integrate partnering into its equipment-supplier projects, Sam Harrell was pressing for it from the SEMI/Sematech side as well.

As part of his contracting responsibility, Erickson established the Supplier Relations Action Council (SRAC) in June, 1989. Composed of senior purchasing and material managers from each of the member companies, the SRAC was designed to network on common issues and to champion strategic relations with U.S. suppliers at their home companies.[1] The SRAC looked at Intel's partnering process and was sufficiently impressed that it formed a task force to study the best aspects of partnering.

The task force considered such basic questions as how to develop a partnership, what it required, what makes it work or not work, and whether Sematech could use partnering not only for dealing with its own equipment and material suppliers, but also to develop a system with the infrastructure in general, making the impact of its projects more than simply technological. The group reviewed eighty partnerships, both successful and unsuccessful, and sifted out three elements that were commonly present in successful partnerships and commonly missing in failed ones. The elements they identified were clear technical roadmaps, clear written expectations of both partners, and an executive review of both sides by a highly placed sponsor.

Using the lessons gleaned from these eighty different partnering experiences, the task force developed a Sematech standard for partnering and distributed it to the industry in late 1989.

## The Need for Quality

The other major aspect of dealing with suppliers covered issues of equipment reliability and quality. This was the responsibility of Intel's Ashok Kanagol, who became Sematech's first Equipment Improvement Program manager by virtue of his unusual background. Kanagol had both a master's degree in industrial engineering and an MBA, as well as specialized skills in piloting improved methods in equipment utilization, improved equipment reliability, higher output, and other related areas. At Intel, Kanagol says he developed programs for "supplier training, and a lot of supplier education on equipment reliability—how to design in reliability so that the equipment that we pay millions of dollars for doesn't turn out to be a dog."

Intel's policy for choosing consortium assignees was entirely competitive. Beginning with the start-up team in 1987, the firm had sent high-caliber personnel who could be entrusted both to deliver Intel's contributions adequately and to bring back valuable information. So Kanagol was persuaded in August, 1988, that coming to Sematech would mean that his work could reach a wider audience. "They told me, 'Hey, you know, you could do that at Sematech,'" he recalls. "'You would probably have more of an impact because you would not be speaking for Intel alone.'" Charlie Farrell, head of manufacturing systems at the consortium, was in the process of creating the Manufacturing Management Science Department, and he offered Kanagol an assignment.[2]

However, Kanagol's arrival was delayed until late November, 1988, by his need to complete a project for Intel. When he finally reported to Farrell, Kanagol says, things had changed: "When I showed up on the doorstep, Farrell said, 'Oh, you're here. Well, we actually dissolved that department. We decided not to go ahead with that. So, what do you think we ought to do with you?' It showed you how unstructured and dynamic things were. Here I am taking a chance, putting my career at Intel on hold, and coming out here, and finding that I don't have a job."

Far from being discouraged, Kanagol saw it as an opportunity to create his own job, and he wound up conducting Sematech's first EQPs. By the time Erickson arrived in 1989, Kanagol had become convinced that the biggest problem equipment manufacturers faced was what he called "The big Q—Total Quality every which way. My focus of equipment reliability just got broadened to deal with the whole quality issue. I took on a different job as the Supplier Quality Manager."

Kanagol was soon reporting directly to Erickson, and their talks led to establishing another task force, this one under Kanagol, to help suppliers develop quality performance methods and skills. This approach was to complement the partnering program, beginning with a quality assessment instrument that employed the Malcolm Baldrige National Quality Award criteria.

In the meantime, Sematech's Partnering Task Force had published Sematech's partnering standards, and the group met again in early December. By the next month, the Total Quality Task Force had also begun work. As the two groups began dealing with many of the same people and grappling with many of the same problems, the notion of their possible convergence started to dawn. Although accounts differ as to where the inspiration for that idea came from, undoubtedly it was an idea whose time had come.[3]

According to Erickson: "About a couple of months into the process, these two different task forces—not related—came up with the idea that these things had to go hand in hand. I don't remember how exactly that happened, but both the Supplier Relations Action Council and the quality organization determined that this had to be together." Kanagol elaborates on this recognition: "We were off working independently, and, within a couple of months, we realized that it was the same job and you can't do one without the other. One hinges on the other. Everything that we, the Quality Task Force, were doing said we had to do better partnering. Everything that the Partnering Force was developing out there said that supplier quality efforts had to improve. So we combined the entire effort."

Combining the partnering and total quality efforts was not as simple as having joint meetings of the two task forces; it meant engineering a two-pronged program that would require acceptance, training, and change in both Sematech's member companies and their suppliers. There were still many customers who had not started partnering yet, as well as many suppliers who had not started working on quality, so it was a good time to introduce the dual approach.

The first thing necessary was to set up training classes, which would require a yet-to-be-determined cash outlay. At this point, Erickson met with Bob Noyce, Turner Hasty, and Sam Harrell to present a program called "Partnering for Total Quality" (PFTQ). He recalls: "Turner and Bob said, 'How much will it cost us?' I said, 'I have no idea. Probably a couple of million dollars per year.' They said, 'Spend it.' That's how easy it was in those days to get the funding. Sematech had $200 million per year, going mainly toward equipment development. So when I said $2 million, that was no big deal." Directing this relatively smaller amount into PFTQ training was made easier by the fact that Sematech had gotten off to a slow start in committing all its designated money to projects on schedule because of the early difficulties in finalizing contracts for equipment development and improvement projects.[4]

Developing the program at Sematech with top-level support was one thing; enlisting member company and supplier participation at the managerial level was something else again. Erickson's experience at Intel had showed him that "It's not a one-sided kind of deal. A real partnership has to be both sides, and you have to give up just as much on the customer side as on the supplier side. It's a lot of work."[5]

By 1989, both partnering and total quality principles were growing trends in U.S. business, but with many differing results. There was resistance on both sides, based on fear of exploitation or dependence on an unequal, unreliable relationship. Disillusioned partners even had a saying—"I've been partnered!"—that described when their relationship resulted in exploitation instead of mutual benefit.[6] The amount of time and resources that quality initiatives demanded were often considered prohibitive by relatively smaller, entrepreneurial suppliers who were scrambling for survival.

In April, 1990, the PFTQ team presented drafts of its first five documents to suppliers on Sematech's President's Day, an annual meeting to host supplier executives. The documents were received with great interest. They also generated considerable skepticism. When the task force then took its program to the chip-maker representatives serving on the ETAB, they again discovered some entrenched resistance, including the objection that PFTQ was too soft because it was based on people skills rather than on technology, which was the ETAB's current focus.

The task force attacked these levels of resistance on all fronts. To begin with, it went right to the top, to Sematech's Board of Directors with a statement of purpose for combining the partnering and total quality initiatives. They convinced the senior member-company executives who sat on the board of PFTQ's value and obtained their signatures on the document. This gave PFTQ its necessary executive sponsorship and clout at other levels, including wary manufacturing managers within member companies.

In order to convince the reluctant suppliers of the need to participate, the task force then turned the semiconductor infrastructure's endangered position into an argument for participating in the PFTQ effort rather than an excuse to avoid investing time and effort in it. The task force used an obituary type of presentation combined with a hope for salvaging the situation, just as Sandy Kane had done with the chip makers in 1987.

Erickson says: "We shared with them some of the purchasing trends over the next five years that member companies' equipment purchases or sales were, vis-à-vis U.S. versus Japan. They hadn't seen them yet in such a straightforward comparison with their equipment. U.S. equipment makers were almost looking at going out of business. We were able to shock them into the realization that it wasn't too late to make major changes, but not technology changes. It was the manufacturing excellence, the quality stuff that mattered. It got their attention."

At the June, 1990, President's Day, final copies of the first five PFTQ documents were presented, and, in one observer's words, "They just blew the SEMI/Sematech members away." By September these papers were printed and ready for distribution. The consortium at first avoided publishing an implementation guide, thinking its restrictions might limit flexibility, but the PFTQ participants soon demanded one. However, no one was sure exactly what was needed, so the task force had to test the process in several sites and create a joint assessment guide, then put out a newsletter to report on the flaws that were discovered. This was a long-term collaborative process, and the implementation guide was the last thing added—nearly eighteen months after PFTQ was introduced.

Everyone working on PFTQ had volunteered for the task force, and the team was given a free hand to design the instrument. Instead of creating a thick, expert-advice type of operations manual, they developed a set of sequential, user friendly pieces, each with an eye-catching graphic color cover. Eventually there was an attractive nine-volume set of detailed booklets, including the partnering, total quality, and training guides, a tool kit, the joint assessment guide, and, later, the implementation guide. These publications were used for the supplier training that now became the main focus of Sematech's PFTQ program.

## PFTQ Training

The original Partnering Task Force, after issuing its guidelines in the fall of 1989, had delayed further distribution of its training materials when the partnering and total quality efforts began to merge. Now, as the combined project began in earnest, the Sematech PFTQ team learned that suppliers needed affordable training programs tailored to their situations and connected to feedback for their participation to be effective. For one thing, when told they needed to get trained in quality methods and partnering techniques, most suppliers said that they simply could not afford it. For another, as Kanagol said, "If all you did was hand them documents and say, 'Go do,' you had little control or encouragement. You don't know if people are really going to go out and improve their quality approaches or not."

The PFTQ booklets had been designed to give suppliers what amounted to a do-it-yourself manual in increments. They contained an entire process by which firms could start to assess themselves, analyze and understand the data, assimilate the data, get the data validated by customers (which helped turn them into partners), and then to act on it. But this was still difficult for companies with no background in quality methods or partnering. Compared to their customers, supplier firms tended to be small with entrepreneurial, technically oriented cultures. Many were also scrambling to survive in their competitive environment. These very characteristics that made partnering and quality training crucially important for them also made it difficult for them to spend the necessary time and resources on it. (It involved, for example, buying repeated plane tickets for personnel to attend sessions in Austin.) As Sam Harrell notes, "Both customers and suppliers needed to change, and we needed to do it like marines hitting the beach and not like a normal culture change that takes three to four years."

As the PFTQ force looked for ways to start partnering quickly and effectively with suppliers, and to get them interested and able to partner, it settled on three strategies: providing convenient, affordable training both at Sematech and several regional sites; bringing supplier development managers on site at critical firms; and presenting awards on President's Days to supplier firms demonstrating a commitment to PFTQ participation.

To provide the convenient, affordable training, the Sematech team set up what it called a "remote-controlled university"[7] for suppliers at sites in the San Francisco Bay area, the Austin-Dallas and Midwest-Minneapolis regions, and in Boston. The formidable logistics required were new to the planners. Kanagol remembers: "None of us had any experience doing anything like this. That was the beauty of it. We didn't sit back and say, 'My God, that can't be done.' There were no paradigms for us."

Kanagol, who was running the training development team, was responsible for procuring courses—either developing them internally or buying or leasing the best available from the outside. Meanwhile, Judith McCracken ran the training deployment organization, making sure that instructors, materials, locations, and participants were available when needed.

Sematech jump-started PFTQ training by giving it away free for the first three months to all suppliers. Later it cost $100 per day per person—a fee that was still a bargain as it cost approximately twice that amount to run a course. The idea was to leave suppliers with no excuse for inaction by saying, in essence, "We'll come to your neighborhood and we'll give it to you cheap."

In an effort to implement its second strategy, the PFTQ team also went to some critical supplier companies where the consortium was investing a lot of money with contracts—beginning with Westech and extending to other companies. Sematech would bring in an experienced supplier development manager for real-time, on-site, participatory quality skills development. The consortium learned an important lesson about partnering here: Unless quality requirements were included in supplier contracts, this effort became a supplier rescue mission rather than training. So the PFTQ team took a step back and included quality development in contracts, which required a heavy resource investment from Sematech, again removing any excuse for noninvolvement.

The third strategy, President's Day awards, was far more successful than expected. During the festive, daylong events, Sematech managers and senior executives gave special recognition to the companies that applied for the award. Firms that showed they were committed to the PFTQ effort and were making progress—even when they had not yet achieved total quality performance—were nominated for these awards. The awards were a form of commendation for taking the right steps, given in front of an audience of supplier peers and their customers, the Sematech member companies.

The PFTQ team was surprised by the impact the awards had on generating interest within the supplier community. Initially, some companies were sincerely interested in the program, but others did it more out of peer pressure. To begin with, they saw that their competitors were being recognized for commitment to quality, and they also wanted a Sematech award to hang in their entrances for customers to see. However, they soon discovered that PFTQ practices were self-rewarding. As Kanagol says: "The award was just a recognition that got them started on the path. Once suppliers realized what it did for them, they said, 'Wow, award or not, this is good. Now, I have something to act on. Now, I know what I've got to go and improve.'" The awards, presented by a consortium of customers to suppliers, also publicly signaled a cultural reconciliation as their relationship changed from adversarial to partnering.

## Partnering Is a Two-Way Street

The chip makers soon began to hear back from their suppliers about one of the most important actions they could take to be better partners: the need to speak with a single voice on quality-assessment standards. Sematech's 1990 EQP was beginning to provide a basis for applying joint assessment and industry standardization in equipment technology. In matters of quality performance, however, when suppliers implemented Sematech's twenty-one-course PFTQ blueprint for everything from quality leadership to joint assessment, they found that each of their chip-making customers still had proprietary processes, criteria, and language for auditing supplier quality. One customer would certify a supplier's quality system at the same time another customer was decertifying the same system.

Mike Werner, a vice president of manufacturing at GCA, which made semiconductor fabrication equipment, was quoted as saying: "The biggest problem is that we are asked to know so many different quality languages. It would make life easier if there were some common way of communicating. As it is, the cost to the industry is not trivial."[8] What was required to make partnering work was the same commitment to change by member companies, through common adherence to a nonproprietary standard, that was being asked of suppliers who committed to PFTQ participation.

Erickson charged Kanagol with standardizing the quality audits that Sematech member companies used to evaluate their suppliers. Erickson knew that this kind of change would be very difficult. Chip makers had developed their own evaluation templates for suppliers over the years, and it would be hard for them to see the value of standardizing them simply because it was what Sematech wanted. However, he was encouraged by an insightful question made by an AMD vice president following a PFTQ presentation in mid-1990. The executive asked, "What are you going to do about the member companies?" Kanagol realized that if the chip makers' quality executives could be made to see the value of networking on common problems, there might be a chance to develop common standards. To facilitate this, Kanagol and AMD assignee Doug Ritchie came up with the idea of creating a Quality Council.

None of the member companies' quality executives knew each other, but Kanagol and Ritchie were confident they were all trying to address the same problems, which had been obscured by the focus on technology. All the member company quality chiefs at the vice-president level were invited to a trial council meeting. It was a hard sell at first, and it took several meetings before the idea started to gel. They asked to be shown that the Council had a mission they could support.

The first part of the mission Kanagol and Ritchie came up with was to find improved ways of dealing with suppliers, of course, but its second part was to demonstrate the potential value of quality partnering to their own firms. Mem-

133

ber companies were spending an estimated $500 million a year training their people—undoubtedly reinventing many courses in the process. Kanagol remembers that IBM alone offered twenty-seven different courses on statistical process control (a basic aspect of quality methods) at one time. At that rate, even a 10 percent improvement rate would offer member companies savings of $50 million a year. That was a projected investment return everyone could appreciate.

The Quality Council supported the development and implementation of a standard called the Sematech/Supplier Quality Assessment. Once the council understood what it could accomplish, it became a catalyst for other cooperative changes, including the creation of related groups such as the Human Resources Council and the Training Council.

By 1992 it was estimated that 110 of the 130 to 140 SEMI/Sematech members were involved with total quality efforts in some way, versus no more than half a dozen in the summer of 1989.[9] Erickson, who returned to Intel in late 1992, was interviewed again in 1995. At that time he continued to see the impact of PFTQ on his parent company, one of the largest buyers of semiconductor manufacturing equipment. "We're still leading teams, being members of teams that go out and do assessments of suppliers and providing honest feedback to the suppliers, and sharing that information with other Sematech member companies," he said. "That is going on today, as an outreach of the Partnering for Total Quality program. I know that Motorola is still strong on that, too. We did thousands and thousands of hours of training,[10] teaching the suppliers the language back in the early days of what total quality is and what the process is. Now they are on their own. Sematech backed away from that on purpose. The suppliers who caught on have the ability to be self-sufficient in that area, and the suppliers who didn't get PFTQ will never get it."

Sam Harrell notes that member companies consider the PFTQ process and the changes coming out of it to be Sematech's second most valuable output (the first being the early workshops). This was because the Partnering for Total Quality process enabled both sides to change in relation to each other, learning to communicate in new ways, shifting to management by data, and then continuing this improvement. PFTQ continued to expand and take on a life of its own in relationships that extended far outside of Sematech. In 1993, for instance, Sematech joined with several *Fortune 500* companies to form a consortium for supplier training for helping small American businesses with affordable training in total quality principles. Consortium members share their own internal quality courses at a network of supplier training centers sited at various community colleges in Texas, New York, Massachusetts and, Arizona, and the consortium provides course material and other guidelines.[11]

At the June, 1992, President's Day meeting Bob Galvin, Sematech's chairman of the board and chairman of Motorola's executive committee, was the keynote speaker. He commented on the change being wrought in the industrial culture by the contagious nature of the cooperation spreading from Sematech through such programs as PFTQ. "There's something happening [at Sematech] that is a fundamental strength of America," he said. "The culture is being ingrained. We are discovering we like to work with each other. We can do it honorably. We can do it in a fashion that is good for our profession and our industry."

## Road Maps for Coordination

Research done by the early PFTQ task force had shown the importance of technology road maps that could demonstrate the simultaneous coordination of multiple interactions among chip makers and suppliers. Sematech soon began to use such road maps more extensively. They were similar in nature to those created at the 1987–88 planning workshops, and by Obi Oberai and his survey team in 1989. However, they now included the intricate coordination required for Partnering for Total Quality with equipment and material suppliers. The Investment Council was still acting as Sematech's engine, the Competitive Analysis Council had become a directional compass, and the technology road maps became detailed guides for specific kinds of expanded collaboration among chip makers and their infrastructure.

Tom Seidel, a primary developer of Sematech's MDV process, became the consortium's chief technologist and was charged with overseeing much of the road-mapping activity. Technology road maps, he says, relate many elements—such as R&D, training, and equipment, resources—that act on each other. The maps include time as a critical dimension by showing anticipated windows of technological and equipment opportunity, as well as the schedules and required deadlines to make it all work together. These maps not only coordinate efforts, they demonstrate how the output from one area becomes the essential input of another in order to leverage their strengths. Eventually, Sematech's technology maps would show cost and market factors as well.

With road maps from different levels, Sematech's competitive analysts could evaluate the consortium's projections against both the industry's future and the global picture. Unfortunately, road maps cannot recommend what strategy to follow because they communicate a "sense of destiny rather than of destination."[12] At Sematech, this job of determining strategic policy was still the task of the OCE and the Board of Directors, aided by the ETAB and FTABs.

In the previous atmosphere of proprietary secrecy, when chip makers and their U.S. suppliers experienced problems, it was easy for them to blame each other, each firm thinking its problems were unique, and not wanting to expose its difficulties to rivals. However, cooperative road mapping laid out the problems and interdependent strategies for the consortium, and everyone had to face up to their responsibilities and determine what they could do to improve the situation. Road maps also continually reminded them that not everything could be done at once with the resources available.

## Charting Milestones

As equipment projects got underway, DARPA appeared reassured by Noyce's leadership and by the consortium's new operational direction. Although the DSB task force had originally supported developing independent domestic DRAM production, the DOD now approved of the shift toward supporting the infrastructure. With the use of the technology road maps, Oberai could show DARPA director Craig Fields how Sematech was "focused on manufacturing, why we were focused on manufacturing, what was the key essence of manufacturing that had to drive us, and how we were going to do it. We were putting down (a) the problem set and (b) clear road maps for now and the next few years. Before Fields saw that, he thought that we were doing what quite often happens in industry: no direction, pick up the target, and shoot. Now he had a rationale that there was a logical, step-by-step process that we were going to follow. He was very helpful to us." The road maps were also useful for charting milestones achieved in work in progress.

Meanwhile, efforts to support the infrastructure at many other levels went on. Even as Sematech was conducting its project with GCA to improve its lithography steppers, it also acted to rescue the Optical Lithography Operations Division of the Perkin-Elmer Corporation, a member of SEMI/Sematech. Lithography is still believed by many to be the weakest and most critically threatened area in U.S. semiconductor manufacture—not because of a lack of progress but because the competition has done so well. It continues to be a major thrust area in Sematech's operation.

In 1990, Nikon attempted to take over Perkin-Elmer's lithography division, thought by many to be the only viable U.S. contender in the optical lithography equipment business at the time (because of GCA's technological problems, described above). Sematech brokered help for SVGL, another SEMI/Sematech member, to purchase more than 60 percent of the American firm, blocking the sale to Nikon and keeping Perkin-Elmer within the U.S. infrastructure. This was significant because even though Nikon could supply excellent equipment, it was believed that its latest models were made available to Japanese chip makers while being withheld from American customers for a generation cycle.[13]

Following this successful U.S. purchase maneuver, SVGL chairman Papken Der Terossian was quoted in a San Jose newspaper article as proclaiming a new breed of national heroes: high-technology executives, with Noyce at the top of the list. In response, Sematech celebrated "Bob Noyce Day" on June 1, 1990, and printed up T-shirts featuring Der Terossian's "Top Hero" quote and Noyce's photo with the words "Teen Idol" emblazoned above it.

Noyce had received many honors and medals, but his biggest smile seen at any ceremony beams out from a photo taken that sunny first day of June as he sits on Sematech's lawn in the midst of thirty-five smiling women colleagues all wearing "Teen Idol" T-shirts. Two days later, he was gone. On the morning of June 3, 1990, Bob Noyce died at home of a massive heart attack.

His passing was so sudden that in areas where his influence and unswerving support had been critical to the success of groundbreaking efforts, the documents do not always reflect his role. On the first PFTQ document, for example, which was signed in June by the entire Board of Directors to legitimize and empower the initiative, Noyce's signature is the only one missing.

## A Most Difficult Time

It is hard to fathom the shock and grief the consortium felt after the loss of its inspirational leader. The gravity of his loss makes Sematech's continuity all the more remarkable. Noyce had been the champion, the one whose image had embodied the vision of freedom to cooperate, to share ideas, and to do something wonderful—not only for Sematech's members, but for the watching world. He had supplied political credibility, scientific reputation, entrepreneurial excitement, and moral stature at a crucial moment, and effectively focused the consortium's turbulent efforts a time it was in danger of tearing itself apart.[14] Now he was suddenly gone.

One of the top-level facilitators, Olivia Miller-Snapp, remembers how people initially coped: "We just sort of kept on keeping on for a while. The board immediately came to the organization and reassured us that we were still together and they were still behind us as an organization." The board publicly assured consortium personnel that the directors were committed to continuity, and to searching for a worthy successor as CEO, and Ann Bowers Noyce even made a personal appearance to speak to the grieving organization.

Sematech held a memorial service "to celebrate Bob's life" the following Saturday, June 9, just eight days after Bob Noyce Day. Sematech founder Charlie Sporck, Noyce's one-time subordinate, later business competitor, and then strong collaborator, opened the memorial ceremony, by saying: "Our goal this morning is to create the kind of environment that Bob would have enjoyed. . . . We're going to thank him for instilling in each of us a sense of caring, a sense of teamwork, and, yes, a sense of humor." Sporck had ordered the flag at his own company, NSC, flown at half-staff on hearing of Noyce's death. Friends and colleagues held a separate service in Silicon Valley.

No one at Sematech wanted to let Noyce down, and the best way to try to live up to his legacy was to continue the cooperation that his leadership had inspired. Shortly after the memorial, management held an off-site goal-setting meeting at which the discussion of Noyce's sudden death was held to a minimum. Attendees agreed it would help if they focused on needed planning, looking to the future by communicating through goals, rather than looking back.

According to Ann Bowers Noyce: "Bob believed in building community and articulated ideas and visions and strategies that other people then took up and made happen. He was in Sematech not because he sought the limelight, but because he was worried about competitiveness before anybody else even thought about talking to Washington about it. Andy Grove once said, 'Bob's ultimate contribution is going to be that he realized that we had to start working together as an industry and with the government, and worrying about being competitive. Bob was always six or ten steps ahead of the rest of us.'"

Those who had known Noyce believed that he would be most pleased by knowing that the organization carried on because of the cooperative philosophy embedded in the organization itself, rather than out of loyalty to him. It is a tribute to Noyce's leadership that Sematech was able to proceed. Turner Hasty, the COO, became acting CEO until the board could find another leader. Hasty had never aspired to fill the shoes of the man he admired so greatly. In fact, in describing his first meeting with Noyce he said: "My first impression turned out to be right. Bob really was ten feet tall. He just appeared five-foot-eight to the untrained observer." Because of his great respect for Noyce, Hasty had always worked hard at turning Noyce's values into Sematech's organizational designs. It was fortunate that he was there to help carry them on.

Noyce's influence had been a catalyst, combining many parts. Miller-Snapp lists some of Sematech's diverse aspects: "The system of assignees—the value of having different people coming here versus having a stable work force. Having a Board of Directors that is representative of many member companies, rather than of one interest. Having focus TABs representing each member company and its thrust area in particular. Having an executive TAB representing every company. Having multiple councils representing all the companies. Having a joint staff representing many, but not all. Diversity is the fabric of Sematech. The tough part is coming up with the unifying force."

Noyce's leadership had been that force.

## Maintaining Momentum

By the time Bob Noyce died in mid-1990 there were hopeful signs that the combined efforts of Sematech and SEMI/Sematech were beginning to help the U.S. semiconductor industry pull out of its death spiral. Market-share hemorrhaging appeared to be halted, and this encouraged the consortium members to believe that the mission could now continue to grow, in spite of Noyce's loss. Nevertheless, finding a new leader was an urgent necessity.

Two months before his death, Noyce had told the board that he wanted to step down as CEO by the end of the year, feeling that his two major goals for Sematech had been accomplished. In a typically modest understatement he named them: solidifying Sematech's external support in Washington, and strengthening the member companies' commitment to the consortium. He had done far more than that, of course, and his would be a hard act to follow.

Meanwhile, the immediate danger was that the organization might simply be satisfied with what it had managed to achieve so far as it sought to steady itself after the shock of losing its leader. Acting CEO Hasty was worried by the possibility that Sematech would lose its sense of urgency, drive, and capacity to adapt. For thirty years he had watched the U.S. semiconductor industry from the inside as it brilliantly, openly, and joyfully invented itself and then choked up on competitive pride, secrecy, and animosity. Hasty knew Sematech must not be allowed to stagnate. He was determined to continue the dream of learning to do things differently through cooperation and sharing until a new leader was found. But the effort to continue the consortium's momentum soon took a new bearing.

By the fall of 1990 the Board of Directors had found its new CEO: Dr. William "Bill" Spencer, who was at the peak of a distinguished career at Xerox. The board's choice of Spencer, who came from outside the semiconductor industry, signaled its recognition that it was time for Sematech to change direction. Noyce's inspiration and nurturing of a novel, fledgling idea had resulted in a vibrant, healthy consortium. Spencer arrived to lead it in October, 1990, bringing in Franklin Squires from Xerox's Palo Alto Research Center (PARC) to serve as CAO, and persuading Motorola to free Bill George to serve as COO in early 1991. Under this totally new OCE, Sematech shifted toward more structure and into a more businesslike stance.

In many ways the time was ripe for such a shift. For instance, by late 1990 the Quality Council's work with suppliers was beginning to make the fact that Sematech itself did not have an internal quality program glaringly apparent. Also, several member companies were beginning to question the alignment and responsiveness of Sematech's mission to their needs. The members of Sematech's new triumvirate faced far different challenges than the consortium's founders had confronted at its beginning.

## CHAPTER 7

# Quality

*Meeting the Customer's Needs*

**T**he announcement of Bill Spencer's selection to serve as Sematech's CEO surprised many observers. Spencer was a physicist employed as group vice president and senior technical officer of the Corporate Research Group at the Xerox Corporation in Stamford, Connecticut. Although he came from outside the semiconductor industry proper, the Board of Directors's mission did not specify that Sematech's new leader must be a semiconductor executive. The search criteria said only that he should have "impeccable technical credentials, a demonstrated track record in the high-tech industrial sector, comfort and proficiency in dealing with the U.S. government, and the ability to follow in Noyce's footsteps."[1]

Bill Spencer was well qualified on all these counts. His early history had a familiar ring. Like Noyce's, Spencer's roots were in the Midwest. He had also attended a small school, William Jewell College in Liberty, Missouri, and assumed he was destined to become a high school basketball coach. Instead, he earned his doctorate in physics from Kansas State. The two scientists' professional paths had taken different turns, however. Spencer began his technology career at Bell Labs, followed by eight years' experience managing government projects at Sandia National Laboratory. Next he had gone to Xerox, where he became group vice president in charge of technology at Xerox's PARC before going to Connecticut and becoming head of the company's worldwide research efforts.

In a parting tribute to Spencer as he left Xerox's PARC, CEO Paul Allaire said: "Bill has been a guiding force in the redirection of the corporation's research efforts for the 1980s and beyond and has been a major influence in accelerating the incorporation of research technologies into new products. We will miss him, but wish him well in this position of major national significance."[2]

Spencer clearly had the requisite technical and leadership credentials, as well as a track record of translating an organization's research efforts into global terms and then turning them into technology applications for competitive advantage. This made Spencer the board's choice to build on the momentum that Noyce had generated at Sematech.

However, unspoken by the board was the fact that the directors had gone outside the semiconductor industry to find Spencer—usually a sign that a governing body thinks it is time for a change in organizational direction. This meant that very few in the specialized world of the semiconductor industry were well acquainted with the new CEO or his accomplishments when he arrived in Austin in the fall of 1990. Almost no one there was aware that Spencer had turned down an offer to become dean of the business school at the University of California at Berkeley to come to Sematech for what he was calling "the most exciting job in the world."[3]

## Spencer's Introduction to Sematech

On the October morning when Spencer was introduced to Sematech in Austin, speculation and curiosity ran high among everyone present. For nearly half a year, everyone had pitched in under Turner Hasty to keep the vision of cooperation alive, and to maintain the fledgling advisory boards and councils. Hasty, as Noyce's COO, had done much to develop the ETAB and then the FTABs into groups that could collaborate on a working consensus for project priorities. They had agreed, for instance, on the technology processes Sematech would use for the Phase II goal of producing a .5-micron circuit feature on chips, and then figured out how to bring the processes into the consortium. That this .5-micron milestone was achieved in August, 1990, only two months after Noyce's sudden death, showed the determination of all Sematech members to keep his vision alive.

The PFTQ documentation and dissemination, which Noyce had just seen begin to blossom, continued apace, and the number of equipment contracts and projects increased, but everyone keenly missed Noyce's influence—Hasty most of all. Now an unknown leader was taking over, and it was hard to see how he could fill Noyce's shoes.

In addition, many people in the bereaved organization were not only personally grieving but also felt close to professional burnout from the enormous effort they had put into founding, building, and sustaining the high-pressure experiment of collaboration to the point where it was beginning to see some results. Other difficulties were looming on the horizon, too, as the consortium's initial funding, both from member commitments and the federal grant, was running out of time—and perhaps also out of justification for its existence. Sematech would very soon need to prove its continuing worth to both its public and private supporters.

As 1990 came to an end, Sematech was prepared to carry on but uncertain about how to proceed. How would a new and unfamiliar leader, and the inevitable changes to follow, affect the consortium's unique nature and its future survival? That was the environment when Bill Spencer received a relieved but somewhat tentative welcome at his introduction to the consortium.

## A Whirlwind Beginning

Bill Spencer did not say a great deal at his Austin introduction that morning. However, what he did say was reassuring. He told Sematech staff members that, while he felt it impossible to fill Noyce's shoes, "Bob Noyce set a vision for us, and it's up to us to implement that vision." Then Spencer was off on a two-day whirlwind tour. First came a nationwide satellite news conference. Immediately afterward, he boarded Noyce's own plane for the first of many Austin-to-Washington flights required of the head of a national experiment dependent on continued political support.

On the plane, Miller Bonner, Sematech's public relations chief, waited to brief Spencer on his full schedule. Right away, Bonner noticed that things were going to be different. In the past, Noyce, who was reportedly not at ease with political networking in spite of the respect shown him, had gratefully followed Bonner's smooth meeting agendas and his suggestions for talking with people. Spencer, however, after expressing his thanks for the help in setting things up this time, said that henceforth he would determine his own agenda. Clearly, Spencer intended to do things his own way.

In Washington, Rep. Jake Pickle, a staunch supporter of Sematech from its most precarious political beginnings, hosted a reception at the House of Representatives for Spencer. House Speaker Jim Wright was there, and Lloyd Bentsen, then the senior Texas senator and another early ally of the consortium, walked over from the Senate side to welcome the new CEO personally.

This day of celebration was followed by a more grueling one of meetings, both with strong Sematech supporters on Capitol Hill, and with more critical members of the Republican executive branch, which had continued to be cool to the idea of industry-government collaboration. These Washington pros and cons were only a foretaste of the "most exciting job in the world" awaiting Bill Spencer back in Austin. He would need strong backing.

## The Importance of Champions

Sematech had always been fortunate to have top industry leaders championing its cause, beginning with Charlie Sporck of NSC, who also served as the consortium's first chairman of the board, and Bob Noyce, whose compelling presence as CEO had bound many disparate parts together. To create Sematech, Charlie Sporck, Sam Harrell, Sandy Kane, Jim Peterman, Jerry Sanders, George Schneer, and many other top SIA and SEMI executives had had the kind of vision—and willingness to work together—that transcended individual corporate ambition. Their stature, skill, and personal involvement had been crucial to negotiating the unprecedented and tricky partnership between industry and an often unenthusiastic government, and to dealing with the ups and downs of a generally more supportive but fractious Congress. Now another industry leader was about to become Sematech's new champion.

In January, 1991, during a meeting that was temporarily interrupted by a bomb threat prompted by the outbreak of war in the Persian Gulf, Bob Galvin, chairman of Motorola's executive committee,[4] was unanimously elected by Sematech's Board of Directors to serve as their next chairman.[5] Galvin found accepting the appointment to be, in his words, "a pleasingly doable assignment," particularly because the board had already recruited Spencer as CEO. He says of Spencer: "I can't imagine anyone with a better mix of energies, talents, dedication, and ability to enjoy what he is doing as CEO than Bill. He is a deep technical thinker, he understands strategy, has the respect of all members of the board, and he can talk up and down as necessary."[6]

For Spencer's part, immediately after being named CEO he had actively lobbied for Sematech to acquire Galvin as board chairman. Although the two men's backgrounds were very different, both were committed to quality methods and practices. Consultant Bill Daniels observed of Galvin, long before he came to Sematech: "He has become an incarnation of Motorola's commitment to quality." Under Galvin's leadership, Motorola was one of the first Malcolm Baldrige National Quality Award winners for its entire worldwide corporate operation, making it the largest technology company to achieve that distinction. Spencer and others believed that Galvin's experience and vision were just what Sematech needed at this critical juncture.

Intel's Craig Barrett described Galvin's value this way: "Galvin brought some very strong things to Sematech. He has credibility in the electronics industry. And, at a time when, I think, because of Bob Noyce's death, and because we couldn't yet see the coming resurgence in the semiconductor and process equipment industries, Sematech needed to generate enthusiasm and confidence amongst its supporters and detractors. Galvin did just that. He brings a calm, reasonable voice to our proceedings. He isn't an active technologist, but he doesn't claim to be, either. He doesn't try to drive any particular agenda other than the big picture of what Sematech should do in the electronics industry."[7]

Sematech would need Galvin's ability to see the "big picture" that extended past the consortium's boardroom and even beyond the whole U.S. semiconductor industry, to the growing national and international importance of microelectronics in the Information Age, and the difficult questions raised by the increasing globalization of their manufacture.

## A New OCE

Meanwhile, back at work in Austin, Bill Spencer was not alone. Turner Hasty, Sematech pioneer and dependable soldier, was there to help a little longer.

However, after a thirty-year career at TI and nearly four years at Sematech, Hasty was ready to retire. Nevertheless, he agreed to stay on long enough to help with the leadership transition. Since he had been at Sematech as long as anyone by that time, had designed and overseen much of the consortium's development, and had provided leadership through several crises, his knowledge and familiar presence provided continuity as the new leaders came in.

The fact that Spencer came from outside the industry with no previous ties to any semiconductor firm gave him certain political advantages, especially in his choice of an executive vice president and COO to succeed Hasty. Sematech's original charter specified that, to avoid any hint of bias, its top three corporate officers must resign from their parent firms. Also, no one serving in Sematech's OCE could return to a parent firm. The COO that Spencer had his eye on to succeed Hasty, though, was not one that his parent company would willingly give up permanently. He was Bill George of Motorola.

George had served that company for twenty-three years. After joining the firm as an engineer in 1968, he held a variety of jobs in device development, engineering, and testing. He eventually moved into management after being awarded seven patents for semiconductor devices. He was elected vice president and general manager of Motorola's MOS Wafer Fab Division in 1984, and in 1987 became vice president and director of the Motorola/Toshiba Alliance. His wide range of technical and managerial experience in engineering design and manufacture, testing, high-level management, and joint foreign alliances was just the combination needed for Sematech's expanding operations.

Bill George had actually had a brief contact with Sematech in 1987, when he participated in one of the early planning workshops. He remembers:

> I had been talking to a lot of Japanese engineers for the six months before that because I was involved with Toshiba, trying to understand what they thought about manufacturing and what was different between the Japanese and American fabs. Every one of them told me that the critical difference that they saw in working in a Japanese fab versus an American fab was not the operators, it wasn't the people, and it wasn't our ability to do things. It was the lack of a partnership between the semiconductor companies and their suppliers. We just didn't work with each other—and we fought all the time. I said, "Here's our opportunity. Finally, we can get together and begin to work together on these things. Sematech has one real opportunity: to get the semiconductor producers speaking with one voice to their suppliers." I ran around preaching that sermon at the workshop, and then went away again [back to the Motorola/Toshiba Alliance] and sort of forgot about it.

Now George was back again, and Sematech was focused on working with suppliers.

The board's acceptance of a member-company assignee in the OCE also signaled the accumulation of collaborative good faith that had built up since

1987, when the founding charter was written. At that early point, even a CEO's unbeholden status and the high regard in which a potential COO was held among his industry peers undoubtedly could not have overcome the suspicion and lack of trust characteristic of that period. The board consented to relax the resignation requirement for the COO, and Motorola said it would let Sematech borrow George for a two-year assignment so long as the company could then have him back. Tommy George (no relation), the executive vice president and general manager of Motorola/Semiconductor Products and Motorola's representative on the Sematech Board of Directors, said it was Motorola's turn to contribute a member to the top leadership. Bill George arrived at the consortium in February, 1991, bringing expert meeting-management skills in addition to his other expertise.

Spencer chose a Xerox colleague, Franklin Squires, to serve as CAO, rounding out the new OCE. Squires succeeded Peter Mills, who joined Sematech in 1988 as its first CAO. Mills had helped develop many of the consortium's internal structures and negotiate the political difficulties of its external relationships, but he was also ready to move on.[8]

Frank Squires had helped to establish Xerox's PARC, and then worked there with Spencer for ten years, reporting directly to him for five. Spencer had confidence in Squires and believed that Sematech had need of his proven administrative ability.

In addition to operating a $200 million business soundly for its public and private stakeholders, the new CAO would be handling the unique complications of a consortium composed of contentious rivals and the government, administering a mixed staff of transient assignees and direct hires, and managing collaboration with the infrastructure and other external agencies. Squires was at first reluctant to leave Xerox, but Spencer finally convinced him that this was an opportunity to, as Squires put it, "come to a company that was small enough so that you could really get your arms around it and personally make a difference for the organization, and be working for a cause that would be beneficial to the country."

By April, 1991, the new OCE of Spencer, George, and Squires was complete, reporting to the board and its new chairman, Bob Galvin. They all had cause for fresh optimism about the U.S. semiconductor industry. Just three months earlier, the microelectronics market-research company Dataquest had announced: "American semiconductor companies accounted for 36.5 percent of the worldwide semiconductor market in 1990, up from 34.9 percent in 1989. This is the first time that American market share has increased since 1979."[9]

Although the international market is obviously influenced by many factors, Sematech was given at least partial credit for the turnaround. The news that the hemorrhaging had stopped and that the patient seemed to be on the mend was heartening, but U.S. market share still lagged behind Japan's, and serious new competition was starting to come from Korea and other countries.

## Facing New Challenges

These new kinds of challenges originated both from within and from without the organization. Some problems were by-products of the consortium's unusual makeup and development; others were related to the rapidly shifting technological, economic, and political environment in which its industry-government collaboration was embedded—and, indeed, to which it was contributing its own changes. Foremost among these problems were the uncertainty and/or dissatisfaction of member companies and DARPA regarding the value they were receiving for their investment in Sematech; an ironic loss of the original sense of urgency as market share began to turn around; the lack of an internal quality program to match the consortium's external PFTQ program; and unexpected difficulties in transferring technology and aligning the consortium's efforts with the realities of a dynamic business environment.

The first of these concerns was undoubtedly the most serious. Sematech faced the very real threat of losing the financial support of its member companies or DARPA or both by the end of 1992 if the DOD was not convinced that Sematech was aligned with its interests and worth renewing its ongoing investment.[10] The diverse Sematech member firms had always differed over what the consortium's focus should be, but in 1987 the shared threat of imminent demise had helped override their differences as agendas were adopted and projects grew.[11] After chip makers had won a little breathing space by the end of 1990, the consortium's majority rule for prioritizing its projects left some companies feeling that their most pressing concerns were not being addressed, and they were considering pulling out. In fact, two letters of resignation scheduled to take effect in 1992—one from Micron Technology of Idaho, and one from LSI Logic in California—were waiting on Spencer's desk when he took office. Another firm, Harris Semiconductor, of Florida, was also thinking of pulling out of the consortium.

Other member companies were disenchanted with the consortium for several reasons. First, with even a small market-share improvement, firms could stop worrying about their immediate survival and start worrying instead about whether they were getting their money's worth. In Abraham Maslow's classic terms, their need level had moved from managing their survival to achieving satisfaction.[12] Even if firms remained in the consortium, complacency could reduce their level of commitment.

The August, 1990, achievement of the Phase II milestone demonstrated an all-American manufacturing line that could produce a chip with .5-micron width features. The Phase III milestone—slated for accomplishment in 1992—called for producing a chip with a .35-micron width using American-made equipment. Achieving that goal would bring the United States up to global technological parity. The industry's previous sense of being left in the dust in the race to capture the world market, and an ambition to lead the pack once again, had driven the consortium's urgency until now. Once that goal was achieved, what would replace it?

Even more disturbing was the discontent among firms that were finding it difficult to calculate transferable, measurable returns on their considerable investment of money and personnel in the consortium. They needed to show results in line and in cadence with their own urgent corporate priorities. Despite the improved overall market-share figures, Sematech's measurable effects and effectiveness on an individual firm's bottom line remained a murky and controversial issue with little hard data available.

Sam Harrell contrasts the satisfaction that member companies felt after the first technological workshops, which had introduced them to possibilities and ideas they could take back home and put to work, with their post-honeymoon disgruntlement: "The member companies, by and large, in the pre-1991 period, were very dissatisfied with Sematech's meeting of its objectives. They were not satisfied with how Sematech was managing its projects."

The problem stemmed partly from the rapid proliferation of peripheral projects once the supplier contracts and equipment initiatives got rolling, and partly from disagreements about the fab operation. But the problem also reflected differences in how the end product was understood by members and by the consortium. Bill George noted that when he joined the consortium in early 1991, "if you asked Sematech what its output was, they'd tell you how many reports they'd published, how many meetings they'd held, and how many documents they'd sent to the member companies. The product was viewed as the report." This view of the product meant that Sematech did not have a clear mechanism to quantify and demonstrate a firm's return on investment (ROI), and however or whatever ROI each individual member company calculated on its own was still closely held proprietary information, not shared with the consortium.

Perception of Sematech's product in ROI terms obviously had to be connected with the transfer of timely, useful technology from the consortium. Despite the help starting to come from Sematech-sponsored standardization and qualification of equipment, better industry cooperation, and the influence of PFTQ on infrastructure relationships, there was still a nearly insurmountable gap between Sematech's product and the actual insertion of the developed technology in a company's production line. Member firms considered this gap to be Sematech's responsibility. Others blamed member firms for a lack of commitment to supporting the product. Nobody owned the problem.

As far as retaining DARPA's support, it was clear that Sematech had traveled far from the 1986 Defense Science Board's recommended mission of rescuing the United States from foreign DRAM dependency. Nevertheless, it could also be argued that the newer focus on strengthening the supplier infrastructure had lessened the likelihood of DRAM dependency in a more fundamental way. But since the government grant was tied to matching funds from the semiconductor industry itself, if Sematech lost industry support—that is, if member companies resigned—it also lost federal funding. Again, Sematech's new leaders were brought back to the challenge of demonstrating a balanced and convincing ROI to all consortium participants.

There were internal changes at DARPA as well. In the spring of 1990, Victor Reis replaced Craig Fields as head of the agency. Fields's skill had helped Sematech through its early attempts to structure a workable partnership with the government and more specifically to develop planning capabilities. The reason given for Fields's removal was that Pentagon officials had opposed his support of high-technology research in specific industries.[13] Later that year Fields was named president and COO of MCC, the Austin-based computer research consortium. At the time, no one could be sure what Field's departure and DARPA's internal changes would mean to Sematech.

## The Environmental Focus

Public scrutiny of government involvement in the consortium was expected to increase as the end of Sematech's first five-year charter approached in 1992. For one thing, the price of visibly achieving some technological milestones meant that environmental groups were turning their attention on the consortium. Perhaps its image was becoming less that of a patriotic savior of the U.S. economy than that of just another domestic high-tech environmental enemy. Or perhaps there was a feeling that government support for the consortium offered environmentalists a fulcrum for leveraging an ecological agenda in an industry whose messy ways were starting to attract more attention.

In May, 1991, in response to a request from the Campaign for Responsible Technology and the Silicon Valley Toxics Coalition, Sematech hosted a meeting where these groups proposed that the consortium should set official environmental standards for its members and for the semiconductor industry as a whole.[14] Not satisfied with Sematech's response, representatives of the Campaign for Responsible Technology—a group of labor unions, environmentalists, and academics—went to Congress in November hoping to pressure Sematech to spend more on developing non-toxic manufacturing methods by making it a condition of renewed funding.[15]

As the funding renewal time in 1992 approached, Sematech could expect increased interest-group pressures on federal decision makers either to attach strings to the previously unfettered grant or to discontinue aid to the semiconductor industry altogether.

Ironically, the improvement in U.S. market share might even have made government support appear less justified, particularly because the number of alliances between member companies and foreign companies had increased during the same period. This undermined the patriotic appeal of a U.S. manufacturing consortium and raised questions in Congress about whether the government's investment in advanced technology development might be leaked away to global competitors through member companies' collaboration with each other and their foreign allies.

All these problems grew out of Sematech's external relationships and support, but another kind arose from within the organization itself. The growing successes of the PFTQ initiative were beginning to reflect back on the unevenness of the consortium's own practices, as well as on its lack of a formal internal quality program. Although it is not unusual for an organization's emphasis on quality to grow from the outside in—that is, to begin with its customer-supplier relationships and then come to be applied internally—Sematech's visible promotion of PFTQ to the industry made it especially vulnerable to criticism in this area.

## Reworking the Internal Organization

Despite the emphasis on cooperation and communication, the workings of the consortium's internal structure had never received attention comparable to that enjoyed by its technological operations and their external connections. When Squires arrived, Sematech had no official organization chart. Harrell comments that at times the consortium resembled a "benevolent anarchy." For instance, at first the human-resources aspect of the organization had been largely ignored, and even later had continued to play the role of poor stepchild to technology issues. As an established organization preaching the quality values of customer satisfaction and continuous improvement through the PFTQ initiative, Sematech appeared overdue for its own systemic application of total-quality principles.

Since a key component of organizational quality is customer satisfaction, by developing quality methods specifically for member companies and DARPA, Sematech could align its operations with the realities of these customers' requirements. In doing so, the consortium would be better positioned to show that it was offering its various stakeholders a good ROI.

It was not startling news that, even as Sematech became a viable organization, reaching its technological Phase I and II goals and running projects and programs credited with helping to turn the competitive tide, many other matters appeared to grow more difficult for the consortium rather than easier. For one thing, the choice to support the infrastructure had taken emphasis and resources away from other efforts where lack of concurrent attention was now creating difficulties.

In November, 1989, Bob Noyce had told a congressional committee: "I think that the job that we have to do has become somewhat more difficult in the two years that have passed since the original plan was put out. As a result of that, we have been moving our emphasis to the semiconductor equipment and material suppliers because we see that as more critical now than the job that we were going to do—more in the manufacturing technology, manufacturing methods, quality methods, the techniques, if you will, of high-volume production. . . . With more money we could do both of those jobs."[16]

Now that Sematech programs designed to strengthen the more critical infrastructure were underway, other problems that had been deferred were looming, and the need for synchronizing Sematech's scattered results was apparent, especially in the face of a fast-moving environment. The market-share trend had just been reversed, but it still needed bolstering. Sematech's new experience and knowledge were developing a potential that was too valuable to relinquish just because it had problems and its first five-year charter was almost up. As Spencer saw it: "The original framers of Sematech underestimated the magnitude of the problem and the severity of the competition. It was probably overly-optimistic to expect that a one-time, five-year experiment could solve all the manufacturing problems."[17]

Frank Squires remembers: "I would say that 1991 was the year in which people began to understand that there would be a Sematech beyond the five-year timeframe. That, in turn, launched a number of transition activities to support the company in moving from a model of being a one-time, five-year experiment into managing itself just like any other ongoing business would."

In February, 1991, President Bush submitted to Congress the FY 1992 federal budget, which included a recommendation to continue funding Sematech at the $100 million level. Giving Sematech even more hope for its continued existence beyond 1992, the two-year DOD budget also sought $100 million for the consortium, extending through FY 1993. This would provide a sixth year of funding and was the first signal that the government might be willing to extend its commitment beyond the original five-year plan.[18] Although not yet a guarantee of funding, it was a public sign of confidence in the consortium—and in its new leadership.

If there was to be life for Sematech beyond 1992, a transition from an experimental to a more businesslike footing was needed—and without delay. Spencer expressed this as he first took office by saying, "If we don't pull together and do business differently, we're going to go out of business."[19]

## Quality Within Sematech

There is an English proverb that says "one should never marry a widow unless her husband was hanged."[20] Spencer appeared to know he was marrying the widow Sematech and he made no attempt to mimic his predecessor's style. Noyce's first gesture upon arriving at Sematech—pocketing his necktie—was that of an egalitarian entrepreneur ready to cooperate in an unprecedented experiment. One of Spencer's first public acts was that of an executive, ready to provide more conventional leadership. He had the OCE offices remodeled with real floor-to-ceiling walls—a far cry from the topless cubicles the previous

OCE had occupied. It was indeed plain that business was going to be done differently under Spencer.

A major and immediate difference would be to map Sematech's internal operations on a Baldrige-style Total Quality approach.[21] "Quality" practices have varying interpretations. The criteria for the Malcolm Baldrige National Quality Award measure different aspects of an organization's comparative excellence in a number of specific applications of Total Quality methods, including a leadership group that promotes quality, the use of information for strategic direction, human-resource practices that promote participation, product quality, and customer satisfaction. An advantage to using the Baldrige Award framework was that it offered a systems approach to simultaneously address many of the problems competing for attention. Spencer had experienced firsthand at Xerox what the application of systemic Total Quality methods could offer to an organization in difficulty.

In 1993 testimony before Congress, Spencer described some specific lessons of his Xerox experience, saying:

> The use of total quality management has been a key issue for us, [at Sematech] and I think benchmarking falls into that.... I was first introduced to benchmarking when I was a group executive at Xerox and had charge of—had responsibility for—technology world wide for that company. In 1981, Japanese competition had been able to take Xerox's market share from about 90 percent when we invented and developed plain-paper copiers down to 10 percent. That's a significant loss in market share, greater than the automotive loss has been, greater than almost any other loss.
>
> Our first reaction to that was one of denial. The Japanese are dumping products. They're selling below cost. They're not making any money. We then turned to looking carefully at what our competition was doing and we found that they were manufacturing things cheaper and better than we were doing.
>
> We did benchmarking not only against our competition in Japan, but also against the best performance by whatever company we thought was better in their activity.

In 1989, Xerox received a Malcolm Baldrige National Quality Award.

The first order in taking the quality approach at Sematech was to create the same kind of operation within the organization that the consortium was preaching to its member companies and suppliers. A few weeks after Spencer's arrival, the OCE and thirty senior managers participated in an off-site, four-day "awareness" session at which a Total Quality model for Sematech was introduced. The meeting became more than an introductory session, however, since the group came to agreement on a shared vision and strategic approach, and even generated a theme: "On Target, On Time, Together." This motto became important enough to eventually be made into a logo with the three *T*s forming a triangle enclosing a capital $Q$ for quality. Later, in 1992, Sematech registered the logo as its first trademark.

Each $T$ in the motto had particular significance for dealing with the problems Sematech's new leaders were taking on. "On target" addressed matters of focusing on and selecting technological deliverables relevant to the projected needs of each stakeholder. "On time" referred to meeting promised project schedules so that deliverables could meet the business-cadence needs of the actual technology generation and fab-equipping cycles of member firms. "Together" meant structuring consensus to give each member company a voice in setting deliverable priorities rather than depending on majority rule. It also meant that each firm must speak with only one voice rather than using the consortium as a forum to hash out its own priority differences.[22] The implications of the three $T$s and their connections grew more apparent as they were put into practice.

A Total Quality steering committee was chosen to lead a series of awareness sessions at which the OCE and directors met with everyone at Sematech to familiarize them with what the Total Quality model would mean in a collaborative organization. For one thing, Sematech had to develop its own quality culture and vocabulary relevant to a consortium, which often differed from the multicultural dialects that assignees brought from parent firms already practicing their own brands of quality. The Sematech model then had to be incorporated into training.

For some at the consortium, Total Quality was a completely new mind-set rather than just a new language. With a few notable exceptions, many firms in the semiconductor industry either had not worked with quality practices before Sematech's establishment, or had only been working to develop them since the mid-1980s.[23] During the early days of U.S. domination of the chip-making market, competition was based largely on innovation. However, with the entry of Japanese commodity production, global competition was forced to focus on price, and with the industry's increasing maturity, competitive advantage was coming down to distinctions in performance and quality. These historical characteristics of U.S. semiconductor competition mirrored the development of the elite status traditionally accorded in the United States to design engineering over manufacturing, and the practices of dividing and beating down equipment and materials suppliers on price.

Sematech's original emphasis on improving and integrating core manufacturing competence, its subsequent inclusion of infrastructure support in the mission, and then the development of the PFTQ program had paralleled the more advanced U.S. chip makers' efforts to set the old competitive bases on their head. These firms also strove to connect quality methods to efficient production and lowered variable costs. Thus, implementing Total Quality methods into the consortium was the next logical move to offset the vulnerabilities of the entrepreneurial U.S. semiconductor industry mind-set.

Still, in early 1991, neither the semiconductor industry in general nor Sematech's own operations yet subscribed to Total Quality. Frank Squires remembers: "There was no internal Total Quality program when I came to Sematech. There had been this very successful Partnering for Total Quality effort that was aimed at improving the operations of the suppliers to our member companies. It was getting rave reviews, and actually making a big difference in that community. But there was nothing going on inside of Sematech that would lead to the use of quality tools and processes being applied to our internal operations. It was kind of like the cobbler's children having no shoes. Again, I can rationalize why that was the case by tying it back to this five-year model [the first five-year charter.] You didn't invest a lot in internal effectiveness if you were only going to be around for five years."

One of Squires's first tasks in the summer of 1991 was to reshape the consortium's organizational structure. Among other things, he made the PFTQ operation independent of Supplier Relations, took Training out of Human Resources, and then created a small team of internal consultants whose job was to create a Total Quality management organization. It would concentrate on two things: maintaining the existing external programs and building on that strength, and introducing Total Quality concepts into the way in which Sematech itself was run.

## A New Five-Year Plan

While Sematech's reorganization was going on in the summer of 1991, the consortium was taking a long-range look at planning for the first time since the original five-year charter was established in 1987. In May, a task force began drafting a long-range plan called Sematech II that was designed to map the consortium's activities beyond 1992.[24] Although DARPA had insisted in 1988 that the consortium draw up an annual operating and business plan, little attention had been given to considering Sematech's future beyond the original 1992 horizon.

A relevant discussion of federal funding, including authorizations for DARPA, was concurrently taking place in Washington during the summer of 1991, and it was a good time for DARPA to help with consortium planning again. Bill George, in particular, worked with Arati Prabhakar, then serving as DARPA's director of microelectronics technology,[25] to define the specifics of the first version of the new long-range plan, which integrated a Total Quality approach to Sematech's future objectives with DARPA's requirements beyond 1992.

The new plan alternated the strategic planning (SP) cycle with an annual planning (AP) cycle. The SP cycle, incorporating customer input, was intended to produce a five-year look forward at technology and support activities. It would occur in the first half of the year and end with an SP Conference, the first to be held in late April, 1991. The SP Conference deliberations would be summarized and published annually as the DARPA's long-range plan. The alternating AP cycle, also incorporating customer input, was to occur in the third quarter and end with a conference producing an AP process to select the programs and funding levels for the following year. Sematech here was also following an important Total Quality Management (TQM) dictum that calls for incorporating specific customer input into strategic business planning.

The five-year business horizon, with long- and short-term cycles, showed the professional acumen and experience with quality practices that Bill Spencer and Frank Squires brought with them to Sematech. Bill George observes, "All of these things collectively have evolved to the conviction that we ought to operate like real companies do. The fact that both Bill and Frank came from outside the semiconductor industry has been very valuable in terms of giving us a different perspective. . . . I think it was a very important addition to the technical repertoire here at Sematech."

## Related Planning

Sematech II planning was not merely for business operations. It was centered on the consortium's technology thrusts as they changed in response to new developments. There were still many urgent technology needs, many of them interdependent, requiring integrated action, and continually generating controversy over their possibilities and priorities. Some technologies, such as lithography, were already part of ongoing thrusts; others, like the pressing issue of environmentally conscious manufacturing, needed to be formally addressed, rather than being included in other areas as previously. Sematech was not the only group concerned with identifying and coordinating the technology requirements for long-range strategic planning. In April, 1991, a historic meeting, called "Microtech 2000," signaled the increasing attention being paid to the integration of the previously largely splintered facets of the U.S. microelectronics community.

The SRC, under the auspices of the NACS and the federal Office of Science and Technology Policy, convened an assembly of ninety U.S. semiconductor experts at Research Triangle Park, North Carolina. Their goal was to identify and map the overall national technology needs to ensure the development of a one-gigabit SRAM with .12-micron line-width feature size by the year 2000. A published report of the group's conclusions included its vision of the products, equipment, materials, and processes required for U.S. semiconductor competitiveness in the first decade of the 21st century.[26]

Microtech 2000 was the first of what was to become a series of increasingly important road-mapping initiatives. This first national road map was criticized on two main points. First, it was still attempting to find a way to leapfrog one full generation of technology capability. Second, Microtech 2000 did not consider either costs or the practicality of some of its "blue-sky" objectives.[27] As Harrell observed, the road map reaffirmed to the industry's less-than-impressed executive community that leapfrogging would be extraordinarily difficult and expensive. Hasty points out that a major danger of leapfrogging is the risk of losing contact with grounding realities, such as customers' needs.

Whatever its flaws, Microtech 2000 marked the beginning of comprehensive semiconductor technology planning for the United States. Later, the NACS asked the SIA and the SRC, along with Sematech, to assume the sponsorship of these road-mapping efforts. The industry-driven meetings would make a point of stressing realism and affordability. The national road maps became an overarching strategic guideline that coordinated the efforts of Sematech, its lab and academic research partners, the semiconductor manufacturing industry, and its materials and equipment infrastructure. However, these comprehensive maps were still in the future.

## Visible Solutions

As Total Quality reorganization and strategic planning for Sematech II proceeded throughout 1991, the organization continued to attract visitors of all kinds, from U.S. officials to other industry executives to foreign trade groups. Among them was Great Britain's Prince Philip, whose stately Sematech photo taken with Bill Spencer hangs in the OCE suite.

With the expansion of global competition in many fields, there was growing interest in the pressing need for various forms of cooperation, including the formation of consortia in other industries. Sematech was beginning to be looked to as a successful model, particularly as it appeared to be the only large consortium able to reconcile the inherent conflicts between operating a manufacturing consortium with a production line while adhering to principles of precompetitive collaboration. Many observers were not really interested in what made Sematech unique, however.

"We frequently get one or two 'consortia,' who come through here wanting to see us as a model—the lessons learned, and that sort of thing," says Harrell. "Most of them have not taken the effort to include all the elements of their industry. They've made no effort to put together a structure where they form a vertical attack on the changes that need to be made to be competitive. That is a distinct difference in Sematech. Even today, there are very few, even after looking at the Sematech model, that attack their problems in that manner."

The importance of this vertical attack—as well as the difficulty of structuring and maintaining it—became visible in 1991 when Sen. Lloyd Bentsen and Sematech released a list of Japanese companies they accused of continuing to purposely withhold advanced manufacturing equipment from U.S. companies in order to give their Japanese customers a competitive advantage. The GAO investigated the allegations by surveying fifty-nine U.S. technology companies.

The GAO discovered twenty-two delays ranging from six months to two years in the delivery of such products as semiconductor manufacturing equipment, packaging materials, and computer components to the U.S. firms.[28]

The subsequent general indignation aroused by these delays gave new ammunition to the consortium's critics, who called Sematech's protest hypocritical. They charged that Sematech's own equipment development contracts allowed or required the suppliers involved to withhold equipment from nonmember customers for up to a year, thus benefiting member firms more than their equipment manufacturers.[29] Suppliers often needed unfettered access to any and all customers interested in their equipment developments to remain healthy.

The original charter's intellectual property provisions that greatly favored member firms over suppliers had been renegotiated with good contracting results in 1989. Now Sematech's practices needed to be reevaluated to bring them in line with its increased infrastructure involvement. This was true not only because of what the consortium was preaching regarding Total Quality and mutually beneficial supplier-customer relationships, but also because of new problems coming in the train of successful equipment testing, development, and improvement.

## Complications Arise

Spencer explains one aspect of these problems: "Centralized equipment qualification means that SME firms working on development or improvement contracts often must wait for approval before being able to ship new equipment, rather than selling prototypes immediately. They benefit from greater eventual sales, but only large SME firms may have the financial resources to endure the delay."[30]

The consortium's SME strengthening and standardizing efforts were beginning to have an impact on the nature and composition of the U.S. equipment infrastructure even beyond the inevitable effects of awarding development projects to the most likely domestic survivors of global competition. To diminish any discriminatory effects and to give suppliers as much opportunity for healthy growth as possible, time and foreign trade restrictions on marketing Sematech-sponsored equipment developments were abolished, with no preferred customer treatment for semiconductor member firms that were customers.

The most obvious advantages of consortium membership now came down to being able to influence the choice and direction of initiatives, and to having assignees from member firms participate in executing projects, while the industry and its infrastructure as a whole unarguably got a free ride. Members had to believe that it was worth their investment to create a tide that would raise all their noncontributing competitors' boats as well as their own.

However, every advance brought its own set of problems. The decision to lift preferential restrictions on suppliers may have deepened some members' sense that the consortium's infrastructure focus was not giving them their money's worth very directly. In fact, the experience of the two firms whose resignations would become effective early in 1992 suggests this.

## Two Members Exit

Micron Technology and LSI Logic were the two smallest of the fourteen firms that joined the consortium in 1987, and Sematech's dues structure—$1 million minimum, $15 million maximum—meant that the cost of participation was relatively higher for small firms than for larger ones. This was especially true when the cost of fulfilling the requirement to join the SRC was added in (a $62,000 one-time sign-up fee, plus capped dues proportional to earnings). Before Sematech, LSI Logic had resigned from the SRC, saying its research agenda did not fit. It had nearly backed out of joining the consortium in 1987 when it learned it would have to rejoin the SRC.[31] Such a proportionately large investment for a relatively small firm had to be weighed very carefully against its own overall corporate strategy.

By 1990, however, LSI Logic's strategic priorities had become concentrated on the expansion of its fab in Japan, and the company's executives felt that they could not afford to support Sematech's focus on U.S. suppliers because the results would not be immediately transferable to their fab in Japan. LSI Logic said it was resigning due to a "divergence in technology directions between LSI Logic and Sematech." The consortium's focus on strengthening the U.S. supplier base, it said, is "too indirect a return on [LSI's] investment."[32]

Micron Technology's 1992 resignation notice cited a similar divergence of interest, based on its "opposition to Sematech's focus on and investment in semiconductor equipment manufacturing firms."[33] In Micron's case, however, the reason for resigning stemmed from a sense of disenfranchisement. Harrell notes: "Micron had significantly different expectations about what the agenda would be. They tried, and tried, and tried to get their agenda worked on. They couldn't convince the others, so finally, in frustration and anger, they left."

Sematech took the underlying reason for these small firms' defections even more seriously than the amount of money they pulled out or the public relations loss. The resignations illustrated a basic flaw of majority rule: Consensus is no guarantee that every member's voice will be heard. Any member firm not being heard had a hard time believing that it was getting the most from its investment.

At the outset it had been hard enough even to arrive at a consensus among member firms. As Sematech was first formulating an agenda, Obi Oberai's diplomatically designed "secret ballot" had been circulated to each firm with instructions to list its top ten project interests from among all the operational possibilities within the sweep of the all-encompassing Black Book and the consortium's overall mission. The top-polling items determined the consortium's choices of project priorities, as well as the composition of the MDL. The previous sense of emergency had made this method acceptable, but it was now apparent that consensus would have to be structured differently if members' commitment was to be retained.

Miller Bonner points out: "You could run the risk—and we did run the risk at first—of taking everyone's secret top ten and taking all the names off it so it was homogenized. A given company's top five projects could totally drop off the bottom of that list, however, specifically if you tended to be a smaller, less advanced company than some of our larger, more technically advanced companies." The one-company/one-vote mechanism had unintentionally allowed what some smaller companies had always feared: that the technology concerns of the larger firms, especially the big four of IBM, Intel, Motorola, and TI, would dominate. It was time to change that trend.

## A New MDL Methodology

The new Total Quality motto, "On Time, On Target, Together," implied that Sematech's deliverables would fulfill all of the member companies' needs. To do this, Bonner continues, "Spencer and George changed the methodology. They basically told the member companies: 'Your top five projects, whatever they are, we're going to do.' Interestingly, it just so happens that, when you do the cut, probably 90 percent of everyone's top five are the same after all." With this method, no matter where a company was on the technology spectrum, its ETAB representative could go back to the parent firm and tell its R&D decision makers that Sematech had projects addressing each one of the firm's top five interests.

To implement this change, the fab would have to improve its productivity and the execution and performance of deliverables[34]—thus getting things done on time, on target, and together. Most projects were being done with suppliers, so the problems often consisted of Sematech, the supplier, and/or the company management either not working in synchronization or not supplying enough resources. Everyone would need to agree on the goals, keep them sufficiently constant, and then deliver them on time. In this light, the MDL began to take on new meaning.

Bonner remembers the new sense of dedication this brought: "One of the commitments that was structured through Bill George's earliest work was that we're going to meet what we say we're going to meet. We're going to execute; we're going to manage. We're going to get results on whatever we say we're going to do." In fact, in April, 1991, this commitment was made publicly visible to the whole organization with the posting of a large poster of the MDL depicting deadlines and their fulfillment by project areas on the cafeteria wall for everyone to see.

George remembers how this commitment began to change the definition of Sematech's product: "We started working in the second half of 1991 to change the mentality of 'Ship them some paper and let them worry about how to use it,' to 'We at Sematech have to do whatever it takes to get the members to use the things we've been working on.' Our job is not done until it is actually being used in the factories—delivering capability that is actually used. The key word was 'insertion.'" It had always been assumed that companies would figure out their own technology transfer if Sematech produced a report. The consortium took pride in the fact that more than a hundred technical reports were distributed in 1990.[35]

Now, for the first time, the step of insertion of technology into the member companies' fabs was formally added as the last item in every Sematech development process. This new step was so crucially important that it required the formation of an Execution and Performance Task Force, led by Gene Feit during the latter part of 1991, to make sure insertion occurred in a timely manner. The new method for formulating the MDL, plus the emphasis on execution and performance of deliverables to include their insertion in members' factories was clearly an attempt to address areas in which member companies had registered dissatisfaction.

## Member Satisfaction Is Key

In late 1991 senior managers met at an important off-site leadership workshop. Not surprisingly, discussion centered on increasing member companies' satisfaction. Now that their dissatisfactions were being addressed, it was easier to see the issues in positive terms. Bill George remembers: "People began to think about making sure that all the member companies got value. The difference lay between just throwing the product out there and hoping the majority gets value, to ensuring that everybody gets value, even if it doesn't maximize the total return. If I were trying to maximize the total return, I'd go after the big guys and make sure they got the highest ratio and therefore when you added it up, the total would be bigger."

It is hard to overestimate the impact of this win-win emphasis. The decision to target individual member satisfaction, rather than going for greater overall return, became a landmark of cooperative competition among rivals, and formed the basis for the next important development in early 1992, the concept of member company ROI.

Bill Spencer is credited with perceiving the need for a basic mechanism that would demonstrate the profitable relationship between Sematech's output and its individual members' interests and investments. In other words, he saw that the consortium needed a system for targeting, measuring, and displaying members' ROI. While waving the flag in a survival crisis had rallied followers in 1987—even if they were secretive about their specific needs—in 1991, demonstrably sound business practice was required to maintain commitment.

"It was through Spencer's brilliance," Tom Seidel believes, "that he established rigorous methodologies to track the return on investment," showing direct and visible results. And Sam Harrell recalls: "Spencer said, 'The only reason somebody should be in Sematech is that you get a return on investment.' There were many of the members who said that they felt good about Sematech, they felt good about how it helped their people, how it helped their competitiveness, and they got all this stuff out of it, but nobody could articulate or quantify why they felt that way. Spencer drove an approach that said, 'Let's get a return on investment: 1X return now, and a 2X by 1992, and a 3X by 1993, and so on.'"

Bill George was already busy shaping up the fab to meet the new performance and execution standards, as well as revamping it to process the new, state-of-the-art, 200 mm (eight-inch) silicon wafers. The project was slated for completion by June, 1992, in time to be used for achieving the Phase III milestone by the end of the year. George now took on the related task of developing a metric for showing member ROI. Results were starting to come in from the supplier-related projects begun in 1989 following the decision to focus on the infrastructure. For the first time, these programs were to be evaluated for their measurable benefits to the chip-making members.

To develop a meaningful yardstick, Sematech did its own appraisals of executed deliverables, which were then compared with data from a member survey on projects done for 1992.[36] The survey asked firms to add up the benefits they received from Sematech, attach dollar values to them, and then report on what they came up with and how they measured it.

## Owning the ROI

The front end of the ROI equation—project choice and planning—obviously had to change, too. Members were at last obliged to clearly define in terms of the projects they had voted for, not only what they expected from Sematech, but also what they intended to do to help the consortium achieve the goal. This took the new MDL methodology to its practical extreme. Both Sematech and its individual members now had to figure out what a measurable ROI would look like for them in terms of the products of cooperative projects. They then had to show how that ROI could be measured, and, even more important, list the resources it would require from each member, from planning to execution. Bill George says: "As we go forward, we try to determine if a program is worth doing from a financial standpoint, rather than it just being a new technical idea."

Two big benefits emerged from these related changes, Harrell says. The first was that they created a communication vehicle for members to say what they wanted. The changes also helped members vote in a disciplined way for things from which they could realistically benefit, rather than for things they could not afford but wanted Sematech to do. This individualized MDL-ROI relationship soon generated another fortuitous advantage.

In late 1992, when member company reports of their Sematech ROIs were first presented to the board,[37] a question was raised about who should be working on the project deliverables. The ETAB agreed to take on the responsibility of staffing designated projects. This resulted in a direct connection between what a member company voted to have on the MDL, what it expected for its ROI, and the choices of the assignees sent to staff the specific projects a company wanted done.

A major hurdle was cleared when the consortium accepted responsibility for executing deliverables on time, and the ETAB accepted responsibility for staffing the projects. There was no point in blaming each other for deficiencies any more. "In other words," says Bonner, "if they [the ETAB] had an interest in getting their assignees on certain projects, it was up to them to give us candidates. It wasn't up to us to go in there and beg for them." The reality of the third leg in the motto—"Together"—gave the other two limbs—"On Time" and "On Target"—the balance they needed to work.

Toward the end of 1993 a gap developed between the completion of many duration-determined personnel assignments and the commencement of project-specific ones, with more assignees going home than coming in. This appeared to threaten the organization's operation. In the first quarter of 1994, though, as the new policy kicked in, the assignee population hit a record high. With better planning and execution of projects, Sematech could better estimate the duration of assignments, and thus tie the length of a new assignment to its relevant project timetable. On the member side, once firms could see a direct proportion between the quality of the assignees they sent and the ROI they expected for their voted interests, the overall caliber of assignees improved.[38]

## One More Loss

Unfortunately, not all these changes came soon enough to forestall another firm's resignation. A third member, Harris Semiconductor, left in December, 1992, claiming that Sematech's concentration on submicron process technology (the Phase I, II, and III goals) was not in line with Harris's focus on analog signal processing and power semiconductors,[39] although the company stated it still felt Sematech was a viable initiative.

Again, as Harrell notes: "The Harris and Micron people each had different agendas, but neither firm was successful at getting their agenda funded. The difficulty all along was to get the right people in the member companies involved, giving the right input, and getting an input which would give the companies a return on investment. We are working on a number of issues today that the companies who left would like to have seen. I don't believe that there are any members today who feel disenfranchised."

Rockwell, which had considered withdrawing from the consortium at the end of 1992, decided to stay on, thus confirming Harrell's opinion. At the time of incorporation, Sematech, with fourteen member firms, represented 80 percent of U.S. semiconductor manufacturing capacity. Membership was now down to eleven firms, but it still represented 75 percent of that same capacity.[40] This test of member commitment now pushed Sematech to reinvent the organization for the next phase of its mission.

## CHAPTER 8

# A New Mission

*Sematech II*

The reorganization of Sematech for its post-1992 incarnation aimed at more than just making the eleven remaining members more satisfied or getting even better assignees. Sematech II would feature Total Quality reorganization, an emphasis on project performance and execution, and ROI assessment and planned improvement. This plan for the consortium, announced in December, 1991, was accompanied by the first in a series of annual publications called *Sematech Accomplishments,* which listed successfully executed projects by their technology thrust areas.

Sematech II had a bold new mission statement: "To create fundamental change in manufacturing technology and domestic infrastructure to provide U.S. semiconductor companies with the capability to be world-class suppliers." The expression "fundamental change," pointedly echoing DARPA's mission statement, revealed the two organizations' close alignment. Says Miller Bonner: "We were showing them that we were going to change and we were going to link with them. We were going to be part of the solution, not part of the problem." Not coincidentally, DARPA's approval of the Sematech II plan would be crucial to winning government support for the next five years.

Also of note, the new mission statement formally acknowledged the materials and equipment infrastructure. It also identified the semiconductor manufacturers as "suppliers" themselves, which of course they are as they supply the essential microchips on which so much of the world runs.

## "Short-loop" Testing as Policy

Sematech II also now recognized, as a matter of policy, some of the developments that had grown out of the consortium's turn toward supporting the infrastructure. One of these was a newly explicit emphasis on short flow or "short-loop" testing—which was the original issue decided by the board in resolving the IBM-AT&T technology choice—to qualify semiconductor manufacturing tools individually, rather than in end-to-end, full-line process testing. Improvements in computer modeling and simulation were making short-loop testing more feasible.

This shift was seen as part of Sematech's "fundamental change"—a total factory approach aimed at speeding up the qualification and development of next-generation tools and at helping member companies upgrade their own processes more quickly in order to introduce new-generation devices 25 percent faster. With full-loop processing, problems tended to show up late, at the end of the line, whereas a factory model would permit more confidence that testing of individual tools could show changes early that would affect the entire line.

Short-loop testing in turn put more emphasis on specific computer-aided processes. These included CIM, CAD, process modeling and simulation, software manufacture, automated material handling, and training systems. Computer-aided processes, especially CIM, grew in importance because they simplified experimentation.

Sematech felt that member firms needed this accelerated development and qualification of new-generation tools more than they needed duplication of their own current expertise in end-to-end, full-line processes. For one thing, members produced far more chips than did the consortium. Also, the new tools would help them bring their own new products to market that much sooner.

In fact, the members' own full-loop, high-volume production lines would prove that Sematech-qualified tools and software systems worked just as the factory model predicted and as the submicron manufacturing vehicles demonstrated. These models ran on specific measurements, which carried risks. However, as Spencer explained: "We felt we had to have measurable goals to be credible. We are going to be Babe Ruth stepping up to the plate and pointing to the left center field bleachers and then hitting our home run."[1]

## New Aims and Objectives

Sematech II's new mission proclaimed it intended "(a) to reduce the time between introduction of new generations of technology by 25%; (b) to use modeling and simulation in the design of new manufacturing equipment development; and (c) to develop the Factory of the Future as a complete system with integrated tools, processes and operating systems."[2]

The statement was precise. The fundamental change would not be a microchip technology breakthrough. It would instead involve quality-driven, continuous improvement of manufacturing equipment and processes, the core manufacturing skills for using them, and even the modeling of their complete factory integration. The mission's three aims were further subdivided into six objectives. Each had its own thrust areas, measurable criteria, and execution strategies, all geared to member-company insertion, cost realities, and leverage of external resources, including the SRC, the SCOEs, the National Labs, and DARPA.[3]

In January, 1992, just a month after the Sematech II plan for extending the consortium's life beyond its original charter was released, President Bush sent Congress his proposed FY 1993 budget. It included consortium funding, thus extending government support of Sematech beyond its original five-year charter. On the down side, however, the budget proposed slashing the 1993 federal contribution to Sematech to $80 million—a $20 million cut.[4] With the consortium expanding its scope to include the infrastructure, Sematech would clearly have to learn how to do more with less.

In August, DARPA announced in a GAO report that it planned to reduce Sematech funding to $80 million in FY 1993, and that beyond 1993 it intended to divide funding for semiconductor manufacturing R&D between Sematech and other competing organizations.[5]

However, before the final vote in September, Sematech's funding was pulled out of the proposed DOD budget as a separate line item and restored to the original $100 million for FY 1993—although with project strings attached for the first time. Congress wanted $10 million earmarked for developing environmentally conscious manufacturing processes.[6] The message was clear: there would be less government support and more government oversight.

Sematech had, in fact, incorporated environmental concerns into all its operations from the beginning. For example, it had completely torn out the old floor of the Data General warehouse in Austin to install five levels of environmentally shielded flooring to protect against possible ground contamination by spilled toxic waste. It was an enormous effort.

Still, in April, 1993, to satisfy the new congressional mandate, Sematech announced a new organizational area for environmental health and safety research. The new department's chief, IBM executive Ray Kerby, had directed IBM's environmental affairs programs for the past decade. At Sematech he would direct the ongoing environmental programs and also create a new Sematech thrust area formally addressing environmental, health, and safety priorities identified by the SIA and the consortium's advisory boards.

Throughout 1992, the FTABs for each of the other thrust areas also updated their analyses and created road maps of their most urgent needs for the next five years. But the consortium's vulnerability to political intervention, as shown by the environmental mandate that had been tied to its continued funding, created an ominous counterpoint to the new road-map planning for Sematech II. This was particularly worrisome since, when all the new FTAB technology road maps were correlated, the urgent needs in semiconductor technology development added up to a staggering $2 billion.

This amount was far greater, and riskier, than even a securely supported consortium could hope to take on. In October, 1992, SEMI/Sematech president Sam Harrell was appointed to the consortium's OCE to fill the newly created post of executive vice president and chief strategy officer. He recalls the challenge he faced: "We looked at this $2 billion problem: How do you get $2 billion supplied for all the things Sematech couldn't do? Out of that began a dialogue of how we leverage the national resources."

## External Connections Help

Fortunately, as the consortium's infrastructure relationships were expanding, some strong external connections had been growing as well. In 1986, at the recommendation of the Defense Science Board, and as part of the original deal for government support, the drafters of Sematech's charter had spelled out plans for collaboration with the various national laboratories and with academia. With the SRC's help, this collaboration began soon after the consortium was founded. Part of Sematech's story is how the numerous Sematech Centers of Excellence (SCOEs) and the various projects at the national laboratories complemented its efforts and leveraged its resources.

The SCOEs, first established in 1988, were starting to produce useful results in the 1990s. For instance, in late 1991 the first SCOE patent—for a lithography process tool—was awarded to John Henry Thomas and Bawa Singh at the David Sarnoff Research Center at the New Jersey SCOE.[7] Because lithography had always been Sematech's major thrust, this newly patented tool represented the kind of help sought from external research collaboration.

However, the SCOEs had been founded not just to do research but also to help remedy the growing scarcity of quality college graduates in the science and engineering fields, and the inability of U.S. graduates to work together effectively. In fact, many of the problems the industry had with graduates from U.S. universities sounded similar to those caused by designing a sophisticated device and "throwing it over the wall" for manufacturers to turn into a usable product.

Because of America's traditional emphasis on individual performance, even graduates from top U.S. programs often had little experience with intellectual teamwork—that is, with the collaborative processes of creating knowledge. The effects of this trend were disturbing enough that in 1989 a Commission on Industrial Productivity sponsored by the Massachusetts Institute of Technology (MIT), devoted part of its report to recommending changes in the individualistic attitudes in U.S. education. The commission believed a new educational emphasis on collaboration would be crucial to any effective program for regaining a productive edge in the United States.[8] Others went so far as to say that the government should actively support a national effort in applied scientific training. Frank Press, president of the National Academy of Sciences in 1989, observed, "A few CEO's have told me they could make a product that almost never fails, but the limiting factor is the quality of the work force."[9]

## Starting Science Earlier

The MIT commission focused on university-level education. The founders of Sematech and the SRC did the same when they developed the SCOE concept. They recognized, however, that cooperation needed to be taught even earlier. In the summer of 1989, the SRC established the SRC Competitiveness Foundation, both to expand its university programs and to develop earlier educational ties to industry—in the kindergarten through twelfth grade years—by bringing science and mathematics teachers into contact with the nation's manufacturing engineers. The foundation runs summer programs that connect elementary and secondary school science and math teachers with applied scientists, letting teachers experience how competitive cooperation and participatory learning work in industry.

In February, 1990, Bob Noyce and Jack Kilby, who had each invented his own type of integrated circuit nearly simultaneously, received the first international Charles Stark Draper Prize from the National Academy of Engineering (NAE). Noyce contributed his $175,000 share of the prize to the SRC Competitiveness Foundation, marking its first major endowment. The gesture demonstrated Noyce's belief that the classroom and the real world needed to be brought closer together. Ralph Darby, executive director of the foundation, noted its powerful symbolism: "A gift of this kind from a man of Dr. Noyce's stature sends the message that K–12 science and mathematics programs are important to the competitiveness stance of this country."[10]

## Sematech Centers of Excellence

Sematech's founders agreed with the MIT commission's recommendations for better preparing U.S. students for the realities of global competition: "Create a new cadre of students and faculty characterized by (1) interest in, and knowledge of, real problems and their societal, economic, and political context; (2) an ability to function effectively as members of a team creating new products, processes, and systems; (3) an ability to operate effectively beyond the confines of a single discipline; and, (4) an integration of a deep understanding of science and technology with practical knowledge, a hands-on orientation, and experimental skills and insight."[11]

The commission drew this conclusion even as Sematech's charter was being written, including its projected industry-academia-government collaboration at the SCOEs and in some of the national labs. In February, 1988, Turner Hasty, the consortium's first director of research, chaired a briefing for universities interested in bidding to become an SCOE. Their selection would hinge on three criteria: the quality of the research programs offered, their relevance to Sematech's needs, and the nature of the school's available resources. (Connection with the University of Texas at Austin was already part of the deal to bring the consortium to Austin, so that university was exempted from the bidding.) As might be expected, university interest—and competition—was high. The first five SCOEs established by May, 1988, sought to focus research in the most critically needed areas of manufacturing: contamination/defect control, optical lithography, single-wafer processing, plasma etching, and metrology.[12] Eventually, more than thirty schools nationwide became involved in the programs.

## The SRC's Role

The SRC, located in Research Triangle Park, North Carolina, was chosen as the oversight agency for the SCOEs. Formed in 1982, the consortium's purpose was to sponsor generic semiconductor research at its participants' sites. By the time of the SCOE bidding, the SRC had been operating for most of the decade, and its member companies had already invested over $100 million in U.S. university research efforts. The SRC became a founding member of Sematech, and Larry Sumney, its president and CEO, acted as Sematech's managing director during part of the yearlong search for a CEO. The SCOE contracts and projects were to be directed by the SRC, drawing on its collaborative experience and connections to link Sematech with academia.

Between February, 1988, and March, 1989, selections for SCOE university sites were made, and $10 million worth of contracts were finalized for the initial research projects. In March, Sematech and the SRC sponsored an initial workshop for SCOE scientists and educators to discuss ways to recover world leadership in semiconductor manufacturing. At that meeting, Sumney claimed that the establishment of the SCOEs "marks a major expansion of the industry's support for university research."[13]

Sematech Centers of Excellence projects deal with the manufacturing aspects of microelectronics in accordance with the effort to integrate research with its practical applications, and to develop the teamwork they require. The ten original SCOE programs in operation by May, 1989, are listed in appendix 2. Sematech and the SRC have continued to work together in supporting educational programs and academic research.

By 1994, the SRC had become a consortium of more than sixty semiconductor companies and government agencies. Since the SRC is not a manufacturing consortium, it never established a central site like Sematech, but from its base in Research Triangle Park it plans and implements an integrated program of precompetitive research conducted at sixty-two North American universities, national laboratories, and research institutions.[14]

The SRC annually provides more than $30 million for semiconductor research in U.S. universities, with roughly a third of that amount coming from Sematech-sponsored projects. These research projects address problems of advanced—but still precompetitive or core—manufacturing technology. In particular, SCOE projects could tackle urgent problems that exceeded Sematech's immediate capabilities, such as the research into X-ray lithography being done at the University of Wisconsin SCOE.

## The X-ray Question

There had been ongoing contention over including X-ray technology in Sematech's agenda from the very beginning. The issue thus provides a good example of the role external projects played. In 1987, most semiconductor manufacturers agreed that the increasing miniaturization of closely packed features on powerful chips would soon force them to use X-rays, deep ultraviolet light (DUV), electron beams (E-beams), or some other energy source with wavelengths shorter than those of visible light for etching circuit lines. As one journalist described the problem: "Trying to make such intricate circuits with light is like trying to paint a thin line with a wide brush. . . . By comparison to light, X-rays, which have a far shorter wavelength, are like a very sharp pencil, and can therefore be used to develop the smaller circuits necessary."[15]

Japanese optical (visible light) lithography equipment makers, notably Canon and Nikon, had begun to dominate that field in the 1980s. By 1989, however, the Japanese were also reported to have more than a dozen X-ray lithography R&D programs either in individual companies or in consortiums. By comparison, in the U.S. that same year only IBM had a major X-ray program, which Motorola was taking part in. (AT&T had a program, too, but it was a small one.) DARPA had been concerned with this problem from the beginning and had pressured Sematech to include X-ray technology development in the 1989 operating plan. However, the DOD agency had hedged its bets by also setting aside $60 million for X-ray lithography research at national laboratories and universities.[16] There was much worry that the United States was falling behind in long-term preparation for the inevitable changes coming in lithography.

In 1989 the Federal Advisory Council report on Sematech noted that Japanese semiconductor makers were ahead in seven strategic areas, including X-ray lithography, and said that consortium planners intended to include accelerated development of commercially feasible X-ray technology on the agenda.[17] However, the advisory council's 1990 survey reported that Sematech's relatively near-term R&D objectives could only allow primary dependence on current-generation (i.e., optical) lithographic technology rather than X-ray and E-beam technologies, even though the latter would probably be required for competitive high-volume production by the end of the 1990s. The dry phrasing in the yearly council reports does not reflect the intensity of the agenda negotiations among member firms and with DARPA over what to do about X-ray technology, and the issue was far from settled.

Despite of the general belief that the laws of physics would eventually dictate using X-ray lithography, and leaving aside Sematech's resource limitations, there were at least three other reasons why the consortium's investment in it remained controversial. First, engineers were unsure whether X-rays would, in fact, turn out to be the best of several alternatives to using visible wavelength light. Second, X-rays came coupled with very high costs. Third, some hopeful progress was being made toward refining current-state optical lithography so as to extend its effectiveness.

In March, 1989, to leverage the consortium's limited capabilities in this costly, long-term, uncertain area, Sematech established a SCOE at the University of Wisconsin at Madison for conducting X-ray lithography research.[18] A connected equipment development project was also set up off site at a U.S. X-ray lithography firm, Hampshire Instruments.[19]

Then, in 1990, just as the submicron line width of miniaturized circuits seemed nearing the limit of optical lithography, an exciting improvement occurred. A manufacturing tool called a "phase-shift mask" was developed. This device—to continue using an earlier analogy—could "paint" not just one thin stripe but two thicker stripes of out-of-phase light that barely overlapped by the desired width of the submicron-sized circuit line needed.[20] The light stripes canceled each other out at the point where they overlapped, thus creating the ultra-fine line of light that escaped to etch the silicon wafer below. This phase-shift innovation, along with the development of new photoresist chemicals for improved etching techniques with deep ultraviolet light (DUV), allowed both Japanese and U.S. manufacturers to delay the costly move toward X-ray lithography.

The phase-shift mask requires a stepper, so the development and use of phase-shift technology were intricately connected with the progress and complications of the stepper initiatives described earlier. (In fact, when the stepper manufacturer GCA failed in 1993, it created a domino effect, taking Hampshire Instruments with it, ending Hampshire's X-ray lithography collaboration with Sematech through the University of Wisconsin SCOE.)

The innovation of phase-shift technology happily extended the effectiveness of optical lithography at least through the 1990s, relieving some of the urgent pressure for immediate development of X-ray or alternative technologies. As Tom Seidel, then Sematech's vice president for manufacturing equipment and materials, noted, "The window for using X-rays keeps getting pushed out."[21]

By April, 1992, Sematech had begun its own program in phase-shift mask operations as part of the consortium's continuing thrust in optical lithography.[22] While pursuing this advance, the consortium also worked on developing other technologies, such as DUV and I-line lithography, as well as continuing to monitor other X-ray research with an eye to possibly using X-rays for etching .25 micron and smaller features. Supporters of X-ray lithography felt that Sematech would still be in a unique position to capitalize on whatever progress had been made in this technology if and when it became necessary in the future.[23]

In a sense, the controversy and difficult choices surrounding the development of X-ray lithography epitomize the drama of Sematech's history to this point. The plot includes a lot of agonizing over where the technology might be headed; over the risk of attempting a costly, long-term, breakthrough technology in view of the consortium's short-term charter and resource limitations; over the intense competitive and political pressures to develop a technology that the Japanese were ahead in and that the DOD wanted; and over how to balance short-term improvements in current-state equipment while leveraging longer-term breakthroughs via external connections. The X-ray tale explains how the external leverage offered by sponsoring high-risk research at the SCOEs could help to fulfill some of the unrealistic early expectations about Sematech that the consortium could not shoulder by itself.

Sematech's connections with academia have continued to grow in importance as Sematech has matured. In January, 1992, just after the Sematech II plan was released, a University Advisory Council was formed. The council consists of the deans of major engineering schools and meets annually to discuss and enhance the collaboration of industry with U.S. research universities and national laboratories.[24] At the 1993 meeting at Stanford University in California, the deans expressed dismay at the overall decrease in U.S. R&D investment and reconfirmed the escalating national need for the real-world, real-time learning offered by industry collaboration combined with enlightened government support, such as Sematech could offer.

## A New Federal Outlook

Sematech's original charter, following the DSB's 1986 recommendation, also provided for leveraging through collaboration with some of the 726 national laboratories run by various agencies of the government, including the National Aeronautics and Space Administration (NASA) and the Departments of Defense and Energy. These labs historically have operated under the kind of specific project oversight that the consortium was able to avoid by receiving its DARPA funding as a grant, as discussed earlier. Still, the dual-purpose nature of much research being done in the national labs complemented Sematech's goals, and a common interface for this extensive national research network with the semiconductor industry could help them both.

Before Sematech, the United States had never had a forum for sharing information about technological problems and their applications among industry and national lab researchers. In fact, industry workers, barricaded in company "silos," had been largely prohibited by antitrust regulation from discussing their work freely with employees of other firms, and corporate secrecy effectively prevented them ever from exchanging much information with academic or lab researchers. The national lab workers had also been sequestered in their own ivory towers, often working on projects that were classified for military or national security reasons. Their constraints, like those of university researchers, historically had been different from the market-driven pressures on those in industry, but that was starting to change.

In 1989, the National Competitiveness Technology Transfer Act established technology transfer as a mission of the national laboratories. The bill permitted them to enter into Collaborative Research and Development Agreements (CRADAs) with U.S. industrial firms. The CRADA, unfamiliar at first, and often cumbersome to negotiate and implement, began to gain momentum in the 1990s. By 1994 there were more than six hundred CRADAs involving national laboratories and U.S. industry. Taken together, they represented a combined R&D effort of more than $500 million per year.[25] This increase reflected the coincidental conversion of a great deal of DOD spending as the Cold War came to an end and the national labs sought civilian projects to replace those being canceled by the military.

In 1993 there was also a new president in the White House. One of President Clinton's first initiatives was his proposed technology plan, which called for federal labs to spend up to 20 percent of their research budgets on partnerships with industry, and offered tax credits along with some direct funding to firms participating in joint research. The rationale for Clinton's plan was that the United States could no longer depend on "the serendipitous application of defense technology to the private sector . . . , but should promote technology as a catalyst for economic growth by directly supporting the development, commercialization, and deployment of new technology, and through fiscal and regulatory policies that indirectly promote these activities."[26]

Predictably, some worried that the president's technology plan would lead to government control of the private sector. Scientists feared that the Clinton team, by emphasizing applied research, might be overlooking the importance of basic research—that is, knowledge pursued without regard for immediate applications.[27] But Clinton's science adviser John Gibbons affirmed that the new program was committed to supporting basic research, increasing the civilian share of the total federal R&D budget from the current 41 percent to 50 percent by 1998.

Three main bases supported specific applications of Clinton's technology plan: better cooperation between industry, labor, universities, and government; government investment in education programs; and government investment in nonmilitary high-tech research. The plan aimed to commit 10–20 percent of the national labs' budget to cooperative R&D projects with industrial firms, and to increase the dual-use ratio of commercial over military projects.[28]

## Cultural Barriers to Cooperation

The actual use of this support still met with cultural and communication barriers, however. Robert Park of the American Physical Society remarked: "A venture capitalist I met once said, 'I never invest with a scientist who is in love with his ideas. I only invest with a scientist who is in love with money.' That's a culture that gets built in at places like IBM. It isn't built in at the national laboratories."[29]

The venture capitalist need not have singled out IBM to make his point that venture capital in the United States has been far more interested in a quick return on investment than in an idea's scientific merit. The inverse is true of scientists, who generally have shown little interest in the profitability of their ideas. The idea of creating a mutually beneficial connection between lab scientists in love with ideas and industrial engineers in pursuit of profits was overdue, as was having a skillful matchmaker. Sematech was uniquely placed and equipped to act as a role model and a broker for research collaboration.

As CEO Bill Spencer noted: "There is no other single place in the nation besides Sematech where as much information exists on the semiconductor industry, the equipment manufacturing industry, and research programs in universities and national laboratories. Individuals at Sematech are involved in programs with our eleven member companies, the government, universities and the national laboratories. They have the opportunity to meet the leading technologists in every aspect of semiconductor manufacturing, and to become acquainted with equipment programs in over 140 U.S. SME companies."[30] By 1992, Sematech was investing $5 million a year in national laboratories.

The 1993 federal technology plan cited Sematech as a role model for future government-industry-academia cooperation, saying that the administration hoped that the program would encourage federal agencies and companies to get involved with projects that companies could not afford individually. The planners credited Sematech's consortium-backed research, supported by industry and the DOD with helping U.S. chip makers increase their share of the global market.[31]

## The Sandia Experience

The growth of Sematech's relationship with the DOE's Sandia National Laboratory in Albuquerque, New Mexico, illustrates the increasing importance of industry-government lab collaboration. In August, 1989, Sematech and Sandia signed their first cooperative agreement—which called for the creation of the Semiconductor Equipment Technology Center (SETEC). Its purpose was to strengthen the U.S. equipment and materials infrastructure by bringing the skills of the national lab to bear on developing new tool designs and methodologies, focusing particularly on equipment reliability research.[32]

Sam Harrell recalls the first years of that partnership: "Over a period of about two-and-a-half years, a lot of give and take, and a lot of pressure, we built a team and learned to work with Sandia in some ways that were very productive." Building on the lessons learned and the positive experience of this first collaborative agreement, Sematech and Sandia signed a second CRADA in April, 1992. The second project called for establishing a contamination-free manufacturing (CFM) research center.[33] Contamination-free manufacturing processes were crucial to the Factory of the Future initiative that was one of the three pillars of the Sematech II mission.

This was followed a year later by one of the largest cooperative R&D agreements ever signed with a DOE laboratory. Cosponsored by the Commerce Department's National Institute of Standards and Technology (NIST), this CRADA allocated $103 million over five years for the joint development of advanced semiconductor technologies for manufacturing the next generation of integrated circuits. The DOE was to provide $ 53.6 million, and Sematech the remaining $49.4 million. Significantly, the effort was to focus not on innovative product breakthroughs but on six crucial areas of core competence: equipment benchmarking and engineering, CFM, equipment and software reliability, equipment modeling and design, materials analysis, and improvements in semiconductor manufacturing processes. Further projects could be added if necessary.[34]

However, the deal was almost torpedoed at the last minute when Sematech's member firms balked at accepting the standard DOE clause guaranteeing "march-in rights," which would have allowed the DOE to repossess intellectual property rights if its industrial partners failed to commercialize the new technology. Secretary Hazel O'Leary of the DOE personally intervened to make an exception to these rights, and the deal went through.[35]

Sandia president Al Narath noted that the agreement "greatly expands and extends Sandia's already close working relationship" with Sematech. According to Bill Spencer, the agreement represented "the first step toward achieving the compelling vision laid down last year by the Semiconductor Industry Association—the creation of a national road map for the entire American semiconductor industry." The kinds of technology to be pursued under the joint accord were aligned with this newest road map, laying out the crucially timed interdependence of many developments. The map was to become an increasingly important consensus, commitment, and synchronization document as more and more organizations began working together.[36]

## A New Image

Balancing out the leverage gained from external collaboration with the national labs, Sematech's emphasis on core manufacturing abilities complemented the more product-focused CRADAs that private firms had increasingly begun establishing with the national labs after passage of the 1989 National Competitiveness Technology Transfer Act. John Preston, MIT's director of technology development, wrote that Sematech had done more than the more traditional government efforts to spur the national economy, thanks largely to its having kept a precompetitive focus on problems that were fundamental to the semiconductor industry. "Collaboration on such critical technologies is nearly impossible because communication is stilted at best," he said. "Several consortia have failed to commercialize new technologies because they attempted to work on the 'crown jewels.'"[37]

This collaborative picture was changing, however. The CRADAs between national labs and private firms, besides complementing Sematech's direct funding and precompetitive focus, represented a real shift in attitude toward mutually beneficial involvement between industry and government agencies—and a practical mechanism for making it work.

Illustrative of the many new CRADAs being formed were two agreements that Intel signed in April, 1994—one with Sandia and the other with Los Alamos National Laboratory. These industry-lab agreements, while not directly involving Sematech, extended the work of the consortium's newest thrust in environmentally conscious manufacturing, established at Sematech in 1993. The CRADA projects at Intel's New Mexico plant were designed to develop highly sensitive microsensors to detect trace quantities of organic chemicals in plant emissions, establish a "smart system" to predict when critical process pumps are approaching failure, use modeling and simulation to reduce particle levels in clean room processing equipment, and transfer technology to Intel for advanced failure analysis techniques that detect microchip defects.[38]

Sematech's environmental thrust had grown increasingly important as the microelectronics industry in general—and some of the consortium's members in particular—had incurred growing criticism for the pollution caused by manufacture of computer parts, including semiconductors. High-tech industries such as microelectronics manufacturers, with their images of sparkling clean rooms instead of belching smokestacks, turned out to be producers of much toxic waste. Environmentalists observed that Silicon Valley had the highest concentration of Superfund cleanup sites for any area of its size in the whole country, with twenty-eight of its twenty-nine documented sites the result of high-technology manufacture.[39] This situation could hardly be ignored by a semiconductor manufacturing consortium.

Indeed, Sematech was the ideal place to tackle the environmental problem. Bill George explains why: "Sometimes, there are new technologies that you'd like to use in your factory, but a real factory making products for real customers has a problem: You can't risk shutting down a fab, so whatever you do has to be proven." A typical example of an unproven technology is the reprocessing of the hydrofluoric and sulfuric acids used in wafer production. Being able to reprocess dangerous, costly materials would clearly decrease a firm's environmental impact and lower its operating expenses—but only if it worked. And that can't be tested in a fab in full production.

George continues: "When I was running fabs at Motorola, we looked very seriously at installing sulfuric acid reprocessing back in 1987. There were tremendous benefits: 95 percent reduction of use, help in environmental situations, all sorts of things." Acid reprocessing recycles hydrofluoric and sulfuric acid, minimizing the need to transport, treat, and dispose of most of the hazardous, costly acids used in chip production. It thus pays to be "green." However, as George says: "We simply couldn't take the risk of shutting down the factory, and it was a nonproven technology at that time. Nobody could prove it. It was sort of gridlocked in the industry. Without some high-volume data, nobody could be the first one to implement. But if the Sematech fab shut down for a week, it wouldn't kill any customer."

As a result, George notes: "Sematech has been able to demonstrate sulfuric and hydrofluoric acid reprocessing in its own fab and gather high-volume data that gives the member companies the ability, in essence, to make risk-free decisions in their own fabs. It improves the intolerable risk that the member companies face." Acid reprocessing was one of the earlier projects in environmentally conscious manufacturing, even before it became a formal thrust area. Sematech's ongoing environmental contributions could be picked up and then further enhanced in CRADAs like Intel's with the Sandia and Los Alamos labs.

## Expanding Cooperative Standards

Sematech's work quickly extended into new areas of collaboration. In July, 1994, the consortium and member-firm TI announced the release of a jointly developed manufacturing specification called the CIM Framework 1. 0. This specification finally offered a standardized interface enabling Manufacturing Execution System (MES) software to "plug and play" on what is known as a "standard software backplane."[40]

The CIM Framework 1.0 allowed software applications from multiple suppliers to "interoperate" with each other in much the same manner as Microsoft Windows–compatible applications operate on a computer. It also offered savings and increased productivity to manufacturers, who would be spared having to install numerous proprietary manufacturing controls that were incompatible with other suppliers' equipment. The use of cooperative equipment standards in an otherwise competitive environment could lessen duplication of effort and increase nationwide productivity without jeopardizing quality.

The CIM Framework 1.0 represented a sophisticated outgrowth of the consortium's early efforts toward industry-wide equipment standards, the first steps toward which had been taken in the 1990 EQP. The CIM thrust under Charlie Farrell—and then the Factory of the Future goal of Sematech II—had taken the idea far beyond the earliest "Sematech Qualified" pieces of equipment that operated with collaborative specifications.

Even more significantly, the CIM Framework 1.0 was then picked up and extended even farther by a larger collaboration—again sponsored by the NIST—that Sematech joined. This $105 million initiative came to be called the Advanced Technology Program (ATP). Besides Sematech, its members included TI, the National Center for Manufacturing Sciences (NCMS), AMD, Digital Equipment Corporation, Intel, AT&T, General Motors, and Rockwell/ Automation, among others. The ATP's goal was to extend the capability of the CIM Framework 1.0 specification into a national standard that could be used in many other manufacturing industries, not just microelectronics.[41] Its mission was a classic example of what Peter Drucker has described as the "application of knowledge to knowledge," which exponentially spreads its effect rather than limiting the application of knowledge to the tools or working practices in which it arises.[42]

Sematech's image as a role model was changing as its external collaboration with other agencies expanded, and also as the idea of collaboration among industry members and between industry and government became less of a feared novelty and more of a practical necessity. In a sense, Sematech was helping to work itself out of a job through its collaborative trailblazing, but in another sense it was creating a different kind of job for itself. The consortium was uniquely placed to serve both as a cooperative clearinghouse for collecting, integrating, and disseminating technological information and as a broker for contacts among private and public agencies as they increasingly looked for ways to work together.

A productive outcome like the jointly generated TI/Sematech CIM Framework 1.0 specification was an impressive, concrete example of what a directly funded consortium could offer to an entire industry and its infrastructure. Even more impressive, however, was the diffuse leveraging potential offered to the entire national manufacturing sector through the multi-industry ATP's collaborative extension of the CIM Framework 1.0.

The technology road map was rapidly becoming the essential mechanism for making visible these kinds of crucial connections among various kinds of knowledge, as well as for demonstrating the interdependence of their applications. Sematech's role in helping to develop such road maps shows how far the consortium had moved beyond its original narrower goal of improving manufacturing competence through cooperation.

## The Importance of Road Maps

In retrospect, we can see how the consortium had used road maps from the very beginning as an ongoing aid to its own internal cooperation—from Obi Oberai's first consensus-building agenda road map, to the ones used to coordinate joint equipment improvement and development projects. Road maps had been used to help coordinate the consortium's ongoing PFTQ efforts with suppliers and were the basis for the 1991 planning for Sematech II. Later still, the consortium had begun participating externally in developing road maps for the larger industry picture, such as the poorly received Microtech 2000 road map of April, 1991, described earlier.

Late in 1991, the NACS, which had sponsored Microtech 2000, announced that it would disband and turned over its road-mapping function to the SIA. In November, 1992, a group of 179 representatives from the semiconductor industry, universities, the federal government, and Sematech drafted a ten-year strategic plan called the National Semiconductor Technology Roadmap (also known as the SIA Roadmap).

This national road map sought to make the best use of available U.S. resources, to rely on the existing R&D structure as much as possible to accomplish goals, and to provide focus to national semiconductor R&D efforts.[43] Although this may sound like simple common sense, it would have been quite impossible in 1987, when Sematech was founded. There had been some fundamental shifts since then.

In fact, it was in December, 1992, just a month after the SIA road-mapping committee convened, that Sematech announced the achievement of its Phase III technological milestone by its target date. The Phase III milestone involved creating .35-micron circuit features on a 200 mm silicon wafer with American-made equipment.[44] That same month, VLSI Research announced that U.S. semiconductor firms, led by Intel and Motorola, would account for 44 percent of worldwide semiconductor revenues in 1992. For the first time since 1984, Japanese companies would come in a close second, with 43 percent of the market. VLSI Research credited Sematech for some of the turnaround.[45]

These accomplishments signaled that the U.S. semiconductor industry had not only scrambled hard to catch up, it had achieved global technological parity and was beginning to regain market leadership. Each of Sematech's three milestones had been accomplished on a two-year timetable. This was faster than the typical three-year technology generation cycle[46] and gave chip makers a head start on manufacturing the new product generation.[47] Industry leaders thus felt ready to take the long strategic view rather than seek desperate short-term measures.

Their long view could now build on three major changes related, in order, to the mission goals listed above for the national road map. First, U.S. chip makers, even while developing more foreign alliances, were finally aware of their reliance on the U.S. materials and supplier infrastructure, and were committed to its health. Second, thanks to the 1989 National Competitiveness Technology Transfer Act, it had become possible to coordinate the efforts of the existing national R&D structures through CRADAs and other means. In other words, it was no longer necessary to create more new organizations in order to collaborate. Finally, although U.S. technology had been nurtured in fiercely proprietary competition, companies were learning to value the power of shared knowledge and to appreciate the fact that any collaborative work would need integration to be fully effective. Sematech, besides contributing to these shifts, was uniquely prepared to continue making them work.

In January, 1993, members from all of Sematech's FTABs, representatives from various other consortium councils, and various industry experts convened to analyze the new national road map and Sematech's role in it. Because of the cooperative practices in place, this effort had a wider scope than the 1991 internal road-map planning session for Sematech II. Bill Spencer now could write to consortium members: "Sematech has proved that government and industry can cooperate on a precompetitive basis to solve technology problems. Now we are participating in this much larger venture (the National Semiconductor Technology Roadmap) that clearly offers the U.S. an opportunity to secure its future as a technology leader and a competitive trading partner."[48]

In February, 1993, Sematech's Board of Directors also took a visible step toward full national road map participation by issuing a new mission statement that read: "Solve the technical challenges required to keep the United States number one in the global semiconductor industry." To address the new mission, the board directed Sematech's management team to broaden the consortium's charter to include the entire breakdown of the specific SIA Technology Committee road maps, and especially to work with the SIA Technology Committee to define an urgently needed national strategy for lithography. Tom Seidel was named the consortium's chief technical officer and given responsibility for coordinating Sematech's strategic plans with the SIA Roadmap.[49]

Including the entire spectrum of the national road map's concerns in Sematech's operations lifted the consortium's sights well beyond its original technology boundary of the wafer fab. The consortium had moved from focusing on better DRAM technology to improving manufacturing equipment sets or processes in partnership with suppliers to creating and inserting standardized technology for a computerized, environmentally sound, total-factory model.

Now the consortium's involvement with the National Semiconductor Technology Roadmap meant expanding the charter to incorporate the ways in which semiconductor manufacturing was related to the national resource base. It meant that planning for manufacturing productivity must recognize its interconnections not only with other parts of the microelectronics industry, but with the country's educational, economic, and political structure. Harrell notes that the semiconductor industry had reached the point in its technological maturity where further gains in productivity would no longer be driven by the diminishing returns of increased yield or equipment improvement, they would depend on other performance and economic determinants.

The wider view was not just a change in outlook, however. In practical terms, it meant including several urgent technical needs in semiconductor manufacturing named in the national road map that Sematech had not previously addressed. No fewer than five new thrust areas would have to be added to the operations side of the consortium—design, test, packaging, CAD, and critical materials—to close what Tom Seidel called Sematech's "silicon systems gap."

During this time NSC's Jim Owens was named COO. He would succeed Bill George, who was returning to Motorola as promised. Owens introduced an overarching methodology for analyzing the total cost of semiconductor production that helped to tie the new thrust areas into the consortium's total-factory orientation. Seidel says the analysis included "the cost for design, the cost for front-end processes which we have modeled, the cost to test, the cost to package. We consider those [production cost] models against a background of a factory environment and make business assumptions about the factory environment. What's the floor space? The overhead? The cost of labor? The cost of materials? From that, we derive the total [production] cost in that environment."

In late 1993, after working for several months under Seidel's direction to establish the new thrust areas, each with its own FTAB, and to tie them into the overall operation, Sematech made two significant decisions: first, to restructure the budget, and second, to reorganize all of its existing thrust areas so as to align with the national road map analyses.[50]

In August, 1993, CEO Spencer announced to the House Committee on Science and Technology that Sematech planned to request $10 million less in funding support from both the federal government and its corporate members, reducing its total 1994 budget by 10 percent to $180 million.[51] Thirty percent of the reduced budget would be applied to the new thrust areas. This financial restructuring—which apparently would accomplish more with less—was made possible by greater leveraging of existing projects by both stronger manufacturers and their healthier suppliers. Both were now able to share more of the burden of joint process and equipment projects. It was also a response to the increased external collaboration in R&D and training with other agencies, such as the national labs and the SCOEs. Sematech's thrust reorganization and budget changes portended a new direction for the consortium—away from direct dependence on government support and toward a more embedded, less singular role in the national technology sector.

## From Role Model to Role Player

Sematech II drew mixed reviews as the consortium entered into its second five-year charter. It was being praised as a model of industry-government cooperation, but it was also threatened with reduced DOD funding and increased congressional oversight. As the consortium continued to expand its external leveraging in an environment generally more favorable to new kinds of collaboration, it experienced declining political support for its status as an organization benefiting a crucial industry—especially since that industry appeared once again to be healthy.

Many members of Congress as well as some members of the Board of Directors remembered that Sematech's founders had predicted that the industry itself would eventually take over the consortium's support. These congressmen thought it was high time. But the board felt that continued government support would be needed for a while longer because the United States was still not in a competitive position in lithography and because Sematech was taking on five new thrust areas.

The consortium's 1994 federal funding approval process was stormy, even though it had slashed its own budget request by $10 million. In October, 1993, the Senate Appropriations Committee voted to freeze Sematech's $90 million in 1994 funding until the ARPA (previously known as the DARPA) approved a plan to reduce federal contributions to the consortium over the next five years. The 1993 Congress also created legislation establishing a Semiconductor Technology Council to replace the Advisory Council on Federal Participation in Sematech. The new council had a broader charter to foster cooperation between government, industry, and academia in the support of semiconductor technology development as a whole, rather than simply focusing on Sematech.[52]

Accompanying the recommended 1994 freeze in Sematech's funding was a critical report citing two reasons for the vote. The first was the unfortunate demise of GCA, a lithography stepper manufacturer. The second was Sematech's financial and technological support of SVGL, the only remaining U.S. optical lithography equipment manufacturer, because SVGL had been trying to negotiate a licensing and joint-development agreement with Japan's Canon since April, 1993.[53]

In November, 1993, President Clinton approved the final DOD appropriations bill, which restored the requested $90 million in funding. However, the report accompanying the bill also warned that the government probably "will not be able to sustain the level of investment that has been made in the past."[54] The handwriting on the wall grew darker and clearer. In large part due to Sematech's efforts, there was greater awareness of the need to maintain the health of crucial national technologies, as well as a political environment more favorable to effective industry-government-academic collaboration toward this end. Ironically, Sematech's own accomplishments were helping to create a situation in which the semiconductor industry might be expected to compete for CRADA-type funding along with other groups, rather than receiving direct support for the consortium.

## Too Far Ahead

Early in 1994, Vice Pres. Al Gore unveiled a new White House technology plan. Reassuringly, the semiconductor research part of the plan included continuing funding for Sematech II. It also called for the establishment of a national semiconductor metrology program, with oversight to be provided by the Semiconductor Technology Council. The council was supposed to replace the Advisory Council on Federal Participation in Sematech at the end of 1993, but no members were appointed to serve on it until late 1994.

Meanwhile, Sematech was headed toward completing another accelerated two-year milestone—a microchip with .25-micron line-width features—by the end of 1994, and was well into the planning for the next generation of .18-micron chips. In June, 1994, Sematech representatives joined with three hundred semiconductor industry experts in Boulder, Colorado, to update the 1992 National Semiconductor Technology Roadmap. Drawing on the information and experience gained from using the first road map, the final draft of the new one, released in November, had a fifteen-year horizon.[55] Publication of this more comprehensive road map created some interesting effects.

First, it was published in the public domain, which meant that foreign competitors had access to the information. According to Seidel: "The advantage of having a national technology road map is that we can all rally to that and focus our resources and be very efficient to achieve just that. Of course, the disadvantage to going public with it is that you arm your competitors with your schedule and your capabilities, and then they are positioned to beat it."

The road map thus was a calculated risk. The timetable also undermined the assumption that Sematech's accelerated generation cycle-time offered the industry an advantage. In fact, the multilevel, interdependent factors of the road map showed that Sematech's milestone demonstrations were outpacing both member companies' business cadence and their readiness to use the new technology. The board acknowledged this fact by voting to go off the two-year cycle and spend an additional year perfecting the .25-micron tool set and processes. This took some pressure off the consortium while at the same time putting pressure on the industry to execute the new generation on time.[56]

## New Life, Not Eternal Life

In October, 1994, shortly after Congress approved the ARPA's FY 1995 funding request, the board decided to forgo federal funding altogether. This stunning decision took everyone by surprise. The *New York Times* report captures the essence of the public's reaction to the news: "Eternal life is one feature of federal programs we have come to expect. So it was a shock last week when a consortium of semiconductor companies volunteered to give up a $90 million-a-year federal subsidy." The article carried this explanation from Bill Spencer: "The industry can now afford to support the consortium and we should. We are setting an example for other U.S. industries and for the world. We never intended direct federal funding to become an entitlement program."[57]

Sematech's board decided to seize the initiative and act from a position of strength while it still enjoyed White House support—which was more wholehearted under President Clinton than that of his Republican predecessors. The decision also gave the consortium time to plan ahead. After FY 1996, Sematech would continue to operate with member companies supplying $90 million each year, but at that point the consortium would begin competing with other agencies for federal research grants to replace the previously appropriated congressional funds.[58]

The DOD, through ARPA, had been consulted on the board's decision and agreed with it. However, Sematech would still need the yearly $90 million ARPA grant through 1996 to complete the technology programs already underway and to ensure a smooth transition into the consortium's next phase of industry-government collaboration. Any reduction in Sematech's funding would disrupt the program and significantly delay its technology goals.

Until then, said Spencer: "The member companies are fully committed to continuing the consortium and have pledged to match the fiscal year 1996 federal grant dollar-for-dollar just as they have always done. After 1996 the member companies will directly fund Sematech's operational costs and will continue to send their most talented engineers to Austin to work on R&D projects that will benefit the semiconductor industry, the equipment industry and the federal government."[59]

The decision to renounce federal grant money won Sematech praise for being a role model for specifically targeted collaboration that would depart from the public trough as soon as possible. The truth was larger than that, however. Although most observers recognized the vital role that Sematech's unique collaboration had played in the U.S. semiconductor industry's recovery, the national road map showed that the consortium's efforts alone would not suffice. Without wider leverage of the nation's resource base than even a well-supported consortium could provide, the U.S. semiconductor industry could not remain competitive.

Thus Sematech, rather than fading away as an historical artifact, as a singular role model for industry-government cooperation, had steadily transformed itself into an ensemble player. It increasingly acted as what Harrell called the "communication vehicle" for the synchronized nationwide development among semiconductor-makers, in coordination with their equipment and materials suppliers, of the cadence plotted on the National Semiconductor Technology Roadmap.

Sematech's leaders intended to expand, not to end, public-private collaboration. Since the consortium would be competing for research grants for specific projects in the same manner as other groups and companies, it was entirely possible it might receive more than the annual ARPA grant. Beyond that, however, in its new role as broker for shared knowledge, Sematech intended to influence a broader spectrum of government spending than ever before, including research programs in the Commerce and Energy Departments as well as in the Pentagon. At this point, as CAO Frank Squires said, "There is little possibility of the semiconductor industry reverting to its traditional arms-length and sometimes adversarial relationship with the federal government."[60]

This final collaborative transformation of Sematech was a far cry from the first unfamiliar steps toward cooperation taken in 1987 by fierce industry competitors suspicious of government partnership. Sematech's own change reflected the changes often laboriously wrought in the national attitude during that period: an appreciation of the value of sharing knowledge and working together, as well as the realization that cooperative productivity could be gained without sacrificing the competitive drive for individual excellence that is so deeply embedded in the American ethic.

America's chip manufacturing industry would never be the same.

## CHAPTER 9

# Learning from the Sematech Experiment

*1987 to the Future*

**B**y 1994, Sematech was operating in a much different environment than the one from which it had emerged in 1987. Fast-moving technological advances, market ups and downs, and political shifts had combined to alter the domestic and global climate in which the American semiconductor industry and its supplier infrastructure were starting to show unmistakable signs of recovery.

One of the most important changes in the United States during this period was a growing appreciation of the rewards of industrial cooperation, especially when faced with the rising costs of high-technology production and increasing global competition. Previously unthinkable forms of collaboration and partnership were starting to become more common in America.

As a highly visible public-private consortium in which competitors cooperated horizontally with each other, partnered vertically with their suppliers, and collaborated with academia and national laboratories, Sematech had helped to create this new cooperative environment. The achievements of its submicron feature goals and joint equipment projects had helped manufacturers and their suppliers to raise core manufacturing competence and to improve processes and equipment, thus enabling the United States to maintain or set the pace of technological advances. The National Semiconductor Technology Roadmap brokered by the consortium represented the synchronization of national resources enabled by such collaboration.

However, just as it would be a mistake to give Sematech the credit for causing all the improvements in the U.S. semiconductor industry's environment or in its competitiveness during this period of rapid change, it would be equally wrong to dismiss the consortium as just one of many participants in the latest management trend. Sematech created a historic role for itself as its members learned by working together to rescue a faltering industry and reconnect it with its splintered infrastructure. The important question is: How can the consortium's unique contributions be identified and what lessons can be learned before the organization is overtaken by the collaborative tide it helped generate?

The consortium's measurable achievements lie in the three areas of interaction mentioned at the beginning of the story. They include Sematech's successful management of horizontal and vertical collaboration, which generated formal and informal cooperative networks nationwide; the maturing nature of its relations with the government, going from being a recipient of direct DOD aid to being the independent broker, sponsor, and/or partner of joint projects with various government agencies; and the accomplishment of the consortium's submicron phase goals, as well as its many equipment and process improvement projects.

The chronological, political, and technological circumstances in which these achievements were reached provide an illuminating context for understanding the significance of the lessons that emerge.

## Signs of Recovery

Recall that in 1980 the U.S. semiconductor manufacturing industry still controlled about 60 percent of the world market it had invented, but Japan was swiftly catching up. Then came the disastrous years of 1984–86, remembered as a "blood bath,"[1] and a "catastrophe" for American chip makers.[2] By 1988, the U.S. share of the world market had dipped to 43 percent, trailing behind the Japanese at 46 percent.[3] Sematech was founded in 1987, but the Japanese continued to gain, adding two more points to their market-share advantage in 1988.[4] The U.S. equipment infrastructure was also sinking on the charts as Japanese capital equipment producers tripled their equipment-making world market share to 40 percent from 1980 to 1988.[5]

By 1991, however, not only had the downward trend for U.S. semiconductor makers halted, but their market share had begun to rise again, for the first time since 1979.[6] By the end of 1992, American microchip makers had regained the lead in world market share,[7] and, despite new competition from countries like Korea, U.S. semiconductor manufacturers were confident they would control about half the growing $77.3 billion global semiconductor market by the end of that year.[8] Indeed, by the time Bill Spencer made his 1994 announcement of Sematech's planned independence from government funding, it was reported that the United States was providing 48 percent of the world's semiconductors compared to Japan's 36 percent.[9] American semiconductor market figures, whether reported in terms of production or of revenue, showed significant increase.

## Equipment Makers Recover

This pattern of dramatic recovery following a serious threat to survival was repeated in the semiconductor equipment-manufacturing sector. According to VLSI Research, between the years 1983 and 1990 American equipment makers' share of the world market dropped steadily, from 66 percent to 44 percent, as Japan took the lead.[10] However, by the end of 1991, U.S. suppliers were starting to pull ahead of Japan.[11]

By 1993, U.S. chip-making equipment sales had ballooned, valued at an estimated $6 billion—an 18 percent increase. At the same time, Japan's share of the market sank from 45 percent in 1991 to 41 percent in 1993. Europe and the rest of the world accounted for the other 8 percent.[12] By mid-1994, Intel, one of Sematech's most supportive members, had become the world's largest microchip manufacturer, and an American supplier, Applied Materials, was the world's largest semiconductor tool manufacturer.[13]

All of this prompted Jim Norling, president and general manager of Motorola's semiconductor business, to claim: "Sematech is the enabler of the U.S. semiconductor manufacturing resurgence." Papken Der Terossian, chairman of SVGL, an equipment manufacturer involved in Sematech research and development projects, added: "It would not be an understatement to say that Sematech saved the [semiconductor equipment manufacturing] industry." Others offered more qualified praise, saying that the consortium's most valuable role was as a catalyst or clearinghouse to get manufacturers and their suppliers talking and working together on common problems.[14]

## Other Strategic Factors

Several other helpful factors occurring between 1986 and 1994 are important to note. First was the SIA-sponsored 1986 Semiconductor Trade Agreement with Japan, aimed at stopping the dumping of cheap DRAM chips on the market and giving the idea of a manufacturing consortium a chance to work. Several related trends also weakened Japan's relative advantage: Korea's emergence as a strong DRAM competitor, Japan's recession in the early and mid-nineties, and the accompanying rise in the yen's value and the price of Japanese exports. Another important element sustaining the U.S. microchip market was the continued American domination of the global personal computer market.

In hindsight, it is clear that many factors influenced the U.S. semiconductor industry's recovery. However, their effects could not have been foreseen, and without Sematech, weakened U.S. chip makers might have been too enfeebled to exploit factors favorable to themselves or to help their suppliers. The consortium's dynamic ability to turn historical trends, politico-economic shifts, and technological circumstances to shared advantage arose from its blend of managed collaboration, public-private cooperation, and commitment to the mutual improvement of core manufacturing competencies and quality.

## Why Sematech Worked

Sematech was an experiment that not only had to work, it had to produce new kinds of knowledge in order to work. The most significant knowledge emerging from the Sematech experiment was the hands-on collective learning about what it takes for competitors to cooperate productively. Specifically, the consortium demonstrated that:

1. Sematech members were willing to change.
2. Sematech members reduced interfirm secrecy.
3. Sematech solved problems with facts and information.
4. Sematech continuously reapplied the cooperative model.
5. Sematech accomplished specific, agreed-upon goals.
6. Sematech members avoided "sandbagging."
7. Sematech leveraged continuous learning.
8. The microchip industry profited by helping itself.
9. The amount of the investment was too big to dismiss.
10. The organization was the optimal size.
11. Leaders were willing to contribute without the assurance of direct payback.
12. Founding members brought with them the confidence of previous success.

Our analysis shows that these twelve principles break down into three areas of experience that overlap in practice. First is the day-to-day operation of the consortium, where people from many different backgrounds learned to work together in an unaccustomed setting. Second is the new organizational design and structure needed to support the unusual nature of the daily operations. Third is the most fundamental of all: the moral vision and code that transformed the idea of making a concerted effort for survival into an ideal of expanding cooperation. This code shaped the development and direction of a new kind of organization, one that not only benefited its own members in the short term but eventually extended the benefits of collaboration in many directions, thus widening and strengthening the economic security of future American generations.[15]

## The Operational Arena

Our discussion of the list of principles explaining why Sematech worked begins with the lessons that emerged from the day-to-day efforts in the operational arena.

## Sematech Members Were Willing to Change

The most important and timely success factor mentioned by everyone involved in Sematech is that unprecedented cooperation among competitors requires an absolute belief in the necessity for collective action—a commonly held conviction that without hanging together, each will surely hang separately. In Sematech's case that conviction was a widely held view that the industry's survival was gravely endangered, and with it, the nation's economic and military independence.

In an evaluative report on Sematech submitted to Congress in 1993, supplier executive Scott Kulicke, an early SEMI/Sematech representative on the consortium's board, made this point: "For these (collaborative) programs to work, they must be supported by a national consensus that transcends partisan bickering or bureaucratic turf wars or interagency spats. One of the lessons our Japanese friends have taught us is that success in this sort of endeavor is based on a collective will to succeed."[16]

Entailed in the collective will to succeed is the willingness to change. For competitive U.S. chip makers, joining forces to work together was already such a large change that the need to change their internal practices was not immediately clear. However, without the added willingness to reevaluate and change their own operations as needed, cooperation among the major semiconductor makers would not have ensured their survival, even with government help. The added commitment of members to change themselves individually *and* collectively at once made the consortium's agenda setting more relevant to members' own strategies and more difficult to agree upon. A common principle to guide collective and individual change was needed.

Sam Harrell remembers that this principle emerged from discussions between Sematech and SEMI/Sematech leaders: "There was a real conscious effort to go through the key issues and say, 'What do we have to change to get more effective here?' Out of that came one standard that has stuck with us through the remaining years. That is: 'If it is not competitive, it has to change.' That's just a small phrase, but it was a very empowering phrase. The first empowerment was the decision to try. The second empowerment was the [planning] workshops, which said, 'Try to do what?' Out of that, we have seen some dramatic changes occur—changes in things that were their practices for a very long time, very dear to their hearts."

## Sematech Members Reduced Interfirm Secrecy

An important early change occurred when consortia assignees began working in regular, direct contact with each other in Austin. They quickly developed insights from their workbench communication that helped to overcome the greatest barrier to interfirm cooperation. The more assignees from different parent firms talked with each other, the more they realized that many of their difficulties were rooted in a lack of communication rather than poor technology. This realization had previously been masked by a self-deluding sense of proprietorship regarding manufacturing practices. As members soon discovered, "The biggest secret is that there is no secret."

April Schweighart, director of Motorola's manufacturing technology group in Austin, tells what this change was like: "Joining a consortium can be an eye-opening experience. The perception of who is ahead on certain technologies may be all wrong. . . . Secrets we thought we had, everybody had. Now we understand what proprietary information we really have."

This early insight at Sematech penetrated all levels of collaboration. Peter Mills, the consortium's first CAO, remembers: "One of the things that we learned at Sematech early on was that all of the secrets we were keeping from each other were basically the same secrets. We discovered that, while there was an awful lot of artful dancing going on to find out as much information as possible from the other guy without giving him any information, there weren't really a lot of true secrets."

Mills credits Turner Hasty, then the consortium's director of research, with identifying the problem: "He recognized what was going on and just put it on the table. 'Guys, the secrets we are keeping from each other are all the same secrets.' Within the first year, that was pretty well resolved, and the rate of productivity increased dramatically."

Eventually, the line between what was and what was not secret was drawn between what could and could not be legally collaborated on—that is, between competitive and precompetitive practices. The prohibited areas of competitive collaboration were related to proprietary product and marketing issues. Legally allowed precompetitive collaboration involved core competencies or generic manufacturing process issues. The approximate proportions of the two types of information were eventually discovered to be a surprising 85 percent generic to 15 percent proprietary.[17]

The emerging recognition, through cooperation, of so much common ground led to a clearer focus on the location of interfirm competitiveness. Frank Squires, Sematech's CAO under Bill Spencer, puts it this way:

> The industry needed to get clear about where each company added its competitive edge or value to products. Some members seemed to believe that manufacturing was part of their value-add to competitiveness. After they were marinated in Sematech for a while they began to understand that world-class manufacturing was an enabler. You either could do it or you were out of the game. Competitive advantage beyond that, for example, in design or customer requirements, goes on only after you are able to make a cost-effective, reliable product. The 80 percent of the semiconductor industry who are our members now understand quite clearly where the line is between precompetitive and competitive technology issues. As a result, the amount of information that they are comfortable sharing has increased dramatically.

"The biggest secret is the one everybody knows" thus became an early say-ing at the consortium.[18] This discovery underscored the unwelcome recognition that U.S. market vulnerability lay in the area of quality manufacturing skills. More importantly, it also meant that addressing core manufacturing compe-tence collectively could raise the competitiveness of the entire industry simulta-neously, without destroying any firm's proprietary advantage.

This lesson was not an abstract issue to the assignees from rival firms who were brought face-to-face daily at Sematech's fab. Squires notes: "It is remark-able to find engineers from AMD and Intel working side-by-side on a deposi-tion tool improvement program while their two corporations sue each other in court left and right about the rights to manufacturing the 386 and the 486 [microchips]." The ability to compartmentalize, to be able to function in differ-ent areas, was an important skill at Sematech.

### Sematech Solved Problems with Facts and Information

Meanwhile, the new openness to change and information sharing made pos-sible the ongoing redefinition of consortium goals through more effective plan-ning and collaborative problem solving. Sematech's first technology road map, which collected information on chip makers' needs, had to be carefully format-ted to mask the identity of corporate informants. This contrasts strongly with the 1992 development of Sematech's newly equitable operating plan for sched-uled projects, based on members' technology choices in relation to their own disclosures of the dollar amounts of their return on consortium investment.

There is also a big difference between the early difficulties of setting up the fab with equipment provided by isolated suppliers who were kept in the dark by rival chip makers and the later openness about mutual supply requirements and equipment standardization made possible through the equipment qualifi-cation and supplier partnering programs.

Sam Harrell points out the parallels between Sematech's internal shift to-ward sharing information horizontally among members and its sharing of information vertically with suppliers through partnering. He notes that the "Partnering for Total Quality program allowed both sides to change, learn to communicate in new ways, to shift to management by data, and to continue these improvements."

Sematech's mission changed repeatedly over the years as more openly shared information became available for tackling problems, and the ability to apply this data to new problems and opportunities grew apace. As AMD's Dick Deininger observed, "One of the crucial features of Sematech was its ability to reinvent itself several times."

### Sematech Continuously Reapplied the Cooperative Model

Once Sematech developed a cooperative system, the organization leveraged the model into as many other areas of influence and kinds of projects as possible—

from disseminating software programs for designing chips and monitoring fab production to helping broker an international agreement on the standardization of the next generation's larger (300 mm) silicon wafer. Bill Spencer described the benefits of cooperating on the wafer change in this way: "This has been an important meeting, because we must have consensus on the next wafer size and also an international standard for those wafers. The (costly) transition will never take place unless there are standards, and a proven cost advantage, which is what these task forces can achieve." Previous wafer size increases had been individually pursued for competitive advantage, but they had become too costly for a single firm to risk alone. The financial benefit from advancing at this high technological level could only be realized through cooperation and standardization.

While Bill George was Sematech's COO, he noted: "The consortium amplified its accomplishments by reimplementing them elsewhere. One thing that I think is very important is the fact that there are two hundred assignees collocated on this site, so you get to work with people from all the other member companies every day for a multiyear assignment. It is an experience that you can't get any other way. It teaches you what you can work together on, it builds a network. The Sematech alumni do network a lot after they go back home. If they have problems, they'll call up a guy that they worked with down here for two years that is in a different company."

Because assignments were typically for two years, a network of Sematech alumni quickly grew. Most had never previously had the chance to know anyone working on similar projects outside their own firms. The trust that these coworkers developed was grounded in a shared conviction of the mutual benefit to be gained from cooperation, reinforced by their personal association. On an individual level, assignees previously steeped in competitive secrecy and adherence to antitrust prohibitions learned that loyalty to their parent firms could be honorably and legally complemented by loyalty to a cooperative purpose.

The benefits of working so openly together eventually extended into the new kinds of quality partnering developed at Sematech between chip makers and their equipment suppliers. They developed supportive relationships that often brought suppliers into the chip makers' facilities, especially during the equipment installation phase, to ensure proper qualification and operation of manufacturing tools. This practice had long been standard in Japanese firms, but America's culture of secrecy and suspicion had previously prevented it.

According to Squires: "I think it is one of the biggest lessons to come out of Sematech. The notion of companies being competitors and cooperating at the same time is not something that comes naturally in our culture or our legal system. The fact that these companies have come together under the umbrella of Sematech and have learned how to do that is quite important." Once people came together, working elbow-to-elbow, one lesson led to another. The discovery of holding common problems in secret reinforced the needed lesson of the importance of improving the industry's core manufacturing skills in close alliance with equipment makers.

Learning to work together on common manufacturing problems produced what many consider to be Sematech's most valuable lesson of all. As Bob Galvin puts it: "Competitors are discovering we like to work with each other. We can do it honorably, in a fashion that is good for our profession, that is good for our industry."[19]

## Sematech Accomplished Specific, Agreed-Upon Goals

Even as the consortium's mission expanded and the organization adapted to its broader scope, the original technological time line remained steady enough so that work progress could be measured and managed. The most visible example of this is the phased planning for reducing the size of chip features. The phase time line remained sufficiently specific that technological progress and achievement were possible to monitor, even as the consortium's overall mission expanded to include the infrastructure.

This level of goal clarity is essential for determining the performance of the management group. As Bill Spencer said, "There has to be proper management in place at the consortium to reach goals, the people who represent the company need a good vision of what they want, and I can't stress enough the importance of milestones along the way to measure progress."

A good example of the usefulness of setting clear goals was that goal clarity helped make it possible to continually redefine the narrow, moving, line between cooperation and competition for consortia members. As fabrication costs continued to rise, so did the willingness to see broader commonalties in core manufacturing processes, as well as to specify a narrower focus on proprietary products.

"Sematech has been successful because it focuses on problems that are fundamental to the industry, but do not involve the 'crown jewels' of the member companies," according to John Preston, MIT's director of technology development. "Collaboration on such critical technologies is nearly impossible because communication is stilted at best." The ability to pose and resolve questions the members had in common while simultaneously holding private their distinctive competence could only happen when the need to change and the need to be specific about what was to change were being addressed simultaneously.

As Robert Galvin, Sematech's chairman of the board, succinctly sums it up: "Cooperation has to be about something." Selecting MDVs and having specific technology goals provided activities in which technological projects could be developed and milestones by which their progress could be measured.

## Sematech Members Avoided "Sandbagging"

"Sandbagging" is a sandlot term for giving less than one's best performance. Individual Sematech firms avoided the temptation to engage in this insidious form of competition. Although the financial obligations of membership were clearly spelled out, members could have withheld resources by sending mediocre assignees to the consortium. This practice would have given a firm a comparative advantage over other members by keeping its best talent back home in production, the very part of the business in which competition was most fierce. But just as Sematech enjoyed proactive senior leadership, its member firms also avoided the kind of silent treachery that would most quickly and easily undermine cooperation and sabotage the consortium's effectiveness.

Intel's COO, Dr. Craig Barrett, advised against sandbagging: "Companies may not be inclined to put the people fundamental to the success of their operation in this environment, especially if it might help competitors. Because it is precompetitive research, the tendency is 'out of sight, out of mind.' It will only work if you invest your very best people."

However, it was hard advice to follow, according to IBM's Sandy Kane: "If the guy is that terrific [to be needed at Sematech], you can't afford to let him go." Nevertheless, Charlie Sporck said: "We [at NSC] are going to put in something like $10 or $12 million [into Sematech]. It would be insanity to do that without putting in good people along with it. We would have to be awful damn stupid to put in that kind of money and not put in good people." Members understood that to withhold talent would be self-defeating.

One of the early problems with MCC, Sematech's predecessor consortium, had been the dearth of qualified assignees provided by member firms. This forced MCC to hire a majority of its technical talent from outside the consortium. Sematech feels strongly that its success at recruiting member firm representatives to staff the consortium was related to the probability that the solutions generated at Sematech would be desired, adopted, and implemented by member companies.

### Sematech Leveraged Continuous Learning

Sematech was constantly importing members' learning and then continuously changing as it incorporated that learning. Sematech did not have time to develop its own organizational R&D base before launching into its urgent mission. The consortium emerged from the SIA forum, drew its members from the SIA, and then drew on their organizational knowledge. Member firms contributed more than dues and personnel, they supplied the consortium with their technological expertise and organizational practices and received an amplification of their contributed learning in return. Says Craig Barrett: "We want to get at least $2 worth of knowledge for every $1 we put into Sematech. It's always difficult to evaluate this, but so far we're not disappointed."

Some of the learning contributions were very specific gifts, such as the equipment qualification process that Dean Toombs brought with him from Intel. Many other operational contributions simply arrived with the ongoing influx of assignees, in the form of their own skills, or their parent corporation's own practices. For instance, Intel assignees brought their custom of engaging in constructive confrontation—that is, challenging anyone's concepts, at any level, in a strictly nonpersonal manner. Some assignees found constructive confrontation irritating at first, but they soon came to value and use the practice themselves.

There is a long list of other member firms' "best practices" that were deliberately imported, beginning with the very first MDV process brought from IBM in 1988 by Obi Oberai. These practices usually came with an incoming expert from the contributing firm. For example, Jim Owens, who succeeded Bill George as Sematech COO in 1994, introduced a methodology used at NSC for analyzing capital productivity. This procedure helped Sematech synchronize its technological developments in response to the rapidly shifting demands of the industry's business cadence. All member assignees engaged in the process took their participatory learning back to their parent firms.

Sematech thus drew on all members' contributions to produce learning for its own operations, as well as to spread learning back to members with returning assignees. The consortium initially attempted to accomplish the difficult task of transferring knowledge gained from projects through the dissemination of reports, but found that the paper transfer was ineffective. With lowering barriers of secrecy and increasing supplier partnering, actual *insertion* of technology into member companies' facilities became the consortium's standard for successful technology transfer, requiring off-site collaboration of teams within member and/or supplier firms.

Sematech also used contributed and developed learning to transform itself repeatedly. A glance at the consortium's mission statements shows that a new statement came out about every two years, reflecting the organization's constantly changing goals in response to the environment while it was affecting that environment. Sematech's expanding sphere of influence through its increasing numbers of joint projects with the supplier infrastructure and with university research and national laboratories, exemplify its own leveraged learning. Member firms leveraged their learning as assignees circulated through the consortium and also through inserted technology transferred from consortium projects.

## The Structural Arena

Knowledge gained from these geographical dispersions also belongs to the structural arena. While Austin remained Sematech's central location, joint equipment projects increasingly began to take place off site in member firms' fabs. National lab and university connections, as well as the PFTQ program also helped Sematech to geographically extend the leverage of its own and its members' learning.

## The Microchip Industry Profited By Helping Itself

During the precipitous U.S. semiconductor market plunge in the mid-1980s that triggered fears of American dependency on foreign supply, the Defense Science Board recommended some sort of concerted action but the federal government had no structure upon which to build collaboration. The semiconductor industry's SIA already existed as a forum where senior leaders could discuss nonproprietary issues and speak with a single voice on trade or other concerns.

Clark McFadden remembers the SIA's role as being fundamental. He says: "Had it not been that the industry at the same time came to essentially the same conclusion as the Defense study, this would probably have had the same fate as countless other studies: 'It is an interesting study; thank you very much.' Then it disappears." Thus, when the DSB's recommendation came, it bolstered industry members' resolve to work together to avert the fate they believed awaited them.

That the industry stood ready to help itself is shown by the personal involvement of senior executives who championed a collaborative effort. The all-consuming work of structuring a collaborative organization in one hectic year, obtaining widespread industry support, and obtaining government authorization and support was accomplished by the industry's top leaders.

McFadden remembers watching them operate: "Top industry leaders were instrumental in it. People of the stature of Bob Noyce and others brought a sense of credibility and confidence to the whole effort. It wasn't left to lieutenants in the company, but senior executives and managers themselves got intimately involved. That gave it a visibility and a sense of credibility that was quite unusual in Washington." The message was that you could not help an industry that does not want to help itself, and this industry did.[20]

This lesson is not as simple as having good timing, exploiting a moment of convergence of industry and government concern. It was a case of the industry having the long-term will and the means to make that convergence work. Organizational commitment came from the SIA, while seasoned executives in the major U.S. microchip makers provided time, effort, and individual company resources. Committed industry resources included the ongoing supply of top-caliber assignees from member firms, sufficient to largely staff the consortium.

The SIA forum was extended as a collaborative instrument, negotiating authorization and support from the government from its own turf to win grant funding, rather than being saddled with meddlesome project oversight. The SIA also provided a nexus for consortium planning and formation. Industry leaders even supplied office space before a site was chosen, and assumed Sematech's total financial support until the promised federal funds arrived.

Finally, even after collaborating with the government, the industry proved its continued eagerness to help itself by moving to wean itself from direct government support as the industry recovered strength, rather than allowing itself to stagnate into permanent dependency.

## The Amount of the Investment Was Too Big to Dismiss

The amount of the resources being invested was too great for member firms to dismiss lightly, or to treat Sematech as a token project. It encouraged members to synchronize their industrial cadence with the consortium's technological time line. The companies that have realized the most benefit from Sematech, believes CAO Frank Squires, have done so by integrating the plan for the consortium's activities directly into their own research plans.

Says Squires: "If the Sematech projects are off to the side, something you don't really rely on, it will hold you back from getting the most out of the relationship. It's like paying your tuition for college and then not attending class. I believe that the forced interaction that Sematech brings to it—that is, that the companies put enough money into it that they can't ignore it and so they send all these assignees down here and therefore the interaction continues—is crucial to the continued interaction of the companies. I believe that if you did away with Sematech and we didn't have a group of people who work in it and the companies weren't putting their money into it, they would quickly revert to the behavior patterns of the past. I really believe that. I think there needs to be some glue to hold it together, and I think Sematech is that glue."

## The Organization Was the Optimal Size

There is always a question about the optimal size for a collective operation. An effort must be large enough to encompass a sizable part of the system it intends to affect, yet laboratory research shows that the larger a system gets, the harder it is to achieve agreement.[21] At Sematech's beginning it was estimated that fairly high membership dues were needed to accomplish the task at hand. Smaller microchip makers complained that the hefty dues structure was prohibitive for them and favored the large, wealthy firms, thus limiting access and making the consortium a rich-boy's club. Nineteen eighty-seven was a hard time in the ailing industry, and Sematech members also had to commit to sending paid assignees, which was proportionately more difficult for small firms. Smaller firms who managed to cough up the membership investment still feared that larger members' agendas would override the smaller firms' needs, lowering the value of what they could expect in return for their contributions.

In spite of the criticisms, it turned out that requiring a considerable financial investment encouraged firms to remain involved with the operation, and to send highly qualified assignees in order to get their money's worth. However, some firms did not renew their membership when their initial commitment expired because they felt the return was inadequate. Even then, the percentage of the U.S. industry involved in the consortium never dropped below 75 percent.

It soon became apparent that the motivation of a large investment would erode without a better supporting mechanism. Sematech thus developed an agenda-setting method based on representation rather than a majority vote.

The new method involved each member—small or large—in the planning projects and assignee choices. This goal-setting procedure was tied directly to individual company needs, to a demonstration of their own ROI calculation, and to the expertise of the assignees they sent.

Under Bill Spencer's leadership, member-defined ROI became the criterion driving the agenda and was used to determine the relative sizes of projects and the use of assignees. The principle of return on every member's investment rewarded their loyalty and opened up greater opportunities for leveraging external resources, such as supplier agreements. Sematech learned that a contribution too large to ignore was a good founding idea, but that it required a mechanism for fairly distributing benefits to maintain incentives for collaborating. This allowed the consortium's size to become a practical effect of fair cooperation rather than an externally imposed ideal.

Bill George sums up the lessons learned about the relation of size to member ROI in this way: "The conclusion we finally drew was that Sematech should be as big as it can be and provide a better return on investment than other potential uses companies have for their funds. That seems to be an obvious answer, but that's the fact. If Sematech can provide a return on $20 million, then it shouldn't be bigger than that. If it can provide a return on $1 billion, it ought to be that big. If it is the best investment for the companies to make, that's how big it ought to be."

## The New Moral Vision and Code

The final, most encompassing arena of learning from experience was the new moral vision and code formed during Sematech's early development, and which continued to expand. This vision grew to mean the increasing inclusion of all of the industry's connections in its efforts to improve everyone's bottom line and not just the members' own. The moral code called for cooperation in improving the situation for the industry's supplier infrastructure, for aiding research in universities and national laboratories, and for supporting the interconnectedness of the American economy and national security with global prosperity.

As mentioned in the first operational lesson above, the willingness to change was basic to managing a cooperative venture among competitors. This new willingness to cooperate was a sound business decision that also reflected a change of heart in an industry that had come to be noted for ruthless competition. It did not mean giving up the drive to succeed, but it did require a reassessment of values: a realization of the vulnerability that could be created by pursuing win/lose values as well as a moral commitment to adopting win/win values as a better way of doing business. This commitment not only supplied Sematech with its original vision, its implications led directly to the consortium's decision to include supporting the recovery of the supplier infrastructure in its efforts to ensure the semiconductor industry's survival.

Expansion of the consortium's mission to focus on supplier recovery also represents a kind of learning leverage, as described above in both the operational and structural lessons. The moral lessons and rewards of expanding horizontal cooperation were leveraged into the wider domain of vertical cooperation with the supplier infrastructure as well.

The third operational lesson discussed above, solving problems with information and data, also required commitment to a shift in vision. While this kind of problem solving may sound like a narrower focus, it demanded an honest self-assessment and a willingness to respond to difficult data in a shared environment by not superimposing proprietary solutions on what might otherwise be perceived as private problems.

In addition to these characteristics that the arena of moral learning shared with the operational and structural arenas, two other important lessons emerged from Sematech's experience.

### Leaders Were Willing to Contribute without the Assurance of Direct Payback

Sematech participants, both at the individual and member firm levels, had the vision and enlightened self-interest to be willing to support the consortium above and beyond what they could individually expect to get back from their investments. High-level contributions are the essence of leadership at Sematech.

The long string of individuals who made these contributions is a continuous link of extraordinary efforts. They are exemplified by Sporck's dedicated drive at the beginning, Noyce's crucial impetus at the go/no-go point, and Spencer's insightful initiative for establishing a sound business basis for the consortium when it was in danger of foundering after Noyce's death.

These leaders and many others set the tone for cooperation in the organization. Interviews with participants revealed an implicit knowledge that most representatives knew who was contributing the most to make Sematech succeed. The high visibility of this culture of contribution made it influential. A sequence of three positive responses to interaction is considered enough to bring potential doubters to cooperation in social science experiments. Given the altruistic examples set by the industry's senior leaders, it is not hard to understand the positive effect that these individual and corporate efforts had on the rest of the semiconductor industry.

### Founding Members Brought with Them the Confidence of Previous Success

The U.S. semiconductor industry, although it had fallen on hard times, still had members that were blessed with the talent, resources, experience, and confidence needed to explore innovative solutions. Necessity may be the mother of invention, but the ability to approach managerial and technical problems also comes from those who have sufficient resources to commit to solving them.[22] While global competition had raised the specter of the gallows, U.S. chip makers' recent experience of world leadership in a technology they had invented was not so far in the past that company representatives were devoid of energy or ideas. Their sense of self-esteem and conviction of their own worth was a valuable and unexhausted resource.

Those in the industry and government who promoted the creation of Sematech had an excellent sense of timing. Conditions were dire enough that the continued trend of lost market share was painful, but the initiative was begun at a time when creativity and hard work could still solve the problem. Market figures since 1987 suggest that Intel, which provided much of the talent and ideas that helped shape Sematech's direction, may have also gained the most from the collaboration. However, interviews with Intel representatives consistently show that they believed Sematech offered them the chance to impact the whole industry through sharing their firm's special attributes. A fundamental rule of innovation is that those who try new things tend to be those who believe they can afford to experiment.

The reciprocal side to industry support for the consortium was the government's contribution, inspired by the high level of industry participation to show an unusual amount of confidence in the project—enough, in fact, to restrain itself from micromanaging it to death. Many of the member companies had previous experience contracting for government production and knew firsthand the dampening effects of inspectors on an operation's external approval chains.

Sematech took on a specific goal and, while asking for the government to support that goal, negotiated for the flexibility to arrive at its own solution for goal achievement without stifling oversight. DARPA, which was responsible for overseeing the government's participation in Sematech, while holding appropriate leverage through its control over the release of authorized funds, had only a nonvoting seat on the consortium's Board of Directors.

## Conclusion: No Blueprint

Although the lessons gained from experience at Sematech were continually translated into new knowledge for the industry, the consortium had no blueprint to follow. It simply invented and reinvented itself, shaping and responding to its environment as it went. This means that the most valuable lesson of all is that the consortium's experience offers insights into the process of how competitors learned to cooperate, rather than a specific formula of success for others to follow.

The insights of Sematech's major practical lessons are rooted in a few abstract principles. These include being open to ongoing self-assessment and willing to change, the recognition of long-term interdependence for survival, the importance of hearing every voice, the necessity of continually learning from learning, and the moral conviction of the win/win rewards of systematically expanding mutual support.

In different circumstances and contexts these principles would undoubtedly result in applications and collaborative configurations that would look much different than Sematech. A consortium founded and operating on the very same principles in 1994 would surely look different from the Sematech that was born in 1987, and just as surely would embark on its own unique history.

The real significance of Sematech is that it played a unique role in the recovery of a crucial U.S. industry through the cooperation of competitors with each other and with their previously scattered and angry infrastructure. In some incalculable way attributable largely to Sematech, between 1987 and 1994 the U.S. semiconductor industry and its supplier infrastructure went from an unhealthy climate of cutthroat domestic competition to a robust condition of synchronized, cooperative, global competitiveness. In doing so, it resumed its world leadership in semiconductor market share.

This shared recovery makes the knowledge gleaned from Sematech's experience relevant to any industry whose survival is threatened. As one analyst observes: "The lesson is that once you lose market share, you don't have to roll over. You can get it back." The importance of this lesson in an era of pressing global competition is hard to overestimate. Turner Hasty, who spent four years helping to establish and manage Sematech, used to say, "Well, you guys, you don't need to worry about getting this right, it's only a matter of whether or not your grandchildren are going to have a job in this country."

# The Complexities of Sematech

## *A Theoretical Summary*

**T**he story of Sematech is the story of cooperation among competitors in the semiconductor manufacturing industry in the United States 1986–94 as told in chapters 1 through 9.[1] Chapter 10 captures the major themes of this story in a theoretical summary.

Competing U.S. semiconductor manufacturers decided to cooperate for two principal reasons: Japan was close to dominating the industry, and it would require pooled resources to respond to that threat.[2] Both of these reasons underlie the foundation of the Sematech consortium in 1987. The fourteen charter members formed the consortium because, as Sandy Kane of IBM put it, no firm could bring about the recovery of the U.S. semiconductor industry alone.[3] Through Sematech, microchip makers could pool their resources in the fight to recover market share from the Japanese and to reestablish their supply and materials infrastructure, which had decayed as U.S. semiconductor sales dwindled.[4]

The desire to save the U.S. semiconductor industry was chiefly economic. Had Japan gained control of the semiconductor industry, it would have been able to dominate the manufacture and distribution of all the products containing microchips. The period was marked by an incredible string of Japanese manufacturing successes. The United States had already seen Japan take over a substantial share of automobile sales and consumer electronics in the 1970s and 1980s, and it did not want to see this achievement repeated on an even larger scale with microchips, the brains of electronic products.

But the issue also had a human side. The integrated circuit, now commonly referred to as the microchip, was simultaneously invented in the United States by Jack Kilby of Texas Instruments, and Bob Noyce, cofounder of Intel.[5] A market that the United States had controlled 85 percent of in the late 1970s was in free fall by the mid-1980s. One market analysis predicted that by 1993 the U.S. market share would shrink to a relatively insignificant 20 percent.[6] So much was at stake that, in addition to the founding firms, the U.S. government contributed to Sematech because the possibility of foreign control of essential computing resources threatened the military and economic security of the United States.[7] This threat became increasingly worrisome in the 1980s as the Soviet Union and its military power dissolved and Japan grew into a powerful global economic competitor.

The story of cooperation at Sematech is set in the context of the increasingly adversarial stance U.S. firms had taken toward each other since the invention of the integrated circuit. Before Sematech was born, the U.S. semiconductor industry conformed to the neoclassical ideal of free-market competition, with individual firms' pursuit of their own goals leading to the efficient and productive use of resources.[8] The notions of free markets and unremitting competition pervade American culture. This was especially true in the semiconductor industry, where entrepreneurial spirit had made some engineers and scientists into millionaire icons in just a few short years.

While the intensity of such competition may favor the founders and the consumer in most instances, this competitive ethos made cooperation between organizations very difficult. More than one of the interviewees for our study marveled at seeing senior industry leaders who were sworn enemies or not even acquainted, and who had not spoken to each other in twenty years, if ever, sitting around the same planning table. There had been historical examples of interfirm cooperation to solve specific problems, but these were driven by national crises, such as world wars.[9] Earlier attempts at cooperation had failed in the semiconductor industry because of a lack of consensus over objectives. Past experience thus suggested that formulating a cooperative strategy would not be easy.[10]

Proprietary, or market-derived, standards were one of the weapons used in the semiconductor industry to dominate products and assure continued generations of usage. Disputes over proprietary standards led to drawn-out court battles, with those involving AMD and Intel being prime examples. Analyses show that, in industries with rapidly changing technologies, proprietary standards create an intense level of competition fueled by the law of increasing returns—an amplifying market phenomenon in which the "firstest with the mostest" increasingly gets farther ahead.[11]

Given this inclination, what we found interesting about Sematech was the chance to learn about how cooperation could arise and persist in such a competitive industry. We knew from the outset that Sematech had achieved a minimal level of cooperation by virtue of the fact that it was established in the first place. Member companies contributed financial and other resources to its support, and most renewed their commitment at the end of its original five-year charter. We also knew that the consortium had both admirers and detractors. The organization has been held up by many, including President Clinton, as the standard for industry recovery. Conversely, T. J. Rodgers of Cypress Semiconductor had railed against Sematech since the organization's inception as being welfare for the rich. We did not set out to resolve these disagreements over Sematech's effectiveness. Rather, we sought to identify and understand from studying this consortium the factors that give rise to, or tend to impede, cooperative relations among organizations, groups, and individuals.[12]

The research for our book employs qualitative methods because we wanted to capture the development of cooperation within Sematech in the rich detail that only the accounts of the organization's founders and early participants could provide.[13] The next section of this chapter presents background information on the research setting, including an overview of research on consortia and a brief history and description of Sematech. We next provide a summary of literature on cooperation and competition that informed our data analysis.

## Research on Consortia

Research on consortia has increased in the United States since 1984, thanks to the Cooperative Research Act. While consortia have in common organizing for joint effort, they take many different forms in the pursuit of tailored objectives.[14] Because consortia attempt to combine the efforts of organizations that frequently have little or no previous experience working together, they must address the following issues: (a) how to set a purpose with proper breadth and focus; (b) how to set the boundaries of who is in and out, as well as determine the attendant costs and benefits for each; (c) how to create value from their joint efforts; and (d) how such an organization is stabilized.[15] Consortia in Western Europe and Japan have developed differently than those in the United States because of the problems they faced. European consortia are more driven by government than industry, and thus tend to consist of independent projects completed by in-house groups of member firms under a directorate, rather than existing in a central facility, as does Sematech. This difference is important to our story. If European consortia tend to arise as a result of government interest, member companies are likely to take less of a leadership role. Sematech happened because senior executives in the major U.S. semiconductor manufacturing firms were committed to obtaining government support for their industry.[16] This comparison is made in a 1995 analysis of Sematech, the Strategic Defense Initiative (SDI), and Eureka, the European response to SDI, by Helmut Willke, Carsten Kruck, and Christopher Thorn.[17] In another international comparison, a survey of U.S. and Japanese consortia found that they differed substantially in structure, with U.S. consortia using a wider variety of mechanisms and generally being more active in information exchange.[18] Also, Japanese consortia are much more likely to conduct research in member firms than are U.S. consortia.[19]

Microelectronics and Computer Technology Corporation, a research consortium, is the most renowned U.S. predecessor to Sematech. David Gibson's and Everett Rogers's 1994 analysis of MCC concluded that its attempts to realize returns on investments by transferring R&D technology projects to the marketplace achieved mixed success. They noted that although the consortium accomplished many technical achievements, it was never vital to the economic competitiveness of its members.[20] The main lessons learned from the MCC experiment were the importance of interfirm collaboration and shared technology.[21] This conclusion may be premature, however, since historically the cycle for commercializing basic research takes fifteen to twenty years from the time of invention, although this cycle time has been dramatically reduced for electronics. The Sematech interviewees for this book showed little interest in comparing themselves to MCC. They saw themselves as having a significantly different mission, and thus had few "takeaways" from MCC that naturally applied to their parent firms' efforts.

Another study of four consortia, including MCC, focused on managerial problems stemming from their separate locations and changing membership.[22] Our study suggests that the central issue in consortia is the level of member cooperation. Resolving this problem has proved difficult for Americans, Europeans, and even the Japanese.[23] One of our earliest impressions of Sematech was the report of one assignee who went home at night with headaches because he felt his cooperative actions were betraying his company. Even with his headache, he was a member of an organization that was successful at answering the cooperation question. Our research focused on the following issues:

- How did Sematech emerge out of the combined efforts of the many members from its diverse set of founding companies?
- How did Sematech's formation and activities enable and encourage cooperation throughout the semiconductor industry?

Our focus on these questions was developed by asking participants who did what, to what effect. Their verbal reports tended to show the interpersonal and organizational communication practices employed in this unique achievement. These practices are summarized in the overview of themes later in this chapter.

## Sematech's Creation, Mission, and Structure

After a year of preliminary development, Sematech was established in 1987 by fourteen firms constituting 80 percent of the semiconductor manufacturing industry and by the U.S. government.[24] Its proclaimed mission was: "To provide the U.S. semiconductor industry the capability of achieving a world-leadership manufacturing position by the mid-1990s."[25] At least three goals emerged in the early days of Sematech: (1) to improve manufacturing processes; (2) to improve factory management; and (3) to improve the industry infrastructure, especially the supply base of equipment and materials.[26] These strategies were to be realized through cooperative research, development, and manufacturing test projects to be completed by Sematech.[27]

Although approached, not all major firms in the industry agreed to participate.[28] The fourteen participating firms agreed to provide financial and personnel support for five years, with each firm's contribution proportional to 1 percent of its annual semiconductor sales, with a cap of $15 million.[29] This was not an easy decision for participating companies since the money in most instances came from their R&D budgets, which usually ran around 10 percent of sales. The Sematech contribution meant taking 10 percent from participating firms' R&D budgets—usually without a corresponding change in performance expectations for the R&D unit. The U.S. government agreed to match that sum, which came to $100 million a year, so that Sematech ended up with a planned operating budget of $200 million annually, or $1 billion over the initial five-year period.[30] (Sematech actually spent about $990 million during that time span). Clearly, this was a substantial commitment on the part of both the industry and the government.

Sematech was officially chartered in 1987 and moved to Austin, Texas, in mid-1988. It occupies space leased from the University of Texas, which was part of the incentive package that induced Sematech to choose Austin. The site, which Michael Dell had once considered as a start-up site for his fledgling computer business, includes a five-story office building and a small fabrication plant.[31] The number of personnel assigned to Sematech from the member companies varies, averaging about two hundred at any one time. Members of the participating firms who are on loan to Sematech for an average of two years are called "assignees." Employees providing support and administrative services are called "direct hires." The total workforce, once Sematech was fully operational, hovered around six hundred from 1989–91. In the early 1990s it grew to more than eight hundred.

The official Sematech mission is updated annually, but certain specific technological goals were evident from the beginning. In order to remain competitive, it seemed obvious that the U.S. industry had to do two things: increase the number of defect-free chips per silicon wafer, and make each chip capable of doing more. Sematech launched efforts to do both, but had more success in developing manufacturing processes for packing more features onto chips. The usual means for doing this is to reduce the width of the etched circuit lines (features) on the chips. The historical development in the industry has been toward smaller chips with greater power through increased features. Responding to this trend was clearly necessary to remain competitive in the future.

Sematech's organization has evolved over time, usually by adding new ways for member companies to collaborate or help shape Sematech's decisions. From the beginning, certain general governance structures were used to bring ideas and information from member companies into the consortium. A Board of Directors, composed of high-level executives from member firms, sets general policy and hires the CEO. An executive technical advisory board (ETAB) sets general priorities for research, development, and testing activities within the consortium. A series of focus TABS approve and advise on specific projects within the general guidelines set by the ETAB. Both types of advisory boards are composed exclusively of representatives from member companies. In addition, a variety of task forces, councils, and other groups have emerged to develop policy on such issues as Total Quality, supplier relations, and the transfer of technology to member firms. Contemporary meeting-management practices are used throughout the organization, with facilitators helping to keep meetings on schedule and topic.

As it developed, Sematech borrowed structures from elsewhere in the industry. Sometimes the structures were deliberately patterned on what top management considered to be the best practices, such as the Intel cases that pervade this book. At other times they came along with assignees given certain task requirements. Three basic features of the structures have proved to be durable in the sense that they were begun under Bob Noyce's leadership and have persisted under Bill Spencer. The first is that the top three executives operate as a team in what is called the Office of the Chief Executive (OCE). They confer frequently, attend important meetings together, and generally work closely together. A second feature is that Sematech has only three levels of management under the OCE: directors, managers, and project managers. The third is that Sematech employees are organized into project teams that work within designated thrust areas. Some thrusts are technical, others are called "enabling." An example of a technical thrust is manufacturing and metals; an example of an enabling thrust is technology transfer. The development of these program structures is described in chapter 6.

### Struggles and Achievements

Although all start-up operations are considered to be difficult managerial achievements,[32] Sematech had a particularly tumultuous beginning. As we detailed in chapter 4, the first major problem was the yearlong search for a CEO to lead the organization. That hurdle was cleared with the appointment of Bob Noyce. Because Noyce was so widely respected in the industry, his appointment was an important early factor in attracting able employees from the member companies—at a time when those member companies harbored considerable doubt as to whether Sematech was a viable venture. Reports of Noyce's behavior and the reactions of many Sematech employees indicate that he exhibited most of the qualities of a charismatic leader.[33] Next was the managerial rift that quickly developed between Noyce and Paul Castrucci, who the Board of Directors had selected as COO. Noyce had not met Castrucci before accepting the CEO position, and their difficulties in reaching agreement resulted in Castrucci's resignation. Then, only two years later, in June, 1990, Sematech experienced the shock of Noyce's sudden death and the loss of its charismatic leader.

Just a few months later, Sematech employees had to adjust again to a new CEO, Bill Spencer, who was recruited from outside the consortium and who had his own ideas about how to build on Noyce's early efforts. That part of the story is told in chapter 7.

Despite the turbulence of these first three years, the organization met all of its "demonstration milestones" on time or ahead of schedule. Phase I achieved .8-micron etched lines on manufactured chips by March, 1989. By the end of Phase II, in October, 1989, the line size was decreased to .5 microns. By December, 1992, Sematech was able to announce that it had completed Phase III by reducing the size of etched lines to .35 microns.

This reversal of fortune for the semiconductor industry has been attributed to several factors including U.S. trade restrictions, the increasing impact of Korean manufacturing competition on the Japanese, the Japan's recession in the 1990s,[34] and Sematech's efforts.[35] Any effects caused by Sematech would, of course, be indirect because, as member-firm executives are disposed to point out, it was ultimately the member companies' factory production that led to the increased U.S. semiconductor market share. Sematech's role has been to develop new manufacturing technologies and methods and transfer them to its member companies, which in turn manufacture and sell improved chips. Sematech's precise contribution to the market recovery is therefore difficult to directly assess. What matters in the context of this research is that eleven of the original fourteen member companies and the U.S. government agreed to extend their membership in Sematech for a second five-year period and committed to new and expanded goals. Their continued commitment to Sematech indicates that they believe Sematech has achieved something worth their investments. As Craig Barrett of Intel notes: "I judge Sematech by results. The organization set out to recover market share from Japan; five years later, market share has been recovered. At Intel we call that a results-oriented successful project."[36]

## Cooperation and Competition

As polar opposites, cooperation and competition are to a degree defined by each other. They coexist in a system highly susceptible to change. Computer simulations show that a disturbance of only 2 percent is enough to move rational players from cooperation to competition. Simulations of the prisoner's dilemma game consistently find that a domino effect results from a single player's defections.[37] Even more surprising is that the converse is also true: In computer simulations, the presence of 2 percent "hard core unconditional givers" moves noncooperation into cooperation.[38] Setting the conditions for cooperation in a culture are especially possible when persons with the propensity for cooperation act consistently with their intentions for a number of time trials. In laboratory studies, three significant acts of unconditional cooperation were enough to induce skeptics to cooperate.[39]

Competition exists when resources are scarce, when those involved have a win/lose relationship, and when the margin of victory is measured by the difference between what one player has and what his opponent has.[40] Competition involves not only the control of scarce resources but also defining the relationship in present terms as though no future interactions or interdependence existed.[41] Furthermore, competition often invokes the use of strategy, with one player estimating the reaction of the other player in response to his action.[42]

Cooperation, by contrast, occurs when people or groups of people act together in a coordinated way in the pursuit of shared goals, the enjoyment of a joint activity, or simply the furthering of their relationship.[43] Cooperation usually involves not only the coordination of activities but also the sharing of benefits that emerge from the cooperation.[44] Cooperation is also said to exist when behavior "maximizes both the individual's and others' interests, whether the situation involves correspondent or noncorrespondent interests."[45] While it is possible to structure conditions that lead to cooperation, some degree of constructive conflict is often useful.[46] Truly cooperative behaviors tolerate conflict and use real-time communication[47] and individual give-and-take discussions to reach productive outcomes.[48] Finally, cooperation defines a relationship with a shadow of the future so that parties treat each other as though their future relationship counted.[49]

## Summary of Book Themes

We found that three conditions enabled the development of cooperation within the semiconductor industry and Sematech: (1) early disorder and ambiguity, which have been described in chapters 1 and 3; (2) emergence of a moral community, which have been described in chapters 3, 4, and 5; and (3) structuring of activities, which have been described in chapters 2, 5, 6, 7, and 8. These conditions emerged as the core categories of our analysis[50] and contributed to cooperation in various ways, as reflected in the selective categories listed in table 1.

### Early Disorder and Ambiguity

The start-up of any new organization is difficult because of the uncertainty surrounding norms, roles, strategies, and structures. These uncertainties mean that people experience a lack of order—they do not know how things fit together. For example, they do not know what is important to do, or what is important about how they do it. Lacking an existing social order for structuring their efforts gives people one advantage, however: They have the opportunity to innovate, either accidentally or deliberately. Karl Weick conceptualizes the organizing process as moving from equivocality to structure.[51] James Thompson points out that organizations thrive on uncertainty by removing it from the

## Table 1. Coding Themes and Core Categories

| Coding Themes | Core Categories | | |
| --- | --- | --- | --- |
| | Early Disorder and Ambiguity | Moral Community | Structuring |
| 1. Early equivocality | X | | x |
| 2. Mixed conceptions of culture | X | x | |
| 3. Valuing continued stage | X | | x |
| 4. Constructive conflict | X | | x |
| 5. Indirectness | X | | x |
| 6. Prior social ties | | X | x |
| 7. Inclusiveness | | X | x |
| 8. Unconditional giving | x | X | x |
| 9. Self-amplifying reciprocity | x | X | |
| 10. Manifold contributions | x | X | x |
| 11. Within-firm communication | | X | x |
| 12. Public actions | | X | x |
| 13. Faith in the outcome | x | X | x |
| 14. Openness | x | x | X |
| 15. Meetings | | x | X |
| 16. Creating new structures | x | | X |
| 17. Standards | x | | X |

*Note:* X = central to core category; x = helps to inform but not central to core category.

system.[52] In this sense, this book is about the organizing process at Sematech, and especially how communication was used to accomplish it.

The selective categories in this core category describe both the state of disorder experienced by Sematech in its early days and some key strategies members devised for coping with it.

*Early Equivocality.* During Sematech's formation, member-company representatives participated in a series of workshops charged with setting technical objectives for the consortium. The end product of this bottom-up planning was a wish list that had something in it for everyone. Consequently, the wish list contained more objectives than the consortium could conceivably fund or accomplish within its designated five-year life span. When Robert Noyce became CEO, one of the issues he faced was to pare down this list into a set of achievable goals. Noyce proved too supportive and enthusiastic to be good at this task, so it eventually fell on Turner Hasty to sell Noyce on a more limited set of objectives, including substantial technical assistance to the supplier industry. Yet the original wish list remained an institutional fact, and keeping people's efforts focused on the narrower set of objectives was not easy throughout the five-year period. Differences over Sematech's goals, for example, were highly visible at meetings we observed in the summer of 1992.

After it moved to Austin, the Sematech organization built up rapidly, but positions were filled unevenly. As one early assignee told us, people were coming in at all different levels. Some people in high-level positions had only one person reporting to them, whereas others in lower-level positions had as many as fifty people reporting to them. These circumstances naturally created ambiguity about individual identity and status. One of the early direct hires tells a story that illustrates this point. At a meeting one day, an employee voiced to Noyce some of his anxiety about his lack of a job title. The insightful CEO jokingly replied, "People can invent their own job titles if they want to." Some people subsequently did. Their doing so suggests that employees felt inadequate without them. Noyce also discouraged the compilation or use of organizational charts. Those that existed were designed to meet the demands of external constituencies.

The early assignee selection process was often as random as posting a job listing on the bulletin board of a member company's fab. In some instances, the assignees who ended up at Sematech were persons who asked to go rather than those who were needed for mission-related tasks. Given those circumstances, many informants agree, there was widespread suspicion that employees who were permitted to go to Sematech were the ones who would be missed least by their parent organizations. This common suspicion made most assignees wonder what being assigned to Sematech meant in terms of their value to their parent firm. Another result of this relatively random selection process was that many assignees came to Austin hoping to get support for pet projects for which they could not get backing in their parent firms. The mix of private agendas, new faces, and an equivocal organizational structure made Sematech's early experience chaotic. This made achieving a cooperative work environment all the more important.[53]

*Mixed Cultural Conceptions.* Because they were drawn from so many different companies, assignees naturally saw their industry and work somewhat differently. Some came from companies reported to have distinctive, strong, celebrated cultures; others came from companies with weaker or less evident cultures. One of the early techniques Sematech used to bridge the cultural differences that assignees brought with them was to compile a dictionary of technical terms and acronyms. Before this attempt at standardization, many firms prided themselves on unique names for things. As a measure of the amount of change the organization has experienced, the dictionary has been updated six times since its original publication in 1988.

According to Sam Harrell, many of the early participants at Sematech felt that they could not afford the luxury of working on the culture because they "needed to do it like marines hitting the beach." The fixed duration initially set for Sematech's existence created a deadline by which a wide variety of ambitious plans were supposed to be realized. Bill Daniels, an early consultant, told Sematech's top management that it takes three to four years to build a culture.[54] Other participants felt that it was impossible to build a culture with assignees, who form the operating core of Sematech, coming and going all of the time. Bill Spencer, who succeeded Noyce as CEO, said that "managing Sematech was like managing a parade."

Yet, for all its uncertainty, Sematech was, from the beginning, a highly normatively charged organization with a strong sense of mission. In other words, it had a set of ideas around which a culture could coalesce. All that was needed to make that culture grow was cultural leadership and appropriate cultural forms.[55]

Bob Noyce proved to be an exceptional cultural leader. His actions fostered an unusually open, egalitarian organizational culture. The story is frequently told about how Noyce, upon arriving at Sematech, took off his tie as soon as he entered the building. It signaled that this would be an informal, we-are-all-in-this-together organization. The staff who accompanied him immediately followed suit. He repeatedly talked of the kinds of people that would be necessary for the job: "We need finishers." Noyce also supported the practice of "dress-down" Fridays, then becoming common in much of the industry.[56] Another symbol of his democratic values was that everyone, including himself, had open offices separated only by low partitions. Even more telling is the fact that there were no designated parking spaces. Hasty and Mills willingly followed Noyce's egalitarian example. And that egalitarianism was only reinforced by the ambiguity of the assignees' prior and current status. The egalitarian culture, in turn, fostered participation and cooperation by treating all contributions as potentially valuable.

*Valuing Continual Change.* Sematech early developed a metacriterion for judging how to respond to a deteriorating industry. Leaders expressed this through the watchword phrase: "If it's not competitive, change it." This phrase tied the member companies and their suppliers together in a "community of fate"—which meant that their common emergency was a greater source of identity than their business differences.[57] If they did not change, their industry would disintegrate. Sam Harrell summarized the challenge: "Sematech empowered every member company, every supplier, and every device manufacturing business to change their own practices. Everybody had to take a stark look at the gallows in 1987 and say, 'I'm willing to make the changes required for the gallows to be for someone else.'"

One of the routes chosen to make the industry more competitive was to develop and continuously raise standards. The old criterion—usually the lowest cost—was debunked as inappropriate in the current competitive environment. A switch was made to a "total cost of ownership" criterion, which took into account installation costs, servicing costs, reliability during manufacturing, and the technological life of the product. This criterion meant that suppliers had to worry about what manufacturers needed, and manufacturers had to cooperate by telling them. Interdependence—a motivation for cooperation— became much more evident.[58] The new criterion also embodied dynamism— people came to accept the idea that standards were ever-changing and that what was competitive today would not be competitive tomorrow.

*Constructive Conflict.* Organization members increase their attention when a structure is in conflict. In this instance, they combined this additional attention with the opportunity, in the absence of structure, to write their own job descriptions and sometimes their own titles. When Turner Hasty tried to structure various research projects into an overarching management plan, as advised by Bill Daniels, he provoked a lot of hostility and infighting. Hasty then checked back with Daniels to see if this was what the consultant had expected. Daniels reassured him that conflict needed to come out and be resolved as a part of members learning how to cooperate.

The meeting-management skills that Intel contributed to Sematech included a specific technique for constructive conflict. This was the so-called "constructive confrontation" technique discussed in chapter 4 (see appendix 3). When using this technique, any person at any level could criticize an idea as long as the criticism was not personal. This had the effect of limiting the ego involvement in disagreements and making them easier to resolve. It also had the effect of making subsequent cooperation easier because members carried fewer unresolved feelings about how they had been affected by previous interactions over what to do and who should do it. Keith Erickson from Intel told us about his early experience at Sematech with this topic. Within the first week of Erickson's arrival, he had a concrete case of how Intel's approach to constructive confrontation might be useful to the consortium as well as the kind of change in practice it might mean for members. People working on the Internal Lithography Program came to him, as a newcomer, and commented on how the program was "split up" at Sematech and on their need for help in sorting it out. The lithography working group included a hundred or so people, and there were strong differences of opinion over the direction the program should take.

Erickson decided to assume a leadership role and called for a dinner meeting: "Let's order a bunch of pizzas and talk it out to deal with the issues directly and immediately." His effort met considerable resistance. The program's managers were not shy in addressing Erickson directly: "How dare you? There is a management structure in place to handle this." Erickson responded by assuring them that he was not challenging their authority. He said his goal was simply to get people to discuss their differences openly and that he did not intend to take over the project or even to take a stand on the issues.

The meeting was a good one. The managers were invited to attend and they did so. They supported Erickson by encouraging open discussion to build trust. The meeting was especially effective at airing concerns about where resources should be allocated. It also addressed the career-limiting doubts members had about being involved in the discussion. Members were concerned about surfacing their professional thoughts about the issues involved in the lithography project. This led to regular interdepartmental meetings with all employees and managers to express their ideas and to get the issues out in the open. This had the effect of eliminating at least one more variable—internal disharmony—from the factors affecting any given problem. Over time, this became one of Sematech's strong cultural strengths: the ability to openly challenge ideas without challenging the individual connected to it.

*Indirectness.* When uncertainty was especially great, openness, directness, and specificity did not always help Sematech participants to reach decisions. Some key events reflected a kind of indirectness that structured events in ways that were not obvious to most participants. This indirectness was especially valuable during Sematech's formation period. The indirectness in this category looks very much like what Weick, in his early writing on self-organizing, calls play.[59]

One early and potentially divisive decision was the choice of Sematech's permanent site. Sematech had already funded a program that supported research programs at the top ten engineering schools in the country, including the population-rich states of California, Florida, New York, and Texas. The legislators from these states actively supported Sematech funding. The selection of the headquarters site became a delicate political issue. IBM's Sandy Kane explained to us that he volunteered to be chairman of the site selection committee because of his concern that IBM would lobby to sell some of the real estate it owned to serve as the consortium's home. He felt that his being chair of that committee signaled to others within IBM that it would be extremely inappropriate for them to try to sell any of their vast and widely dispersed holdings to Sematech.

Another example of indirectness was Bob Noyce's habit of asking questions—approximately five questions for every direct statement, according to one observer's estimate. Noyce was a curious genius who liked to hear about and act on almost any topic—from tort reform to managerial theory. This curiosity and his informal leadership style made him very approachable. His attentive listening also was a form of cooperation.[60] These qualities had the effect of empowering people to act on the clarity they gained from conversations with him. As Ann Bowers Noyce commented, "Bob just assumed a person would act on what needed to be done." People came out of these conversations with the notion that Noyce expected them to go out and "do something wonderful." Because people wanted to please him, they were "motivated by the expectation of emotionally-prompted social approval."[61] In this way Noyce's curiosity indirectly increased individual commitment and cooperation.

*Summary.* Perhaps the most basic condition that created ambiguity at Sematech was the organization's inherently unstructured mission, which was no less than to revitalize the entire semiconductor industry. No one knew exactly how to do this, and experimental actions were therefore tolerated and valued. Changes in practices appeared to be imperative. The whole organization thus grew around the central idea that change was inevitable, must be confronted, and must be anticipated. The criterion that guided decision making was the need to change everything that did not compete in the international market. Because Sematech was a start-up, no one had the same experience before, and uncertainty and disorder could not be avoided. Indirectness and various other devices for limiting conflict and chaos provided some continuity and redirected energy when needed. A key input into this process was the series of amplifying inputs made by the early leaders.[62]

## Moral Community

One of the requirements of cooperation is a willingness to attend to the well being of all rather than a select segment of community members, which is what we mean by the use of Amitai Etzioni's term, "moral community."[63] He sees the moral community as a giving place where members perceive a "we" rather than an imposing, restraining "they."[64] This notion of inclusion was a pattern at Sematech. Sam Harrell, for example, is unusually proud that this consortium included the entire industry, both horizontally (the member manufacturers) and vertically (the supply chain that provides equipment and materials to make the microchips). The moral community at Sematech was driven by the tone set by the founders. The root metaphor for the consortium was selfless contribution. More important than the financial support provided the organization was the time and information given to it by member firms. In order to bring about the creation of a consortium, leaders in that industry had to behave as members of a community with the higher goal of preserving their industry.

*Inclusiveness.* Cooperative communities cannot be established if some members are excluded or relegated to out-groups.[65] By the time it was formed, Sematech included fourteen firms accounting for 80 percent of U.S. semiconductor manufacturing.[66] When three small firms later withdrew, Sematech still included 75 percent of the industry.[67] Sandy Kane reports that when Sematech's mission statement was finally agreed upon, Charlie Sporck made a point of inviting all members of the planning group—not just those whose positions were reflected in that decision—to the meeting in which the decision was announced.

Early members of Sematech's executive group were also sensitive to the issue of inclusion. Peter Mills reports that he and others advised Noyce to make a point of looking around at others around the room, even when he was part of an audience, so that speakers would not focus only on him. Peter Mills and Ann Bowers Noyce both volunteered that it was important to Noyce that Sematech not be a "star culture," with connotations of elitism.

Another important facet of inclusiveness at Sematech was the way in which it increased the size of the total pie subject to its influence. Rather than restricting the chance to influence the direction of the industry by including only parts of it, everyone felt that they had a greater say in the agenda.[68] Sam Harrell, who served both as president of the supply association and as Sematech's chief strategist, claims that the dollars spent by Sematech are minuscule in comparison with the amounts being spent in member companies' R&D labs. This serves to demonstrate Sematech's leverage. Its goal of alignment with the member companies' labs meant that the resources of the whole industry were being focused on the same purpose: saving the industry.

Inclusiveness extends to the public agencies included in Sematech's original charter. At its founding, the NACS charged the consortium with establishing SCOEs in top U.S. universities. Sematech also was to establish cooperative microelectronics manufacturing research projects at some of the 726 national labs run by government agencies, including NASA and the Departments of Defense and Energy. By 1990, when Bill Spencer became head of the consortium, many felt it had done all it could to help the industry weather its acute global market-share crisis, and it was time to disband when the five-year charter expired in 1992. Spencer, a visionary leader, saw how Sematech's worth to the country as a whole could expand through developing national inclusiveness. At a time when the consortium's continued existence was in question, Spencer, with the help of COO Bill George, was able to convince nearly all of the member companies to renew their commitment and to persuade the government to renew its financial obligation, thus giving Sematech at least a second five-year lease on life. By 1992, Sematech was investing $5 million a year in national laboratory programs, and the continued future growth of their collaboration looked probable.[69] With a narrowly focused vision on industry market share rather than Spencer's more inclusive vision, this national benefit could not have been realized.

*Unconditional Giving.* As Sandy Kane and others told us, Charlie Sporck, the CEO of National Semiconductor, is known as the father of Sematech because he took an entire summer off to poll members of the industry and hammer out an agreement among them that led to its founding. His was a pure gift because it conferred benefit on others, imposed a net cost on him (his inattention to his own company), and was voluntary.[70] His contribution was not an exchange. It was, in Kenneth Boulding's terms, a one-way transfer or gift from his generation to his grandchildren's. He often repeated, "What is at stake are jobs for

America's grandchildren." This level of contribution is what establishes community.[71]

Another crucial contribution was made by Bob Noyce, who came out of retirement to be Sematech's CEO at a time when, several informants felt, his not doing so would likely have meant failure for the consortium. Early Sematech executives and assignees mention three things that help explain his value: (1) His personal reputation and fortune were such that he had nothing to gain or prove by leading another organization; (2) with him at the helm, Sematech could gain support from Congress and member companies; (3) he gave luster and credibility to the whole effort. In addition, he contributed a participatory management style that tolerated complexity and a degree of chaos that allowed the processes described here to unfold. Since cooperation is affected by the role models for behavior, the leaders of this moral community established a reciprocal and self-reinforcing relationship.

Texas Instruments's contribution to the leadership group was Turner Hasty, who joined Sematech during its formative phase and acted as COO both before and after Noyce's death. Although Hasty told us he was initially far from sold on Sematech, he gave prodigiously of his energy and emotion. Other major contributions of managerial talent occurred after Noyce's death when Motorola permitted Bob Galvin to serve as chairman of Sematech's Board of Directors and Bill George to become the consortium's COO. In the words of the top executive who sent George, "It was our turn."

There were, of course, many other contributions mentioned by our interviewees. For example, IBM and AT&T contributed technology to start the fabrication facility in Austin; Intel contributed the methods of setting standards; and various companies allowed Sematech researchers to use their factories for testing. Our interview data with people at lower levels in the member companies indicates that they cooperated in a manner suggesting they had learned the norms their leaders modeled.

*Self-Amplifying Reciprocity.* The biggest worry for a consortium made up of volunteers from member firms is that some companies will send second-tier performers when others are providing their best. According to the lawyer who represented the SIA in Congress, some participants and observers initially expected that such "free riding" would be a problem at Sematech. But it did not happen. Interviewees recounted how Intel, the least threatened of Sematech's member companies, took the lead and contributed additional top-notch performers when other member companies were threatening to pull out if their vision of the mission was not accepted. According to Hasty, Craig Barrett, Intel's director of manufacturing, called him and asked, "How can Intel have more of an impact on Sematech?" Hasty's said Intel should send more high-quality performers, and Intel complied. In doing so, Intel did not wait upon the contributions of others, as traditional economic theory would predict. From then on, Intel made a series of interlinked contributions that set in motion a Kantian model for giving in which all felt obliged to make at least "the minimal cooperative contribution" they hoped others would make.[72]

As individual firms contributed to the efforts to found and operate Sematech, the contributions of each built on and enlarged the contributions of others. Individual contributions had a multiplier effect in terms of cooperation because they established and reinforced norms that required all to join in. Sematech was in the limelight, and the actions and contributions of each member firm were highly public. One issue to be worked out was the sequence of contributions:[73] "If I make a big contribution now, can I count on you taking a turn later?" This problem was met with an unspoken sense of fairness. Gifts of valuable resources tended to occur sequentially, as if the member companies were taking turns.[74]

The reciprocity practiced at Sematech soon established a group-based trust that allowed members to cooperate with "the expectation that others will respond favorably."[75] Norms of reciprocity and cooperation persisted as participants' exercise of trust led to further trust in the predictability of others' future actions.[76] These norms were not invariably operative at Sematech, however. At a workshop for Sematech's Human Resources group, one of the industry experts we interviewed reported a visible amount of secrecy and competition. This appears to be a theme in the semiconductor industry: social scientists and therapeutic specialists are less able to cooperate than the hard scientists and engineers.

*Manifold Contributions.* The enlightened contributions of several of Sematech's early leaders enabled the consortium's development to go forward. Without their input, the organization might have disintegrated or become frozen in a form that did not change. Moreover, the formation of a moral community created normative expectations that member companies and individuals would all take their turn making their unique contributions. The emerging norm of reciprocity ensured that Sematech did not wither or die for lack of new ideas and energy.

The very visible contributions of Sematech's top management also set a tone for contributions from everyone else within the organization. People who worked there reported they came to feel that every contribution was valued. A notable feature of the organization was the way in which women's contributions were valued, whether they worked as scientists or as secretaries. Bill Daniels described a practice that symbolized this inclusiveness: executive secretaries were invited to teamwork training meetings with the top management team. In effect, they were treated like peers. Structuring working relationships as peer relationships encouraged cooperation.[77]

Bob Noyce's wife, Ann, was herself a high-powered industry executive. Prior to meeting him, she had been a human resource executive at Apple and a key player at Intel. She reported to us that she influenced Noyce to take women seriously and give them opportunities. She served as a positive example to him of what women could contribute in a male-dominated industry and also as a catalyst for changing the treatment of other women.

Another important group of contributors was the so-called direct hires— the persons who worked directly for Sematech primarily in support roles and who were hired for indefinite terms. The egalitarian, open-ended culture at Sematech let many of these people make contributions that they would not have been allowed to make in more traditional business cultures. Our direct-hire informants reported feeling that they could realize their potential at Sematech. Assignees also realized they were being given more latitude and responsibility at Sematech than they were likely to have when they returned to their parent companies. Another unusual and valuable role was played by a group of facilitators who acted as third parties and thus helped defuse the early distrust and hostility in the organization.[78]

The level of effort was so high while Noyce was CEO that many interviewees reported they could not have sustained it much longer. People worked around the clock and on weekends. The parking lots were never empty. Direct hires who have been there for a long time reported to us that the early instability and disorder bred ingenuity, persistence, and Herculean effort because those things were vital to getting things done. Over time, these traits seem to have become ingrained in many people there. An extreme example of this extraordinary dedication is the case of the woman who chose to deliver her baby via Cesarean section when it would not interfere with work commitments.[79] Such remarkable degrees of energy and effort mobilized growth, preventing stagnation.[80]

*Intrafirm Communication.* Sematech's member firms varied considerably in their own skills and styles of internal communication. Effective intrafirm communication enabled better alignment between managers' and assignees' conceptions of what Sematech was about and how to work with it, enhancing cooperation at Sematech.

The two firms most noted for their ability to resolve internal differences and to manage conflict constructively were Intel and Motorola. They were also, in many observers' opinions, the most influential in shaping practices at Sematech. According to one early Intel assignee, Intel had influence because it used vertical communication structures that enabled its managers to agree internally on what they wanted. Other firms—notably Texas Instruments, with its history of military contracts—were more secretive internally as well as externally.[81] Participants were well aware of their relative communication skills. Bob Galvin commented that one reason he joined Sematech was to transfer Motorola's internal learning about cooperation to Sematech and other firms in the industry.

Another way member intrafirm communication proved important was in the transfer of technical information from Sematech back to member companies. Hewlett-Packard had spent more time than other member companies in designing and managing such interfaces. We learned from one Hewlett-Packard executive that his company set up not only a Board of Directors for interactions with Sematech but also an internal network that covered the entire span of Hewlett-Packard-relevant technical areas to receive and pass on information from Sematech.

*Public Actions.* Public behavior, generated at Sematech in part through government involvement, can increase participants' commitment to action.[82] Even before connecting with the government, however, key members agreed on the need to educate the industry in general on the grave danger it faced and took the risk of going public to communicate it. Sandy Kane, for example, recalls how he developed and delivered a presentation on the imminent peril, first within IBM, then going outside the firm, with John Akers's approval. During the first half of 1986, Kane gave his briefing twenty-five times to executives of major U.S. semiconductor firms. His "obituary," was a general alarm call about the crisis. Other informants reported that much ferment and talk about the situation were simultaneously erupting into the public view.

All of this public talk culminated in the 1986 SIA decision to ask Charlie Sporck to spearhead a consortium initiative.[83] This was followed by the public pledge by SIA leaders to financially support a consortium and an avowal to pursue specific goals. The public nature of these actions made them less revocable and increased the SIA members' commitment to the new consortium.[84]

As these examples show, the actions taken to found Sematech were highly public, at least by semiconductor industry standards. This perhaps explains why openness also became the norm at Sematech—so much so that when members of the consortium discovered Sematech's first COO, Paul Castrucci, had made private decisions allocating vast sums for equipment and other ventures, they considered his actions insubordination. The consistent story shared with us by several informants was that Castrucci's authoritarian management style and penchant for private decisions were inimical to Noyce's vision for an egalitarian, open organization, and eventually led to Castrucci's resignation.

*Faith in the Outcome.* People are more likely to cooperate when the future casts a long shadow.[85] Cooperation occurs when gains from future dealings are "highly valued in relation to current ones."[86] Put another way, "If people think that their future is not important compared with their present, they cannot cooperate."[87]

When Sematech was formed in 1987, conventional wisdom had it that if the present trend in loss of market share continued the U.S. share would drop to only 20 percent by 1993. Instead it rebounded to 47 percent, placing the U.S.

ahead of the Japanese for the first time since 1986. Early joint planning among members set a five-year term for industry membership in Sematech, which ran in concert with the five-year federal funding approval (subject to yearly review). Under the leadership of Bill Spencer, most of the member companies continued to exhibit faith in Sematech's mission and effectiveness. Sematech won another five years' support from most of the original member companies and Congress in 1992.[88]

*Summary.* All of the factors just described enabled Sematech to achieve—and maintain—a moral community. It was a feat that few could have predicted given the extreme competitiveness of the semiconductor industry. It was unclear at the outset whether its manufacturing firms would be able to achieve even minimal cooperation in this new consortium. The executives who founded and supported it came from differing company cultures, and they often expressed conflicting notions about the consortium and how it would help the industry. In addition, there was a pervasive issue of potential cultural misunderstanding and conflict. What was clear, however, was that a lot needed to be done, and the need was *urgent.* People poured themselves into jobs and activities that were accomplished at incredibly fast rates. So, despite a high potential for conflict, members were somehow able to achieve cooperation and change the industry. How and why is this so?

## Structuring

Many structures were created at Sematech to realize its goals, among them were internal task forces, new standards for supplier equipment and materials, and a U.S.-only supply organization carved from the international supply association.[89] The key structures evident in the development of Sematech follow.

*Openness.* One issue that needed to be resolved early in Sematech's history was the general belief that information about member firms' manufacturing processes was value-added and thus proprietary—hence secret. Many initial meetings therefore experienced long periods of silence.

Turner Hasty was the first to voice the view that the secrets being kept were not really secrets at all—that the differences between firms were primarily cultural, not technological. (An early assignee from Intel later agreed. He estimated that "almost 85 percent of the information is generic; only the top 15 percent is truly proprietary.") Peter Mills tells us that Hasty raised the whole issue in a single dramatic moment when he asked others at a meeting, "Can't you see, we're all talking about the same thing?"

Thereafter, assignees began to confer with their companies about what they would share at Sematech, sometimes by calling "home" at breaks during meetings to inquire about sharing a particular piece of information. Resolving the secrecy issue early meant that meetings were productive and produced outcomes.

Because we learned early in our interviews that proprietary secrets had been an issue, we checked with all subsequent informants to see whether any member companies had incurred costs from secrets revealed at Sematech. We could find no evidence that this had ever happened. This evidence of trust is a key element of cooperation at the consortia. In the language of probability for considering the veracity of a hypothesis, does one trust too little and risk the possibility of a missed opportunity? (A Type II error.) Or does one risk becoming a sucker and trust too much? (A Type I error.) We found no evidence that anyone ever trusted too much; no evidence that anyone at Sematech had made a Type I error.[90]

*Meetings.* One of the responses to the early chaos within Sematech was to import meeting-management practices that had worked well at Intel. Bill Daniels, a private consultant used by that company, told us how he trained the Sematech organization in meeting management in 1988. The problem-solving orientation the consortium learned from Daniels encouraged explicit information exchanges in meetings rather than expressions of individual agendas.[91] It also fostered cooperation.[92] The meetings involved "face-to-face interactions" in which members could express their positive interdependence in visible behaviors.[93]

External observers sometimes criticized Sematech for wasting its effort on "a bunch of meetings." The participants themselves saw it otherwise. For example, Sam Harrell, the president of SEMI/Sematech and later a member of Sematech's OCE, reported that the supplier community thought Sematech's workshops were "the most valuable deliverable in the first three to four years of Sematech." In this sense, as long as meetings were tied to resource allocation, they were a good investment.

Our own observations of meetings at Sematech confirm interviews with meeting-management staff that Sematech's meetings were both efficient and purposeful. The meeting-management program emphasized concrete outcomes, and to achieve that end it employed agendas, deliverables, strict use of time, and equalizing the opportunity to speak. We also found that facilitators were used to keep meetings on track. Participants reported to us that meetings produced valued outcomes, reinforcing what we call their "faith in the outcome" and thus also supporting a moral community.

*Creating New Structures.* The early meetings at Sematech focused on creating consensual frameworks—that is, goals, technological road maps, rules, contracts, position descriptions, and new organizations. Informants reported, and documents show, that one such agreement reached quite early in Sematech's history was to work on strengthening the U.S. supplier industry. Members realized that U.S. manufacturers could not be competitively secure without a strong domestic supplier industry. Because of the importance of the timeliness of technical information, there were widespread fears that too much dependence on Japanese firms in particular left U.S. manufacturers vulnerable if the Japanese delayed informing them of any new technological developments while informing their own companies. This fear was exemplified by a comment from a Nikon representative at a SEMI (suppliers') meeting, recounted by Craig Barrett, then executive vice president of Intel. He said, "I was at a SEMI meeting in Japan and the representative from Nikon stood up and said: 'When appropriate, we may even tell our foreign customers about our new equipment.' I can't say it any better. . . . A public statement like that to a bunch of U.S. and Japanese folks says it pretty clearly. Nikon happens to be our supplier, and it's nice to know that 'when appropriate' they might even tell us about the next generation."

To realize the goal of timely information, though, a structure had to be found through which Sematech could influence the suppliers. The solution was SEMI, an international association of suppliers to the semiconductor manufacturers that included foreign firms, whereas Sematech's agreement with the U.S. Congress was to support only the U.S. industry (Public Law 180–80, Section 171, Part C). To allow Sematech to work with the supplier community, a U.S.-only organization of suppliers called SEMI/Sematech was formed through Sam Harrell's efforts.[94]

Not all of the structures that emerged had their start from the stimulus of rational planning. Turner Hasty and Peter Mills reported that the Investment Council, for example, was created in response to Paul Castrucci's private dealings mentioned earlier.[95] In response to the emergency situation caused by Castrucci, the Investment Council was structured to execute contracts in a fashion that did not disenfranchise or alienate people in the industry, as well as to ensure fairness, and became, unpredictably, an invaluable "engine" driving the organization.

The PFTQ program is another example of the unforeseen structures that emerged from cooperative interaction at Sematech. Program staff explained to us that two groups were formed initially—one for partnering and the other for Total Quality. But because their members communicated, they soon realized that their domains and efforts overlapped, and they decided to merge. The PFTQ group sought to improve quality and to encourage partnering between suppliers and semiconductor manufacturers. A highly influential early assignee commented that one criticism of the U.S. supplier industry was that firms were too focused on costs and not enough on quality. The PFTQ group in Sematech developed an extensive program of training and created training materials for suppliers that emphasized the interactions between partnering and Total Quality.[96] Through the training program, as well as through regular audits by their customers—many of whom were also members of Sematech—suppliers were urged to find out more about what their customers wanted. They were also urged to adopt the ideologies, tools, and practices of Total Quality Management.

*Standards.* Before Sematech was founded, each firm in the semiconductor industry demanded manufacturing equipment uniquely designed for its own proprietary processes and chip architectures. A firm's ultimate objective was to be able to set the proprietary market standard through successful innovation, forcing consumer compatibility. Firms competed by trying to develop a standard they could own and use to either collect licensing fees or seize market share from competitors. (The practices of the software firm Microsoft epitomize this strategy.) Manufacturing equipment specifications were kept as secret as other intellectual property, such as product design.

Such practices fragmented the semiconductor industry, through rapid and continuous spin-offs for each new innovation, with their resultant drain on investments, human capital, and effort. This exclusive emphasis on proprietary innovation also fragmented the materials and equipment supplier infrastructure, through proliferation of secretive demands from manufacturers for uniquely designed equipment; often, in effect, a reinvented wheel for each firm's new chip design generation. This excessive fragmentation, along with lack of attention to pursuing manufacturing competence at a level of quality to match the brilliance of innovation, has been blamed for the U.S. semiconductor industry's vulnerability to aggressive global competition.

The creation of Sematech helped semiconductor manufacturers arrive at precompetitive manufacturing standards, such as standardization of tool specifications.[97] One example of how such standards emerged occurred when Intel sent Dean Toombs to introduce its equipment qualification procedures to other member companies. Intel had developed this standard-setting process in 1986, after it was badly burned by attempting to open a new fabrication facility with what turned out to be unreliable U.S. equipment. Some suppliers had resented Intel for being "strange and arrogant" when it imposed rigorous qualification requirements on all subsequent new equipment, but many had learned to value Intel's requirements for continuous improvements. These procedures were now introduced in the cooperative forum of Sematech, where members were relieved of the pressures of antitrust threats and associated secrecy requirements. Intel's program for standardizing specifications and for achieving quality standards in manufacturing equipment eventually was implemented as Sematech's Equipment Qualification Program, and standardized, quality-certified equipment was made available to the U.S. semiconductor industry for the first time.

*Summary.* While the structuring we have described was clearly a product of the early cooperation discussed in our section on moral community, these new structures, once in place, allowed for still more refined practices of cooperation, such as Sematech's later Partnering for Total Quality program, greatly extending the chipmaker/supplier cooperation on standardization as well as quality. Current meetings at Sematech routinely incorporate the cooperative practices that were established with such conflict and difficulty earlier. For example, early discussions of needed equipment were often guarded, exploratory probes to discover a possible source without betraying members' own usage. By 1993 these discussions had become routinely open.

Today, when the need for equipment is identified, the group is asked directly, "Does any firm here have equipment to share with Sematech?" If the answer is yes, the information is shared; if no, the group selects a supplier to develop the standardized equipment to be made available to all members. According to present-day assignees, this practice does not present a conflict between proprietary (competitive) and non-proprietary (pre-competitive) information. When asked about it, they responded, "Everyone understands the difference."

## Overview of Complexity Theory as It Informs This Book

The next step in theorizing from qualitative data involves finding meaningful relationships among the core and coded categories that help to explain the phenomenon of interest. This theorizing step summarizes the content of the body of this book. In the beginning, what seemed most remarkable to us and in need of explanation in the story of Sematech's creation and development was how cooperation could emerge from such a competitive setting as the semiconductor industry. It was evident that the Sematech story revolved around several phenomena that are not new in organizational research: competition, cooperation, and change. What might be new is how these phenomena came together to influence Sematech's founding and early functioning.

The literature on change suggested several more specific streams of theory as relevant. In particular, theories of self-organization seemed pertinent, since a coherent system emerged from such a large number of participants in such a wide variety of organization levels and locations.[98] Related to theories of self-organization, descriptions of organizational systems as dissipative structures[99] also seemed to apply, since the semiconductor industry was under make-or-break pressure that forced a qualitative change of state in the system. Theories of self-organization, dissipative structures, and, in addition, complex adaptive structures, are addressed in a larger, overarching framework—called complexity theory—that describes the mechanisms for radical changes in complex adaptive systems (systems that repeatedly incorporate their own effects, according to internal rules, to generate new states). A hallmark of this process is the emergence of persistent new structures, qualitatively greater than the sum of their parts. The new states of a system thus incorporate increasing complexity within a coherent whole.

SEMATECH

## Complexity Theory

Ilya Prigogine pioneered the systematic description of how ordered systems arise from apparent chaos with his work in physical chemistry. No small part of the reason he was awarded the Nobel Prize in 1977 is that he also understood the wide-ranging philosophical implications in his discoveries—for example, that they offered a new way of understanding how systems emerge in ways and with patterns that are not intended. Other researchers extended this understanding into social processes by studying their emergent orders as self-organizing systems in which innovative cultural patterns and increasingly complex structures repeatedly emerge.[100] These structures may stabilize, continue to evolve, self-destruct, or do all three in cycles. The central message of complexity theory is that the self-organization of complex, ordered systems from apparent chaos happens all the time—even when it is misunderstood, unappreciated, or unwanted.

Complexity theory fit our data on the development of Sematech in important ways. We saw the following correspondence between complexity theory and the events we observed in Sematech:

1. Complexity theory describes many of the ways in which order can arise out of apparent chaos.[101] Sematech was conceived in an industry that was in decline and disarray, if not complete chaos. We will refer to these conditions as irreversible disequilibrium.

2. Complexity theory describes the dynamics of complex adaptive, i.e., self-reinforcing, systems that repeatedly build on the results of their own interactions to achieve a more richly ordered complexity, rather than repeatedly damping their own effects in an effort to remain stable. Each self-reinforcing repetition or set of interactions amplifies the possibilities of the one before, to the point where a very small input may apparently trigger a "quantum leap" to a more complex whole. Sematech certainly developed many self-reinforcing processes from its internal and external interactions. We will describe these developments under the more familiar heading of self-organizing systems.

3. According to complexity theory, along with a change of state of a system comes unpredictability and novelty, and the chance for something new to emerge into the world.[102] What emerges is qualitatively different instead of just larger, because when the complicated interactions of many previously separate agents coalesce to function as a system, the new whole exhibits unaccustomed characteristics. Sematech certainly constituted something new in the world.[103] The founding and activities of this consortium, while not entirely unprecedented, has encouraged a new and apparently irreversible level of cooperation within a highly competitive industry.

The sheer size of the contributions made by each member company and by the federal government created the critical mass for interaction that complexity theory describes as necessary for qualitative change. The magnitude of contributions helped to ensure that some fundamental change would take place to justify those investments. Furthermore, the results of its founding and activities were highly unpredictable. Many observers predicted failure and many skeptics still question what the consortium has accomplished. We will discuss these points further in a subsection below entitled "A New Order."

*Irreversible Disequilibrium.* Only because the state of the semiconductor industry in the mid-1980s was such that its leaders feared its demise were they likely to open themselves to the possibility of a radical change in their practices. The obituary delivered by Sandy Kane[104] was an important specific example of a growing consensus that the situation in the industry was so severe that members of the community did not see returning to the "original set of equilibrium conditions" as possible.[105] They had reached what complexity theorists call a bifurcation point or point of singularity, where a system changes state. Because of the pressures building in the conditions leading to this point, the semiconductor industry needed to operate in a manner that was qualitatively different from the past.

According to complexity theory, a bifurcation signals a break with past patterns, where participants' interactions take on a different character and may exhibit newly coherent values.[106] In the case of Sematech, participants discarded the values associated with cutthroat competition, proprietary secrecy, and exploitative fragmentation. In the process, members committed themselves to facing the unknown, including whether cooperation would lead to recovery of the industry, and what it would take to achieve cooperation within the consortium.

*Self-Organizing Processes.* The events and activities described using Anthony Giddens's concept of structuring[107] in our results section seem even more descriptive of what various theorists have called self-organizing processes. Early activities and events within Sematech spawned new patterns of activities and events that in turn served to organize still other activities and events that followed.

However, the Sematech example departs somewhat from typical conceptions of self-organizing, which usually describe processes of generating new structures from elements *within* a system.[108] What happened at Sematech was that new structures were often created within the organization by borrowing practices from *outside* the organization—primarily from member companies and the supplier industry. We want to point out, however, whether structuring elements in a self-organizing system are seen as coming from inside or outside the system obviously depends on how system boundaries are drawn.[109] Sematech was an organizational system with very porous boundaries operating within a larger industry. At the industry level, most of the inputs were from within the system, while at the organizational level, many came from the outside. Also, most innovative structuring within any system is probably at least a partial imitation of something someone in the organization has seen somewhere else before, making the source of practices doubly unclear.

These distinctions aside, the Sematech case contributes to fleshing out the concept of self-organizing by showing (1) how members systematically searched the industry for the best practices to use internally and as models for the industry, and (2) how member companies and their suppliers were willing to give their practices to this cooperative effort.

One characteristic of a complex adaptive system, as described by complexity theory, is that its emergent structures not only persist, but through the interaction of their participants combine in novel ways as building blocks for the next, more complex, emergent structure. A clear example is seen in the experience of the two teams that were formed at Sematech, one to study quality issues and one to address supplier partnering. The teams were not isolated in separate "silos" as they might have been in a more conventional organization. Instead, they communicated, began interacting, and the Partnering for Total Quality structure emerged from their efforts, one of Sematech's most successful and effective programs. Although this outcome was not foreseen, its participants could feel a sense of accomplishment and pride, because it directly resulted from their interactions and learning.

Another factor that was exceedingly important in Sematech's self-organizing process was the relatively nondirective leadership style used by its early top management team.

As CEO, Bob Noyce was clearly an influential articulator of the mission and an inspiring role model at Sematech, but he seldom instigated structures.[110] Most treatments of founding leaders assume they both inspire followers and structure the organization.[111] However, one analysis of charismatic leaders concluded that such leaders tarnish their charisma when they become involved in routine matters because their charisma is derived partially from their being seen by followers as exceptional and in touch with matters on a higher plane.[112] Noyce exerted powerful influence over people connected with Sematech, but he avoided exerting direct control by delegating administrative detail. When Noyce was CEO at Intel, our informants told us, Andy Grove handled most administrative matters for him. At Sematech, Turner Hasty filled this role. Noyce's avoidance of detail allowed his charisma to grow and flourish.

Noyce's nondirective leadership style also created opportunities for others to structure situations and activities according to what seemed to be needed. In this sense, Sematech became genuinely self-organizing. The consortium's viability was enhanced because people throughout the organization could "create structures that fit the moment."[113] This flexibility and fluidity allowed Sematech to modify structures it found useful and to keep inventing new ones.

*A New Order.* Complexity theory suggests that, following a bifurcation point, the old system may appear to chaotically disintegrate prior to coalescing in a more complex and appropriate alignment—a new ordering.[114] In order to achieve and sustain this emergent process, the system must remain open to change and continuously attract high levels of new energy inputs. Systems capable of such dynamical emergence are called dissipative because of their ability to attract resources and skills in sufficient quantity to offset the potential disorganization stemming from new ways of operating.[115]

Our results showed that Sematech's founders came to recognize that a new order was required in their industry if they were to avoid its demise. Their solution showed how open they were to radical change. They decided to do what they had never done before: create a new organization—whose form was not completely predictable, having been previously unavailable to them because of legal restrictions—which would facilitate cooperation in solving common problems. They backed up that risky decision with substantial commitments of their own financial resources.

Much of what subsequently happened was not envisioned by all members of the founding group, and thus was, in accordance with complexity theory, unintended to a degree. Three of the major unintended consequences were:

1. A large portion (about half) of the consortium's resources would be used to help the supplier industry in SEMI/Sematech rather than directly helping the member companies.
2. The consortium would develop more commitment and cooperation than many members expected because free-riding behaviors became discredited as both counternormative and inimical to gaining full benefits from membership.
3. The consortium's life would be extended beyond its initial five years because of its perceived success.

Although some of Sematech's founders may have had the ideal of helping the supplier industry, others did not. The pursuit of this mission and the addition of SEMI/Sematech as a sort of collateral organization also had the unintended consequence of making Sematech more complex than originally envisioned. Few of the hardheaded managers in the founding group were idealistic enough to fully intend the last two consequences. There were plenty of skeptics at every step, but their skepticism was gradually overcome. Some of the founding companies understandably adopted a wait-and-see policy toward Sematech, but most were eventually drawn into the cooperative system that emerged.[116]

Another correspondence between Sematech and complexity theory is the way in which the consortium's emergent development depended on attracting and generating new energy. One important source of energy was the many individuals who contributed their efforts in the early years. We feel that the two most crucial individual energizers were Charlie Sporck and Bob Noyce. Sporck selflessly devoted himself to gaining commitments from his peer CEOs in the semiconductor industry to form Sematech. Noyce gave up his retirement to take over as CEO when it became evident that Congress would not fund the consortium without an acceptable CEO in place. Their high-level contributions helped to set a norm for cooperation and giving that was necessary to get the new organization off the ground.

Yet normative behavior alone is insufficient to explain cooperative systems.[117] Something must set the norms in motion.[118] That something is often one or more cultural leaders who "originate or recognize rationales that will reduce people's uncertainties, make them understandable and convincing, and communicate them widely so that others come to share them."[119] Sporck, Noyce, and others were Sematech's cultural leaders.

In Sematech's case, the matching funding from the federal government was also a necessary, if not sufficient, energizer. For a more complex order to emerge, a critical mass of input must be present, whether of enough resources, enough participants who are adequately interconnected and interacting simultaneously, or whatever. While the semiconductor firms did not really want government involvement, early planning indicated that without it, firms could not commit sufficient revenue, or legally connect with each other. Government assistance, both legal and financial, was essential for critical mass, as was the participation of a majority of industry players.

Complexity theory does not yet tell us the sources and pattern of new energy needed to lead a system toward a new order. Indeed, dissipative and complex adaptive systems are open to their environments and must draw energy from them. Our results show that such energy may come from many sources. Also, our results show that a rather surprising pattern of implicit turn taking emerged in this competitive industry. Different member firms contributed different kinds of resources at different times as those particular resources were seen as needed. In this respect, our results support Peter Ring's and Andrew Van de Ven's contention that contributions do not necessarily come in a pattern of calculated, equal exchanges.[120] Complexity theory also fails to specify the sources of new energy. Our data dramatize and strongly support that, in good part, this new energy must come from the efforts of key individuals, again supporting Ring and Van de Ven's analyses.

### Other Implications for Research and Practice

Complexity theory, as it has been applied to organizations, is a contrast to the homeostasis of systems theory in that it allows for radical change through an organization's own restructuring. More organizational applications of the model are needed to determine the value of complexity theory as a framework for understanding and analyzing organizational change. It is clear that complexity theory fits and helps to illuminate this research case. It remains to be seen how much this general framework will benefit future research. The turbulence of the environments that many organizations currently face and the radical changes that many are attempting to adapt to that turbulence suggests that this framework has relevance for future research and may be applicable to many more instances of organizational change.

Our results suggest that the interdependencies involved in interorganizational arrangements can pay off, but require some degree of trust and someone to start the contributions flowing.[121] They also show, as Michael Argyle suggested, that cooperation is easier among peers.[122] Sematech exemplified this suggestion by structuring interactions to take place among persons at the same organizational levels. Sematech's management formed countless committees and task forces to do this at every level of the organization. Peer-level communication was achieved primarily through meetings, and Sematech took care to be sure that its participants were trained in proven meeting management and participant skills. As Andy Grove pointed out, the meeting is where the business of the organization is done and where individuals take the risk of giving over to the group their singular views to achieve a joint effort.[123] This giving is an act of trust that must be met with success if meetings are going to retain a reputation for being successful.

Our data show that sequences of contributions do not necessarily follow an exchange model of equal value of outcomes for value of inputs for all parties. Instead, they may conform to the oldest assumption of trust: that it is almost impossible for everyone to get equal value at all times, and that it is necessary to have faith that one's efforts will be rewarded at a later, undefined time, and that these choices to offer and risk are tied to individual honor and pride.

The data from Sematech also illustrate the problems some leadership styles pose for efforts at cooperation. In particular, overbearing styles, such as William Shockley was reputed to exhibit at Shockley Labs,[124] or a penchant for unilateral, secretive decision making, such as Castrucci exhibited at Sematech, undermine cooperative efforts. On the other hand, such behaviors can galvanize cooperative efforts in others. Shockley's overbearing style led bright young engineers and scientists to leave and become the "Fairchildren" who colonized Silicon Valley. Castrucci's behaviors led to the formation of Sematech's Investment Council. Sometimes , the pressure of problems triggers the emergence of new solutions that would not otherwise have surfaced, or would have done so at a significantly different pace.

The leadership that galvanized effort at Sematech was established through visible and highly symbolic actions. In this instance, the organization had the advantage of a charismatic leader—an advantage not all organizations can count on. But the care Noyce devoted to symbolism and the participatory and democratic management style he used can be adapted by other leaders to other organizational settings.

## Conclusion

Sematech's continued viability demonstrates that cooperation among competitors can be achieved under certain conditions. The consortium's presence and activities have not eliminated competition in the semiconductor industry. Rather, Sematech has provided a sort of neutral ground on which "blood enemies" could and have cooperated within certain agreed-upon boundaries. The consortium has become the symbol and the catalyst for many cooperative efforts. What complexity theory contributes to our understanding of this account is to help us to understand how small, discrete events can, under certain conditions, amplify into large consequences. It gives hope for other organizational systems facing turbulence, apparent chaos, and even imminent demise, by demonstrating that (a) through effective communication, (b) that enables connected individual interactions, (c) undertaken by a critical mass of participants, (d) who exercise enough good faith, a new order—a more powerful new whole—may be brought forth and sustained. Individual contributions became self-amplifying in this case because they gave birth to a moral community and because they created structures that in turn created other structures. Initial disorder made innovation mandatory, and the egalitarian culture Noyce and others created allowed innovation to flourish.

Complexity theory also serves to highlight the importance of an initial crisis or state of chaos that marks a break with the past and stimulates openness to radical new ideas. Members of the semiconductor industry clearly recognized that they could not continue to prosper unless they drastically changed their practices. Such recognition is relatively rare in organizations and in industries and seems to be a necessary precursor to radical change. In this and other ways, Sematech provides an unusual or outlier example. Clearly, complexity theory would not inform all instances of change.

Ring and Van de Ven argue that a central question for organizational theory is how interorganizational relationships emerge and grow over time, and that the way to begin to understand such relationships is to focus on the sequence of events and interactions among the organizational parties involved.[125] Our study has done this. Our results indicate, as Ring and Van de Ven predict, that trust is an important factor in establishing and maintaining such relationships.[126] Our data also demonstrate the crucial importance of individual efforts. As Ring and Van de Ven argue, "these relationships only emerge, evolve, grow, and dissolve over time as a consequence of individual activities."[127]

Other factors were undoubtedly crucial to the founding and support of Sematech. These include the widespread conviction that something had to change, the fear and pain the U.S. semiconductor industry experienced as it watched its market share drop, the emergence of a charismatic leader who could inspire unusual efforts and cooperation, and the faith and courage of the many participants who worked tirelessly to accomplish the mission set for them.

# Chronology

1971: Semiconductor Equipment and Materials Institute (SEMI) formed by U.S. industry suppliers, goes on to become international.

1977: Semiconductor Industry Association (SIA) formed by five merchant microchip makers: LSI Logic, Intel, Advanced Micro Devices (AMD), National Semiconductor (NSC), and Motorola.

1982: Semiconductor Research Corporation (SRC) established by the SIA to do collaborative research and support education in silicon-related areas.

1984: National Cooperative Research Act exempts joint research and development projects from treble damage and per se rules of antitrust law.

1985: Global market-share bust for semiconductor manufacturers.

June, 1986: SIA commissions Charlie Sporck to poll members on need for a collaborative effort.

November, 1986: SIA forms a steering committee, coins the acronym for a SEmiconductor MAnufacturing TECHnology consortium (Sematech), begins lobbying efforts for government support, and steps up lobbying for trade sanctions against Japanese dumping to buy time.

December, 1986: Defense Science Board (DSB) task force report on U.S. semiconductor dependency is leaked to the media. Report calls for a Semiconductor Manufacturing Technology Institute involving government-industry collaboration.

March, 1987: Operating in Santa Clara offices donated by Sporck's NSC, the steering committee names task forces for operational planning and developing "Black Book." Original twenty-two (later forty-four) assignees from potential members begin working on plans.

May, 1987: SIA adopts Black Book and business operating plan for Sematech consortium, sets technology Phase I–III objectives.

June, 1987: Kickoff for series of ongoing technology planning workshops to be conducted industry-wide through early 1988. Lobbying for government support, industry membership recruitment, negotiating antitrust and intellectual property issues all intensify. Difficulty negotiating participation agreement.

August, 1987: Sematech incorporates with thirteen semiconductor manufacturing member companies. (One additional firm joins in 1988.)

September, 1987: Separate Sematech board formed, SEMI/Sematech branch established, with seat on Board of Directors. Work begins on formation of representative Technical Advisory Boards (TABs).

December, 1987: Legislation authorizing federal funding through DOD for Sematech.

January, 1988: Austin, Texas, selected as Sematech's new home.

April, 1988: Sematech moves from Santa Clara to Austin, recruits assignees and direct hires.

July, 1988: Board names Bob Noyce CEO and Paul Castrucci COO. Noyce brings in Peter Mills to serve as CAO.

October-November, 1988: Major reorganization effort from the top down, leading to February, 1989, conference with bottom-up manager feedback. Decision made to focus on suppliers. Meeting management training conducted. Restructuring is done to bring objectives in line with budget, new supplier focus, and job descriptions.

November, 1988: Fabrication facility dedicated, built in record thirty-two weeks. Castrucci wheels and deals for equipment, GAO investigation begins, Investment Council established.

March, 1989: "First silicon"—fully processed wafers. One hundred tools brought into production. Castrucci resigns, Hasty becomes COO. First Sematech Centers of Excellence (SCOEs) established.

March, 1989: Phase I milestone achieved: The manufacturing technological ability (equipment and processes) to etch .8-micron feature lines on 4Mb DRAM and 64K SRAM chips.

November, 1989: Supplier Relations Action Council (SRAC) and Total Quality task force established.

1990: Programs for Joint Development Projects (new equipment) and Equipment Qualification Projects (existing equipment) established. Cover four major technology areas: lithography; furnace and implant; multileveled metals; and manufacturing methods, processes, and systems.

1990: Partnering task force and quality task force combined in Partnering for Total Quality (PFTQ) program with suppliers.

June, 1990: Bob Noyce Day celebration in Austin; Noyce dies suddenly two days later.

1990: PFTQ self tests and guidebooks delivered, training workshops begin.

November, 1990: Bill Spencer and Frank Squires from Xerox become CEO and CAO, with Bill George of Motorola as COO.

1990: Threatened nonrenewal of government funding with defense cutbacks.
    Three members announce resignation. Reorganization effort, with new formulas for establishing return on investment (ROI) and agenda determination by remaining members.

1990: Phase II milestone achieved: .5-micron feature line etched on a silicon chip, a global benchmark.

May, 1991: Planning for Sematech II begins.

1991: Development, with member companies of a master list of fifty-eight "deliverables" more directly related to their agendas and supplier issues.

January, 1992: Government funding renewed for next five years. Ties to national labs, National Institute of Standards and Technology (NIST), and SRC strengthened as defense conversion begins.

August, 1992: Sematech II begins, with new mission statement reflecting restored competitive position: "Create fundamental change in manufacturing technology and the domestic infrastructure to provide U.S. semiconductor companies the continuing capability to be world-class suppliers."

SEMI leader Sam Harrell is first chief strategy officer.

January, 1993: Phase III goal achieved: .35-micron feature device. Motto: "On Target, On Time, Together."

March, 1993: Sematech helps develop National Semiconductor Technology Roadmap.

April, 1993: Announcement of a new thrust area addressing environmental issues in semiconductor manufacturing.

1994: COO Bill George returns to Motorola, new COO Jim Owens arrives from National Semiconductor.

1994: CEO Bill Spencer announces Sematech will relinquish dependence on federal funding.

# Sematech Centers of Excellence

| | |
|---|---|
| Arizona | University of Arizona and Sandia National Laboratories: research on contamination/defect assessment and control in the manufacture of semiconductors. |
| California | University of California at Berkeley and Stanford University: research on lithography and pattern transfer. |
| Massachusetts | Massachusetts Microelectronics Center, Massachusetts Institute of Technology, Boston University, and Northeastern University: research related to single-wafer processing for flexible integrated circuit manufacturing. |
| New Jersey | David Sarnoff Research Center, New Jersey Institute of Technology, Rutgers University, Stevens Institute, and Princeton Plasma Physics Laboratory: research in advanced plasma etch processing technology. |
| New Mexico | University of New Mexico and Sandia National Laboratories: research in all phases of metrology important to the semiconductor industry. |
| New York | Rensselaer Polytechnic Institute: research on multilevel metallization. |
| North Carolina | North Carolina State, University of North Carolina at Chapel Hill, Duke University, Research Triangle Institute, North Carolina A&T, and University of North Carolina at Charlotte: research on single-wafer processing. |
| Texas | University of Texas at Austin: research on submicron CMOS; Texas A&M University: research on manufacturing systems. |
| Wisconsin | University of Wisconsin at Madison: research on X-ray lithography. |

# Intel's Four-Step Model for Constructive Confrontation

I. Preparation. Identify the issue, set a goal, prepare for the approach.

1. Define the issue; focus on root problems; gather factual data, define the issue in one sentence.
2. See it from their viewpoint; seek a solution that meets your needs and the needs of Intel; be aware you may not be accurate in assessing their view; you will ask for their view in the initiation phase.
3. Write your goal. How will I better my job at Intel after the confrontation? How will business at Intel be improved?
4. Decide if it is worth confronting. Decide on issues of criticality, business goals, customer service, joint ownership and commitment to goal, data accuracy, and problem definition.
5. Pick a place to confront. Pick privacy over too public a setting; when possible confront issues as they arise.
6. How you approach the problem can lead to collaboration or defensiveness.
7. Describe your issue to them using the following criteria: Objective, factual, focused on outcomes not personal attacks, and on your ability to do your job.

II. Initiation. State your issue, listen to participants, summarize.

1. Follow your plan. Meet with individuals; use the positive approach in your plan.
2. Describe your issue. Use "I" statements; state calmly how the issue is affecting Intel's business; address importance; be specific; focus on the present and the future; communicate your interest in solving the issue together.

3. Ask them for their view of the issue and then listen. How do they see it? What is their perspective? Is this how you thought they viewed the issue?

4. Active listening skills to use. Attending—show them you want to hear their side via nonverbal behavior including eye contact, body language, and gestures. Clarifying—asking questions to assure the message you heard was the one intended. Empathizing—showing persons that you understand their feelings on the issue. Paraphrasing—summarizing what the other person said so that you both know you have heard and understand what was meant.

5. After listening, summarize positions. If the issue remains, agree that it exists by summarizing your view and their view of the problem.

III. Negotiation. Ask for solutions, consider options, choose one, commit to a written plan.

1. Ask for solutions. They may have a solution that meets both needs; they will be more committed if they own solving the problem with you.

2. Listen with respect. Keep an open mind; concentrate on their ideas; send messages that you are listening.

3. Suggest your possible solutions. Have an open discussion about how possible solutions meet both of your needs. This is critical.

4. Consider third options. Look for alternatives neither of you has mentioned; ask: "are there options we haven't considered?"

5. Pick a solution that will meet both of your needs.

6. Integrate their needs. Tell them why it will meet your needs; ensure they see the benefit of the solution; the solution should meet both of your needs and the needs of Intel.

7. Is the solution best for Intel? Step back and look at the big picture. Is this best for Intel, or does it just meet both of your needs?

8. Clarify and commit to a written plan.

IV. Follow-up/evaluation. Set date to discuss progress, ensure goal is reached, ensure process works for both parties.

1. Determine evaluation strategy. How will you know you are making progress? Have you achieved the goal of your solution plan? Record all agreements reached. Know who will do what. A person must own each agreement reached. Groups cannot own agreements reached.

2. Follow up by setting dates. Set milestones to check progress; set a meeting on your calendar to discuss progress.

3. Send plan out via electronic mail. This will reaffirm plan and ensure both have the same copy of the agreement.

4. Show discipline in follow-up. Most solutions require follow-up, measure-

ment of progress, and tweaking to ensure they solve the problem; be persistent—the effort is wasted unless the problem is solved.

5. Write a contingency plan. Brainstorm things that could cause your agreement to fail—allowing the problem to persist; write a plan to keep you on track; continue working your agreement and solve the problem.

# Notes

## Preface

1. "Topic of the Times," *New York Times,* Oct. 12, 1994, Late Edition, Final, reproduced in Lexis-Nexis.

2. *Reuters Financial Report,* Mar. 2, 1994, BC Cycle.

3. Tim Green, "Spencer Joins Sematech Team," *Austin Business Journal,* sec. 1, p. 1, reproduced in Lexis-Nexis.

4. Elizabeth Corcoran, "Competitive Climate: Industry Leaders Look to the Government for a New Era," *Scientific American,* Mar., 1989, p. 70, reproduced in Lexis-Nexis.

5. T. J. Rodgers, president of Cypress Semiconductor, interview on the *MacNeil/Lehrer News Hour,* Jan. 1, 1993.

6. Sematech was allowed to register as a manufacturing consortium under the 1984 National Cooperative Research Act. Under that act, activities that are deemed precompetitive are protected from the risk of treble damages and liability for a plaintiff's attorneys' fees. In June, 1993, the act was further expanded and renamed the National Cooperative Research and Production Act.

7. David Gibson and Everett Rogers, *R&D Collaboration on Trial: The Microelectronics and Computer Technology Corporation.*

8. Sematech's mission statement was amended several times, with a trend toward defining a clearer focus with a wider application, particularly to the semiconductor industry's supplier infrastructure.

## Chapter 1

1. T. R. Reid, *The Chip.*

2. We make extensive use of direct quotations from the interviews conducted for this book. We have edited these statements to increase clarity and reduce redundancy.

3. SEMI is based in Mountain View, California, with offices in Brussels, Moscow, Tokyo, Seoul, Boston, and Washington.

4. Miller Bonner, Lane Boyd, and Janet A. Allen, "Robert N. Noyce, 1927–1990," Sematech Archives, Austin, Tex. (hereafter Sematech Archives).

5. Micael L. Dertouzos, Richard K. Lester, and Robert M. Solow, *Made in America: Regaining the Productive Edge, The MIT Commission on Industrial Productivity.*

6. Steven Brull, "Japan-U.S. Microchip Makers Join Forces Warily," *Reuters Financial Report,* Dec. 26, 1988, reproduced in Lexis-Nexis.

7. IBM's Sandy Kane makes this distinction between forward pricing and dumping: "Forward pricing occurs when you charge less than it is costing you to make a part because you know that as the learning curve goes up, your additional knowledge will allow you to make the part cheaper. As a result of this knowledge, a company can charge less for a product initially—knowing that they will make it

up as their manufacturing becomes refined. Dumping occurs when a firm sells a product below cost in some markets for the purpose of driving out competition."

Kane went on to say that this distinction is important because the dumping caused U.S. manufacturers and the U.S. government to intervene. The Japanese strategy to take over the industry would have been effective had the dumping not triggered the U.S. response.

8. This meant that telephone "monopoly money" could no longer be used to support the AT&T's renowned Bell Labs, the conglomerate's well funded, Nobel Prize–winning research arm where in 1947 William Shockley (along with Walter Brattain and John Bardeen) invented the first practical transistor, called the "junction transistor." The electronic transistor replaced the cumbersome vacuum tube, and in 1959 led to the integrated circuit, a single semiconducting chip made of silicon (invented by Bob Noyce) or of germanium (invented by Jack Kilby) that could contain many transistors.

9. Vertical integration can motivate quality control since integrated firms bear the costs of their own defective products directly rather than passing them on to their customers.

10. David Yoffie, "How an Industry Builds Political Advantage," *Harvard Business Review*, May-June, 1988, p. 82, reproduced in Lexis-Nexis.

11. Ibid.

12. A captive semiconductor manufacturer designs and manufactures proprietary chips for its own microelectronic products. IBM, for instance, produces the microchips for IBM computers. A merchant manufacturer designs and manufactures microchips for sale to makers of other microelectronic products. Intel, for instance, during the period this chapter covers, did not make computers but instead designed and made microchips for others (they advertise "Intel inside" on other firms' computer brands). Captive firms may also buy special chips, and sometimes they sell chips or license their own designs. Some firms do both all the time. The terms merchant and captive thus are not always definitive. However, the distinction is not unimportant since it also refers to the scope and characteristics of a firm's market strengths and vulnerabilities, as well as determining their attitudes toward both domestic competition and foreign trade. (For instance, the semicaptive chip maker of a computer firm, designing and making its own patented microchips, might also buy its memory chips from a Japanese supplier and benefit from cheap dumping, whereas a straight semiconductor merchant might be opposed to all foreign chip dumping.) It is hard to define the merchant-captive distinction in either/or terms.

13. John Alic, Lewis Branscomb, Harvey Brooks, Ashton Carter, and Gerald Epstein, *Beyond Spinoff*.

14. Ibid.

15. Ibid.

16. Michael Borrus, *New York Times*, July 31, 1988, sec. 3, p. 3, reproduced in Lexis-Nexis.

17. Barbara Gray and D. J. Wood, "Collaborative Alliances: Moving from Practice to Theory," *Journal of Applied Behavioral Sciences* 27 (1991).

18. Jan Mares, *Business America*,

19. Ibid.

20. Dertouzos et al., *Made in America*.

21. Interview with Jim Peterman by the authors.

22. *Financial Times*, July 18, 1986, reproduced in Lexis-Nexis.

23. U.S. Department of Commerce, "1984 Industrial Outlook" (Washington, D.C.: 1984), pp. 30–4 and 30–8; and International Trade Administration, "U.S. Technology Trade and Competitiveness" (Washington, D.C.: Department of Commerce, 1985), pp. 5–11, 17.

24. "The High-Tech Commodity: A Text-Book Market? Two Ways to Stay in Business," *The Economist*, Nov. 22, 1986, p. 78, reproduced in Lexis-Nexis.

25. Steve Lohr, *New York Times*, Jan. 24, 1993, sec. 4, p. 2, reproduced in Lexis-Nexis.

26. Ken Jacobson, *Federal Technology Report*, Feb. 4, 1993, reproduced in Lexis-Nexis.

27. Steve Lohr, *New York Times*, Jan. 24, 1993.

28. Jack Robertson, *Electronic News*, Dec. 8, 1986, p. 1, reproduced in Lexis-Nexis.

29. "Pentagon Advisers Call for U.S. Aid to Chip Industry," *Wall Street Journal*, Dec. 10, 1986.

30. U.S. Department of Defense, "Report of the Defense Science Board Task Force on Defense Semiconductor Dependency" (Washington, D.C.: 1987) (emphasis in original).

31. Shintaro Ishihara, *The Japan that Can Say No: Why Japan Will Be First among Equals*, p. 21.

32. "Administration Policy Groups Split on Need for Aid to High-Tech Industry," *Inside U.S. Trade,* Nov. 28, 1986.

33. The manufacturing demands and high-volume production of technology drivers (e.g., DRAMs) allow the producer to learn new techniques that apply to the next generation of products. By losing capacity in such technology drivers, manufacturers lose out on the chance to be competitive in the next generation of devices. The National Security Council panel could not agree on a definitive list of such drivers that merited support.

34. U.S. Department of Defense, "Report of the Defense Science Board Task Force."

35. This forum was different from the plans for Sematech and was conceived as a much smaller initiative.

36. IBM's Sandy Kane noted in a follow-up interview that the quick coordination to get representatives together on a task force in a single week's time was a strong signal of how important and critical firms viewed the Sematech start-up task.

37. Dertouzos et al., *Made in America,* p. 106.

38. In 1993, as part of President Clinton's technology plan, production consortia were also to be exempted. (See Carl P. Leubsdorf, "Clinton Details Technology Policy; Plan Calls for $17 Billion Federal Effort," *Dallas Morning News,* Feb. 23, 1993, p. 1A.)

39. The Malcolm Baldrige National Quality Award was established by Congress on Aug. 20, 1987, as a memorial to Baldrige following his untimely death in a rodeo. The purpose of the award is to help improve the quality and productivity of U.S. businesses. (See R. C. Palermo and G. H. Watson, eds., *A World of Quality: The Timeless Passport, Xerox Quality Solutions.*)

## Chapter 2

1. Dewey, Ballantine weekly report, May 8, 1987, Sematech Archives.
2. Report of the Federal Advisory Council on Federal Participation in Sematech, 1989, ES-4.
3. A unit of measure equal to a thousandth of a millimeter or .000039 of an inch—1/100th the diameter of a strand of human hair.
4. John Thompson, "Sematech Aim: Tie Sematech, Gear Expertise, *Electronic News,* Feb. 22, 1988, p. 20, reproduced in Lexis-Nexis.
5. Dewey, Ballantine weekly report, May 22, 1987, Sematech Archives.
6. Dewey, Ballantine weekly report, May 29, 1987, Sematech Archives.
7. *Electronic Business,* May 1, 1988, p. 32, reproduced in Lexis-Nexis.
8. Dewey, Ballantine weekly report, May 22, 1987, Sematech Archives.
9. Committee roster, July 23, 1987, Sematech Archives.
10. Interview with Turner Hasty by the authors.
11. Board of Directors roster, July 23, 1987, Sematech Archives.
12. Michael Smitka, *Competitive Ties: Subcontracting in the Japanese Automotive Industry.*
13. Tim Green, "Austin on SEMATECH," *Austin Business Journal,* Jan. 11, 1988, reproduced in Lexis-Nexis.
14. *Business Wire,* Jan. 25, 1988, Sematech Archives.
15. A comparative description of chip types is provided in chapter 3. (See ibid.)
16. *Electronic News,* Nov. 24, 1986, p. 1, reproduced in Lexis-Nexis.
17. Sematech Archives.
18. The letter was signed by Sens. Pete Domenici (R-N.M.), Jeff Bingaman (D-N.M.), Alfonse D'Amato (R-N.Y.), Dennis DeConcini (D-Ariz.); Jim McClure (R-Ida.); John McCain (R-Ariz.); Pete Wilson (R-Calif.); Harry Reid (D-Nev.); Lawton Chiles (D-Fla.); Tim Wirth (D-Colo.); and Lloyd Bentsen (D-Tex.).
19. Dewey, Ballantine weekly report, Sept. 11, 1987, Sematech Archives.
20. IBM, TI, and Micron were the only U.S. firms still actively manufacturing DRAMS at this time.
21. Dewey, Ballantine weekly report, Sept. 19, 1987, Sematech Archives.
22. Andrew Pollack, "Chip Pioneer to Head Consortium," *New York Times,* July 28, 1988, p. D1, reproduced in Lexis-Nexis.
23. Sematech Archives, Oct. 22, 1987.
24. Dewey, Ballantine weekly report, Oct. 9, 1987, Sematech Archives.

## Chapter 3

1. NCR was later acquired by AT&T but retained its voting membership in Sematech.

2. Jeffrey Mayer et al., Advisory Council Report on Federal Participation in Sematech, 1989, p. 13, Sematech Archives.

3. Ibid.

4. David Sanger, *New York Times,* May 26, 1987, p. A1, reproduced in Lexis-Nexis; Yoffie, "How an Industry Builds Political Advantage."

5. They were known as technology drivers because they were produced in such high volume and with such tight process control of their increasing miniaturization that they supported R&D while bringing down the learning curve.

6. Yoffie, "How an Industry Builds Political Advantage," p. 82.

7. Since 1986, with the growing importance of microprocessors and logic chips, and the resulting increase in the volume of their production, DRAMs have grown proportionately less important. Intel, for example, now produces a volume of microprocessors equivalent to the output of most DRAM manufacturers. Sematech's establishment occurred just as the industry's dependence on DRAMs was beginning to shift. (From Turner Hasty interview.)

8. Mayer et al., 1989 Advisory Council Report, p. 21, Sematech Archives.

9. While CIM refers solely to the integration of computer control and monitoring into a manufacturing process, CAD can refer both to the process of designing a part or assembly with a computer to capture the designer's intent, produce drawings, and analyze the behavior of the object, and/or to that area of data processing concerned with the design, supply, operation, and support of systems performing such functions. Therefore, CAD is concerned not only with chip design but also equipment and process design. (Definitions taken from the Sematech Official Dictionary, Revision 2.0, Sematech Archives).

10. Perry was then the undersecretary for research and engineering at the DOD. He became secretary of defense in 1993 under President Clinton.

11. Dewey Ballantine memo to the SIA Public Policy Committee, Dec. 10, 1986, Sematech Archives.

12. Turner Hasty interview.

13. Ironically, the mere knowledge that IBM had a unique planarization technique led directly to its generic development and dissemination at Sematech. Thus even sharing the existence of an untold secret had value. This is easier to see in hindsight; no one realized it at the time.

14. The term "fab" is used loosely, like the term "factory," sometimes simply meaning only the building itself, at other times referring to the whole operating facility of the building and equipment together. At this point, we are considering the equipping process separately.

15. *Federal Contracts Report,* Mar. 14, 1988, vol. 49, no. 11, p. 451, reproduced in Lexis-Nexis.

16. "SEMATECH Goes to Austin," Dataquest *Research Newsletter,* Feb., 1988.

17. Andrew Grove, *High Output Management.*

18. Interview with Sam Harrell by the authors

19. Turner Hasty interview.

20. George Leopold, "Computer Chip Group Could Serve as Model for Hi-Tech Cooperation," *Defense News,* Jan. 7, 1991, p. 10.

21. The transformation that CAD could have on easing the problems of specialized manufacturing requirements, particularly through the use of more standardized equipment, was not yet widely appreciated. Computer-aided manufacturing to automate flexible production of specialized chips looked more promising.

22. David Sanger, *New York Times,* May 26, 1987.

23. Mayer et al., 1989 Advisory Council Report, p. ES-3, Sematech Archives.

24. Sematech Archives.

25. Mayer et al., 1989 Advisory Council Report, p. 12, Sematech Archives.

26. This characterization does not reflect the distinction made at Sematech between "tool" and "equipment." Tool is a more comprehensive term, including any device used to execute an operation, including computer modeling, software, and metrology mechanisms. Equipment means a specific apparatus used to execute an operation: Sematech glossary.

27. Turner Hasty interview.

28. Mayer et al., 1989 Advisory Council Report, p. 22, Sematech Archives.

29. One report said: "The situation is proving to be an early political problem for Sematech, and the first test of whether a cooperative consortium of highly individualistic American semiconductor companies can work. Although committed to loaning some of their key employees to Sematech and providing tens of millions of dollars in funding, the founding firms are loath to see a mass defection of talent to the consortium." (Robert Ristelhueber and John Thompson, *Electronic News,* Mar. 14, 1988, p. 1, reproduced in Lexis-Nexis).

30. Thompson, "SEMATECH Aim."

31. Gibson and Rogers, *R&D Collaboration on Trial.*

32. Because of the limited duration of the Sematech charter, these employees were never referred to as "permanent hires."

33. A disconnect refers to an area in planning for which no one is taking responsibility.

34. Mayer et al., 1989 Advisory Council Report, p. 23, Sematech Archives.

## Chapter 4

1. Mayer et al., 1989 Advisory Council Report, p. 22, Sematech Archives.

2. Public Law 100-180.

3. In distinction to more typical project type oversight, in which there might be an officer in each major area.

4. Mayer et al., 1989 Advisory Council Report, p. 45, Sematech Archives.

5. *Electronic News,* August 1, 1988, reproduced in Lexis-Nexis.

6. Bonner, Boyd, and Allen, "Robert N. Noyce, 1927–1990."

7. Ibid.

8. Mayer et al., 1989 Advisory Council Report, p. 23, Sematech Archives.

9. Within a month after Noyce's appointment, the Japanese firm NEC expressed interest in joining the consortium, but officials confirmed its intention to remain all-American. (Sematech Press Review, May–Sept., 1988, Sematech Archives.)

10. Tom Wolfe, "The Tinkerings of Robert Noyce," reprinted from *Esquire,* Dec., 1983, by Intel Corporation, Santa Clara, Calif.

11. Recall that a micron is 1/100th the diameter of a human hair and that Sematech's first three objectives were already in the submicron range—from .80 to .35 of a micron.

12. There are two Motorola fabs in Austin. One is in suburban Oak Hill, southwest of the city, and the other is on Ed Bluestein Boulevard on the city's east side.

13. Sematech Press Release, Nov. 15, 1988, Sematech Archives.

14. Mark Langford, "Sematech dedicated; officials unveil parts of high-tech clean room," United Press International, Texas Regional News, Nov. 16, 1988.

Other guests included the Texas supporters who helped make it all come together at both the federal and state levels. Several members of Congress participated in the dedication ceremony: Sen. Phil Gramm (R-Tex.); Rep. Les AuCoin (D-Ore.), a member of the House Appropriations Committee; Rep. Bill Chappell (D-Fla.), chairman of the House Appropriations Defense Subcommittee; Rep. Ron Coleman (D-Tex.); Rep. Charles Wilson (D-Tex.); and Rep. J. J. "Jake" Pickle (D-Tex.), who played such a key role in negotiating the winning proposal for Austin.

15. "1990 Financial World Partners," *Financial World,* Mar. 20, 1990. Actually, billion dollar fabs were common by the early 1990s.

16. Mayer et al., 1989 Advisory Council Report, p. 20, Sematech Archives.

17. Sematech 1989 Strategic Operating Plan, p. 4-2, Sematech Archives.

18. Mayer et al., 1989 Advisory Council Report, p. 22, Sematech Archives.

19. Ibid.

20. Ibid.

21. Sematech 1989 Strategic Operating Plan, p. 1-4, Sematech Archives.

22. Mayer, et al., 1989 Advisory Council Report, p. ES-4, Sematech Archives.

23. Ibid.

24. Sematech 1989 Operating Plan, Sematech Archives.

25. Because of his concern for confidentiality, we were unable to obtain an interview with Cecil

Parker, who facilitated many meetings at Sematech. Our interviews with Olivia Miller-Snapp, the other principal facilitator, failed to produce usable details from her observations at meetings. Their point of view is a missing ingredient from our analysis.

26. Andrew Pollack, "Conflict at Sematech Forces Out No. 2 Man," *New York Times,* Mar. 21, 1989, Late City Final Edition, p. D1, reproduced in Lexis-Nexis.

27. Parker was to have been permanently hired but could not come due to other obligations. He later expressed regret at having to miss his opportunity to work more closely with Bob Noyce.

28. Sematech 1990 Operating Plan, p. 6, Sematech Archives.

29. Ibid.

## Chapter 5

1. November, 1989, testimony, House Budget Committee.

2. Sematech 1990 Strategic Operating Plan, p. 1-1, Sematech Archives.

3. Mayer et al., 1990 Advisory Council Report, p. 17, Sematech Archives.

4. Ibid.

5. Ibid.

6. Ibid.

7. During a Jan. 1, 1993, interview on the *MacNeil/Lehrer News Hour,* persistent critic T. J. Rodgers repeated his allegations of Sematech's lack of wisdom in subsidizing comparatively successful firms by asking, "Why should we be giving suckers to 300-pound kids?"

8. Interview with Deepak Ranidive by the authors.

9. In the organizational and psychological literature, such a set of relations is called a moral community. (See Morton Deutsch, "Educating for a Peaceful World," *American Psychologist* 48 (1993): 510–17; and Amitai Etzioni, *The Moral Dimension: Toward a New Economics.*)

10. Muzafer Sherif, *In Common Predicament: Social Psychology of Intergroup Conflict and Cooperation.*

11. Ibid.

12. Interview with Tom Seidel by the authors.

13. This understanding was especially clear in Applied Materials, a supply firm that had patterned its entire organization on what it had learned from supplying to Japanese firms. (See James C. Morgan and J. Jeffrey Morgan, *Cracking the Japanese Market: Strategies for Success in the New Global Economy.*)

14. David Teece, "Information Sharing, Innovation and Antitrust," *Antitrust Law Journal* 2 (1994): 465–81.

15. Interview with Sam Harrell by the authors.

16. The 1990 Advisory Council Report stated flatly: "The task of restoring independence is not only a matter of developing world-class manufacturing technology. It also involves restoring or sustaining the commercial strength of financially pressed U.S. equipment and materials suppliers. To meet the latter requirement, new or improved equipment and materials must be developed *in phase with chipmaker's purchasing cycles* for the next two generations of semiconductor device technology. . . . reflected in the time lines for Phases 2 and 3." (Mayer et al., 1990 Advisory Council Report [emphasis in original], Sematech Archives.) For additional views related to timing and cadence in organizations, see J. Hassard, "Aspects of Time in Organization," *Human Relations* 44 (1991).

17. Mayer et al., 1990 Advisory Council Report, p. 7, Sematech Archives.

18. Dertouzos et al., *Made in America,* p. 253.

19. *Electronic News,* November 28, 1988, p. 26, reproduced in Lexis-Nexis.

20. Mayer et al., 1990 Advisory Council Report, p. 10, Sematech Archives.

21. Ibid.

22. Ibid.

23. Jack Robertson, "IBM Thinks Ahead," *Electronic News,* Mar. 20, 1989, p. 12, reproduced in Lexis-Nexis.

24. Sematech Press Review, Jan. 27, 1989, Sematech Archives.

25. Sematech Press Review, May 23, 1989, Sematech Archives.

26. Sematech Press Review, Apr. 20, 1990, Sematech Archives.

27. Sematech 1989 Strategic Operating Plan, Technical Appendices, p. 3, Sematech Archives.

28. Sematech 1990 Strategic Operating Plan, p. 1-5, Sematech Archives.

29. Mayer et al., 1990 Advisory Council Report, p. 18, Sematech Archives.

30. Ibid., p. 19.

31. Ibid., p. 20.

32. Sematech 1990 Operating Plan, Sematech Archives.

33. Ibid., p. 7–9.

34. Interview with Franklin Squires by the authors.

35. Sematech Press Release, May 23, 1989, Sematech Archives.

36. Andrew Pollack, "Ideas & Trends: High-Tech Business Loses a Friend at the Pentagon," *New York Times,* Apr. 29, 1990, sec. 4, p. 5, reproduced in Lexis-Nexis.

37. John Schneidawind, "Explosive Growth Ahead for Industry," *USA Today,* Jan. 22, 1993, p. 1B, reproduced in Lexis-Nexis.

38. For another analysis of this issue, see Larry D. Browning and Janice Beyer, "The Structuring of Shared Voluntary Standards in the U.S. Semiconductor Industry: Communicating to Reach Agreement," *Communication Monographs* 64 (1998): 1–25.

39. *Electronic News,* Oct. 29, 1990, reproduced in Lexis-Nexis.

40. Ibid.

41. *Business Wire,* Jan. 9, 1990, reproduced in Lexis-Nexis.

42. Ibid.

43. Scott Pendleton, *Christian Science Monitor,* Jan. 25, 1993, reproduced in Lexis-Nexis.

44. Mayer et al. 1990 Advisory Council Report, pp. ES-4–ES-5, Sematech Archives.

45. *Investor's Business Daily,* June 17, 1993, reproduced in Lexis-Nexis.

46. *Los Angeles Times,* Apr. 30, 1993, p. A1, reproduced in Lexis-Nexis.

47. *Boston Globe,* May 11, 1993, City Edition, Metro/Region sec., p. 1, reproduced in Lexis-Nexis.

48. *Los Angeles Times,* Apr. 30, 1993, p. A1.

49. Turner Hasty interview.

50. *Boston Globe,* May 11, 1993.

51. Ibid.

52. Jack Robertson, "Sematech Sumo Match," *Electronic News,* Oct. 29, 1990, p. 12, reproduced in Lexis-Nexis.

53. *Electronic News,* Jan. 25, 1993, reproduced in Lexis-Nexis.

54. Peter Dunn, "Motorola Selects Canon Steppers for MOS-11 Fab," *Electronic News,* Oct. 22, 1990, reproduced in Lexis-Nexis.

55. *Los Angeles Times,* Apr. 30, 1993, A1.

56. Robertson, "Sematech Sumo Match."

## Chapter 6

1. Mayer et al., 1990 Advisory Council Report, p. 26, Sematech Archives.

2. Ashok Kanagol remarks: "Just to give you a feeling of how unstructured things were in those days, people didn't really have designations or titles. Very few people did at that point. The senior managers were all vice presidents." Turner Hasty says that the title of vice president was mostly used for off-site image, and had less meaning on site than the actual work that managers did. This in part reflected the early lack of structure, and in part the egalitarian culture.

3. Richard Gerstner, a writer working on documents for both task forces, claims to have been one of the first to see and call attention to the overlap. The interview with Ashok Kanagol indirectly supports Gerstner's claim. The best explanation of the development of PFTQ is that of a project with crucial contributions at all levels, from bottom to top.

4. "Sematech's current Operating Plan projects expenditures in calendar year 1990 totaling $260 million. This amount includes a sizable carry-over from 1989." (Mayer et al., 1990 Advisory Council Report, pp. ES-3–ES-4, Sematech Archives).

5. Both sides giving 50/50 is also a cooperative assumption in Peter Block's *Flawless Consultation: A Guide to Getting Your Expertise Used.*

6. Christopher Avery, Debra R. France, Larry D. Browning, and Michael S. Oswald, "Best Customer and Supplier Partnering Practices in the U.S. Semiconductor Industry," Sematech Technology Report no. 93031544AXFR, Austin, Tex., 1993, Sematech Archives.

7. Many industrial firms establish "universities" for their personnel, who may already have advanced academic degrees, to receive specialized training. For example, the Motorola University in Schaumberg, Ill., with regional campuses in Phoenix and Austin, in 1992 delivered 102,000 days of training to employees, suppliers, and customers. (Ronald Henkoff and Andrew Erdman, "Companies that Train Best," *Fortune,* Mar. 23, 1993, reproduced in Lexis-Nexis.) The amount spent by industry on the training and education of employees is at least equivalent to the national budget for higher education.

8. Peter Burrows and Garret DeYoung, "Recipe for Success: Keep Your Customers Smiling; Electronics Suppliers Who Put the Buyer First Will Survive the Quality-Conscious '90s," *Electronic Business,* Oct. 15, 1990, p. 85.

9. Interview with Richard Gerstner by the authors.

10. By the end of 1991, more than thirty-five hundred people from seventy-one U.S. companies had participated in sixteen PFTQ classes. (Sematech 1991 Annual Business Report, Sematech Archives.)

11. Sematech *Update,* July-Aug., 1993, p. 3, Sematech Archives.

12. Ralph Stacey, *Managing the Unknowable: Strategic Boundaries Between Order and Chaos in Organizations,* p. 146.

13. *Federal News Service,* Nov. 29, 1989, reproduced in Lexis-Nexis.

14. An indication of the power of Noyce's reputation in Washington is represented by the response to a call he made to Sen. Sam Nunn (D-Ga.), chairman of the Senate Foreign Relations Committee. Senator Nunn is reported to have returned Noyce's call within five minutes.

## Chapter 7

1. Green, "Spencer Joins Sematech Team," *Austin Business Journal,* p. 1.

2. Ibid.

3. Ibid.

4. Robert Galvin succeeded his father, Paul, who founded Motorola in 1928, first as president in 1956, then as chairman in 1965. Robert Galvin stepped down as chairman in 1990, retaining the chairmanship of the Executive Committee.

5. Sematech Press Release, Jan. 17, 1991, Sematech Archives.

6. Telephone interview with Bob Galvin, Aug. 1, 1993.

7. Interview with Craig Barrett by the authors.

8. Mills went on to become CEO of the U.S. Display Consortium (USDC) in 1994, established to coordinate the development of a domestic flat panel display in the United States.

9. Sematech Press Review, Jan. 11, 1991, Sematech Archives.

10. According to the charter, member firms were required to submit their intent to resign two years in advance. Since original memberships ran through 1992, late 1990 was the first time members were within the timeframe for signaling their intent to resign. The DARPA grant was also authorized for five years—from 1987 to 1992—although as a government program it continued to be subject to yearly evaluation and federal budget approval.

11. Charles F. Sabel, "Studied Trust: Building New Forms of Cooperation in a Volatile Economy," *Human Relations* 46 (1993).

12. Abraham Maslow, *Motivation and Personality.*

13. Sematech Press Review, Apr. 27, 1990, Sematech Archives.

14. Sematech Press Review, May 24, 1991, Sematech Archives.

15. Sematech Press Review, Nov. 8, 1991, Sematech Archives.

16. Hearing of the Defense Industry and Technology Subcommittee of the Senate Armed Services Committee, Subject: National Advisory Committee on Semiconductors Report, Nov. 29, 1989, Sematech Archives.

17. Jack Robertson, "Sematech Confirms Shift in Test from End-to-End to 'Short Loop,'" *Electronic News,* Dec. 23, 1991, reproduced in Lexis-Nexis.

18. Sematech Press Review, Feb. 15, 1991, Sematech Archives.

19. *Business Week,* Dec. 10, 1990, reproduced in Lexis-Nexis.

20. Robert Ziller, "Toward a Theory of Open and Closed Groups," *Psychological Bulletin* 64 (1965): 164–82.

21. Sematech 1991 Annual Report, Sematech Archives.

22. For example, coming from the multidivisional member firm of IBM, there were three competing agendas for Sematech project investment: either the GCA or the Micrascan optical lithography steppers, or the development of X-ray lithography.

23. For example, Hewlett-Packard and TI won the Deming Award for quality in Japan even before Sematech. The Motorola Corporation (not just the semiconductor division) was an early Malcolm Baldrige National Quality Award winner. IBM and Intel began developing quality practices early.

24. Sematech Press Review, May 10, 1991, Sematech Archives.

25. Prabhakar later became the director of the National Institute of Standards and Technology (NIST).

26. *The Microtech 2000 Workshop Report,* Sematech Archives.

27. Jack Robertson, "SIA Roadmap Accents MCM, Low-Power Ics, Semiconductor Industry," *Electronic News,* Jan. 18, 1993, p. 1, reproduced in Lexis-Nexis.

28. Sematech Press Reviews, May 10 and Sept. 27, 1991, Sematech Archives.

29. Sematech Press Review, Aug. 2, 1991, Sematech Archives.

30. William Spencer, unpublished paper, Sematech Archives.

31. "The Haves versus the Have-Nots," *Electronic Business,* May 1, 1988, p. 32, reproduced in Lexis-Nexis. In 1987, LSI Logic and Micron Technology were the two smallest companies to join Sematech, with FY 1987 sales of $262 million and $91 million, respectively. Relatively speaking, a smaller, perhaps $20 million company's base fee amounts to 5 percent of sales, whereas for Sematech's larger members, dues only come to roughly 1 percent of their semiconductor sales. This proportion affects the weight of a firm's decision to invest in a consortium, relative to its overall corporate strategy.

32. Sematech *Update,* Feb., 1992, Sematech Archives.

33. Sematech Press Review, Jan. 17, 1992, Sematech Archives.

34. Some critics charged that Sematech reduced the scope of its goals whenever it was unable to meet them on time. Beginning with the grandiose aspirations of the Black Book, a case could be made that the consortium had experienced a running series of reality checks, with numerous subsequent adjustments to formulate realizable and affordable goals. For whatever reason, it was generally recognized that in 1991 Bill George took over an unnecessarily "dysfunctional" fab that was having trouble producing deliverables on schedule.

35. Sematech 1991 Strategic Overview, p. 1-13, Sematech Archives.

36. Bill George comments in his interview that every company reporting in 1992 said it had received more benefits than it paid in dues. The goal is to keep increasing this several-fold, perhaps even to eight or nine times, if possible.

37. According to Bill George, the results of the 1992 survey showed that all members who reported (about half at first) said they got back in benefits at least what they had put in, making membership at least cost-neutral. The goal was to look for ways to continue increasing the ratio of return.

38. The quality of Sematech's assignees had always been considered high in general, but uneven, as some firms tended to contribute more talent than others. Now, "free riding" offered less of a payoff in this area.

39. Sematech Press Review, Jan. 15, 1993, Sematech Archives.

40. "Sematech Consortium Says Rockwell Stays," *Financial Report,* Jan. 6, 1993, BC cycle, reproduced in Lexis-Nexis.

## Chapter 8

1. Robertson, "Sematech Confirms Shift."

2. Sematech *Communiqué,* Special Issue, Dec., 1991, Sematech Archives.

3. Sematech 1991 Strategic Overview, pp. 3-2–3-11, Sematech Archives.

4. Sematech *Update,* Feb., 1992, Sematech Archives.

5. Sematech Press Review, Aug. 21, 1992, Sematech Archives.

6. Sematech Press Review, Oct. 2, 1992, Sematech Archives.

7. Thomas and Singh had developed a three-electrode plasma reactor using phase modulation to control the plasma. (Sematech *Update,* Feb., 1992, Sematech Archives.) By 1993, fifteen patents had been generated at Sematech itself, with thirty-six patents pending. At least two engineers, Dick Anderson

and Franz Geyling, had received three patents each for work done at Sematech. (Amy Smith, "Finding Patent Success," *Austin Business Journal,* Jan. 18, 1993, sec. 1, p. 5, reproduced in Lexis-Nexis.)

8. Dertouzos et al., *Made in America.*

9. Corcoran, "Competitive Climate," p. 70.

10. *San Francisco Chronicle,* Feb. 22, 1990, p. C3, reproduced in Lexis-Nexis.

11. Dertouzos et al., *Made in America,* p. 157.

12. Sematech Press Release, May 31, 1988, Sematech Archives.

13. *PR Newswire,* Mar. 29, 1989, reproduced in Lexis-Nexis.

14. *PR Newswire,* Aug. 4, 1994, reproduced in Lexis-Nexis.

15. Andrew Pollack, "New Chip Method May Be Put Off," *New York Times,* Dec. 12, 1990, p. D1, reproduced in Lexis-Nexis.

16. Ibid.

17. Mayer et al., 1989 Advisory Council Report, p. ES-4, Sematech Archives.

18. Sematech Press Review, May 5, 1989, Sematech Archives.

19. Glenn J. McLoughlin, "SEMATECH: Issues in Evaluation and Assessment," Congressional Research Service, Library of Congress, 92-749 (spring, 1992).

20. Out of phase lights are lights of different wavelengths.

21. Pollack, "New Chip Method."

22. Sematech Press Release, Apr. 27, 1992, Sematech Archives.

23. McLoughlin, "SEMATECH."

24. Sematech *Update,* Feb., 1992, Sematech Archives.

25. "Oak Ridge in Transition: A Perspective from the Solid State Sciences," *Solid State Technology,* Apr., 1994, p. 34, reproduced in Lexis-Nexis.

26. *Federal Contracts Report,* The Bureau of National Affairs, Inc., Mar. 1, 1993, reproduced in Lexis-Nexis.

27. *Newsday,* Feb. 28, 1993, reproduced in Lexis-Nexis.

28. *Federal Contracts Report,* The Bureau of National Affairs, Inc., Mar. 1, 1993.

29. "Clinton's Design on Technology; Sparks Debate over 'Meddling,'" *Newsday,* Feb. 28, 1993, reproduced in Lexis-Nexis.

30. Spencer, unpublished paper, p. 19, Sematech Archives.

31. "Clinton's Design on Technology," *Newsday,* Feb. 28, 1993.

32. Sematech *Update,* Sept., 1989, Sematech Archives.

33. Sematech *Update,* June-July, 1992, Sematech Archives.

34. Sematech Press Release, Apr. 7, 1993, Sematech Archives.

35. *Federal Technology Report,* Apr. 15, 1993, reproduced in Lexis-Nexis.

36. Ibid.

37. *Federal Technology Report,* Apr. 14, 1994, p. 4, reproduced in Lexis-Nexis.

38. Ibid., p. 14.

39. *Earth Action Network* 5, no. 2 (Apr., 1994): 28.

40. *Business Wire,* July 18, 1994, reproduced in Lexis-Nexis.

41. Ibid.

42. Peter Drucker, *Post-Capitalist Society,* pp. 22–30.

43. Sematech *Update,* Jan., 1993, Sematech Archives.

44. Sematech *All Hands Memo,* Dec. 18, 1992, Sematech Archives.

45. Sematech Press Review, Dec. 11, 1992, Sematech Archives. Earlier in 1992, VLSI Research had also released final survey results showing that in 1991 U.S. semiconductor equipment suppliers actually pulled ahead of Japan in world equipment market share with the U.S. claiming 46.7 percent to Japan's 44.9 percent. (Sematech *Communiqué,* July-Aug., 1992, Sematech Archives.)

46. Three years from development to manufacturing was the time usually figured into the road maps.

47. Tom Seidel notes that the competitive pressure to accelerate technology generation cycles was great. Samsung Electronics in Korea, for example, had completed five two-year generations, culminating in the demonstration of a 256-megabit, fully functional DRAM, announced in Aug., 1994.

48. William J. Spencer, "A Roadmap for a Competitive Industry," Sematech *Update,* Mar.-Apr., 1993, Sematech Archives.

49. Sematech *All Hands Memo,* Feb. 22, 1993, Sematech Archives.

50. Sematech *All Hands Memo,* Oct. 5, 1993, Sematech Archives.

51. Sematech Press Review, July 16, 1993, Sematech Archives.

52. Sematech Press Release Nov. 16, 1993, Sematech Archives.

53. Sematech Press Review, Oct. 15, 1993, Sematech Archives. The consortium intended to provide support for SVGL's Micrascan stepper until it could develop an adequate market. In late 1994, SVGL announced that its Micrascan II stepper had been used successfully by Samsung Electronics in the creation of a 256-megabit DRAM. Shortly thereafter, however, SVGL's licensing and joint development negotiations with Canon broke off with no deal concluded.

54. Sematech Press Review, Nov. 12, 1993, Sematech Archives.

55. Sematech *Update,* Nov.-Dec., 1994, Sematech Archives.

56. From interviews with Sam Harrell and Tom Seidel by the authors.

57. "Topic of the Times," *New York Times,* Oct. 12, 1994, Late Edition, Final, reproduced in Lexis-Nexis.

58. Sematech Press Review, Oct. 7, 1994, Sematech Archives.

59. "SEMATECH Seeks Final Direct Funding," Sematech *Update,* 1st Quarter, 1995, p. 1, Sematech Archives.

60. *Financial Times,* Oct. 6, 1994, reproduced in Lexis-Nexis.

## Chapter 9

1. Interview with Craig Barrett by the authors.

2. *PC Week,* Feb. 1, 1993, reproduced in Lexis-Nexis.

3. *San Diego Union-Tribune,* Oct. 9, 1994, reproduced in Lexis-Nexis.

4. Sematech Press Review (figures from Dataquest, Inc.), Jan. 6, 1989, Sematech Archives.

5. Charles Ferguson, "From the People Who Brought You Voodoo Economics," *Harvard Business Review,* May-June, 1988, reproduced in Lexis-Nexis.

6. Sematech Press Review (figures from Dataquest, Inc.), Jan. 11, 1991, Sematech Archives.

7. Sematech *Update,* Jan., 1993, Sematech Archives.

8. John Markoff, *New York Times,* Oct. 6, 1994, Late Edition, Final, p. D1, reproduced in Lexis-Nexis.

9. *San Diego Union-Tribune,* Oct. 9, 1994, reproduced in Lexis-Nexis.

10. "Behind the news of cyclically rebounding profits shines a larger truth: U.S. economic preeminence looks more secure than it has in a generation." ("The Economy," *Fortune,* Apr. 18, 1994, Domestic Edition, p. 52.)

11. Sematech *Update,* June-July 1992 (figures from VLSI Research), Sematech Archives.

12. *San Diego Union-Tribune,* Oct. 9, 1994, reproduced in Lexis-Nexis.

13. "Financial Focus," *Defense News,* July 25–31, 1994, p. 25.

14. *Financial Times,* Feb. 9, 1993, reproduced in Lexis-Nexis.

15. The theoretical literature that is the scaffolding for our understanding of the moral code is developed more fully in the final chapter.

16. *Federal News Service,* Nov. 29, 1989, reproduced in Lexis-Nexis.

17. Interview with Deepak Ranidive by the authors.

18. Interview with Joan Yaffe, a Sematech facilitator and trainer, by the authors.

19. Quoted in "U.S. Semiconductor Research Seeing Impact," Sematech *Update,* July, 1991, Sematech Archives.

20. Scott Kulicke, congressional testimony quoted in *Federal News Service,* Nov. 29, 1989, reproduced in Lexis-Nexis.

21. Michael Argyle, *Cooperation: The Basis of Sociability.*

22. D. Levinthal and J. G. March, "A Model of Adaptive Organizational Search," *Journal of Economic Behavior and Organization* 2: pp. 307–33.

## Chapter 10

1. This chapter has been adapted from an earlier publication in the *Academy of Management Journal* 38 (1995) with Janice Beyer as our coauthor. We extend our thanks to her for that article's contribution to this chapter and for her professional guidance on this research project.

2. Pooling resources and responding to a threat are two conventional reasons for establishing cooperative efforts. See Robert Axelrod, *The Evolution of Cooperation*.

3. J. J. Barron, "Consortia: High-Tech Co-ops," *Byte,* June, 1990, p. 269, reproduced in Lexis-Nexis.

4. Ferguson, "From the People," p. 55.

5. Jack Kilby and Bob Noyce are usually listed as "coinventors" of the semiconductor. See Reid, *The Chip*.

6. VLSI Research, Sematech Archives.

7. U.S. Department of Defense, *Report of the Defense Science Board Task Force on Defense Semiconductor Dependency* (Washington, D.C.: 1986).

8. Etzioni, *Moral Dimension,* p. 31.

9. Harry Trice and Janice Beyer, *The Cultures of Work Organizations*.

10. Yoffie, "How an Industry Builds Political Advantage," p. 82.

11. B. Arthur, "Positive Feedbacks in the Economy," *Scientific American,* Feb., 1990, pp. 92–99.

12. Gray and Wood, "Collaborative Alliances"; Peter Ring and Andrew Van de Ven, "Developmental Processes of Cooperative Relationships," *Academy of Management Review* 19 (1994): 90–118.

13. In the first part of this methodological footnote we cover sampling. As is appropriate in qualitative research, this study used theoretical sampling, which means we sought out different perspectives on what happened until few outlying points of view remained uncovered. To assure that our interpretation of what happened at Sematech was not only a report of leaders' views, we invited all employees to participate in the study via Sematech's electronic-mail system. Our response to this request was quite small, possibly because the organization's norms imply that it is appropriate to be modest and asked about such topics as Sematech's development and what made it successful. As a result, only six individuals from this open appeal volunteered. They were interviewed during the first two months of the study. We subsequently interviewed fifty-four founding and current leaders, who were selected by invitation after reviewing records and requesting interviewees to identify other important sources. Those interviewed included fourteen semiconductor industry executives, eight Sematech executives, twelve Sematech assignees, fourteen Sematech direct hires, and six industry experts who had some contact with Sematech on such topics as development of the technology and human resources.

The next methodological topic is data collection. Interviews were private and structured to begin with a brief professional history of each interviewee and a description of how they and their firms became involved in Sematech. The narrative from this part of the interview lasted approximately ten–fifteen minutes and was used as a base for follow-up questions. The interviews ranged in length from 25 to 120 minutes and were audio or video taped and transcribed for analysis. Throughout the data collection we had the advantage of access to Turner Hasty, who was then at the University of Texas College of Engineering, as a key informant. Hasty had worked with the original Sematech formation group of forty-four in Santa Clara, Calif., as COO under both Noyce and Spencer, and as interim CEO following Noyce's death.

To verify the interview data with the official facts of Sematech's history, we also reviewed, primarily on our own and occasionally jointly with Hasty, documents in ten bank boxes of organizational archives from the files of key early executives and from original records collected by the Sematech librarian. In addition, we read, sorted, and abstracted over five thousand reports and news articles on Sematech identified from a full-text Lexis computer search. We worked with the Sematech librarian to develop a time line of events from this material. The product of this review is a twenty-five-page chronology of Sematech's history. In addition, we observed and recorded our responses to fifteen Sematech meetings in 1992 and 1993.

The next methodological topic is data analysis. Given an opportunity to analyze a novel and apparently successful instance of interorganizational cooperation, we wanted both to develop a theoretically interesting example and to identify behaviors and strategies that might be applicable to other interfirm settings. We chose grounded theory methodology (Anselm Strauss and J. Corbin, *Basics of Qualitative*

*Research: Grounded Theory Procedures and Techniques;* Anselm Strauss, *Qualitative Analysis for the Social Sciences;* Larry D. Browning, "A Grounded Organizational Communication Theory Derived from Qualitative Data," *Communication Monographs* 45 [1978]: pp. 93–109; and Barney Glaser, *Theoretical Sensitivity*) primarily because we aspired to derive new theoretical insights from the data we gathered on this unprecedented and unique effort at building cooperation.

We coded the transcripts using constant comparative analysis in which each different incident was assigned to an emergent open-coding scheme until all interviews had been coded. The authors jointly produced 130 codes, which they subsequently collaborated to reduce by stages into increasingly abstract categories through axial coding. This stage of the analysis produced twenty-four categories. In a process of selective coding, with the assistance of Janice Beyer, we further collapsed and renamed the categories to yield the seventeen categories presented in table 1 and described in the results section of this chapter.

While all sources of data proved useful for cross-checking purposes, the fifty-two interviews are the primary source of data for this study. Archival and observational data are used here to verify and provide context to the reports of the interviewees. As it turned out, our interviewees—especially the engineers, chemists, and physicists who played a role in Sematech's development—had surprisingly clear recall about the facts of what happened. Many of them brought calendars and meeting records to the interview and were quick to provide verification of events, dates, and outcomes. Those few apparent discrepancies of fact that arose were reconciled through additional interviews with the original informants involved.

The validity issues of the research were covered in the following way. The processes involved in the constant comparative method we used in this study had internal checks on the validity of the data. As data were collected and coded, investigators developed conceptual categories, and tentative hypotheses about them emerge. Questions about certain matters of fact also arose that were important to understanding and interpreting the data. Additional data to test the bounds of conceptual categories, matters of fact, and tentative hypotheses could then be collected from additional informants or from other data sources. As the research proceeded and new data were collected, they were constantly being compared to prior data in terms of categories and hypotheses. When new data yielded new or inconsistent information, conceptual categories and the emerging theory were modified to take them into account. This process was repeated until theoretical saturation was reached—that is, until no new categories emerged and no new information inconsistent with the categories and tentative hypotheses was being generated.

Our methods also permitted some within-and-between-method triangulation. We could compare data obtained from interviews with data available from newspaper clippings and other documents or from our observations of the settings involved. As mentioned above, the authors independently coded all of the interview data. They then compared their coded categories for overlaps and disagreements and arrived at a common set of categories, which were then used to recode all of the data. This process helped to assure that the coders interpreted the data similarly and did not miss relevant information. Similar checking and reconciliation processes were used during axial coding. Janice Beyer participated with the authors at the selective coding stage, and played the role of questioner and devil's advocate. At this final stage of coding, no categories were changed, but several were merged, many were renamed to fit the emerging theory, and the relationships among some were clarified.

In qualitative research, the primary checks on validity are among informants and between their reports and archival sources. Only data that were consistent across informants and sources are reported here. To further verify the accuracy of our statements and interpretations, the draft of this book was submitted to a number of key participants for review. A few minor factual corrections were made in response to their suggestions.

14. E. Raymond Corey, *Technology Fountainheads: The Management Challenge of R&D Consortia;* Helmut Willke, Carsten Kruck, and Christopher Thorn, *Benevolent Conspiracies: The Role of Enabling Technologies in the Welfare of Nations, The Cases of SDI, SEMATECH, and EUREKA;* Peter Grindley, David Mowery, and Brian Silverman, "Sematech and Collaborative Research: Lessons in the Design of High-Technology Consortia," *Journal of Policy Analysis and Management* 13 (1994): 723–58.

15. B. Borys and D. B. Jemison, "Hybrid Arrangements as Strategic Alliances: Theoretical Issues in Organizational Combinations," *Academy of Management Review* 14 (1988): 234–49.

16. Grindley et al., "Sematech and Collaborative Research"; Willke et al., *Benevolent Conspiracies.*

17. Willke et al., *Benevolent Conspiracies.*

18. Howard Aldrich and T. Sasaki, "Governance Structure and Technology Transfer Management in R&D Consortia in the United States and Japan," unpublished paper presented at the Japan Technology Management Conference, Ann Arbor, Mich., July 21–22, 1993, Sematech Archives.

19. Ibid.

20. Gibson and Rogers, *R&D Collaboration on Trial*.

21. Ibid., p. xvi.

22. W. M. Evan and P. Olk, "R&D Consortia: A New U.S. Organizational Form," *Sloan Management Review* (1990): 37–46.

23. Grindley et al., "Sematech and Collaborative Research."

24. Sematech internal memo, 1992, Sematech Archives.

25. Jim Peterman, "An Address to the Industrial Research Institute at the National Academy of Sciences, Oct. 25, 1988," *PR Newswire*, Mar. 19, 1989, reproduced in Lexis-Nexis.

26. Ibid.

27. Sematech Black Book, 1987, Sematech Archives.

28. For example, T. J. Rodgers, the CEO of Cypress Semiconductor, and his firm did not join when approached. Another firm that was asked but did not participate was Delco.

29. Each contributed 1 percent of its annual semiconductor sales, with a cap of $15 million.

30. Delays in the start-up and other factors led to some departures from this planned budget.

31. Peterman, "An Address to the Industrial Research Institute."

32. Henry Mintzberg, D. Rasinghani, and H. Lebleboici, "The Structure of Unstructured Decision Processes," *Administrative Science Quarterly* 21 (1976): 246–75.

33. Trice and Beyer, "Cultural Leadership in Organizations," *Organization Science* 2 (1992): 149–69.

34. This change in economic fortune changed so drastically that by 1997 one estimate concluded that the assets of the country had depreciated by a third from their earlier peak in the late 1980s.

35. *Financial Times,* 1993, reproduced in Lexis-Nexis.

36. Interview with Craig Barrett by the authors.

37. Axelrod, *The Evolution of Cooperation*.

38. Tetsuo Kondo, "Some Notes on Rational Behavior, Normative Behavior, Moral Behavior, and Cooperation," *Journal of Conflict Resolution* 34 (1990): 495–530.

39. Craig Parks, Robert Henager, and Shawn Scamahorn, "Trust and Reactions to Messages of Intent in Social Dilemmas," *Journal of Conflict Resolution* 40 (1996): 134–51.

40. Jonathan Bendor, R. Kramer, and Roderick and Suzanne Stout, "When in Doubt: Cooperation in a Noisy Prisoner's Dilemma," *Journal of Conflict Resolution* 35 (1991): 691–715.

41. Axelrod, *Evolution of Cooperation*.

42. Bowers, Gilchrist, and Browning, "A Communication Course."

43. Argyle, *Cooperation*.

44. Morton Deutsch, "Educating for a Peaceful World," *American Psychologist* 48 (1993): 510–17.

45. Delega and Grzelak, *Cooperation and Helping Behavior*.

46. Richard Walton, *Interpersonal Peace Making and Third Party Consultation*.

47. Peter Vaill, "Towards a Behavioral Description of High-Performing Systems" (paper presented at the Organizational Development Network Conference, Hartford, Conn., Apr., 1980).

48. Deutsch, "Educating for a Peaceful World."

49. Axelrod, *Evolution of Cooperation*.

50. Strauss and Corbin, *Basics of Qualitative Research*.

51. Karl Weick, *The Social Psychology of Organizing*.

52. James Thompson, *Organizations in Action: Social Sciences Bases of Administrative Theory*.

53. Bendor et al., "When in Doubt."

54. Bill Daniels was an intellectual grandchild of Likert (1967) in that Daniels's chief mentor, Pat Waters, had learned his consulting skills directly from Likert. For details on this issue see Raymond Miles, "From Prudential to Sematech: A Lifetime of Organizational Research, Experimentation, and Change—An Interview with Charles A. "Pat" Waters," *Journal of Management Inquiry* 5 (Mar., 1996): 60–66.

55. Trice and Beyer, *The Cultures of Work Organizations*.

56. Many firms in the computer industry allow informal dress like blue jeans, sports shirts, and

tennis shoes all of the time in jobs that do not involve contact with customers. Dress-down Fridays tended to allow this dress for everyone. At Sematech, Noyce himself followed this practice while on site.

57. Sabel, "Studied Trust," p. 1135.

58. Deutsch, "Educating for a Peaceful World."

59. Karl Weick, "Organization Design: Organizations as Self-Designing Systems," *Organizational Dynamics* 6 (1977): 30–46.

60. Deutsch, "Educating for a Peaceful World."

61. Heinz Hollander, "A Social Exchange Approach to Voluntary Cooperation," *American Economic Review* 80 (1990): 1157–67.

62. Margoah Maruyama. "The Second Cybernetics: Deviation-Amplifying Mutual Causal Processes," *American Scientist* 51 (1963): 64–179.

63. Etzioni, *Moral Dimension,* p. 31.

64. Ibid., p. ix–x.

65. Marcel Mauss, *The Gift: Forms and Functions of Exchange in Archaic Societies.*

66. Sematech internal memo, 1992, Sematech Archives.

67. Sematech internal memo, 1992, Sematech Archives.

68. Arnold Tannenbaum, *Control in Organizations.*

69. William J. Spencer and Peter Grindley, "SEMATECH after 5 Years: High Tech Consortia and U.S. Competitiveness," *California Management Review* 35 (1993).

70. Hollander, "A Social Exchange Approach."

71. Kenneth Boulding, *A Preface to Grants Economics: The Economy of Love and Fear.*

72. Hollander, "A Social Exchange Approach," p. 1163.

73. Deutsch, "Educating for a Peaceful World."

74. D. G. Pruitt, and P. D. Carnevale, "The Development of Integrative Agreements," in *Cooperation and Helping Behavior: Theories and Research,* ed. V. J. Delega and J. Grzelak.

75. Bendor et al., "When in Doubt," p. 716.

76. C. Bicchieri, "Norms of Cooperation," *Ethics* 100 (1990): 838–61.

77. Argyle, *Cooperation.*

78. Deutsch, "Educating for a Peaceful World."

79. The report of the woman's joy in having a Cesarean section was reported by her supervisor, not her. In fact her nonverbal response to having this mentioned was ghastly, as though this choice came under pressure. For an excellent treatment of this specific issue, see Joanne Martin, "Deconstructing Organizational Taboos: The Suppression of Gender Conflict in Organizations," *Organization Science* 1 (1990): 339–59.

80. Of course, such extreme levels of effort and commitment to work had a dark side in terms of health and nonwork life.

81. Joel Wiggins, "Players at Work, Workers at Play: An investigation of the Relationship between Work and Play" (unpublished paper, Department of Speech Communication, the University of Texas at Austin, 1994).

82. Larry D. Browning, Karl Weick, and Sue Powers, "Quality Shock: Cross-functional Commitment at Motorola" (paper presented at the Best Paper session at the annual conference of the Academy of Human Resource Development, San Antonio, Tex., Apr., 1994).

83. The first Sam Harrell interview differs from this account in that he reports that he, through SEMI, the supplier industry's association, made an extensive effort to find a champion to address infrastructure issues. He said that Sporck was consciously identified and educated by SEMI on the issues in order to place him in a position to assist the industry.

84. P. S. Goodman, E. Ravvlin, and M. Schminke, "Understanding Groups in Organizations," *Research in Organizational Behavior* 9 (1987): 121–73.

85. Axelrod, *Evolution of Cooperation.*

86. Sable, "Studied Trust," p. 1135.

87. Kondo, "Some Notes on Rational Behavior," p. 504.

88. McLoughlin, "SEMATECH."

89. The definition of structures used in our analysis was taken from Giddens, whose major categories for analysis are frameworks and interaction. Interaction includes the discussions and speech behav-

iors that are necessary to build and maintain cooperation. Frameworks are the structures that emerge to bound and give meaning to the interactions. Giddens sees interactions as leading to frameworks that allow new interactions that can create new structures. He calls this interactive sequential process "reflexivity." Our data on Sematech's development yield many examples of reflexivity. For an overview of Giddens's work, see P. Cassell, *The Giddens Reader* (Stanford, Calif.: Stanford University Press, 1993).

90. Bender et al., "When in Doubt," p. 713.

91. Pruitt and Carnevale, "The Development of Integrative Agreements."

92. Argyle, *Cooperation.*

93. Deutsch, "Educating for a Peaceful World," p. 510.

94. Peterman, "An Address to the Industrial Research Institute."

95. Sematech Investment Council, June 9, 1989, Sematech Archives.

96. "Partnering for Total Quality," vols. I–IX, Sematech Archives.

97. The Cooperative Research Act of 1984 relaxed prior antitrust restrictions on competitors sharing information.

98. Weick, "Organization Design"; G. Morgan, *Images of Organization.*

99. Smith and Gemmill in *Human Relations* (1991); R. Leifer, "Understanding Organizational Transformation Using a Dissipative Structure Model," *Human Relations* 42 (1989); Gemmill and Smith in *Human Relations* (1985).

100. E. Jantsch, "From Self-Reference to Self-Transcendence: The Evolution of Self-Organizing Dynamics," in *Self-Organization and Dissipative Structures: Applications in the Physical and Social Sciences,* ed. W. C. Shieve and P.M. Allen; Weick, "Organization Design."

101. This phenomenon has been described in physical systems such as chemical solutions (Nicolis and Prigogine, 1989; Prigogine, 1981, 1984), in natural systems such as biological evolution (Kauffman, 1990), and also in social systems (Axelrod, *Evolution of Cooperation;* Jantsch, "From Self-Reference to Self-Transcendence").

102. J. A. Wheeler, "Information, Physics, Quantum: The Search for Links," in *Complexity, Entropy and the Physics of Information,* ed. W. Zurek (Redwood City, Calif.: Addison-Wesley, 1990), pp. 3–28.

103. While MCC was already an established consortium in the computer industry, its mode of operating and structure were markedly different from Sematech's.

104. It also drew IBM into the semiconductor manufacturing community in a way that was unprecedented.

105. Leifer, "Understanding Organizational Transformation," 705.

106. Ibid.

107. Ibid.

108. Smith and Gemmill in *Human Relations* (1991).

109. Some analysts suggest that organizational boundaries are in an increasing state of flux.

110. Interestingly, his creation of the Office of the Chief Executive embedded his role in a team with others who could play the structuring roles.

111. E. H. Schein, *Organizational Culture and Leadership,* pp. 228–53.

112. Trice and Beyer, *The Cultures of Work Organizations.*

113. Margaret J. Wheatley, *Leadership and the New Science: Learning about Organization from an Orderly Universe,* p. 90.

114. Gemmill and Smith in *Human Relations* (1985).

115. Leifer, "Understanding Organizational Transformation."

116. Our informants indicated that the companies leaving Sematech after the initial five-year charter expired did so because they were farther back in the technology chain than other member companies and thus could not put Sematech's research and testing to immediate use.

117. Kondo, "Some Notes on Rational Behavior."

118. Maruyama, "The Second Cybernetics," pp. 164–79.

119. Trice and Beyer, "Cultural Leadership," p. 151.

120. Ring and Van de Ven, "Developmental Processes," pp. 90–118.

121. Mauss, *The Gift.*

122. Argyle, *Cooperation.*

123. Ibid.

124. Rogers and Larson, *Silicon Valley Fever*.
125. Ring and Van de Ven, "Developmental Processes," pp. 90–118.
126. Our interviewees did not specifically use the term "trust," and it often broke the rapport established in our interviews if we injected the language of trust. Nevertheless, trust was illustrated repeatedly in what they told us.
127. Ring and Van de Ven, "Developmental Processes," p. 95.

# Bibliography

**Archives and Manuscripts**

Aldrich, Howard, and T. Sasaki. "Governance Structure and Technology Transfer Management in R&D Consortia in the United States and Japan." Paper presented at Japan Technology Management Conference, Ann Arbor, Michigan, July 21–22, 1993.

Avery, Christopher M.; Debra France; Larry Browning; and Michael Oswald. "Best Customer and Supplier Partnering Practices in the U.S. Semiconductor Industry." Sematech Technology Report no. 93031544AXFR. 1993. Sematech Archives, Austin, Texas (hereafter Sematech Archives).

Bonner, Miller; W. Lane Boyd; and Janet A. Allen. "Robert N. Noyce, 1927–1990." Sematech Archives.

Browning, Larry D.; Karl E. Weick; and Sue Powers. "Quality Shock: Cross-Functional Commitment at Motorola." Paper presented at the Best Paper session at the Annual Conference of the Academy of Human Resource Development, San Antonio, Texas, April, 1994.

Dewey, Ballantine memo to the SIA Public Policy Committee, December 10, 1986. Sematech Archives.

Dewey, Ballantine weekly reports for May 8, 22, and 29, September 11 and 19, and October 9, 1987. Sematech Archives.

Mayer, J., et al., Advisory Council Report on Federal Participation in SEMATECH, 1989. Sematech Archives.

————. Advisory Council Report on Federal Participation in Sematech, 1990. Sematech Archives.

*The Microtech 2000 Workshop Report.* Sematech Archives.

Sematech *All Hands Memo,* December 18 and 30, 1992; February 22, 1993; October 5, 1993. Sematech Archives.

Sematech Annual Report, 1991; Board of Directors roster, July 23, 1987; Committee roster, July 23, 1987; Strategic Overview, 1991. Sematech Archives.

Sematech Black Book, 1987, Sematech Archives.

Sematech *Communiqué,* Special Issue, December, 1991; July-August, 1992. Sematech Archives.

Sematech Operating Plan, 1990, Sematech Archives.

Sematech Press Releases, May 31, 1988; May 23, 1989; January 17, 1991; April 27, 1992; April 7, 1993; November 16, 1993.

Sematech Press Reviews, January 27, 1989; May 5 and 23, 1989; April 20 and 27, 1990; January 11, 1991; February 15, 1991; May 10 and 24, 1991; August 2, 1991; September 27, 1991; November 8, 1991; January 17, 1992; August 21, 1992; October 2, 1992; December 11, 1992; January 15, 1993; July 16, 1993; October 15, 1993; November 12, 1993; October 7, 1994. Sematech Archives.

"SEMATECH Seeks Final Direct Funding." Sematech *Update,* 1st Quarter, 1995, p. 1. Sematech Archives.

Sematech Strategic Operating Plan, 1989. Technical Appendices. Sematech Archives.

Sematech Strategic Operating Plan, 1990. Sematech Archives.

Bibliography

Sematech *Update,* September, 1989; February, 1992; June-July, 1992; January, 1993; July-August, 1993; November-December, 1994. Sematech Archives.

Senate Armed Services Committee. National Advisory Committee on Semiconductors Report. November 29, 1989. Sematech Archives.

Spencer, William J. "A Roadmap for a Competitive Industry." Sematech *Update,* March-April 1993. Sematech Archives.

————. "In Hearings before the Subcommittee on Technology, Environment and Aviation." Washington, D.C.: GPO, p. 10–11. Sematech Archives.

"U.S. Semiconductor Research Seeing Impact." Sematech *Update,* July, 1991. Sematech Archives.

Vaill, Peter. "Towards a Behavioral Description of High Performing Systems." Paper presented at the Organizational Development Network Conference, Hartford, Conn., April, 1980.

Wiggins, Joel. "Players at Work, Workers at Play: An Investigation of the Relationship between Work and Play." Unpublished paper, Department of Speech Communication, the University of Texas at Austin, 1994.


**Books and Articles**

"Administration Policy Groups Split on Need for Aid to High-Tech Industry." *Inside U.S. Trade,* November 28, 1986.

Aldrich, Howard, and T. Sasaki. "R&D Consortia in the United States and Japan." *Research Policy* (forthcoming).

Alic, John; Lewis Branscomb; Harvey Brooks; Ashton Carter; and Gerald Epstein. *Beyond Spinoff.* Boston: Harvard Business School Press, 1992.

Argyle, Michael. *Cooperation: The Basis of Sociability.* London: Routledge, 1991.

Arthur, B. "Positive Feedbacks in the Economy." *Scientific American,* February, 1990, pp. 92–99.

Axelrod, Robert. *The Evolution of Cooperation.* New York: Basic Books, 1984.

Barron, J. J. "Consortia: High-Tech Co-ops." *Byte,* June, 1990, p. 269. Reproduced in Lexis-Nexis.

Bendor, Jonathan; R. Kramer; and Roderick and Suzanne Stout. "When in Doubt: Cooperation in a Noisy Prisoner's Dilemma." *Journal of Conflict Resolution* 35 (1991): 691–719.

Bicchieri, C. "Norms of Cooperation." *Ethics* 100 (1990): 838–61.

Block, Peter. *Flawless Consultation: A Guide to Getting Your Expertise Used.* La Jolla, Calif.: University Associates, 1981.

Borrus, Michael. *New York Times,* July 31, 1988, sec. 3, p. 3.

Borys, B., and D. B. Jemison. "Hybrid Arrangements as Strategic Alliances: Theoretical Issues in Organizational Combinations." *Academy of Management Review* 14 (1988): 234–49.

Boulding, Kenneth. *A Preface to Grants Economics: The Economy of Love and Fear.* New York: Praeger, 1981.

Browning, Larry D. "A Grounded Organizational Communication Theory Derived from Qualitative Data." *Communication Monographs* 45 (1978): 93–109.

Browning, Larry D., and Janice Beyer. "The Structuring of Shared Voluntary Standards in the U.S. Semiconductor Industry: Communicating to Reach Agreement." *Communication Monographs* 64 (1998): 1–25.

Browning, Larry D.; Janice M. Beyer; and Judy C. Shetler. "Building Cooperation in a Competitive Industry: Sematech and the Semiconductor Industry." *Academy of Management Journal* 38 (1995): 113–51.

Brull, Steven. "Japan-U.S. Microchip Makers Join Forces Warily." *Reuters Financial Report,* December 26, 1988. Reproduced in Lexis-Nexis.

Burrows, Peter, and Garret DeYoung. "Recipe for Success: Keep Your Customers Smiling; Electronics Suppliers Who Put the Buyer First Will Survive the Quality-Conscious '90s." *Electronic Business,* Oct. 15, 1990, p. 85.

Cassell, P. *The Giddens Reader.* Stanford, Calif.: Stanford University Press, 1993.

"Clinton's Design on Technology Sparks Debate over 'Meddling.'" *Newsday,* February 28, 1993. Reproduced in Lexis-Nexis.

Corcoran, Elizabeth. "Competitive Climate: Industry Leaders Look to the Government for a New Era." *Scientific American,* March, 1989, p. 70. Reproduced in Lexis-Nexis.

Corey, E. Raymond. *Technology Fountainheads: The Management Challenge of R&D Consortia.* Boston: Harvard Business School Press, 1997.

Delega, V. J., and J. Grzelak, eds. *Cooperation and Helping Behavior: Theories and Research.* New York: Academic Press, 1982.

Dertouzos, Michael L.; Richard K. Lester; and Robert M. Solow. *Made in America: Regaining the Productive Edge: The MIT Commission on Industrial Productivity.* Cambridge, Mass.: MIT Press, 1989.

Deutsch, Morton. "Educating for a Peaceful World." *American Psychologist* 48 (1993): 510–17.

Dicken, P. *Economic Geography* 70, no. 2 (April, 1994): 101. Reproduced in Lexis-Nexis.

Drucker, Peter. *Post-Capitalist Society.* New York: Harper Business, 1993.

Dunn, Peter. "Motorola Selects Canon Steppers for MOS-11 Fab." *Electronic News,* October 22, 1990. Reproduced in Lexis-Nexis.

*Earth Action Network* 5, no. 2 (April, 1994): 28. Reproduced in Lexis-Nexis.

"The Economy." *Fortune,* Apr. 18, 1994, Domestic Edition, p. 52.

Etzioni, Amitai. *The Moral Dimension: Toward a New Economics.* New York: Free Press, 1988.

Evan, W. M., and P. Olk. "R&D Consortia: A New U.S. Organizational Form." *Sloan Management Review* (1990): 37–46.

Ferguson, Charles H. "From the People Who Brought You Voodoo Economics." *Harvard Business Review,* May-June, 1988, p. 55. Reproduced in Lexis-Nexis.

Ferguson, Charles H., and C. R. Morris. *Computer Wars: How the West Can Win in a Post-IBM World.* New York: Times Books, 1993.

"Financial Focus." *Defense News,* July 25–31, 1994, p. 25.

Gibson, David, and Everett Rogers. *R&D Collaboration on Trial: The Microelectronics and Computer Technology Corporation.* Cambridge, Mass: Harvard Business School Press, 1994.

Glaser, Barney. *Theoretical Sensitivity.* Mill Valley, Calif.: Sociology Press, 1976.

Glaser, Barney, and Anselm Strauss. *The Discovery of Grounded Theory.* Chicago: Aldine, 1967.

Goodman, P. S.; E. Ravvlin; and M. Schminke. "Understanding Groups in Organizations." *Research in Organizational Behavior* 9 (1987): 121–73.

Gray, Barbara, and D. J. Wood. "Collaborative Alliances: Moving from Practice to Theory." *Journal of Applied Behavioral Sciences* 27 (1991): 3–21.

Green, Tim. "Austin on SEMATECH." *Austin Business Journal,* January 11, 1988. Reproduced in Lexis-Nexis.

Grindley, Peter; David Mowery; and Brian Silverman. "Sematech and Collaborative Research: Lessons in the Design of High-Technology Consortia." *Journal of Policy Analysis and Management* 13 (1994): 723–58.

Grove, Andrew. *High Output Management.* New York: Random House, 1983.

Hassard, J. "Aspects of Time in Organization." *Human Relations* 44 (1991).

"The Haves versus the Have-Nots." *Electronic Business,* May 1, 1988, p. 32. Reproduced in Lexis-Nexis.

Henkoff, Ronald, and Andrew Erdman. "Companies that Train Best." *Fortune,* March 23, 1993. Reproduced in Lexis-Nexis.

"The High-Tech Commodity: A Text-Book Market? Two Ways to Stay in Business." *The Economist,* November 22, 1986, p 78. Reproduced in Lexis-Nexis.

Hollander, Heinz. "A Social Exchange Approach to Voluntary Cooperation. *American Economic Review* 80 (1990): 1157–67.

Hornstein, Harvey. "Promotive Tension: Theory and Research." In *Cooperation and Helping Behavior: Theories and Research,* ed. V. J. Delega and J. Grzelak. New York: Academic Press, 1982.

International Trade Administration. "U.S. Technology Trade and Competitiveness." Washington, D.C.: Department of Commerce, 1985.

Ishihara, Shintaro. 1989. *The Japan that Can Say No: Why Japan Will Be First Among Equals.* New York: Simon and Schuster, 1991.

Jacobson, Ken. *Federal Technology Report,* February 4, 1993: McGraw-Hill, Inc. Reproduced in Lexis-Nexis.

Jantsch, E. "From Self-Reference to Self-Transcendence: The Evolution of Self-Organizing Dynamics." In *Self-Organization and Dissipative Structures: Applications in the Physical and Social Sciences,* ed. W. C. Shieve and P.M. Allen. Austin: University of Texas Press, 1982.

263

Bibliography

Kondo, Tetsuo. "Some Notes on Rational Behavior, Normative Behavior, Moral Behavior, and Cooperation." *Journal of Conflict Resolution* 34 (1990): 495–530.

Langford, Mark. "Sematech Dedicated; Officials Unveil Parts of High-Tech Clean Room." United Press International, Texas Regional News, November 16, 1988.

Leifer, R. "Understanding Organizational Transformation Using a Dissipative Structure Model." *Human Relations* 42 (1989): 705.

Leopold, George. "Computer Chip Group Could Serve as Model for Hi-Tech Cooperation." *Defense News,* January 7, 1991, p. 10.

Leubsdorf, Carl P. "Clinton Details Technology Policy; Plan Calls for $17 Billion Federal Effort." *Dallas Morning News,* Feb. 23, 1993, p. 1A.

Levinthal, D., and J. G. March. "A Model of Adaptive Organizational Search." *Journal of Economic Behavior and Organization* 2:307–33.

McLoughlin, Glenn. J. "SEMATECH: Issues in Evaluation and Assessment." Congressional Research Service, Library of Congress, no. 92–749 (spring, 1992).

Martin, Joanne. "Deconstructing Organizational Taboos: The Suppression of Gender Conflict in Organizations." *Organization Science* 1 (1990): 339–59.

Maruyama, Margoah. "The Second Cybernetics: Deviation-Amplifying Mutual Causal Processes." *American Scientist* 51 (1963): 64–179.

Maslow, Abraham. *Motivation and Personality.* New York: Harper and Row, 1954.

Mauss, Marcel. *The Gift: Forms and Functions of Exchange in Archaic Societies.* New York: Norton, 1967.

Miles, Raymond. "From Prudential to Sematech: A Lifetime of Organizational Research, Experimentation, and Change—An Interview with Charles A. "Pat" Waters." *Journal of Management Inquiry* 5 (March, 1996): 60–66.

Mintzberg, Henry; D. Rasinghani; and H. Lebleboici. "The Structure of Unstructured Decision Processes." *Administrative Science Quarterly* 21 (1976): 246–75.

Morgan, G. *Images of Organization.* Beverly Hills, Calif.: Sage, 1986.

Morgan, James C., and J. Jeffrey Morgan. *Cracking the Japanese Market: Strategies for Success in the New Global Economy.* New York: Free Press, 1991.

"1990 Financial World Partners." *Financial World,* March 20, 1990.

"Oak Ridge in Transition: A Perspective from the Solid State Sciences." *Solid State Technology,* April, 1994, p. 34. Reproduced in Lexis-Nexis.

Palermo, R. C., and G. H. Watson, eds. *A World of Quality: The Timeless Passport, Xerox Quality Solutions.* Milwaukee: ASQC Quality Press, 1993.

Parks, Craig; Robert Henager; and Shawn Scamahorn. "Trust and Reactions to Messages of Intent in Social Dilemmas." *Journal of Conflict Resolution* 40 (1996): 134–51.

"Pentagon Advisers Call for U.S. Aid to Chip Industry," *Wall Street Journal,* December 10, 1986. Reproduced in Lexis-Nexis.

Peterman, Jim. "An Address to the Industrial Research Institute at the National Academy of Sciences, Oct. 25, 1988." *PR Newswire,* March 29, 1989. Reproduced in Lexis-Nexis.

Pollack, Andrew. "Chip Pioneer to Head Consortium." *New York Times,* July 28, 1988, p. D1. Reproduced in Lexis-Nexis.

———. "Conflict at Sematech Forces Out No. 2 Man." *New York Times,* March 21, 1989, Late City Final Edition, p. D1. Reproduced in Lexis-Nexis.

———. "Ideas & Trends: High-Tech Business Loses a Friend at the Pentagon." *New York Times,* April 29, 1990, sec. 4, p. 5. Reproduced in Lexis-Nexis.

———. "New Chip Method May Be Put Off." *New York Times,* December 12, 1990, p. D1. Reproduced in Lexis-Nexis.

Pruitt, D. G., and P. D. Carnevale. "The Development of Integrative Agreements." In *Cooperation and Helping Behavior: Theories and Research,* ed. V. J. Delega and J. Grzelak. New York: Academic Press, 1982. Reproduced in Lexis-Nexis.

Reid, T. R. *The Chip.* New York: Simon and Schuster, 1984.

Ring, Peter, and Andrew Van de Ven. "Developmental Processes of Cooperative Interorganizational Relationships." *Academy of Management Review* 19 (1994): 90–118.

264

Robertson, Jack. "IBM Thinks Ahead." *Electronic News,* March 20, 1989, p. 12. Reproduced in Lexis-Nexis.

———. "Sematech Confirms Shift in Test from End-to-End to 'Short Loop.'" *Electronic News,* December 23, 1991. Reproduced in Lexis-Nexis.

———. "Sematech Sumo Match." *Electronic News,* October 29, 1990, p. 12. Reproduced in Lexis-Nexis.

———. "SIA Roadmap Accents MCM, Low-Power ICs: Semiconductor Industry." *Electronic News,* January 18, 1993, p. 1. Reproduced in Lexis-Nexis.

Rogers, Everett, and Judy Larson. *Silicon Valley Fever: Growth of High Technology Culture.* New York: Basic Books, 1984.

Sabel, Charles. F. "Studied Trust: Building New Forms of Cooperation in a Volatile Economy." *Human Relations* 46 (1993): 1133–70.

Schein, E. H. *Organizational Culture and Leadership.* 2d ed. San Francisco: Jossey Bass, 1992.

Schneidawind, John. "Explosive Growth ahead for Industry." *USA Today,* January 22, 1993, p. 1B. Reproduced in Lexis-Nexis.

"SEMATECH Consortium Says Rockwell Stays." *Financial Report,* January 6, 1993, BC cycle. Reproduced in Lexis-Nexis.

Sherif, Muzafer. *In Common Predicament: Social Psychology of Intergroup Conflict and Cooperation.* Boston: Houghton Mifflin, 1966.

Smith, Amy. "Finding Patent Success." *Austin Business Journal,* January 18, 1993, sec. 1, p. 5. Reproduced in Lexis-Nexis.

Smitka, Michael. *Competitive Ties: Subcontracting in the Japanese Automotive Industry.* New York: Columbia University Press, 1991.

Spencer, William J., and Peter Grindley. "SEMATECH after 5 Years: High Tech Consortia and U.S. Competitiveness." *California Management Review* 35 (1993): 9–32.

Stacey, Ralph. *Managing the Unknowable: Strategic Boundaries between Order and Chaos in Organizations.* San Francisco: Jossey Bass, 1992.

Strauss, Anselm. *Qualitative Analysis for the Social Sciences.* Cambridge: Oxford University Press, 1988.

Strauss, Anselm, and J. Corbin. *Basics of Qualitative Research: Grounded Theory Procedures and Techniques.* Newbury Park, Calif.: Sage, 1990.

Tannenbaum, Arnold. *Control in Organizations.* New York: McGraw-Hill, 1968.

Teece, D. J. "Information Sharing, Innovation and Antitrust." *Antitrust Law Journal* 2 (1994): 465–81.

Thompson, James. *Organizations in Action: Social Sciences Bases of Administrative Theory.* New York: McGraw-Hill, 1967.

Thompson, John. "SEMATECH Aim: Tie Sematech, Gear Expertise." *Electronic News,* February 22, 1988, p. 20. Reproduced in Lexis-Nexis.

"Topic of the Times." *New York Times,* October 12, 1994, Late Edition, Final. Reproduced in Lexis-Nexis.

Trice, Harry, and Janice Beyer. "Cultural Leadership in Organizations." *Organizational Science* 2 (1992): 149–69.

———. *The Cultures of Work Organizations.* Englewood Cliffs, N.J.: Prentice Hall, 1993.

Walton, Richard. *Interpersonal Peace Making and Third Party Consultation.* Reading, Mass.: Addison Wesley, 1969.

Weick, Karl. "Organization Design: Organizations as Self-Designing Systems." *Organizational Dynamics* 6 (1977): 30–46.

———. *The Social Psychology of Organizing.* Reading, Mass.: Addison-Wesley, 1979.

Wheatley, Margaret J. *Leadership and the New Science: Learning about Organization from an Orderly Universe.* San Francisco: Berrett-Koehler, 1992.

Wheeler, J. A. "Information, Physics, Quantum: The Search for Links." In *Complexity, Entropy and the Physics of Information,* ed. W. Zurek. Redwood City, Calif.: Addison-Wesley, 1990.

Willke, Helmut; Carsten Kruck; and Christopher Thorn. *Benevolent Conspiracies: The Role of Enabling Technologies in the Welfare of Nations, The cases of SDI, SEMATECH, and EUREKA.* New York: Walter de Gruyter, 1995.

Bibliography

Wolfe, Tom. "The Tinkerings of Robert Noyce." Reprinted from *Esquire,* December, 1983, by Intel Corporation, Santa Clara, Calif.

Yoffie, David. "How an Industry Builds Political Advantage." *Harvard Business Review,* May-June, 1988, p. 82. Reproduced in Lexis-Nexis.

Ziller, Robert. "Toward a Theory of Open and Closed Groups." *Psychological Bulletin* 64 (1965): 164–82.

# Index

*Kenneth E. Montague Series in Oil and Business History*
*Joseph A. Pratt, General Editor*

Buenger, Victoria, and Walter L. Buenger. *Texas Merchant: Marvin Leonard and Fort Worth.* 1998.

Hyman, Harold M. *Oleander Odyssey: The Kempners of Galveston, Texas, 1854–1980s.* 1990.

Malavis, Nicholas G. *Bless the Pure and Humble: Texas Lawyers and Oil Regulation, 1919–1936.* 1996.

Margavio, Anthony V., and Craig J. Forsyth. *Caught in the Net: The Conflict between Shrimpers and Conservationists.* 1996.

Miles, Ray. *"King of the Wildcatters": The Life and Times of Tom Slick, 1883–1930.* 1996.